Russia's Military Way to the West

Also by Christopher Duffy

Siege Warfare

Christopher Duffy

Russia's Military Way to the West

Origins and Nature of Russian Military Power 1700-1800

Routledge & Kegan Paul
London, Boston and Henley

First published in 1981
by Routledge & Kegan Paul Ltd
39 Store Street, London WC1E 7DD,
9 Park Street, Boston, mass. 02108, USA and
Broadway House, Newtown Road,
Henley-on-Thames, Oxon RG9 1EN
Set in 10/12pt Press Roman by
Columns, Reading
and printed in Great Britain by
St Edmundsbury Press, Bury St. Edmunds, Suffolk
© Christopher Duffy 1981
No part of this book may be reproduced in
any form without permission from the
publisher, except for the quotation of brief
passages in criticism

British Library Cataloguing in Publication Data

Duffy, Christopher
Russia's military way to the West.
1. Russia — History, Military, to 1801
I. Title
947'.046   DK51

ISBN 0-7100-0797-3

First published as a paperback in 1985
ISBN 0-7102-0535-X

Contents

	Preface	xi
One	So Many Russias	1
Two	Peter I, 'the Great' 1682-1725	9
Three	The Age of Marshal Münnich 1725-41	42
Four	Elizabeth Petrovna 1741-1761/2	55
Five	The Russian Soldier	125
Six	The Russian Officer	136
Seven	The Cossacks	157
Eight	Catherine II, 'the Great' 1762-96	165
Nine	Paul I 1796-1801	200
Ten	Conclusions	233
	Appendix	242
	Select Bibliography	243
	Index	251

Illustrations

1	Peter the Great	9
2	*Zar und Zimmermann* – Peter the Great in the guise of a shipwright on his Western travels	12
3	Fusilier of the Preobrazhenskii Regiment, 1700-2	13
4	James Bruce, creator of the modern Russian artillery	18
5	Aleksandr Danilovich Menshikov	33
6	Grenadier, 1700-2	34
7	Infantry officer, 1700-2	39
8	Burchard Christoph Münnich	44
9	Elizabeth Petrovna	55
10	Petr Shuvalov	60
11	Cornet of cuirassiers, Seven Years War	65
12	Dragoon, Seven Years War	66
13	Artillery of the Seven Years War	68
14	Artillery of the Seven Years War	69
15	Artillery of the Seven Years War	69
16	Artillery of the Seven Years War	70
17	Artillery of the Seven Years War	70
18	Artillery of the Seven Years War	70
19	Details of the Shuvalov secret howitzer	71
20	Stepan Fedorovich Apraksin	74
21	Grand Prince Peter and Catherine, leaders of the 'young court'	92
22	Fusilier and sergeant of infantry, Seven Years War	97
23	Infantry officers, Seven Years War	99
24	Grenadier of a regiment of musketeers, Seven Years War	100
25	Captain of a regiment of grenadiers, Seven Years War	101
26	Cuirassier on dismounted sentry duty, Seven Years War	101
27	Artilleryman, Seven Years War	102
28	Petr Semenovich Saltykov	105
29	Peter III	122
30	Peter III and his suite	123
31	Russian infantry of the later eighteenth century	127
32	Grenadier, period of Catherine the Great	134
33	Officer of the *Leibkompagnie*	141
34	NCO and officer of the Chevalier Garde, 1764-96	141
35	Officer of the Cadet Corps, 1732-42	143
36	Generals of Catherine the Great	149
37	Kiril Razumovskii	150
38	Cavalry officer, after 1769, probably a carabinier	152
39	Infantry officer, period of Catherine the Great	152
40	General of the 7th Jaeger Corps, 1797-1801	153
41	Nikolai Vasilevich Repnin	155
42	Hussar of the Slobodskaya Ukraine, Seven Years War	157
43	Volga Cossack	160
44	Charge of the Don Cossacks at the battle of the Trebbia, 1799	163
45	Catherine the Great	165
46	Grigorii Grigorevich Orlov	166
47	Zakhar Grigorevich Chernyshev	167

48	Field-marshal, period of Catherine the Great	167
49	Central divisional squares at Kagul	170
50	Rumyantsev in battle against the Turks	171
51	Musketeer, 1763-c.1786	173
52	Jaegers, 1765-c.1786	177
53	Grigorii Aleksandrovich Potemkin	180
54	Musketeers in the 'Potemkin' uniform, c.1786	183
55	The 'Potemkin' cap	184
56	Suvorov the man-manager	193
57	Suvorov in English caricature	193
58	Aleksandr Vasilevich Suvorov	194
59	Catherine tempted by the Devil	195
60	Catherine the Great with her family and leading courtiers, 1782	197
61	Grenadier and musketeer of the Gatchina Corps, 1793	200
62	Inspection of the guard indoors at Gatchina	201
63	Paul I	202
64	Paul I in front of the Winter Palace	203
65	Paul I	203
66	Musketeer, period of Paul I	204
67	Paul I and Suvorov	206
68	Grenadier of the Shlyushelburgskii Musketeer Regiment, period of Paul I	211
69	Novi Castle	220
70	Base of the interior tower at Novi Castle, looking at the western side	221
71	At the gates of Switzerland	223
72	Forcing the Devil's Bridge, Andermatt	225
73	Descent to the Muotatal from the Kinzig Pass	227
74	Convent of St Joseph, Muotathal village	228
75	Eastern end of the Klöntalersee	229
76	The entry to the Panixer Pass	231

Maps

(by the author)

Western Russia: political	3
Western Russia: physical	5
Narva, 19 November 1700	16
The Baltic theatre in the eighteenth century	19
The way to Poltava, 1708-9	21
Poltava, 27 June 1709	25
The Turkish campaigns, 1736-9	52
The invasions of East Prussia	75
Gross-Jägersdorf, 30 August 1757*	76
The central theatre	84
Campaign of 1758	85
Zorndorf: Prussian turning movement*	87
Zorndorf, 25 August 1758*	88
Campaign of 1759	106
Paltzig, 23 July 1759*	107
Kunersdorf, 12 August 1759*	109
Kunersdorf: the defence of the Kuh-Grund*	110
Kunersdorf: victory*	111
Campaigns of 1760 and 1761	113
Rumyantsev's War, 1768-74	174
Kagul, 21 July 1770: attack in divisional squares	175
The Turkish War, 1787-91/2	186
North Holland, 1799	210
Italy and Switzerland, 1799	213
Novi, 15 August 1799	219
Suvorov in Switzerland, 1799	224
Rosenberg in the Muotatal, 1 October 1799	230

*There is a key to these maps on page 77.

Preface

There can be no doubt that the great and increasing military might of Soviet Russia has become one of the dominating issues of international affairs in the last four decades. The present study attempts not to explain this remarkable phenomenon, but to provide the reader with historical perspectives, by taking him back to the time when Russia acquired and began to exercise modern military power.

A perceptive historian has noted that 'with military scholars of the eighteenth century concentrating on central and western Europe, the study of war in eastern Europe ... was and remains an unjustifiably ignored field' (Longworth, 1965, 301). The omission is all the more surprising when we consider that Russia, although the youngest significant member of the European community, played a leading part in smashing the Swedish Baltic empire, and went on to find herself heavily engaged against the two states that threatened most to disturb European repose – the Prussia of Frederick the Great, and the resurgent France of the Revolution.

The title of my book has been plundered from Mediger's fine study of Russian mid-eighteenth-century statesmanship, *Moskaus Weg nach Europa*. At once concise and ambiguous, the phrase, translated into military terms, indicates all the avenues which I have set out to explore, namely:

(a) what you might call the 'snow on the boots' question, asking whether you can establish a direct relation between the application of military force by Russia, and the westward advance of Russia's borders and influence in the period under consideration;
(b) the issue of how far the new Russian army assimilated Western techniques and structures;
(c) the question of the relative importance of western European and native Russian influences on the Russian army;
(d) and finally the evaluation of the performance of the Russian armies in Western theatres of war.

In the concluding chapter I also touch on the historiographical treatment of Russian military affairs in the eighteenth century, and venture some comments on the much-debated theme of continuities between Tsarist past and Soviet present.

The present high costs of printing threaten to put the purchase of books entirely beyond the means of private individuals. I have therefore established a number of firm priorities for space in the present volume, giving just the bare minimum of information on subjects which have been treated in detail by expert authorities elsewhere. For naval affairs I refer the interested reader to the works of R.C. Anderson and N.E. Saul and Chapter 6 of the recently published work by A. G. Cross, *Russians in Eighteenth-Century Britain*, Newtonville, 1980. The proper study of military costume also has significance, for it reveals a great deal about the morale and discipline of armies, and the impression which sovereigns desire to make upon the world. Here I recommend the well-illustrated volumes by the Funckens, the Mollos and Zweguintzow. Copies of the huge old standard text by Viskovatov are available in the British Library and the library of the Victoria and Albert Museum.

Likewise, the blow-by-blow narrative of the Great Northern War can be readily retrieved from the histories of Peter the Great by M. S. Anderson, and of Charles XII by R. M. Hatton. For detail on the reign of Catherine the Great, please consult the monumental work by I. de Madariaga.

The Tartar and Turkish campaigns, for the same reason, are examined here principally to help to explain what was specifically non-European about the Russian art of war. Conversely, I devote a goodish amount of space to the still little-known stories of Russia's intervention in the Seven Years War and the War of the Second Coalition, and to the work of that much-misrepresented gentleman, Paul I.

At the risk of appearing pompous, I must also clarify my historiographical standpoint. I would certainly not deny that what is rather arrogantly called 'the new military history', with its emphasis on social, economic and political considerations, has done much to make for a more complete and satisfying kind of study than the old histories of the 'battles and kings' variety. At the same time, I am beginning to suspect that the vogue for 'war and society', which lies at the heart of the new enthusiasms, is in danger of commanding a disproportionate amount of attention. A few of the protagonists of 'the new military history' appear to proceed from the assumptions that campaigns and battles are unworthy of serious attention, that everything worth knowing about them has already been established, and that their outcome (as far as it is relevant at all) is somehow determined without conscious human intervention. These are presuppositions which I cannot share. Indeed, I would contend that 'war and society', as an historical exercise, is by its nature local, descriptive rather than analytical, and oddly inert — explaining possibly less of what actually happened than do the neglected subjects of military organisation and military decision-making.

As a useful corrective to the excesses of military sociology, I recommend a reading of the article by Dennis E. Showalter, 'A Modest Plea for Trumpets and Drums' (*Military Affairs*, 1979), John Keegan's masterful study of the experience of combat (*The Face of Battle*, 1976), and the long section of Michael Roberts's *The Swedish Imperial Experience* (1979), in which, after carefully turning over every possible alternative explanation, he concludes that the loss of Sweden's eastern Baltic provinces was an avoidable catastrophe, the responsibility for which lies squarely with the Swedish kings. Writing of this standard gives one the confidence to assert that it was indeed a matter of some moment that a Rumyantsev commanded armies on the Danube in the 1770s, or that a Survorov led the Russians in Italy and Switzerland in 1799.

The circumstances of my employment precluded me from pursuing research in the Soviet Union. As some compensation, the Lenin Library in Moscow kindly leant me a generous amount of otherwise inaccessible material. Moreover, the fund of relevant printed documents and contemporary memoirs at hand in this country has turned out to be almost limitless, equalling in range the sources relating to the Prussian army of the period, and foreshadowing in its descriptive power and psychological accuracy the oeuvre of the Russian nineteenth-century novelists.

Rather more frustrating has been the business of evaluating the recent secondary material. Not only do the general historians, almost without exception, lack the military historical knowledge required to distinguish between what is true and what is tendentious in Soviet writing on eighteenth-century warfare, but non-socialist authorities are in fundamental disagreement on some quite weighty matters of more pacific nature. Is it correct, for example, to say that the concessions made by Russian monarchs in the matter of noble service obligations were an intelligent response to changed social conditions (Raeff), or merely the product of weakness? Were the later partitions of Poland really powered by the land-hunger of the Russian nobility, 'concealed behind the lofty slogans of "national tasks"' (Pipes)? Terms like 'feudalism', 'aristocracy' and 'autocracy' are liable to explode under the boots of the military historian, who must look about him with care and tread as lightly as he can.

An especially sharp controversy concerns the very nature of the Russian body politic. Richard Pipes, in his beautifully written *Russia under the Old Regime* (1974), claims to have identified a 'patrimonial' character in the public affairs of ancient Muscovy, which set it apart from the institutions of western Europe, and which, transmuted through the centuries, helps to account for the emergence of the police state of the later nineteenth century, and the totalitarian regime of modern times. Aleksandr Solzhenitsyn, at the other extreme, accuses Pipes and his followers of racialism, and, by attributing every evil to a basically non-Russian Soviet despotism, he categorically denies any survival from the earlier period. The debate is of more than historical interest, for American politicians are unaccountably ready to lend an ear to academics and visionaries. While I am in no way qualified to intervene in this battle of heavyweights, I must say that I find both schools of thought equally uncongenial. On instinctive rather than scholarly grounds, I distrust the all-embracing Pipes interpretations, and suspect that they are unduly influenced by a dislike of things Russian. On the other side, the Solzhenitsyn thesis is tenable only if you are ready to ignore the mass of evidence which clearly points to significant continuities in the life of his great nation.

I owe a great deal to the facilities made available by John Hunt the librarian of the R.M.A. Sandhurst, and to the staffs of the London Library, the British Library, and the library of the School of Slavonic and East European Studies.

Profitable avenues of investigation were suggested by Philip Longworth, my colleagues Michael Orr and Christopher Donnelly, and Lieutenant-General Pavel Zhilin, the President of the Soviet Commission on Military History. Professor Bruce Menning introduced me to the considerable amount of work now going ahead on related themes on the far side of the Atlantic. At a moment's notice Herr Albert Schmied left his occupations, and conducted me around the Muotatal, so unexpectedly rich in the sites, relics and living traditions of the passage of the Russians in 1799. I look back on those hours as some of the most enjoyable I have ever spent as an historian.

Two people unselfishly read through the typescript of this book — a labour which was the literary equivalent of hauling a barge one hundred miles up the Volga. One was Richard Woff of the Foreign and Commonwealth Office. The other was Dr Isabel de Madariaga, Reader in Russian Studies at the University of London, who not only knows more about Catherine the Great than probably anyone else, but also, as people say, shares some of the characteristics (the good ones) of that remarkable woman. I benefited greatly from their constructive criticisms, and from their eagle-eyed vigilance which exorcised the work of that devil who unerringly guides you to write 'up' when you mean 'down', or 'east' when you really intend 'west'. All remaining mistakes and misjudgments are entirely my own responsibility.

This work was undertaken as a private venture. No passage therein should be taken as an expression of official opinion.

One So Many Russias

The bloody mire of Mongol slavery ... forms the cradle of Muscovy, and modern Russia is but a metamorphosis of Muscovy. (Marx)

From time immemorial the government of Russia has borne a despotic character. The liberty of a Russian subject has never extended so far as to permit him to discuss the respective rights of sovereign and people ... it is possible that no Russian has ever conceived that his country could be governed otherwise than by an absolute sovereign. (C. H. Manstein)

Not many areas in historical study offer quite so much opportunity for unverifiable speculation as the origins and nature of The Russian Soul. The influence of foreigners has always claimed much attention in this respect, if only because it can be endowed with seeming authenticity by referring to places and dates.

In search of trade and plunder, the Norsemen of the ninth century drove and hauled their longships over the great tract of Slavonic lowlands between the Baltic and the Black Sea, founding the northern trading centre of Novgorod, and setting themselves up in 882 as princes in the southern city of Kiev. The legacy of these Scandinavians was out of all proportion to their small numbers. They founded the *druzhinas*, or bands of feudal retainers, which were the remotest ancestors of the Russian military forces. They left the name of 'Rus' to the land as a whole, as well as adding to the fair-haired stock among the population at large. Families like the Dolgorukov (lit. 'long arm') and Obolensky are still fond of tracing their lines back to Rurik and his compatriots, while the Nordic 'Helgas' were the etymological ancestresses of all those Russian girls called 'Olga', who conjure up fantasies (according to one's mood) of sultry spies, or brawny female tractor-drivers.

If Novgorod was increasingly drawn to the North over the centuries, the city of Kiev became the main channel by which the culture of Byzantium reached Russia, after Grand Prince Vladimir was baptised in 989. The Greek alphabet, culture, liturgy and belief helped to transform relationships and institutions, fusing the present with a timeless eternity, binding people and church together, and welding spiritual and temporal authority into an indissoluble whole.

In the middle decades of the thirteenth century the Russian heartlands underwent a conquest of a much less gentle nature. Having consolidated their power in the East, after Genghis Khan conquered Pekin in 1215, the Mongol hordes turned west into Slavonic Europe in what became known as the Great Raid of 1237-9. Kiev was totally devastated in the process, and the Mongols established themselves along the Volga, from where they demanded tribute from all the princes of the land of Rus.

If we except the inhabitants of Kiev and Little Russia, lying in their heaps of whitened bones, no population was more radically transmuted by the Mongol presence than the folk of what later became known as Great Russia — the area of heavy forest that extended around little settlements like Moscow. The princes of Muscovy became the most enthusiastic and shameless of the Mongol surrogates, and much that was distinctive and unattractive about the Russian character and Russian institutions has been attributed to this experience. Mongol influence has been held variously responsible for the destruction of the urban classes, the brutalisation of the peasantry, a denial of human dignity, and a distorted sense of values which reserved a special admiration for ferocity, tyrannical ways and slyness. More specifically, we can point to the Tartar derivation of many words concerning trade, communications and repression, and to the Mongol influence on the Muscovite military forces, which found ready-made models in Tartar weapons, formations and tactics, and borrowed the useful idea of entering people on conscript rolls for military service and taxation.

Muscovite notions of representative government were likewise derived from the heirs of Genghis Khan, extinguishing any hope of the emergence of the concept of land or peoples as entities distinct from the personal property of the ruler. The Great Russian populations, if they were not actually born to be serfs, have certainly, over the centuries, inclined themselves to accept a degree of direction which elsewhere might be regarded as frankly tyrannical. They justified it to themselves as, variously, a safeguard against foreign invasion, a curb on their anarchical instincts, or as a spur to a passive temperament which could supply no initiatives of its own.

No less marked was the Muscovite inclination towards communal living and collective action. Here we can probably detect the working of the physical conditions of Great Russia. Only a community labouring in concert could put forth the intense effort needed to exploit the brief growing season and clear the dense and matted forests. Conversely, a resigned, almost comatose passivity was the only reasonable response to the long periods of the year when there was little of any use to be done in the open air. Once the heaviest snows had fallen, the notorious winters were actually less paralysing in this respect than the seasons of the spring thaw and the torrential autumn rains.

The Russian language was itself profoundly influenced by the forest experience. The word *izba* (log hut) originally bore the significance of 'heated building', and like the Russian vocabulary describing fire and the colour red it bore overtones of a welcoming warmth, calling to mind the traditions of hospitality among rustic neighbours, and the dedicated feasting of their princes. Other usages remind us of the isolation and fears of the Russian communities. The collective name for something that was strange or alien, *chuzhoi*, had strong pejorative implications. *Nemets* was even worse, meaning a speechless foreigner, and more especially a German one.

It is of the greatest importance for our story that the power which came to represent 'Russia' to the world was the Muscovy of the forest and the Mongol absolutism, and not Kiev or Little Russia, with their outlook on Byzantium and Catholic Poland, or Novgorod, with its openings to Scandinavia and Hanseatic Europe. Indeed, a person of an uncharitable and legalistic turn of mind might be inclined to claim that Muscovite Russia survived into the twentieth century as the last remnant of the Mongol empire, for the grand prince of Muscovy simply ceased to pay tribute to the Golden Horde in 1476, without having evicted the Mongols by force, or renounced his allegiance. In the seventeenth century families of Tartar origin accounted for almost one in five of the service nobility, and they comprised names as well-known as Apraksin, Leontev, Rostopchin and Turgenev.

The principality of Moscow had gradually asserted its mastery of Great Russia during the eclipse of Kiev, and with the decline of Mongol power in the fifteenth century the Muscovites began to behave towards their more distant Russian neighbours in a notably high-handed style. Grand Prince Ivan III (1462-1505) made use of the opportunities to the full, and not only annexed Novgorod in 1478, but appropriated the double eagle insignia and other trappings of the defunct Byzantine empire for himself. This exercise helped to lend credibility to Moscow's claim to be

So Many Russias 3

considered the 'Third Rome' – after Byzantium, as the 'Second Rome', had disgraced itself by compounding with the Latin Christians in 1439, and undergone condign punishment when it was wiped out by the Turks in 1453.

Emerging from their forest refuge, the Muscovites found the landscape of Russia seamed with meandering watercourses. A march of no more than 160 miles from their capital brought them to the little rivers of the Valdai uplands, or the regimes of the Volga, the Don and the Dnieper, and so offered them the potential of access to the Gulf of Finland, the Black Sea and the Caspian. In each of these directions, however, there existed peoples whose obduracy offered the kind of barrier which geography had failed to supply. To the west, the very formidable military power of Poland disputed the Ukraine, Little Russia and White Russia, and retained the means of striking at the Muscovite heartland. Competition became more intense the closer the Muscovites approached the Baltic littoral, for there they had to contend not just with the Poles, and their Lithuanian and Livonian associates, but with the newly arrived and aggressive Swedes. Livonia was abandoned to the Poles in 1582, and Estonia to the Swedes in 1595. Moscow itself underwent a period of Polish occupation in the anarchic 'Time of Troubles' early in the next century.

From 1654 Tsar Aleksei Mikhailovich took the risk of committing Muscovy to the fringes of the series of great wars that raged through Europe in the middle decades of the seventeenth century. The young Muscovite armies suffered appallingly at the hands of the Poles, especially in a run of defeats at the turn of the 1650s and 1660s, when 10,000 men might be lost in a single battle. The Muscovites could not sustain the conquests that they made from the Swedes in the Gulf of Finland in the concurrent war of 1656-61, and the cost of the thirteen years of struggle was disproportionately high, even taking into consideration the fruits of the peace treaty of 1667, which advanced the borders of the state across the Ukraine to the Dnieper, and, on the far side, gave Aleksei Mikhailovich the city of Kiev, in all its tarnished glamour.

With such experiences awaiting them in the west, it was scarcely surprising that the Muscovites should sometimes have turned their eyes to the Don and the 'dear mother' Volga as they wandered through woods, grasslands and desert steppe to the southern seas. The prospect was all the more tempting because the cohesion of their former overlords, the Tartars (Mongols), had dissolved in the course of the fifteenth century. In the process the Golden Horde broke up into a number of khanates, only one of which, that of the Crimea, had the power to withstand the Muscovites.

One of the doomed khanates had its seat at Kazan, ensconced amid magnificent oakwoods at the great bend of the Volga, where it finally settled on its southward course. After two years of effort, Prince Ivan IV 'the Terrible' conquered the place in 1552. This was an event of crucial importance in Muscovite territorial expansion, unlocking as it did the avenues eastwards across the Volga into central Asia, and southwards towards the Caspian. Both routes were exploited with astonishing speed, with the help of water transport. In 1556 the Muscovites reduced Astrakhan, where the Volga branched out for its final push to the Caspian Sea – an acquisition which gave them the entire course of that great river, and an outlook on Persia and the back door of the Middle East. The corresponding advance eastwards was spearheaded in the 1580s by parties of Cossacks, who pointed the way for trading posts and settlements that were to extend thousands of miles across Siberia to the Pacific.

The one surviving khanate was that of the Crimea, which comprised the peninsula proper, which was the home of the 'settled' Crimea Tartars, and the steppes of the Nogai nomads on the adjacent mainland. In 1475 the Crimean Tartars became vassals of the aggressive Ottoman Turks, who enjoyed direct access to the Crimea and the estuary of the Dnieper across the Black Sea, and to the mouth of the Don by way of the Straits of Kerch and the Sea of Azov. These circumstances help to explain why the Crimean Tartars, instead of being pushed into the sea by the Muscovites, entered a new career as a strategic bridgehead of militant Islam.

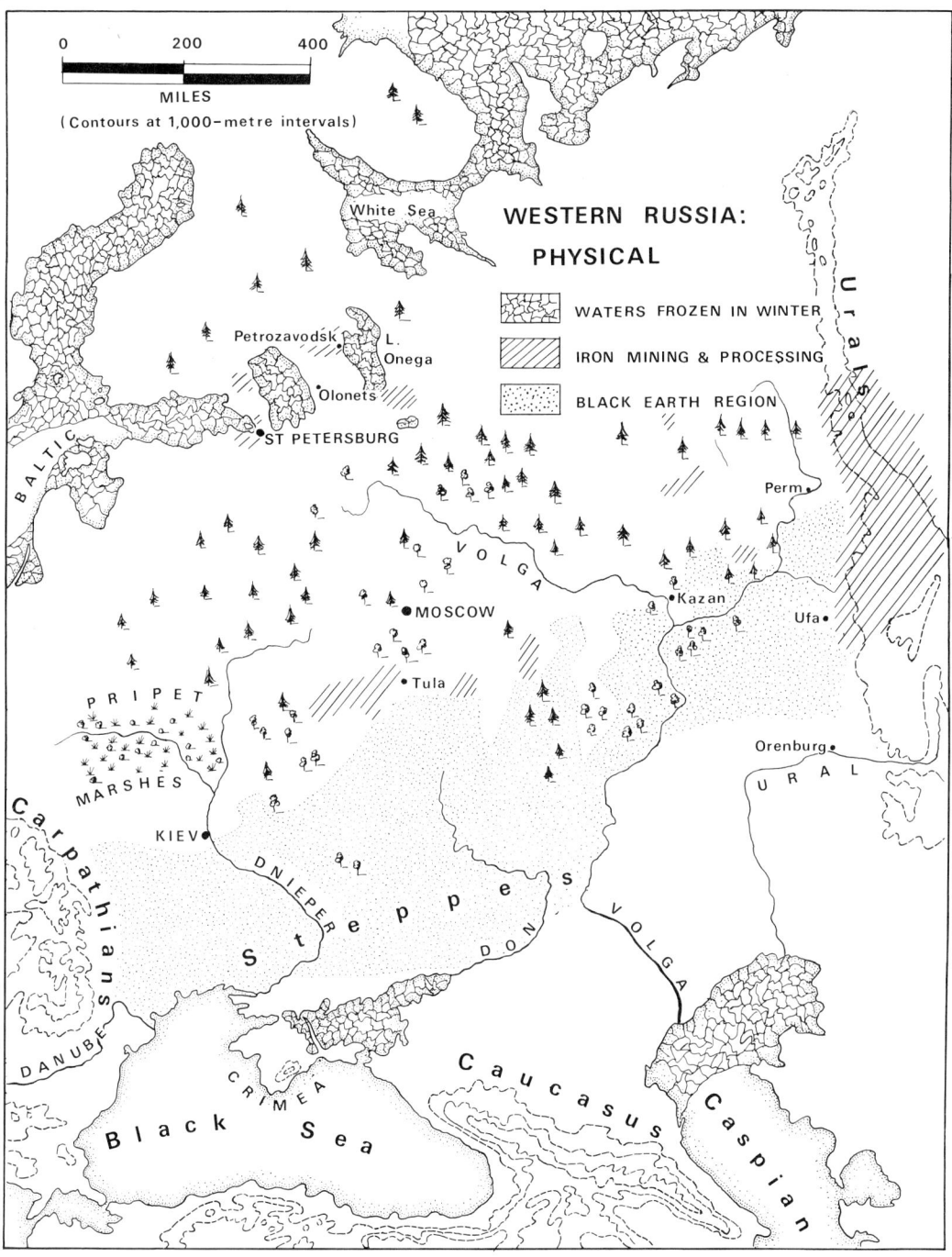

The reasons for Muscovite annoyance with the Crimean Tartars remained remarkably constant over the years. For three centuries the Tartars were in the habit of raiding deep into Russia and the Ukraine, in search of slaves for the Levantine market. On the defensive, the Tartars could embarrass the Russians simply by sitting behind their massive Lines of Perekop, astride the narrow isthmus connecting the Crimea with the mainland. Here they were neatly positioned on the flank of any Russian drive around the shores of the Black Sea. The Russians consequently had to detach considerable armies to storm the Perekop Lines, or to stand watch on the steppes outside, which was a hardly more attractive prospect.

These considerations, taken together with the great physical effort involved in bringing the Russian armies across the steppes in the first place, made the decision to fight on the southern theatre a matter of some moment, implying a major and perhaps permanent diversion of forces from the north-western borders, where they might be needed for use against folk like the Poles, Swedes or Prussians. Experience showed that in order to gain solid results in the south, Russia had to make the commitment not just for a decade, but for a whole generation at a time.

With the young Muscovite state engaged along so many frontiers, we have to examine the fitness of its institutions to stand the strain.

By the middle decades of the seventeenth century, the army had evolved into an extraordinary rag-bag of formations, representing so many survivals from the past, borrowings from the West, and experiments and expedients, expressing a general principle of setting the new alongside the old, without any attempt to transform the whole.

The most ancient and in every way the most unsatisfactory element was represented by the noble cavalrymen and their armed serfs. The greater landed boyars (numbering about 6,000 males) derived prestige from their closeness to the person of the tsar, but now scarcely even went through the motions of providing the state with an effective military force. They were greatly outnumbered by the 50,000 or so males of the Middle Service Class — the *dvoryane* and the *deti boyarskie* (lit. 'children of the boyars'), who owned an average of five or six peasant households each, in return for an obligation to perform wartime service. This petty nobility was assiduous in its efforts to improve its social standing — in 1649, for example, it won the full legal enserfment of its peasants — but it became of less and less account in warfare. In terms of numbers, its contribution was not very significant, comprising in 1667 only about 19,000 out of the total of 42,500 cavalry. Moreover, with its feeble, gun-shy horses, and its bows and arrows, lances and rusty swords, it proved to be inadequate for combat against the Tartars, and almost completely useless when faced with regular Western armies.

The failings of the feudal levy left the *Streltsy* (lit. 'musketeers') for many years as the only reliable source of native troops. They were founded by Ivan the Terrible in 1550, and soon proved their worth in the conquest of Kazan. Clad in their distinctive long coats, and armed with muskets and halberds, they did excellent service for the rest of that century and for much of the next, and even survived to give Peter the Great some of the best stock for his regular army. Their numbers had risen from the first 3,000 in 1550 to 33,775 in 1632, and to no less than 50,000 in 1681, comprising 45,000 infantry and 5,000 cavalry. By then, however, the formation was failing to measure up to the needs of the times. While maintaining a very high sense of self-importance, the *Streltsy* lacked good native leadership, and their commitment to the military life often gave second place to their peacetime civilian trades.

Long before the reign of Peter the Great, the tsars of Muscovy were alive to the importance of acquiring useful military technology and skilled manpower from the West. Foreign gunfounders and military engineers had been active as far back as the reign of Ivan the Terrible in the middle of the sixteenth century. Modern ideas on military organisation and the art of war were also prized. In 1621 Onisim Mikhailov produced a manuscript *Code of Military and Artillery Practice*, after many years of study in foreign languages, and in 1649 the young Tsar Aleksei Mikhailovich published a volume of infantry regulations deriving mainly from the example of Maurice of Nassau – a document which Peter the Great himself recognised as the foundation of the regular army of Russia.

Over the middle decades of the seventeenth century the endemic wars of western Europe bred up generations of ambitious, discontented or dispossessed military men, many of whom found their way to Muscovy – English or Scots, made homeless by the defeat of Charles I, perhaps, or Dutch, Danes, Germans and Swedes who had been thrown out of work by treaties of peace.

The first large batch of foreigners was enrolled in the early 1630s, as part of a recruiting drive in north-west Europe. The results did not entirely meet expectations, for the foreign regiments did not acquit themselves particularly well on campaign, and the nobles of the Middle Service Class were unwilling to serve under or alongside the newcomers. In 1647, however, Aleksei Mikhailovich had the inspiration of cutting loose from the past, and forming a body of native conscripts who were summoned for service on the basis of census rolls. The recruiting of foreigners went ahead, but now with the particular purpose of buying individuals to officer the conscript army.

The new regiments were formed in the early 1650s as units of infantry, heavy cavalry and lancers – all in addition to an existing corps of regular dragoons. In wartime the new formations supplied a mass of up to about 60,000 infantry and 45,000 cavalry, who were supposed to be armed and organised on the Western model. In time of peace, however, both the numbers of men and the cadres were greatly reduced, and only a few units were kept at a high standard of training.

Not surprisingly, the state was thrown into a convulsion whenever the tsar committed it to war. The noble cavalrymen groped around in dusty cupboards for their weapons, while generals for the conscript forces were sought out, or promoted on the spot, and severally assigned districts 'from which, according as the necessities of war may demand, the serfs are to be driven from their huts into the ranks, until the requisite number be filled up'. The product was all too often 'a mob of the lowest and most uncouth ragamuffins' (Korb, 1863, II, 138).

By the 1670s, Muscovy could certainly put forth vast forces, which amounted, according to some estimates, to 200,000 or 300,000 men, but in almost every other respect the rest of Europe remained unimpressed. An Austrian diplomat claimed that 'from a slothful genius and habits of slavery, they have neither stomach for great things, nor do they achieve them' (Korb, 1863, II, 35). The boyars disliked campaigning, and thought only of returning to home comforts once the danger of invasion was past, while the *muzhik* infantry let themselves be herded forward in battle, then lost heart and were cut down in their thousands.

In the early 1680s a small group at the court of the juvenile Tsar Fedor Alekseevich tried to carry through a last reform of the old Muscovite forces. In November 1681 a conference of generals, boyars and leading citizens came together under the presidency of Prince Vasilii Golitsyn to devise measures 'for the better organisation and direction of the army'. On 12 January of the next year it proclaimed the most ambitious of its resolutions, which abolished *mestnichestvo*, the 'system of places' according to which the old nobility had taken its place in the army according to elaborate tables of ancestry. As had long been the case with the foreigners, ranks were now to be filled by the serving families regardless of their origins.

It was not easy to discern any beneficial effects on the army, which needed nothing so much as firm discipline and a period of peace. Instead, Russia joined itself in 1686 to the Holy League of Austria, Poland and Venice against the Turks. The army was twice directed towards the Crimea, in 1687 and 1689, marching in a single unpaid and hungry mass. I. T. Pososhkov recalled how 'Prince Vasilii Vasilevich Golitsyn moved against the Perekop, accompanied by an army which some say amounted to 300,000 troops. The Tartars on their side had but 15,000 men all told, yet our force for all its size did not dare give battle to such a tiny band' (Pososhkov, 1951, 262).

What had gone wrong? In the introduction to his Military Code of 1716 Peter the Great acknowledged the pioneering work of Aleksei Mikhailovich, whose army had accomplished 'glorious deeds' in the wars against the Poles and Swedes.

And what happened then? The army proved incapable of standing not just against civilised nations, but even against barbarians, of which we still have fresh memories ... not only of what happened ... in the Crimean campaigns, but of more recent events as with our experiences at the hands of the Turks at Azov, and at the beginning of the present war at Narva.

He traced the cause to a fundamental lack of 'good order'.

Two Peter I, 'the Great' 1682-1725

The young tsar

The early years of Russia's greatest ruler were fraught with enough shocks and excitements to derange the mind of a more stable person than the juvenile Peter Alekseevich Romanov. The story is a very familiar one, but it bears a little repetition.

The very fact that Peter came into the world at all placed him in some peril. He was born in 1672, as a fruit of the second marriage of Tsar Aleksei Mikhailovich. During the subsequent reign of Fedor Alekseevich, the young Peter lived in constant danger from his violent and jealous half-sister, Sophia, who was a product of the first marriage, and in 1682 he and his mother retreated to the doubtful safety of the village of Preobrazhenskoe outside Moscow. Preobrazhenskoe signifies 'Transfiguration', and there was indeed something almost miraculous about the way this retarded, awkward and nearly uneducated boy found the way to teach himself, and ultimately his entire nation, about the basics of armed power.

Inspired partly by a youthful enthusiasm for military games, and partly by a highly developed instinct for self-preservation, Peter slowly formed a miniature army about his person. To begin with, the company lived up to its name of the *Poteshnyi* Company — plaything or entertainment — being recruited from childhood playmates and the servants and retainers of his dead father. The first adult to present himself was the young groom Sergei Leontev Bukhvostov, who in 1683 was

1 Peter the Great

entered on the books as the 'First Russian Soldier'. The necessary hardware was hauled up from wherever it could be found — artillery and stands of arms from storerooms and the Kremlin arsenal, and an ancient English or Dutch sailing boat which had been lying forgotten in the village of Izmailova. Peter had once shuddered at the sight of anything so large or so wet as a pond, but the little craft at Izmailova became the inspiration for a whole navy.

As Peter progressed through his teens, the military games assumed a more professional air. The *Poteshnyi* were organised as a company of bombardiers, and they embodied a strict principle of promotion according to merit. Peter was 'concerned from the start to wean the nobility of his state from their prejudices about birth. They believed it was insulting for a man of illustrious family to have to serve under a general of lower condition' (Manstein, 1860, II, 360). Peter had himself enrolled as nothing more grand than the 'First Bombardier', and he put all promotion in the hands of Prince Fedor Romodanovskii, who, until his death in 1718, solemnly advanced the tsar up through all the ranks of the military hierarchy. Something approaching regular manoeuvres were held around a miniature fortress, and in 1687 the corps received a significant accession of strength in the form of drafts from the three elite *Streltsy* regiments from the Butyrki district of Moscow. These were formed into two complete regiments, the Preobrazhenskii and the Semenovskii (pron. 'Semionovsky'), so-called after Peter's refuge and one of the nearby villages. The original bombardiers of the *Poteshnyi* Company were assigned to them in two companies of fifty each.

All of this helped to draw down on Peter and his party the attention of Sophia, who identified a threat to her tenure of power as regent. To put his person beyond the reach of her plots, Peter fled in 1689 to the sanctuary of the massive walls of the Troitse-Sergiev monastery, to the north of Moscow. The 'play regiments' lay at Peter's disposal, as was only to be expected, but of far greater importance in building up his power base was his success in winning over the prominent boyars, the Western officers from the Foreign Suburb, and the mass of the *Streltsy*. Sophia was left without support, and Peter returned to Moscow in the autumn as acknowledged master of Russia.

Nothing is more surprising in Peter's development than his reluctance to assume a post of ultimate responsibility. Just as he did not take up active field command until well into his war with the Swedes, so now the process of fitting himself to lead the army and state continued regardless of his victory over Sophia.

From the Dutchman Franz Timmermann the young tsar absorbed the principles of fortification, ballistics and other mathematically based arts. The Swiss Franz Lefort gave him an outlook on the wider world and its ways, as well as many useful notions on military affairs. From the unlikely background of a staid Genevan family, the latter gentleman had found his way through the French, Dutch and Prussian services to Russia, where he ended up penniless in the Foreign Suburb. Lefort saved himself by marrying a rich heiress, but he did not hesitate to put his career at risk by presenting himself as one of the first supporters of Peter at his monastic stronghold. Peter prized Lefort for his cheerful and energetic character, as much as for his expertise and loyalty, and he made him his first general and admiral, and the first of the knights of the Order of St Andrew, which he founded in the same year of 1689. Lefort was capable of matching Peter bottle for bottle, and his dissolute habits were said to have hastened his death ten years later.

A calmer, more staid and reflective influence emanated from the Catholic Scotsman, Patrick Gordon, who had come to Muscovy in 1661. However, both Gordon and Lefort were active in helping Peter to stage the very realistic manoeuvres that were held outside Moscow in the early 1690s. A 'great and terrible battle' took place in the autumn of 1691, and the series culminated in a combat in September and October 1694, when six regiments of *Streltsy* tried to defend a fortress against 15,000 troops of the new foundation – the original Preobrazhenskii and Semenovskii Regiments, two new regiments set up respectively by Gordon and Lefort, and Colonel Scharf's regiment of conscripts. Many were the men who were skewered by bayonets and swords, or blown up by the cardboard bombs and pottery grenades.

The next year the carefully nurtured new formations were pushed with the unregenerate old army into war in earnest against the Turks, and the experience was to show how very far both elements still fell short of measuring up even to these half-barbaric enemies. Peter had made up his mind to put new life into the War of the Holy League which he had inherited from Sophia the regent. He was actuated less by crusading zeal than by the desire to crack open the Turkish fortress of Azov, and thus open the way through the mouth of the Don to the Sea of Azov, and so perhaps ultimately to the Black Sea. He had been entranced by two recent visits to his bustling port of Archangel on the aptly named White Sea, but he appreciated that these far northern waters, which were frozen for most of the year, would never give him a fitting avenue to the wider world.

While 120,000 of the 'old' troops were sent towards the Dnieper, a force of more than 30,000 men of the new regiments made their way by barge down the Volga, and thence a short distance overland to the regime of the lower Don. In July 1695 all the forces arrived before Azov. It soon transpired that there was no way of stopping the Turks from replenishing the fortress by way of the river, or of curbing the sorties of the unusually frisky garrison. Peter impatiently ordered a general assault, over the protests of Gordon, and when the attack went in on 5 August it was repulsed with a loss of more than 1,500 killed. In September a second assault met with no greater success, and in cold and damp weather the army undertook the seven-week journey home.

Peter and his army made their way back to Azov in 1696. This time the preparations were much more thorough. From the experience of the last campaign, Peter had learnt that 'in order to take a fortified place' it was necessary to have suitable forces, directed by 'an expert in the art of attacking towns' (Fabritsius, in Skalon, 1902 – c.11, VII, pt. 1, v). He therefore appealed for help to the Christian powers, and in the course of the campaign, large numbers of German technologists arrived at the trenches before Azov – Brandenburgers like Kober and Schuster, and the gunners Schmidt and Rosen who had been sent by the Emperor of Austria. The attack went through the due processes of regular siege, and the Turks capitulated in July, without putting Peter to the necessity of storming the place. Peter at once repaired the fortifications of Azov town, but preferred to plant his new harbour a little way out along the northern shores of the Sea of Azov at Taganrog.

Dissatisfied with having had to learn so much about Western ways at second hand, Peter left Russia in March 1697 under the thin guise of one 'Peter Mikhailov', a gentleman. He spent well over a year in foreign parts, energetically questioning soldiers, sailors and technicians, measuring fortifications against his own large frame, and leaving behind him a succession of smashed-up apartments and gardens, and a slug-like trail of members of his own party of 250 or so, who were left behind to investigate matters of interest. Vasilii Kochmin was one of the five bombardiers who stayed in Brandenburg to learn more about bombardiering, and he wrote pathetically to Peter

our master [a lieutenant of artillery] is a good man; he knows a good deal, and teaches us well. The one thing that stands in the way of our good relations is that he asks for money for his teaching, and without payment our instruction cannot proceed. (Strukhov, in Skalon, 1902-c.11, VI, bk 1, pt 1, 28)

After making an unannounced stop at Riga, in Swedish Livonia, Peter proceeded to East Prussia (where he got on very well with the Elector of Brandenburg), and then by way of Berlin to Holland to discover how to build ships. Britain was the westernmost destination of the grand tour. Here he found further opportunities for practical shipbuilding, in the Thames dockyard at Deptford, as well as for researches into astronomy a little way downriver at Greenwich Observatory, and into gunfounding at Woolwich Arsenal.

Peter planned to make a leisurely return journey by way of Austria and Venice, but an accumulation of bad news from home forced him to break off the tour in Vienna in July 1698, and head immediately for Moscow. He took back with him an incalculable store of knowledge, and a set of standards by which his transformation of Muscovy would have to be judged.

2 *Zar und Zimmermann* — Peter the Great in the guise of a shipwright on his Western travels

The reason for the sudden curtailment of the western tour lay in the unrest among certain of the *Streltsy*, who had been encouraged in their grumblings by Sophia, who had retained all her worldly ambitions during her banishment in a nunnery. Peter returned to Moscow in such an agitated and unpredictable mood that it was physically dangerous to stand anywhere near him. He regarded the *Streltsy* malcontents not merely as traitors, but as representatives of an old political, social and military order which he was determined to crush. The interrogations, tortures, hangings, decapitations and breakings on the wheel extended over five months, and claimed the lives of probably more than one thousand wretches.

Four regiments of the Moscow *Streltsy* were disbanded without more ado for their part in the rebellion. The men of the remaining sixteen Moscow regiments were held to the obligation of service, but scattered over the country as peasants, while the regiments of provincial *Streltsy* were absorbed over the years into the new regular army.

'The soldiers' hut at Preobrazhenskoe' — the creation of the standing regular army of Russia, 1699-1700

Peter's foreign tour and the gutting of the *Streltsy* represented two stages in the tsar's process of winning free of the legacy of ancient Muscovy. As the new century approached, Peter believed that the time had come to endow his Russia with one of the most important attributes of a modern state — a standing army of regular troops, 'most sagely considering that it is only the veteran soldier who has been broken in by many years of training that is worthy of the glory of real warfare' (Korb, 1863, II, 141).

To begin with, the recruiting embraced both volunteers and conscripts. The first published notice relating to the new army appeared on 8 November 1699:

Concerning the enlistment of all willing men into service as soldiers. Whoever wants to join up, is to have himself enrolled at Preobrazhenskoe, at the soldiers' hut. Such men will be given eleven roubles per annum, and they will be engaged in the Moscow regiments as soldiers. When they are on His Majesty's service, and wherever they happen to be, they will receive rations of flour, fodder and wine on the same basis as the soldiers of the Preobrazhenskii and Semenovskii regiments.

These terms were by no means unattractive, for eleven roubles represented a very good working wage, and military service offered a means of escape to peasants from a servitude that was becoming more and more oppressive. The enlistment of volunteers was made the particular responsibility of General A. M. Golovin, who by the spring of 1700 had collected more than 10,000 men in his 'division' at Moscow.

Interestingly enough, Peter was forced from the

cavalry expressed the abhorrence of the petty nobility for service under foreigners. The *deti boyarskie* were guaranteed against such an affront by being formed into regiments of dragoons, officered and manned almost exclusively by people of their own kind.

The establishment of the new regular army comprised the two veteran regiments of Preobrazhenskii and Semenovskii, twenty-seven, mostly newly raised, 'soldier' regiments of infantry, and the two new regiments of dragoons, making a paper total of about 32,000 men. In fact, the complements of the infantry regiments fell very far short of the target of 1,100 each, and the officers and men alike were direly inexperienced. It is easy to imagine the scenes of disorder as the few veteran officers and NCOs assembled the hordes of *muzhiks* at Preobrazhenskoe, depriving them of their comfortable baggy clothes, and their beards and flowing locks, and arraying them in the unfamiliar 'German' gear of tricorn hat, green coat, cross-belt and cartridge pouch, breeches, gaiters and stiff black shoes.

The process took place without the help of Peter's early mentors, the trusty Lefort and the beloved Gordon, both of whom were dead by 1700. Fortunately, some basic written guidance was at hand. The essentials of Western practice were transmitted through the agency of the young Adam Adamovich Weide (1671 or 1677-1720), who was to become one of the most valued of Peter's servants. Weide was born in Moscow of German parents who had settled in Russia. He was originally intended for a medical career, but he opted instead for the military life. He was sent abroad as a major to observe the newest military developments, and was fortunate enough to serve as an aide-de-camp to Prince Eugene in the campaign of Zenta in 1697. Weide returned to Russia in time to advise on the formation of the new army, and to be captured in the disastrous battle of Narva. Peter ransomed this useful fellow in 1710, and over the following years made him field-marshal and the Second President of the War College. Weide expired in 1720 'very much regretted by both their majesties, and by all ranks of people; but more particularly by the army, who

3 Fusilier of the Preobrazhenskii Regiment, 1700-2. Green coat with red cuffs, buttonholes and lining; red breeches, light green gaiters or stockings; hat with silver lace (Viskovatov, 1844-56)

outset to make a number of concessions to Russian ways and conditions. By raising conscripts, as well as volunteers, he harked back to the levies of the old Muscovite host, if not to the Tartar way of doing things. This measure was aimed especially at sweeping up some of the vast numbers of feudal servants and hangers-on, who were to be recruited from clerical landlords at the rate of one man from every twenty-five households, and from the men of the secular lords at the rate of one from every thirty to fifty households. General Weide saw to the recruitment of these people at Moscow, and Prince Repnin did the same in the little towns to the south and east.

Likewise, the character of the new regular

adored him, notwithstanding his strict discipline' (Bruce, 1782, 204).

Of more immediate relevance for our theme were the regulations of 1698, in which Weide summed up for a Russian audience what he had learned in Austria and elsewhere. The first section emphasised the importance of regular armies, which depended on sound rules and assiduous training to gain their victories. Weide then showed how armies were organised in the West. He took nothing for granted among his readership, and carefully explained that modern armies were 'organised into various subdivisions, namely companies, battalions, regiments and brigades', and that such armies were essentially made up of 'infantry and cavalry'. Next came an elucidation of the hierarchy of Western ranks, and Weide finished with a section on tactical formations. Peter reviewed the document with care, if he did not actually re-write some of it himself, and one of the passages certainly expresses a sentiment which he made his own: 'The term "soldier" applies to everyone who belongs to the army, from the highest general to the last man.' Weide's work was circulated in the army in manuscript form, and officers were expected to copy sections into their individual 'military books'.

Further information was available from the pen of A. M. Golovin, who was another of the 'divisional' commanders of 1699-1700, directly concerned with the formation of the regular army. In his *Military Articles* (*Voinskie Artikuly*), published in March 1700, Golovin went into some detail about the formations and tactics of infantry, but since neither he nor Weide had much to say about the formation of raw troops, the best of their teachings were incorporated with the current experience of training the army into a comprehensive *Short Standard Instruction* (*Kratkoe Obyknovennoe Uchenie*) for infantry regiments, which held good until 1708.

Many years later the Prussian diplomat Vockerodt tried to bring home to his Crown Prince Frederick (later 'the Great') something of the impact of Peter's new army upon Russian society, which saw the regular troops as so many shackles 'placing them without defence at the mercy of the despotic will of their sovereign, however bizarre and unjust it might be'. Peasants found themselves banished from their families for years or life, while the comfortable old nobility could not understand why the tsar wanted to meddle with ways that had served Russia perfectly well in the past. They bore no grudge against the Swedes or anybody else, and by the same token they were reasonably sure that nobody else had a quarrel to pick with them, as long as Russia minded its own business. 'But now we will have to abandon any such thoughts of repose, now that foreigners have imbued our sovereign with the principle that the army must be kept perpetually on foot in peacetime as well as war' (Mediger, 1952, 110-12).

The one Russian to respond with public enthusiasm for the new order was I. T. Pososhkov, in his essay *On the Conduct of the Army* (*O Ratnom Povedenii*) of 1701. He wrote scathingly about the shortcomings of the feudal host, but he suggested that the boyars and other folk might be tempted into the service if skill at horsemanship were properly rewarded.

Foreigners were never in any doubt that the emergence of the new force was a matter of moment. The Swedes rightly saw the army as a direct threat to themselves, while the Austrian ambassador reported that Peter was making ready sixty or even eighty regiments, each with a complement of 1,000 men. This exaggeration was testimony to his concern, if not the accuracy of his arithmetic.

Débâcle at Narva, 1700

Peter was putting his army together with all the more urgency because a concatenation of circumstances seemed to present him with the opportunity of doing something spectacular and advantageous on the northern theatre. The Baltic princes resented the pre-eminence of the Swedes, who by a long process of conquest in the seventeenth century had wrested large pieces of territory from their neighbours – Scania from the Danes on the great Scandinavian peninsula, western Pomerania with the mouth of the Oder in north Germany, and, of more immediate moment to Russia, Karelia and Ingria at the eastern end of the Gulf of Finland, and Estonia and Livonia on the southern shores. These last acquisitions cut off Muscovy from the sea and deprived it of direct access to northern Europe.

Towards the end of the seventeenth century, a refugee Livonian nobleman, Johann Patkul, stimulated the Baltic powers into positive measures to put an end to this unsatisfactory state of affairs. The first of Patkul's converts was the massive figure of Augustus, who ruled the north-east German state of Saxony as elector, and the semi-anarchical state of Poland as King Augustus II. Augustus found little difficulty in winning over the Danes, who had some very old scores to settle with the Swedes, and he sent General Karlovich to Peter to outline the advantages of joint action. Peter fell in quickly with the scheme and promised his support, asking only for time to make an accommodation with the Turks (which he actually reached in July 1700). Nobody expected very serious opposition from the object of all these calculations. Sweden's great days seemed to lie in the past; its present ruler was the eighteen-year-old lad, King Charles XII, who was notorious for his irresponsible and sadistic ways.

It is perhaps timely to take brief stock of Russia's own young ruler, who was about to push his country on to the wider stage of European events. So much about the man called to mind not just the appalling experiences of his youth, but the stirrings of his nation as a whole, emerging as if from a long sleep like the giant of Lermontov's poem. This latent strength lay at the command of a variety of alarming and unpredictable impulses. There was the drive of curiosity, which produced a navy from the sight of the boat in the old storehouse, or created the persona of Peter the savant, directing a correspondence with Leibniz on the origins of the Russian nation. There was the demand for physical action, expressed in the image of the 'worker-tsar' and 'skipper Peter', or in the shocking personal brutalities. There were the lingering insecurities, which had the power to reduce the despotic master to a state of shrieking panic. There was Peter the emperor, and Peter the buffoon.

All the same we have good reason to call Peter 'the Great', when we deny the title to Louis XIV. The magnitude of his achievement is undiminished, even when we call to mind the creative ferment of Muscovy earlier in the seventeenth century. More impressive still is the total lack of vanity and self-seeking. His monuments and statues are the work of his successors, not of himself. Even his great ferocity was probably a necessary measure of state, in the context of the goals which he had set before himself. 'We must establish a distinction between bourgeois virtues, and the necessary attributes of sovereign lords and the leading men in cabinet and in the field. What could have been achieved by gentleness and goodness alone?' (Helbig, 1917, 19).

With so many attendant circumstances that were fresh and promising — the approach of the new century, and the advent of the new regular Russian army to Western warfare — the near-catastrophic failure of the Baltic campaign of 1700 was to prove all the more painful.

On 9 August 1700 the Russians declared war on Sweden. By that time the basis of the joint plan of operations had already been overset. Exploiting the advantages of seaborne mobility and his central strategic position, Charles XII of Sweden had descended on Denmark with a small elite army, and almost simultaneously with the Russian declaration, he forced the Danes to abandon the alliance. King Augustus and his Saxons worked almost as feebly as the Danes, and they committed themselves to a half-hearted siege of Riga, the fortress-capital of Livonia. All of this left Peter, at the eastern end of the Baltic, as the sole immediate target for the Swedes and their energetic king.

Peter's own objective was the strong new Swedish fortress of Narva, which stood on a little river a dozen miles from the Gulf of Finland in Swedish Estonia. The Russian contingents were pushed forward with some difficulty from Novgorod and Pskov, but by the middle of October Narva was surrounded by a mass of 34,000 men — regiments of the new formation, *Streltsy* and noble cavalry.

Two prominent Westerners were borrowed for

16 Peter I, 'the Great' 1682-1725

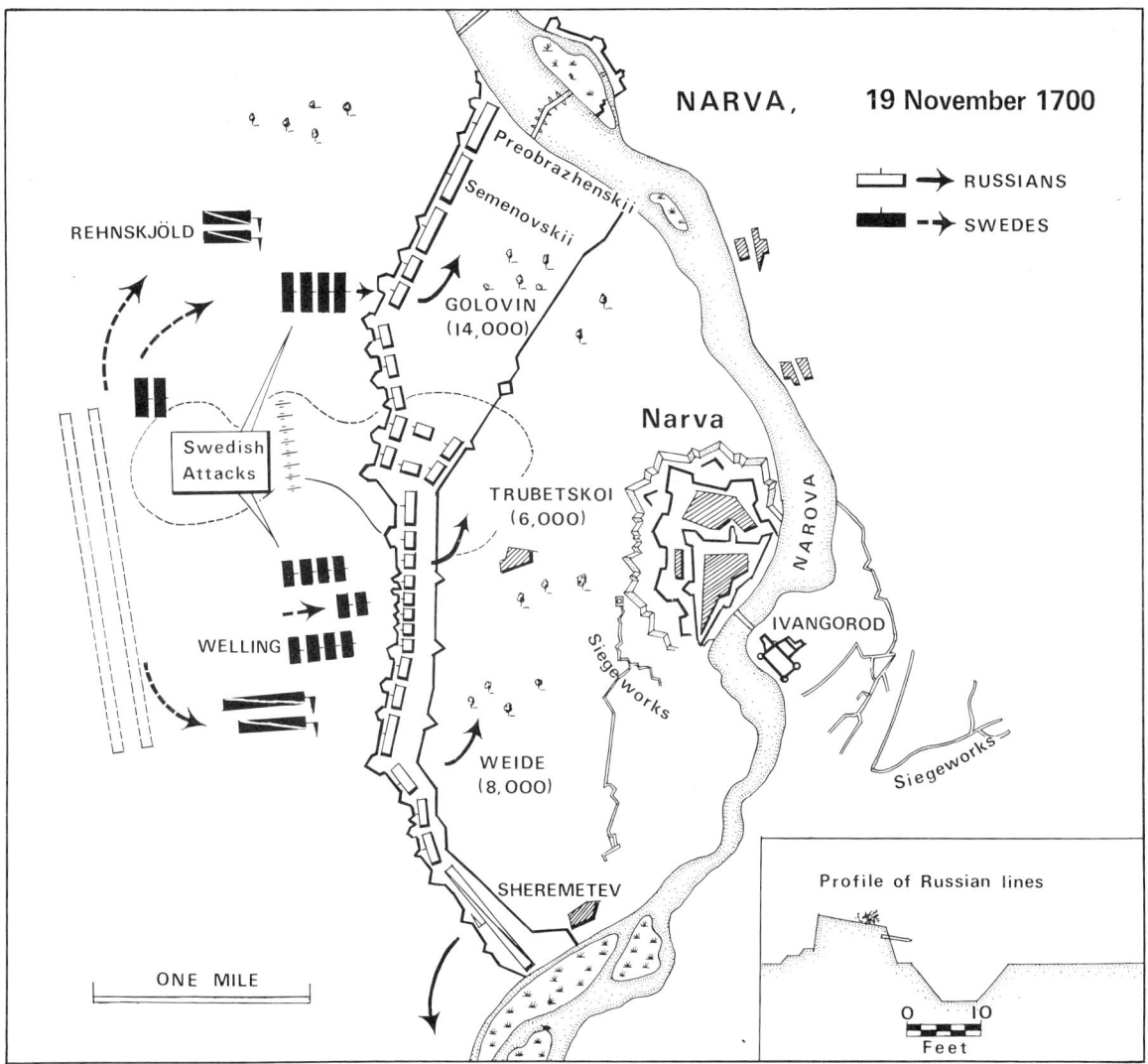

the occasion. The veteran Duc de Croy came from the Emperor of Austria to act as field commander, while King Augustus sent Lieutenant-General Hallart to supervise the technical side of the operation. In the event, the siege artillery performed badly, while the covering army was strung out in the narrow space between two lines of earthworks, lacking alike in depth for manoeuvre and in co-ordination along its length.

Peter sensed that the doom of the Russians was pronounced when Charles landed with his army at Pernau, and moved rapidly to the relief of beleaguered Narva. Peter now found that all sorts of urgent business demanded his presence elsewhere, and he made off early on 19 November, leaving everything in the hands of de Croy. By the rules of war, the tiny Swedish army of about 11,000 men should now have approached the Russians with some circumspection, and settled into a fortified camp of their own. Instead, eight hours after Peter's departure, the Swedes emerged from the woods, and without checking their stride they broke into the Russian entrenchments in two columns.

The feudal cavalry on the Russian left fled in the snowy tracks of their leader, Boris Sheremetev, and before long they were spilling into the black waters of the river Narova. The corresponding heroes on the right, or northern, flank stampeded towards the Kamperholm bridge, which broke under their weight. The remaining divisions were forced to surrender one by one. The Swedes relieved them of their weapons and their senior officers and then, as an ultimate insult, left the rank-and-file free to go back home.

Possibly as many as 8,000 Russian regular troops were killed or wounded in the battle, in addition to the drowned feudal cavalry and untold members of *canaille*. The entire artillery, consisting of 145 cannon and thirty-two mortars and howitzers, was abandoned to the Swedes, who themselves lost a mere 2,000 men. The Russian high command had disappeared, and Peter was so short of officers that he had to promote Sheremetev to field-marshal (only the second of this rank in the army to date), and entrust him with guarding the border.

The restoration of Russian striking-power, 1701-7

Long afterwards Peter wrote:

The Swedes certainly beat us at Narva, but you have to ask yourself what kind of an army they overcame. There was just one veteran regiment, that of Lefort. The two regiments of the Guard had been in two attacks on Narva town, but they had never fought a battle in the open field, let alone one against a regular army. In the rest of the regiments, a few colonels excepted, officers and men alike were the merest recruits. Is it therefore surprising that such an army as the Swedish, veteran, trained and experienced, should have attained a victory over such an unskilful force as ours? It is true that at the time the defeat constituted a heavy blow — a desperate setback to our hopes that was ascribed to the anger of God. Now, however, when we look back on the affair, we must confess that it was a sign of the grace of God, not His disfavour. (Beskrovnyi, 1958, 43-4)

The defeat certainly had the negative advantage of clearing the ground for rebuilding on new foundations. In terms of crude numbers, the 34,000-odd troops who were available in October 1700 had approximately doubled by January the next year. The recruiting system was reorganised in 1705 (see p. 38), and two years later Peter had a total of about 200,000 men under arms.

Some of the hardest work was put in by Prince Boris Golitsyn, who had the job of creating dragoons (the sole category of Peter's regular cavalry) from an unresolved mass of 27,326 men. The first of the new regiments seem to have reached Sheremetev at Pskov in the spring of 1701, and every year saw the formation of fresh units. Twelve regiments were set up in the period 1705-7 alone. The noble character of the dragoons was already being diluted, and 'if we may form an estimate from these fellows from the rash audacity of their crimes, they are fitter for robbery than for rightful war' (Korb, 1863, II, 142-3). The last unflattering sentiment comes from the Austrian secretary of legation, Johann-Georg Korb, who in 1700 published the first account of the new army to reach the Western world. Peter tried in vain to track down and destroy every copy.

The artillery was another arm which had been wiped out at Narva. The aged Andrei Vinius, the Director of Posts, was commissioned to confiscate bells from churches and monasteries, for the sake of the metal, and compel the town artisans to make the necessary gun carriages. His authority was backed by all the force of the Muscovite despotism, and in the early spring of 1701 the first batch of gleaming new ordnance was sent to Sheremetev, in the form of 243 cannon, thirteen howitzers and twelve mortars. Hundreds more pieces were produced by November, when Vinius reported that 'never before has such a quantity of artillery been cast in such a short time and by such "experts" ' (Korb, 1863, II, 75).

It proved easier to replace the vanished hardware than to find good people to direct the artillery. Until then, nearly all the senior gunner officers had been foreigners, lent by other states 'as a proof of amity' (Korb, 1863, II, 144). Vinius was too old, too corrupt and too limited to take

4 James Bruce, creator of the modern Russian artillery

over the superior direction, and Peter instead placed all his trust in Major-General James Bruce. This excellent man was born in 1670, and represented the third generation of his Scottish family to live in Russia. He had served in the two Azov campaigns, and accompanied Peter on his Western tour, when he took the opportunity to study the process of artillery manufacture at Woolwich Arsenal.

Bruce was in every sense a member of the wider European scientific community, and he brought his knowledge to bear on the technical improvement of the Russian ordnance. In 1705, for example, he adopted as the basis of his calculations the *scala*, or system of measurements, which had been devised by the Nuremberg mechanic Hartmann in 1540. He was able to reduce the weight of the 12-pounder field gun from 112 *puds* to thirty, and together with Peter he worked out accurate plans for all the gun carriages and artillery vehicles — a principle that was not taken up in a country like France until as late as 1732. On the organisational side, Bruce arranged the field personnel into an artillery regiment, which first appeared in the lists in 1702, and which received a firm establishment in 1712 in the form of twelve companies of gunners and one of bombardiers.

A generation later, Manstein emphasised the debt which the Russians still owed to the work of Bruce:

I confidently assert that the Russian artillery is in such good order, and so well served, that I truly believe that there is no other which is its equal, let alone its superior. It is . . . the one branch of the military art to which the Russians apply themselves industriously, and in which they have able native-born officers. (Manstein, 1860, II, 368-9)

Peter turned to another of his 'Scotsmen' for advice on how to give some shape to the army as a whole. This was the ex-Austrian Lieutenant-General G. B. Ogilvy, who entered the Russian service at the age of sixty on 14 November 1702. After a study of Russian conditions, he approached Peter in 1705 (some say 1704) with a thirteen-article *Plan and Arrangement for the Army According to Foreign Practice*. Peter accepted the principle of organising the standard infantry regiment as a unit of about 1,400 officers and men, arranged in two battalions. The corresponding organisation for the dragoon regiment became one of six squadrons of two companies each. The tsar, however, decided that Ogilvy's proposals for the size of the army were too modest, and settled on an establishment of two regiments of Guards, forty-seven of line infantry, five of elite grenadiers, thirty-three of dragoons and one of artillery. It was vital to have some bearings of this kind during those years, when so many regiments were being formed and re-formed, or simply extinguished in combat. Peter would probably have been well advised to put the individual regiments on a larger establishment as well, bearing in mind the heavy attrition of manpower in the Russian service (see p. 235).

There remained the problem of acquiring

combat experience in the field. In retrospect, one of the central themes of the Great Northern War might appear to be a personal duel between the tigerish young kings, Peter and Charles, which culminated in the campaign and battle of Poltava. In fact, the activity of the two parties was not congruent. Charles, the active army leader, spent most of the period chasing the Saxons around central Europe, and paid little heed to the doings of the Russians in the eastern backwaters of the Baltic. He had let the Russians go, when they stood at his mercy at Narva, and, like the Israelis after their comparable victory in 1967, he was suffering from the affliction of 'wanton conceit'. Peter, who excelled at organising the work of others, was glad to have six years respite in which to marshal his forces. He fed his armies cautiously into his chosen theatre of war in the Baltic provinces, whenever possible giving battle only when the odds were overwhelmingly on the Russian side, and all the time learning by experience and training the army accordingly.

Field-Marshal Boris Petrovich Sheremetev (1652-1710) proved to be a steady and brave commander, after his lapse from grace at Narva, and with his superior forces he beat the Swedes at Eristfer on 30 December 1701, and again at Hummelshof on 17 July the next year. The open country and little towns of Livonia now stood at the mercy of the Russians, who devastated them

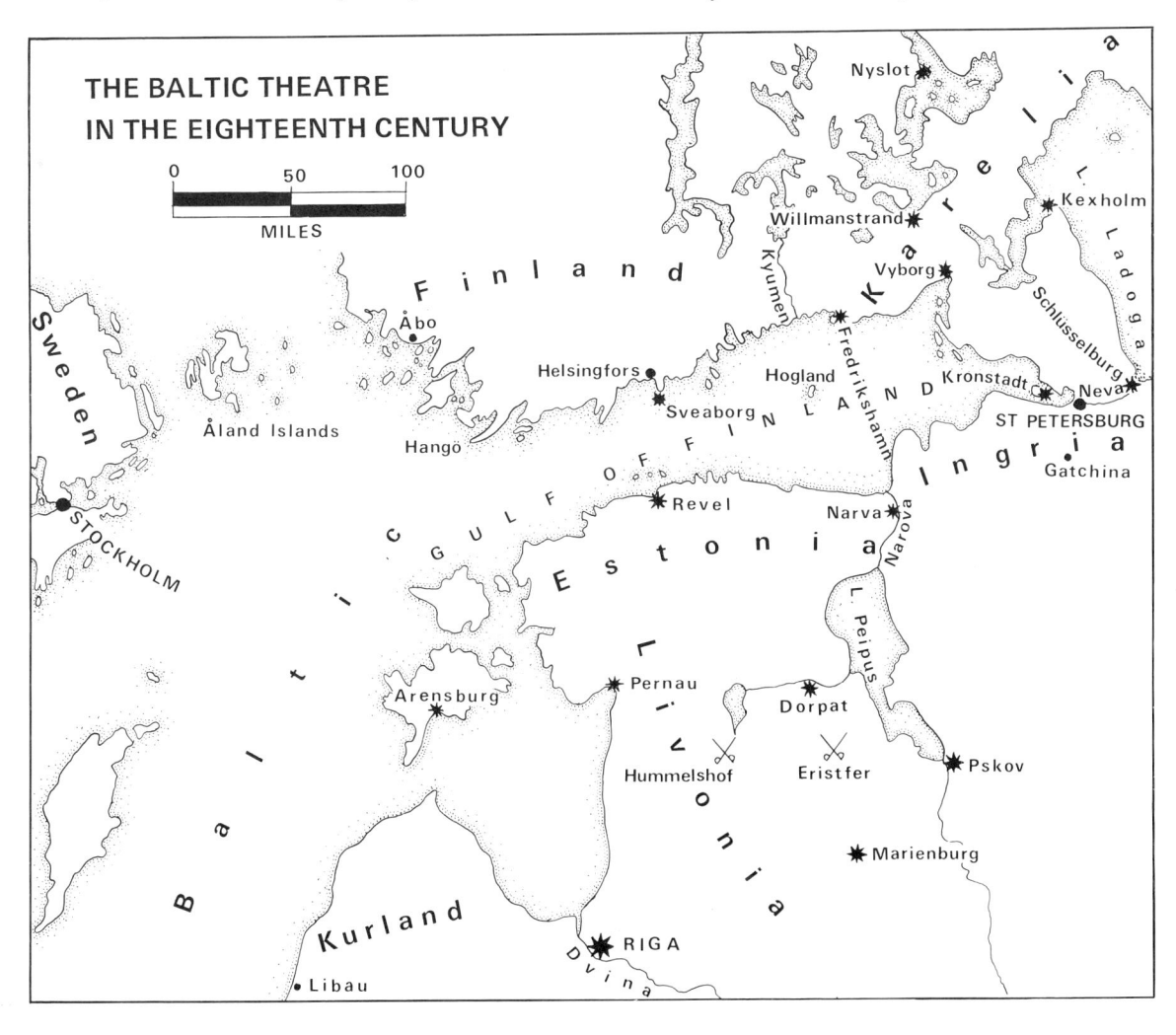

THE BALTIC THEATRE IN THE EIGHTEENTH CENTURY

in a systematic fashion. Among the desirable items which Sheremetev carried away from Marienburg was the seventeen-year-old girl, Catherine Skavronska, who was to become the wife of Peter and ultimately the Empress Catherine I.

Sheremetev was now ordered to move into the northerly province of Ingria, and concentrate his 30,000 men against the little fortress of Nöteborg, which stood on an island just where the waters of the River Neva left Lake Ladoga on their way to the Gulf of Finland. The place was taken by storm on the night of 10-11 October 1702, and this conquest became:

> of the greatest importance for operations against the Swedes, opening as it did the avenue to the Neva and the Baltic, and serving as the centre of the strategic communications for both the right and left shores of the Gulf of Finland, as an alternative to the uncertainties of the sea route. For these reasons Peter called the place 'Schlüsselburg', signifying 'key to the sea', and after he surrounded it with new earthen fortifications he returned to Moscow. (Bestuzhev, 1961, 93)

The slow workings of Peter's cumulative strategy gave him the whole of the course of the Neva and the neighbouring southern shore of the Gulf of Finland in the course of 1703. The Russians had now completely secured the eastern end of the Gulf of Finland, and Sweden's Baltic empire was cut in two.

These acquisitions gave Peter the impetus to move his capital away from Moscow, so hopelessly sunk in the ways of the past, and plant it instead on the woody and marshy islands at the estuary of the Neva. 16 May 1703 saw the laying of the foundations of a guardian fortress on Yanni-Saari (Hare Island). The work was called the Petropavlovsk Fortress, and was carried out at first in timber, and then in more permanent style in bricks of a startling orange-red. The growing settlement round about was given the name of 'Sankt Piter Burk', and the creation of this new city helped powerfully to advance Russia into the ranks of European powers. 'Built with ruthless symmetry on the side of an old Swedish fortress and given a Dutch name, Petersburg symbolised the coming to Muscovy of the bleak Baltic ethos of administrative efficiency and military discipline which had dominated much of Germanic Protestantism' (Billington, 1966, 114).

1704 was a year of sieges, designed to crack open the major Swedish fortresses in the country to the south of the Gulf of Finland. Dorpat was stormed on the night of 12-13 July, and ill-famed Narva received the same treatment on the afternoon of 9 August. However, the Russians enjoyed less success when they began to intervene in the main theatre of war. A large Swedish garrison was entrenched impregnably in the great fortress-port of Riga, and in the early months of 1706 the Russians were lucky to escape intact into the Ukraine, after the main Swedish army hounded them from Poland. Now that his rear seemed to be free, Charles turned back west to settle accounts with Augustus, leaving behind a command of just 8,000 troops to confront the Russians.

At the bidding of Peter, an independent corps under the command of Aleksandr Menshikov attacked the isolated Swedes at Kalicz on 1 October 1706. At the end of three hours' fighting the Swedish general, Mardefeld, was in Russian hands, together with 1,760 of his men. This was the most convincing victory so far attained over the Swedes in the open field, and the first combat in which the Russian dragoons had operated to good effect, charging home with cold steel instead of popping off with their firearms. It was all the more galling to learn that Augustus of Saxony had already come to terms with the Swedes, and that all the good work had gone for nothing. The humiliating Treaty of Altranstadt was made public in November. Augustus renounced the alliance and his claim to the Polish throne, and he delivered up Patkul, the author of the coalition, to the savage retribution of the Swedes.

The way to Poltava, 1707-9

For a time the whole gallant enterprise of a modernised Russia stood within measurable distance of the abyss, now that the Saxons were

Peter I, 'the Great' 1682-1725

THE WAY TO POLTAVA, 1708-9

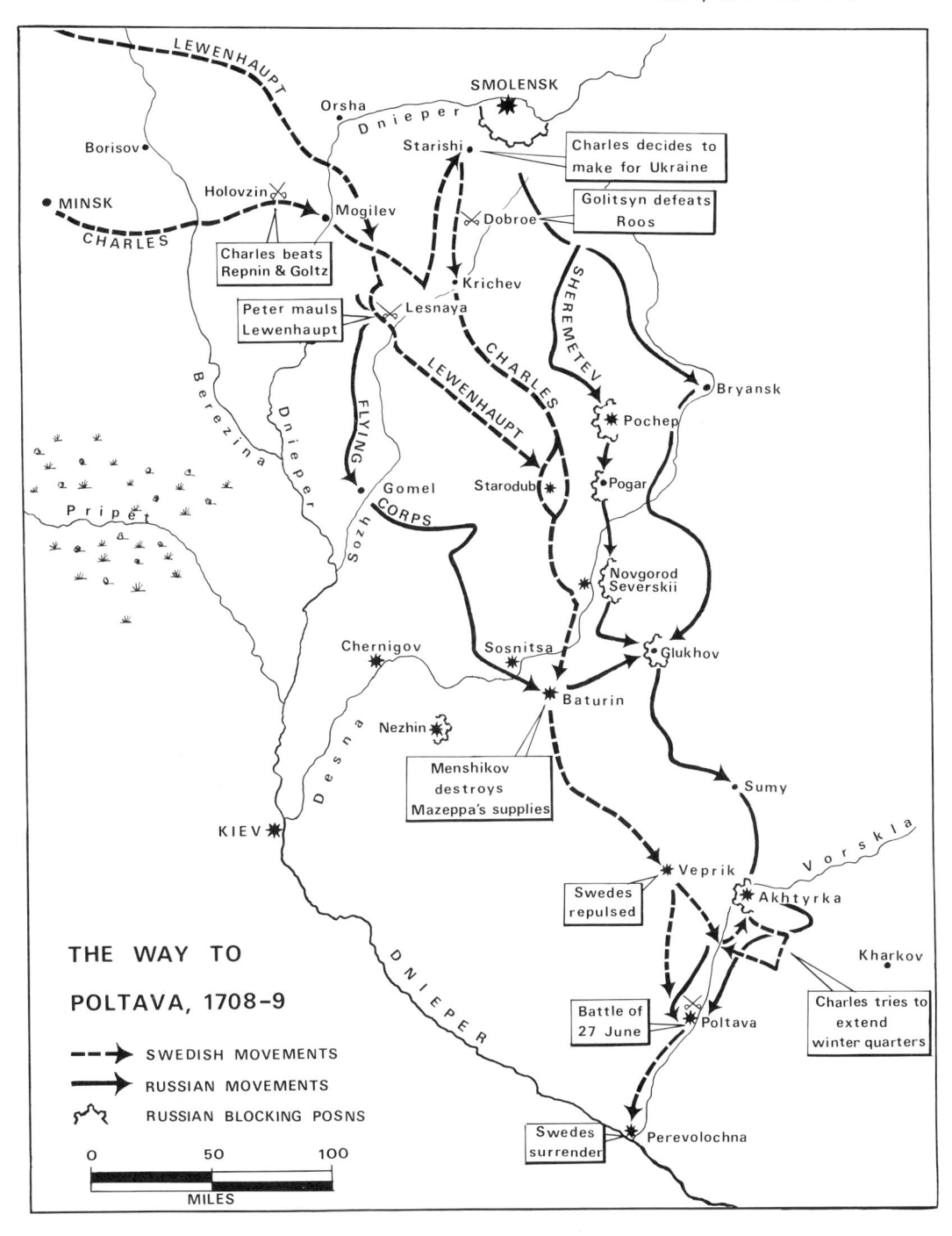

knocked out of the alliance, and the Russians were left to face the Swedes alone, very much as had happened in 1700, the terrible year of Narva. Peter's infantry were in a passable state, but the dragoons were badly commanded and understrength. At home the population was groaning under the full weight of the new taxes and the new recruiting system, and armed rebellions were breaking out among the peoples of the Volga and the Don. Worst of all, the able Hetman Mazeppa was secretly making plans to throw the support of the Dnieper Cossacks behind the Swedes.

As he waited for the Swedes to erupt from Saxony, Peter disposed his forces as best he could to cover both Moscow and St Petersburg. In general terms, the strategy for the defence of Russia was worked out in the early months of 1707. Peter and his councils of war did not need much persuading to adopt the principle 'not to give battle in Poland, for if we suffer a reverse in such an action, it would be difficult to retreat' (Beskrovnyi, 1958, 198). This was a helpful suggestion of Sheremetev's. With a stand-up battle therefore ruled out, the Russians sought instead 'to exhaust the enemy by denuding the country of provisions and fodder' (Meshcheryakov, in Beskrovnyi, 1969, 101).

Charles too was making his preparations. At this stage his plan already diverged somewhat from the Russian expectations, for he seems to have intended to make his main effort not on the northern flank against St Petersburg, but straight through the centre towards the ancient capital of Moscow. Forty-four thousand fine troops were to be devoted to the principal thrust, while Adam Lewenhaupt was to hold himself in readiness to move down from the Baltic in support. Lewenhaupt had 12,500 men under his command, and it was hoped that the supply train that he brought with him would keep the main army amply provided, even if the Russians were ruthless enough to lay waste their own countryside.

In January 1708 a first, short bound brought Charles XII and the advance guard of his army to the Niemen at Grodno, compelling Peter to scamper off in some haste. Charles was on the move again in June. By speed and fraud he effected an easy crossing of the Berezina, and he pushed on through sodden woods in search of the Russian army. Peter at this time was still far to the north, where he had expected the main Swedish attack, and the job of guarding the direct route to Moscow was left in the hands of Menshikov and Sheremetev, who commanded the principal army of 38,000 men. These were strung out east of Holovzin along more than six miles of the east bank of the marshy little river Babich. The articulation of the line of battle was not a whit better than it had been at Narva, and Prince Repnin's division, in the centre, was separated by boggy ground from Sheremetev's division to the right, and from the cavalry division of Lieutenant-General Goltz to the left.

In the event the Russians fought like men paralysed, except when it came to retrograde movement. Early on the morning of 3 July the Swedes waded the river under cover of a most effective cannonade, and engaged the Russian centre and left in a lively combat. By seven in the morning Repnin had lost control of his troops, who had exhausted their ammunition and were falling back in some confusion, and he looked in vain for support from his left, where Goltz's troopers were fighting a series of private battles with the Swedish cavalry under Rehnsköld. Repnin lost ten guns and more than 700 men, and with the collapse of the centre the entire army made off into the marshes and woods.

The combat at Holovzin forced Peter to re-examine the state of tactical preparedness of his army. Over the years, the articles of Weide and Golovin had been followed by a series of detailed instructions, relating to the execution of drill movements, and the responsibilities of officers. What was still lacking was a tactical overview, showing how each formation and arm could make the most effective contribution to the fighting of an action as a whole. This was now supplied by the *Rules of Combat* (*Pravila Srazheniya*, Peter the Great, 1887-1975, vol. VIII, pt 1, 7-13), a document which reveals in almost every paragraph the painful lessons of Holovzin, and gives the misleading impression that Peter had been present in person on the unfortunate 3 July.

The first three paragraphs were concerned with the means of nullifying or carrying off the enemy artillery, which had worked such execution in the early stages at Holovzin. The *Rules* then proceed to the main battle:

The infantry must not fire too often, and when they do fire they must aim low . . . also they must not jump to the conclusion that everything is lost, when the cavalry are separated from them; on the contrary, they must offer a steadfast resistance, so as to give time for the cavalry to join up again (point 4).

This was founded on the experience of Repnin's division. The next four articles relate just as clearly to the loss of discipline among Goltz's horse: 'Our cavalry must not go straight out and chase the enemy over a long distance, after defeating them. Instead they must assemble instantly by squadrons in good order, and await the instructions of their commanders (point 5).'

One of the articles (point 12) was devoted to the management of the heavy field artillery (the 6- and 12-pounders), which were to be sited on elevations, and change position from time to time. Two further articles (9 and 12) sharply reminded the generals that, 'it is essential to observe mutual support, so that if the enemy attacks one wing, the other will take him in the rear or flank. . . . None of the generals are to leave the field of battle until they receive an order to that effect from their commander.'

It was not very long before the chastened Russian troops were put to the test. Still hesitating a while at the gateway to Russia, Charles rested his army at Mogilev on the Dnieper, then crossed to the east bank between 4 and 8 August 1708. The bluecoats hung around on the far side, waiting for Lewenhaupt to drop down from Livonia with his train of supplies, which before long might be urgently needed in view of the way the Russians were devastating the countryside.

For only the second time in the campaign to date, the Russians took the initiative. The objective in this case was a little Swedish division standing in an isolated position at Dobroe on the Chernaya Napa, which came under a heavy Russian attack early on 29 August. The marshy terrain prevented all the Russian detachments from arriving on the scene, but M. M. Golitsyn was able to commit eight battalions to the action, and push the Swedes back to the support of their main army.

The encounter at Dobroe was more important for what it signified than for what it achieved. Peter wrote: 'Since I first entered military service, I have never seen or heard of our soldiers having kept up such a heavy fire, or maintained such order in their operations' (Peter the Great, 1887-1975, vol. VIII, pt 1, 111). Peter's assessment was realistic and balanced, as always, and it was supported by the testimony of an Englishman in the enemy army:

'tis true their [Russian] cavalry is not able to cope with ours, but their infantry stand their ground obstinately, and 'tis a difficult matter to separate them or bring them into confusion if they be not attacked sword in hand; nevertheless 'tis most probable they will not hazard a battle with us, but endeavour by surprises and by cutting off of our provisions to moulder away our army. (Hatton, 1968, 266)

This was probably the first time the new Russian army had come off better in a comparison with a Western one.

The campaign of Poltava is famous as one of the classic invasions of Russia, and it highlights some of the salient features of warfare in that vast land. Given the great depth and breadth of the theatre, and the shortness of the campaigning season, the invader's choice of direction has always been of absolutely crucial importance, for once an army or corps has been committed along a particular avenue, it can be retrieved only with difficulty for other purposes before the end of the campaign. (Hence the German failures before Moscow and Stalingrad in 1941 and 1942, when the armoured spearheads of Guderian and Hoth were diverted to the southern flanks.) Thus Charles XII made a fateful decision in the middle of September 1708, when he renounced the direct route eastwards to Moscow, with its endless prospect of burning villages, and instead turned his army south-east. He aimed first to reach Moscow by way of the untouched province of Severia, but after the Russians reached Pochep and Starodub before him he plunged on in the direction of the Ukraine, there to join forces with the Dnieper Cossacks under the hetman Mazeppa, and recruit his strength amid relative abundance for a fresh advance on Moscow in 1709.

Later in Russian campaigning seasons, a vital significance is liable to be attached to some apparently insignificant encounter, if it happens to affect the reinforcement or supply of the invading army, operating at such a distance from its homeland. This was why the little battle of Maloyaroslavets in 1812, which forced Napoleon back along the exhausted route that he had followed on the outward journey, decided much more than the vast bloodletting of Borodino beforehand. In the same way, a great deal hung in 1708 upon the fate of Lewenhaupt's corps, struggling through muddy roads to join Charles in southern Russia. Lewenhaupt's supply train did not matter quite so much as before, since the main army was heading for the fertile Ukraine, but Charles stood in desperate need of the reinforcement of 12,500 men, to add to his own depleted force, which had sunk to 25,000.

Now that the Swedish intentions were declaring themselves more clearly, Peter sent Sheremetev with the main army to dog Charles on a parallel course, to prevent him breaking through to the Kaluga road by way of Bryansk. Peter himself held back a 'flying corps' of 11,625 men and thirty guns, as a personal weapon with which to destroy Lewenhaupt before he could join Charles.

Peter caught up with Lewenhaupt as he was making for a crossing of the River Sozh, and mauled him so badly at Lesnaya (28 September 1708) and over the following days that the Swede was left with just 7,000 combatants to bring to Charles. The events at Lesnaya not only had an important strategic dimension, but actually signified a Russian success over superior forces, which was a novelty to Peter's army. 'This may be termed our first victory, for never before have we overcome a regular force . . . it was the first test of our army, and greatly encouraged the men; it was the mother of Poltava' (Beskrovnyi, 'Strategiya i Taktika', in Beskrovnyi, 1959a, 39).

In the winter and spring of 1708-9 the most important campaign in Russian eighteenth-century history congealed into a struggle for strongpoints and supplies in the Ukraine, as Peter sought to hem in the 30,000-odd Swedes and 8,000 Dnieper Cossacks by a strategic blockade, while Charles tried to create a base for an advance northwards on Moscow in the following summer. Towards the end of April 1709 the Swedes clapped a siege on Poltava, a little fortress standing on the Vorskla, and a place which, in Swedish hands, would give Charles a covered communication back through Cossack territory to the Crimea, and an avenue by way of Kharkov and Kursk to the prize of Moscow.

The siege of Poltava was crude and prolonged, and the delay imposed on the Swedes allowed the Russians to build up their forces in the offing, and meditate how best to bring relief to the beleaguered fortress, which lay on the far, or western, side of the Vorskla. Peter arrived on the scene on 9 June, and for the first time in his career he took personal command of the main Russian army. On 16 June he called together a council of war, which decided to 'cross the river and, with the help of God, seek our luck in combat with the enemy' (Peter the Great, 1887-1975, vol. IX, pt 1, 215). The main force duly effected the passage of the Vorskla just over six miles north of the fortress.

It is evident that we are dealing with a new style in Russian warfare, and that after all the years of humiliation and preparation Peter was at last willing to stake everything on a confrontation between the two hostile armies. Certainly the odds were stacked heavily on his side. He now had under his command a markedly superior force of 45,000 men and a mass of 102 guns. The Swedes, on the other hand, were even worse off than their numbers might suggest. Many of their forces were tied down in the siege of Poltava, leaving them with only 24,000 or 25,000 troops free to give battle. They were short of powder (the reports of their undercharged muskets sounded like the slapping of gloves), and their leader King Charles had been wounded on 16 June, and had to be

POLTAVA, 27 June 1709

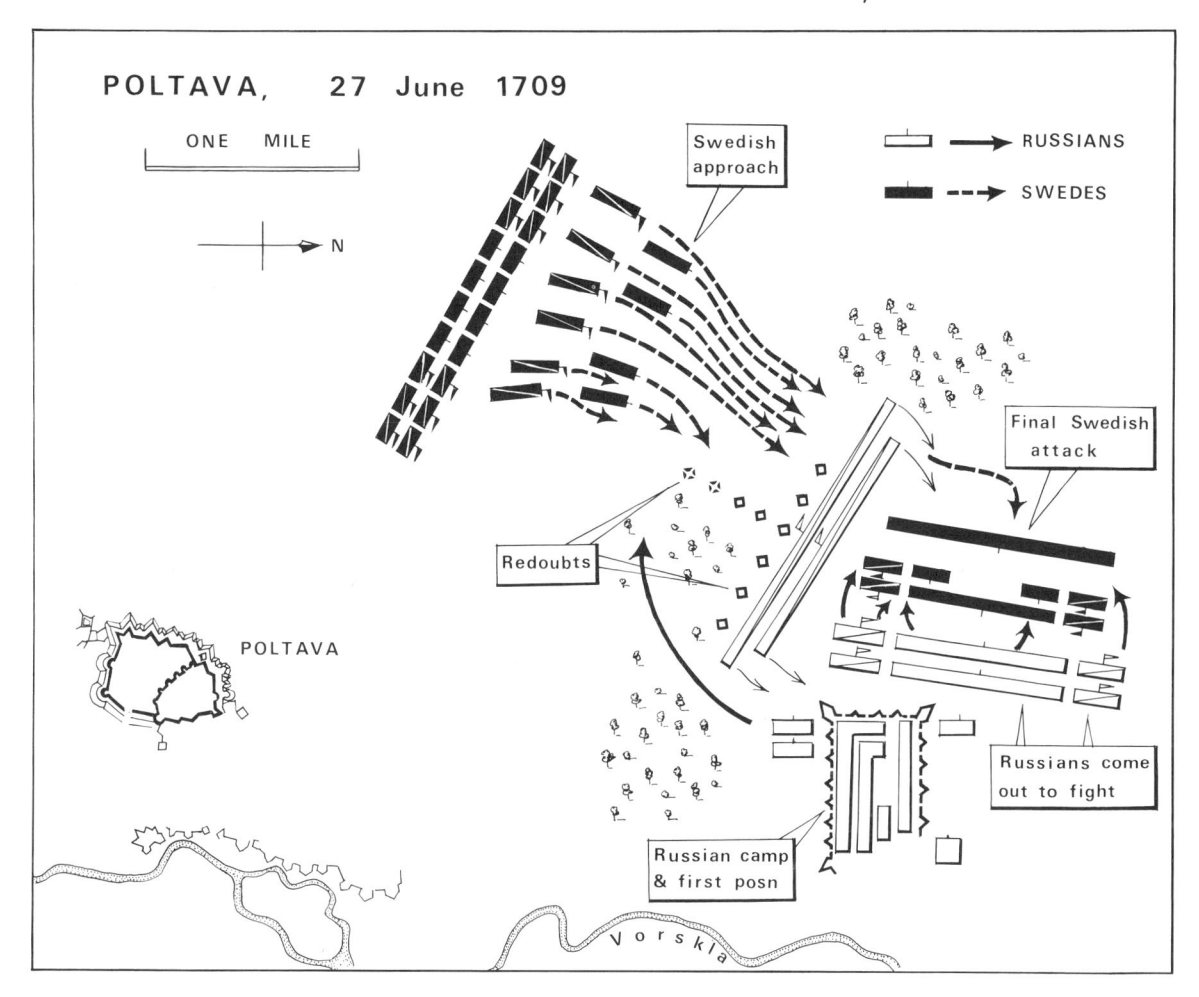

carried around on a litter.

The first fortified camp of the Russians on the west bank of the Vorskla was in the nature of a bridgehead to their crossing point. From here Peter moved south on 25 June as close as he dared to the Swedish positions before Poltava, and planted himself three miles north of the town. The earthworks of the new camp were almost complete by the morning of the 26th, and they represented a marvel of military engineering. The main position was roomy and well-sited, and gaps were left in the fortifications to permit the launching of counter-attacks. In front, the only avenue of approach was obstructed by an inverted 'T' of redoubts (self-contained strongpoints). Altogether the Russians had both security and freedom of movement (something lacking in their positions to date), and the means of breaking up a Swedish attack before it could reach the main position.

Charles made up his mind to attack before the balance of forces swung still more to his disadvantage. At two in the morning of 27 June 1709 Menshikov's dragoons detected the Swedes moving to the assault from the south-west.

In broad outline the subsequent battle may be divided into two phases. The first began at about three in the morning, and ultimately carried the Swedes to the ditch of the Russian camp, with their forces disrupted and heavily depleted. There was a lull as the Swedes gathered their forces for a final attack, and they were astonished to see the Russians winding out of their camp to give battle in the open field. The Russians still had things well in hand (which would have seemed incredible in their earlier battles), and Peter arranged his army in two lines in front of the position.

The single weak line of Swedes moved forward some time after nine in the morning, and the challenge was answered by a corresponding advance on the part of the Russians. The superiority of the Russian artillery soon made itself felt in the tussle that followed, and the bluecoats were in no state to withstand a final general advance of Peter's army. The Swedes made off in the direction of their baggage train, leaving behind 10,000 dead, wounded and prisoners, 137 colours and standards, and four guns. Russian losses amounted to 1,345 dead and 3,290 wounded, giving a total butcher's bill of 4,635.

Charles and a small knot of followers got across the Dnieper and Bug into Turkish territory, not to re-appear on the northern theatre of war until 1714. On 30 June Menshikov overhauled Lewenhaupt and the rest at Perevolochna on the Dnieper, and bluffed him into surrendering his entire force of 16,254 men, with twenty-eight guns and 142 colours and standards. This brought the total Swedish losses up to an estimated 9,234 dead, 18,794 captured, thirty-two guns, 264 colours and standards, and all the baggage, which spelt the ruin of the royal army.

In England Defoe was struck by what he saw as a frightening combination of Peter's brutal methods and Russia's vast resources, and he maintained that there was something almost unfair about the way the battle of Poltava had gone: 'an army of veterans beaten by a mob, a crowd, a mere militia; an army of the bravest fellows in the world, beaten by scoundrels, old alms-women, or anything what you please to call them' (M. S. Anderson, 1958, 58). The captured Swedish generals did not see things in the same light. Peter invited these brave gentry to dine with him, and drank to the health of 'my teachers in the art of war'. Karl Rehnsköld asked who these mentors were. 'It is you, gentlemen', was the royal reply. 'In that case,' said Rehnsköld, 'the pupils have delivered a good return to their masters.' The Swedish officers were released on parole, and many of them earned their keep in Russia by teaching music, the dance, languages and other accomplishments. They earned respect through their quiet industry, and brought the first knowledge of western manners to many noble households.

On a wider theatre the stupendous victory of Poltava helped significantly to advance the end of the sequence of Baltic wars in which Russia had been engaged, with some interruptions, since the 1620s. The whole of the non-Swedish north once more sprang into life, with Saxony-Poland, Denmark, Prussia and Hanover all showing an interest in the resurrection of the old alliances. Poltava had been won deep in the Ukraine, but Peter was right to remark: 'Now indeed has the foundation stone of St. Petersburg been laid' (Peter the Great, 1887-1975, Vol. IX, pt. 1, 231).

First exploitation, 1709-10

The prosecution of the war against Sweden was now essentially the affair of the siege trains and the fleet. The field armies merely stood at hand to support and occupy. After his first success in the south, Peter turned his attention to the task of breaking through to the open waters of the Baltic, from the first Russian holdings at the eastern end of the Gulf of Finland. These operations make for dull reading, but they were an important part of the process of wearing down the considerable enemy resources which still remained on the northern theatre. 'The Swedish power was not broken, and indeed could not have been broken by the battle of Poltava' (Myshlaevskii, 1896, 3).

On 13 June 1710 a powerful siege train accomplished the reduction of Vyborg, a Swedish strongpoint that was sited on the northern shore of the Gulf within easy reach of St Petersburg, 'and so', wrote Peter, 'the capture of this place has put St. Petersburg in complete security' (*SIRIO*, 1878, XXV, 203-4). Nearby Kexholm also fell into Russian hands.

On the southern shore of the Baltic, the Livonian fortress-port of Riga capitulated to Sheremetev in July, after a prolonged blockade and a short but violent bombardment — a process typical of the crude Russian siege methods. The smaller strongholds of Pernau and Revel succumbed in August and September, which completed a useful corridor of conquests stretching back to Ingria.

Riga and Livonia were useful prizes on their own account, since the flax, hemp and other products of the hinterland had a convenient outlet in the excellent port, and before long a timber town in the Muscovite style sprang up around the walls of the old Hanseatic city. More important still for our story was the fact that the acquisition of Livonia and nearby Estonia helped to accentuate the Germanising tendencies within the emerging Russian state. The Livonian and Estonian upper classes were Baltic Germans, lineal descendants of the crusading Teutons of the middle ages, and being practical, hard-driving folk, who were given a favoured position by their new Russian masters, 'they gained (out of all the foreign elements) the most important role in the directing class' (Amburger, 1966, 514).

Misadventure on the Pruth, 1711

While matters were shaping in such an encouraging way in the north, Peter found himself compelled to turn aside once more to the southern theatre, where the Crimean khan and the refugee King Charles XII prevailed on the Turks to declare war in 1711.

Russia was still unacquainted with some fundamental truths about campaigning against the Turks (see p. 6), and Peter committed himself to a plan of operations which in hindsight must appear rash in the extreme. The Russian army of 44,000 men no longer took the relatively familiar route down the south-eastern rivers, but instead executed a wide sweep around the western shores of the Black Sea, with the intention of raising the Christian peoples of Turkey's Danubian principalities. Peter did not know a great deal about the theatre of war, but he trusted that the army would be able to find all the supplies it wanted in the liberated lands.

Everything ultimately depended on the speed with which the Russians could seize the Danube crossings. In the event, Field-Marshal Sheremetev moved too slowly to anticipate the enemy at the river barrier, and the Turks poured on to the north bank. Peter came to join the army in person, but he could do nothing to stay the flood of Turks and Tartars, who finally trapped him against the River Pruth. On 10 July the Russians beat off a series of fanatical assaults, but Peter was caught without hope of redemption, and two days later he was forced to make a costly peace, by which he bought his army's freedom at the price of ceding Azov, Taganrog and their hinterland. Thus the Russians lost the mouth of the Don and all their other gains of 1699, and they were once more totally sealed off from the Black Sea. There was no means of retrieving the ships at the fine new naval establishment at Taganrog, and the craft were therefore burnt on the spot.

Russian historians like to attribute the sorry episode of the Pruth campaign to the failings of Peter's foreign officers, and they claim that he used the opportunity to rid the army of these alien elements. In fact there was every incentive for foreigners to quit a service which seemed to have become notably hard and dangerous, and a large number of officers of all ranks left the army without taking the considerable back pay that was due to them. General Ginsberg went off proclaiming that 'the Muscovite army has suffered so badly that it cannot possibly be re-established for several years to come' (Baluze to Louis XIV, *SIRIO*, 1881, XXXIV, 89).

Final exploitation and triumph, 1712-21

The diversion to the Pruth only served to postpone the reckoning with the Swedes, and the new two-pronged advance along either side of the Baltic was carried much further than in 1710. Peter put an army into the field in north Germany to aid his Danish and Saxon allies in the work of evicting the Swedes from their holdings on the southern shores. The Swedish fortress of Stettin surrendered to the allies in September 1713, and Peter handed the place to the Prussians as a bribe, over the angry protests of the Danes. Both Prussia and Hanover joined the alliance in 1715, but the internal dissensions remained as deep as ever, and the consequence was that the Russian troops were actually absent when the major fortress-port of Stralsund capitulated on 12 December. Great affront was caused by some further schemes of Peter's, when he tried to build up a power base in the duchy of Mecklenburg, and when he urged — and then arbitrarily abandoned — a grandiose plan for the invasion of the Swedish mainland from Denmark.

The Russians had a much freer hand on the northern side of the Baltic, where they acted on their own account, and enjoyed all the advantages of sea-borne mobility. They seized Helsingfors in 1713, which gave them an operational base halfway along the southern shore of Finland. In the following year Golitsyn consolidated the earlier successes on land, while the new Russian fleet annihilated a powerful Swedish squadron at Cape Hangö on 27 September. The victory afforded Peter every bit as much satisfaction as the triumph of Poltava. Not only did he capture one frigate and nine galleys, but he now had strategic control of the Åland Islands and the direct sea route to Sweden. Under the protection of the main fleet, the Russian galley flotilla went on to raid the Swedish mainland in July 1719, and again towards the end of the year and in the early summer of 1720.

Never before had Russian military power reached so far to the west. Charles XII had been killed before the Danish fortress of Fredriksten in Norway on 29 November 1718, which contributed towards the general impression of Swedish powerlessness, and the danger to the northern balance of power was such that the overmighty Peter was deserted by his allies one by one. British squadrons began to appear in the Baltic, but they were unable to defend the Swedish coasts, or summon up the resolution to attack the Russian shore defences.

A final raid helped to dispose the Swedes to agree to terms of peace at Nystadt on 30 August 1721. The Russians evacuated nearly all Finland, but in return they gained Swedish recognition of the other conquests made in the late war, extending for about six hundred miles of coastline from the inner corner of the Gulf of Finland to the Baltic province of Livonia. The Muscovites had cast off the muzzle which had been clapped on them by the kings of Sweden, to use an image of olden times, and the Hanoverian statesman Joachim von Bülow wrote anxiously:

for Germany and the whole Northern world, affairs have never looked so dangerous as at the present time. The Russians are indeed much more to be feared than the Turks. The Turks at least remain sunk in their hoggish ignorance, and go back home after they have ravaged abroad. The Russians, however, grow in their knowledge and experience of military and international affairs all the time, and actually surpass many other nations in slyness and dissimulation. (Mediger, 1952, 58)

The British, quite apart from their new Hanoverian connection, were unhappy to see Peter build his new fleet, and plant fortified bases at Kronstadt (an island off St Petersburg) and Revel. Already in 1713 the Tory *Examiner* expressed the fear that the success of the Russians in the war might be 'the occasion of bringing down a foe upon Europe, more formidable than the Goths and Vandals, their ancestors' (M. S. Anderson, 1958, 59).

On 22 September 1721, in the name of the people, the Senate offered Peter the titles of *Father of the Fatherland, the Great*, and *the Emperor*. Prussia and Holland recognised the imperial title almost immediately, and Sweden did the same in 1723. England and the proud Habsburgs finally unbent in 1743, and so did the French and Spanish in 1745. By then the Russians had diplomatic representation at almost every major foreign court, and the House of Romanov had renounced its custom of marrying into Russian noble families, and instead sought dynastic matches in the West.

It is not easy to assess the internal benefit to Russia of her participation in the Great Northern War. The drive of the military machine undoubtedly advanced the Russian metal industries into a leading place in Europe, and Peter was convinced that he had effected a radical transformation of

Russia as a whole, by dint of organising institutions and society to serve the ends of the war.

However, the cost must seem excessive, if we once allow human happiness any weight in our calculations. To the men lost in action we must add the untold thousands who died of disease, and the probably still greater numbers who were expended to build Peter's fortresses and naval bases, and the huge enterprises of St Petersburg and the Ladoga Canal, which were an essential contribution to Russia's status as a Western power. Some time afterwards, Field-Marshal Münnich calculated that in the process there had scarcely been a family in Russia which had not lost at least one son or brother in these years.

None of this deterred Peter from risking substantial forces in a new adventure, this time for the sake of advantages which were by no means so obvious as in the last war in the north. The destination in this case was the western and southern shore of the Caspian Sea, where the rule of the ancient empire of Persia was weakening under the impact of civil disturbances, and intervention by the Turks and Afghans. Peter resolved to lead an army of his own to that part of the world, and plant garrisons along the Caspian. He hoped thereby to divert the oriental silk trade through Russia instead of through Turkey, and perhaps ultimately to establish Russia as the principal intermediary for commerce between Asia and Europe.

The emperor sent a powerful flotilla and heavily laden ammunition transports down the Volga, and advanced by land and sea to the port of Derbent, which he seized on 23 August 1722. Peter returned to Moscow in a state of bad health, but his subordinates completed the work of conquest by taking Reshut and Baku in 1723. The Russians won the recognition of their gains from the Persians in September 1723, and again, after a threat of war, from the Turks in June 1724.

Russian parties had meanwhile pushed through southern Siberia in the teeth of opposition from the Ustyak Tartars, and planted forts along the Irtysh, Ob and Eniseisk. Russian posts now stood on the far distant Kamchatka peninsula, and Peter sent Captain Behring on a voyage to discover whether a land bridge existed between Asia and the American Continent. Nearer to home, a defensive line was built against the Crimean Tartars across a neck of land between Pavlovsk on the Don and Tsaritsyn (Stalingrad, Volgograd) on the Volga.

The creator of this and so much more died in his city of St Petersburg on 28 January 1725.

Peter the Great and the art of war

When every allowance is made for foreign models and foreign assistants, it is evident that the final and determining force in Peter's conduct of war came from his own intelligence and sense of purpose. Again and again in his codes we encounter phrases like 'because I saw it in the last action', indicating the extent to which hard-won experience went to shape the way the Russians were going to fight the next battle or campaign.

As the immediate threat from Sweden began to decline, Peter meditated how to construct a more permanent framework that would support the army through war and peace. As early as 1712 Peter had started to put together a large military code 'to which he devoted several hours every evening', and four years later there was published the great *Military Code of the Year 1716* (*Ustav Voinskoi 1716 goda*). An historical introduction paid tribute to the pioneering work of Tsar Aleksei Mikhailovich, while stressing how much had still remained to be done in the way of creating a regular army. The body of the work comprised:

 (i) a 'military code';
 (ii) a set of 'military articles and processes';
 (iii) a 'book of drill'.

The original manuscript was written out in German and Russian versions (indeed the Russian may well have been a translation of the former), but in spite of its misty origins the language is remarkably clear and unambiguous, and compares favourably in this respect with the kind of material that was later penned by Peter Shuvalov, or Emperor Paul and his cronies.

At the same time, the *Military Code of the*

Year 1716 serves to illustrate the characteristically cumulative nature of Russian official military writing. It was intended to complement, not replace, the early tactical prescriptions, which were already incorporated in the army's routine, and so it has much less to say about drill than about the details of marches, supply and everyday routine of service in garrison and in the field. In their turn, the subsequent codes of 1755 and 1763 left these matters largely untouched, and so the 1716 code had enduring value, being reprinted thirteen times between its first appearance and 1826.

The co-operative nature of the Petrine literary oeuvre is also of some significance. Peter put his name to many memoranda and other productions that were plainly the work of other people, but by the same token he assisted fellow writers through his advice and criticism. His indirect contribution is particularly noticeable in the translations of foreign works on fortifications and artillery which appear after 1706. We encounter editions of Rimpler (1708), Braun (1709), Sturm (1709), Brink (1710), Borgsdorf (1710), Coehoorn (1710), Buchner (1711) and Manesson Mallet (1713). Peter told his translators to cut short the long-windedness they would find in the German texts, and he kept a close eye on every stage of production, so as to eliminate any ambiguities in the translation, and correct mistakes in the printing and typefaces.

The historical compilations of the period served variously for propaganda, or Peter's self-instruction. The element of publicity was foremost in the accounts of battles, sieges and campaigns which first appeared in 1713 under the title of *The Books of Mars* (*Knigi Marsovoi*). The author was M. P. Avramov, the director of the St Petersburg printing works. Peter's achievements as a whole were glorified in Vice-Chancellor P. Shapirov's *Discourse* (*Rassuzhdenie*). The first printing of 1717 was succeeded by a second in 1719, and a third (to the number of 20,000) in 1722. It was something of a novelty for a Russian ruler to justify his doings in this way to the public at large. Later in the century, however, Russia's case was abandoned by default, and enemies like Frederick the Great were left with a clear run of the field.

A more reflective tone was evident in Peter's *Journal or Daily Note* (*Zhurnal ili Podennaya Zapiska*). Here Peter made a careful evaluation of the reasons for his early failures, and showed how a series of small advantages culminated in the crowning triumph of Poltava. The *Journal* was not published until 1771-2.

From all of this it is possible to reconstruct Peter's notions on the management of his armies in some detail. Following the western European practice, Peter recognised no permanent sub-divisions between the mass of the army as a whole, and the multitude of the individual component regiments. Formations like divisions and brigades were *ad hoc* groupings, made and re-made in the course of campaigns, and (in the case of divisions) existing in peacetime purely for administrative convenience. The *Code of 1716* defined the division as 'an army formation, in which several brigades come together under the direction of a single general'. The brigade, in turn, comprised two, three or more regiments.

Much more original was what Peter had to say about the kind of self-sufficient mobile formation which he used to smash Lewenhaupt at Lesnaya in 1708. He describes it as a light force,

detached to lie at the disposal of the general, whether to cut the enemy off, deprive them of a pass, act in their rear, or fall on their territory and make a diversion. Such a formation is called a 'flying corps' [*korvolan*], and it consists of between six and seven thousand men. A force so constituted can act without encumbrance in every direction, and send back reliable information of the enemy's doings. For these purposes we employ not only the cavalry, but also the infantry, armed with light guns, according to the circumstances of time and place. (*Code of 1716*)

A flying corps on the Petrine model captured Berlin in 1760, and these distinctive formations have reappeared in Russian strategy over the centuries.

Peter applied the word *Generalität** to the

---

*With the publication of the *Table of Ranks* it referred specifically to the first four ranks, down to major-general inclusive.

whole body of 184 generals, and their supporting staff, and French and German terminology was in fact applied in transliteration throughout the structure, resulting in the appearance of dignitaries like the *Generalkvartirmeister*, or the *Kapitan Degidya* (*Capitaine des Guides*). Supreme command was exercised by a generalissimo, or more normally by a field-marshal. This individual was responsible in one direction immediately to the sovereign, and in the other to the body of his generals assembled in council of war: 'Every important and weighty matter, and every enterprise, is always to be decided with the council of generals, and never at his own pleasure' (*Code of 1716*). Diplomats and other civilian officials joined in the councils of war, when the deliberations turned on wider matters, and Peter sometimes submitted projects for his codes to the examination of those present. Hence Russian councils of war assumed a more important role than the councils in foreign armies, where they were a favourite resort of weak commanders. The Petrine version was designed partly to curb the arbitrary will of independently minded generals (like Ogilvy at Grodno in 1706), and partly as a means of educating the monarch and the senior officers.

A prime objective of the *Code of 1716* was to ensure that the holders of every rank were aware of their exact duties. At the lower level the regimental hierarchy stood under a colonel, aided by a lieutenant-colonel and first and second majors who controlled the captains. The company officers were reminded in their turn of their responsibility for the discipline and progressive training of their men. A decree of 1722 told them that they must behave like strict but kindly fathers, and 'as far as lies in their power work for the good of their soldiers, and not just concern themselves with overloading them with unnecessary ceremonial, sentry duties and the like' (Stein, 1885, 77).

The stipulated tactics were of the linear kind, and were borrowed straight from the Western practice. The original six-rank line was reduced between 1704 and 1706 to the more handy one of four ranks, and the men were trained to fire in mass volleys, both by individual ranks, and by whole platoons at a time according to the contemporary English and Prussian fashion. The dragoons were expected to master the intricacies of dismounted fire, as well as the charge with cold steel and fire from the saddle. Peter stressed the importance of dragoon fire-power during the Turkish campaign of 1711, but at other times the emphasis was on the attack with the sword, as at Kalicz and Poltava, and in Menshikov's dragoon *Artikul* of 1720.

After the excellent enunciation of principles in the *Rules of Combat* of 1708 (see p. 22) Peter was disinclined to enter into any great detail on the arrangement of the army in battle, for 'all of this depends on the prudence, skill and courage of the general. It is up to him to acquaint himself with the nature of the terrain, and the strength and methods of the enemy, and to manage his army accordingly' (*Code of 1716*). He recommended in general terms that the army should be drawn up in two main lines and a reserve, with the cavalry on either flank (which approximates to the conventional Western practice). The commander was to put the baggage in a safe place, and he 'inspects the surrounding terrain, and the lie of the ground, and, if it proves necessary, he arranges for the construction of redoubts and entrenchments' (*Code of 1716*).

Peter explained that there were three methods of moving across the theatre of war, depending on the proximity of the enemy. If there was no danger of an encounter, the army was to march by widely separated corps, so as to alleviate the burden of supply on the country. When the enemy were in the offing, the corps were still to march in columns along separate roads, but take care to bunch together more closely so that they could concentrate when necessary. Lastly, when very close to the enemy, the way ahead was to be sounded by a powerful advance guard or force of massed cavalry. Peter was proud of the way he had carried out the march through difficult terrain to attack the Swedes at Lesnaya, and he wrote afterwards to Apraksin: 'I beg you to operate not just in the open field but in woods as well, which can be extremely useful, as I saw myself' (Peter the Great, 1887-1975, vol. VIII, pt 1, 183).

If the army was to rest for some time in any one place, it encamped in three lines in formation of battle. Peter devoted much space to the details of routine service in these and other locations, and the soldiers were to be instructed in all the minutiae of sentry duty and the paying of 'compliments'. All ranks were to be kept up to the mark by ferocious and comprehensive articles of war, which made up the second section of the *Code of 1716*, and subsumed all the previous disciplinary regulations. Peter himself put together the 209 paragraphs relating to the various punishments. Executions were carried out through hanging and quartering, breaking on the wheel, burning or beheading, and the victim might be put in the mood for the ordeal by having a red-hot iron bored through his tongue beforehand. Lesser punishments comprised old Muscovite delights such as the knout, as well as practices like running the gauntlet, sitting astride a sharp plank (*Eselsreiten*), and standing or walking on sharp stakes, which came from the Danish or Swedish practice.

Otherwise the main external influences on Peter's codes stemmed from the example of the:

finest two services of the Europe of the time, namely the Austrian and the Prussian, the former having been founded by Montecuccoli and brought to perfection by Prince Eugene, and the second set up by the Prince of Anhalt-Dessau, who created the Prussian army in the reign of the father of the celebrated Frederick. Peter the Great, however, as a man of exalted intellect, was careful to select only what was strictly suitable for adoption by his army. He correctly appreciated that the climate, manners and ways of his country dictated some fundamental modifications (Vorontsov 'Zapiski', *AKV*, 1870-95, X, 469-70).

Peter's military machine

It is remarkable how a person of Peter's eccentricities and animal energy was able to devise a military system that survived in some basics until the next century.

On the human level, Peter made a wise choice of assistants, which by itself ensured an important element of continuity. When he was absent from St Petersburg on campaign, Peter lived in simple style, accompanied by a small Personal Field Chancellery (*Blizhnyaya Pokhodnaya Kantselyariya*), through which he exercised control of the army. Aleksandr Ivanovich Rumyantsev (legal father of the famous Petr Aleksandrovich) and other likely junior officers were assigned to the person of the emperor as general-adjutants. Other folk appeared under the odd name of 'batmen'. These were in fact a collection of resourceful and nimble-witted young men who were enrolled for form's sake in the Guard, and who carried out an almost infinite variety of tasks — galloping off with messages, perhaps, reconnoitring enemy fortresses and camps, organising the baggage, or preparing confidential reports on officials. After such a useful grounding, a man like Vasilii Suvorov could rise in later years to the rank of *generalanshef*, while Aleksandr Buturlin became a field-marshal.

Three of Peter's associates deserve special mention. Much that was good in the reign derived from the counsel of Prince Yakov Fedorovich Dolgorukov (1639-1720), who had studied Swedish laws and institutions during eleven years of captivity after the battle of Narva. Altogether less respectable were the origins and ways of Prince Aleksandr Danilovich Menshikov (1673-1728). According to a widely accepted story, he made his public début on the streets of Moscow, selling the revolting Russian fish pies from a tray which he carried around on his head. Peter was much the same age, and he listened with delight from his apartment windows, while Menshikov directed telling retorts at the *Streltsy* who were trying to provoke him. Peter made him into an intimate friend, and thereafter Menshikov's rise paralleled that of the new Russian state. He did service in Peter's company of boy soldiers and in the Azov campaigns, and he accompanied Peter on his journey to western Europe. In 1709, as prince and lieutenant-general, he contributed mightily to the victory of Poltava, whereupon Peter hugged him in front of the army, and promoted him to field-marshal. Menshikov's military career was

5 Aleksandr Danilovich Menshikov

crowned by the reduction of the fortress of Stettin, and in 1714 he returned to St Petersburg to begin his ascent in the administration, becoming First President of the new War College when it was opened six years later.

Menshikov was polished and hospitable to foreigners, and indeed to anyone who could promote his interests, but his behaviour towards people who crossed his path was coarse and vengeful in the extreme. These contradictions contributed towards his downfall. He survived a first disgrace in 1724, and his power began to reach almost imperial heights under Peter's immediate successors. At last, however, his enemies bore him down, and he died in discredit in 1728.

Both Menshikov and Peter had a hand in promoting the ascent of the most unlikely of all the parvenus of eighteenth-century Russia. This was the Ethiopian negro, Abraham Petrovich Hannibal, who came to Russia as a slave. 'The young Moor had a sharp intellect, and showed a great gift for acquiring knowledge of the science of fortification. His industry was quite exceptional' (Helbig, 1917, 135). Peter sent him to France to study at the feet of the foremost experts, and in the course of his long career Hannibal became *generalanshef* and director of the scientific researches of the engineering corps. A Russian in all but colour, he was a friend of Vasilii Suvorov, and established a family which produced the poet Pushkin as a great-grandson. Hannibal retired at the time of the Seven Years War, and he died in 1782 at the age of ninety-two.

Hannibal and very many others helped to ensure a living survival of Petrine tradition into the second half of the eighteenth century. All the same, an army cannot be run on memories alone, and Peter's work would have gone for nothing if he had not taken good care to collectivise and depersonalise the direction of military affairs.

In the early years of the century the organs of state administration still bore something of the character of departments of the royal household. In 1711, however, Peter set up a supreme executive organ, the Senate, which had the particular responsibility of directing the war effort and raising money when he was away on campaign. The same year saw the foundation of a powerful reorganised *Kommissariat*, to manage the supplies of the army.

Towards the end of the Great Northern War Peter went on to establish the 'collegiate' system of administration, the principle upon which Russian civil and military affairs were to be run for the rest of the century. The inspiration seems to have derived variously from the councels of war (see p. 31), the advice of the German savant Leibniz, and the workings of the Swedish college administration, which Dolgorukov had seen at first hand. However, the essential point was to run every department like a miniature cabinet, in which authority was shared among the members of the college. The organisation was a cumbersome one, to be sure, but it was well suited to the Russia of the time, when many of the officials were of doubtful expertise or honesty.

The War College was entirely typical of the animal. The First President was duty-bound to act in concert with a Second President, and later with one or more Vice-Presidents. The other permanent or semi-permanent members were represented by a lieutenant-general, a major-general, a colonel in charge of the Secretariat, and a procurator who kept order in the administration of the College and at the meetings of its members, 'and if, during their consultations, the members fall out or lose their tempers, the procurator bangs on the table with his mallet and reduces them to silence' (Anon., *Anecdoten ... des Fürsten Potemkin*, 1792, 37).

Further military men were seconded on a temporary basis, and every now and then the War College was told to set up a special *ad hoc* military reform commission, to see to the overhaul of the army, such as those which came together in 1730-1, 1754-7, 1762 and 1763-5. The ordinary competence of the College was wide in any case, and embraced the collection of the poll-tax, promotion of all but the most senior officers, the granting of leave, the running of courts martial, the procurement of arms from factories, the determining of camps, quarters and march routes, and the forwarding of money to the army on campaign.

The War College was formed in the years 1718 and 1719, and opened on 1 January 1720 with Menshikov as First President. It got to work very speedily indeed, and already on 9 February it was able to issue a new establishment for the army, as well as financial statements and a new code of dress regulations. The old-fashioned surviving departments of military administration were hard put to it to hold their ground. Bruce reorganised his Artillery Chancellery on collegiate lines, as the best protection against the mighty newcomer, but the *Kommissariat* was less adaptable, and in 1724 it forfeited its important food supply department.

The local administration of army affairs resided in the hands of mixed civil and military administrations in territorial units called 'governments'. The newly-conquered province of Ingria was organised as such a 'government' in 1702-3, and seven other governments were set up on the same pattern from 1708. A rearrangement of Russia into eleven governments followed in 1719, and one into five huge 'general governments' between 1725 and 1727.

The new Russian army, the object of all this weight of administration, was organised with a few notable exceptions along conventional Western lines. The infantry was the heart of the force, and it was given a stable organisation in 1711, in the shape of two regiments of Guards (the Preobrazhenskii and Semenovskii), five of elite grenadiers, and thirty-five of ordinary fusiliers, making up a total of 52,164 combatants and 10,290 non-combatants. Contrary to the German practice, Peter deliberately fostered local loyalties by endowing the regiments with the names and arms of their local provinces, and not the names of their colonels.

The dress was of a sober and surprisingly uniform character throughout the infantry, and

6 Grenadier, 1700-2. Green coat with red cuffs and turn-backs; green waistcoat; green breeches; green mitre cap (Viskovatov, 1844-56)

the dark green of the coat offered a marked contrast to the whites, reds or blues of the other European armies. Peter rejected the false economies he had observed in Prussia, and he gave his troops cloaks and boots as protection against the weather.

The Russian infantry regiments retained a complement of pikes in the 1720s, as a reliable short-range weapon against hordes of bloodthirsty Turks. The principal arm was, however, the flintlock musket. The original Model 1700 was an odd weapon, rather heavy and short by Western standards, with a large calibre (26-28.2mm), and a conical constriction towards the breech — a Russian peculiarity that was reproduced in the artillery in the 1750s. The bayonet was of an old-fashioned design, being a stout two-edged knife that was planted in the muzzle of the musket by its wooden handle. In the middle of the reign the old muskets were officially supplanted by the Model 1709, which was an up-to-date design of 18.5 mm (.78 inch) calibre, and weighed a tolerable fourteen pounds. The matching bayonet was a slender triangular-sectioned sleeved weapon, also in the modern fashion. In practice the supply of weapons from the factories was tardy and irregular, and for the rest of the century the Russian infantry went to war with a variety of old and unreliable muskets.

Peter's cavalry could in no way compare in quality with his sturdy, long-enduring infantry. The troopers on the whole were a mixed crew, despite the noble pretensions of the arm, and they were commanded by colonels who were notorious for their irresponsibility, greed and professional ignorance even in the Russian army, which must have made them very monsters of infamy by Western standards. To compound these fortunes, Russia was incapable of producing horses powerful enough to carry armoured cuirassiers for any distance, let alone across the vast tracts of ground which Russian armies had to traverse in order to reach their enemies. Peter therefore opted for the type of light regular cavalry called 'dragoons', which appear on the Establishment of 1711 to the number of thirty-three regiments, with a nominal complement of 34,320 combatants and 33,000 horses. The dragoons were supposed to be able to fight equally well on horseback and on foot, and for all their inadequacies they spared Peter from total dependence for light cavalry work on the unreliable hussars and Cossacks.

It was some compensation that the artillery was already showing signs of the immense power that it was to develop in the Russian army (see p. 000). Likewise, if native Russians did not show the same aptitude or interest in tedious subjects like siege-work or permanent fortification, they became masters in the art of throwing up light fortification on the battlefield, as they showed at Poltava and again at Saltykov's camp at Kunersdorf fifty years later.

Fortresses and frontiers were notorious for the rate at which they sucked in manpower, but Peter appreciated just how many troops he was losing in this way only in the years 1707 and 1708, when he was hard pressed to find the forces to put down the rebellions of the Cossack Bulavin and the Bashkirs. In 1711, therefore, he founded a separate Garrison Army of 58,000 men, drawn from the existing regiments on garrison duty, with the addition of invalids, veterans and spare troops from the field army. In the 1720s the force reached a strength of more than 70,000 infantry and dragoons, and in specific areas like the Baltic provinces and the Ukraine it could be reinforced in time of war by a newly created Land Militia of local levies.

We have the opportunity to deal only very briefly with the subject of the new Russian navy, which was such a useful adjunct to the land army. Three fleets came into being in the course of Peter's wars — those of Azov, the Caspian and the Baltic. By its nature the Baltic fleet was the one of the greatest consequence. The first of all its ships was the 28-gun frigate *Shtandart*, which took to the water on 22 August 1703. The first of the corresponding ships of the line, the *Poltava*, was launched in 1712, and by the end of the Great Northern War the strength of the Baltic fleet stood at 124 Russian-built sailing vessels, and fifty-five craft which had been taken from the Swedes.

Peter had learnt the employment of galleys in his Azov campaigns, and he recognised how useful these shallow-draft self-propelled vessels could prove amid the islands and channels of the Baltic, where they could manoeuvre in combat, carry out reconnaissances and raids, bombard shore targets, and transport troops and supplies. The coastal woods offered almost unlimited timber for galley construction, and the handy Russian peasant-soldiers showed that they were able to build, row and fight these vessels with the minimum of supervision. Such was the weapon which enabled Peter to carry the war to Sweden in the last years of the war, which he ended with a force of 416 galleys.

Galleys were unable to stay at sea for very long, which was one of the reasons why it was so important for Peter to establish naval bases along the coasts at reasonably short stages. The seat of Russian naval power in the Baltic was to be found in the innermost waters of the Gulf of Finland, at the naval base on Kronstadt Island and the Admiralty Yard at St Petersburg. For more far-reaching operations, bases were established at Revel and Vyborg in 1710, and along the shores of Swedish Finland – at Helsingfors (1713), and at Åbo and in the Åland Islands (1714).

The Russian navy was possibly the proudest of Peter's creations, but it was in every respect also the most perishable. The efforts were inevitably dispersed among separated seas (the bugbear of Russian naval power), and the timbers of the principal concentration of vessels rotted with disturbing ease in the brackish waters of the Gulf of Finland. Moreover, there was virtually no Russian merchant navy which could have engendered a reservoir of nautical expertise, and freed Russia from a dependence on foreign naval officers.

The material base

Every now and then foreigners were reminded of the immense potential of the Russian empire, and of the apparently boundless writ of the sovereign, which seemed to be able to set ordinary considerations of economy at naught. It was perhaps fortunate for the West that the vastness of the land and its locked-in power were so exactly balanced by a countervailing paucity of physical and organ-isational means of tapping those resources. Peter explored all the frustrations that lay in store for Russian rulers, for he was seeking in a single generation to set on foot a regular army and make his country self-sufficient in manufactures.

The story of the military finances is enlightening. Peter's work of modernisation increased about seven-fold the expenditure on the armed forces in his time. Thus the following figures:

	Revenues	*Military expenditure*
1680	1,500,000 roubles	c. 750,000 (total)
1701	2,500,000	1,839,600 (total)
1710	3,133,879	2,566,324 (army)
		433,966 (fleet)
1724	8,546,000	4,003,348 (army)
		1,400,000 (fleet)

A great deal lies behind these bare and possibly not very accurate statistics. No reliable means was ever evolved of furnishing the army with what it needed in the way of pay, quarters and kind. In the absence of barracks for all but the Guard, the army was scattered in peacetime in quarters among the civilian population, which was common practice even in the armies of the West. What was peculiarly 'Russian', however, was the extent to which the regiments were expected to feed and pay themselves from their localities. This circumstance, together with the cheapness of certain basic commodities, helped to eke out the state income.

Otherwise, the burden of supporting the defence of the great empire rested on the bowed shoulders of about five million taxable folk, comprising the state peasants and privately-owned serfs, and an urban population which had nearly doubled between 1652 and 1722. These were entered first as 'households', and then for the purposes of the new poll-tax as 'souls', but throughout the reign the process of enrolment was attended with extraordinary difficulties. The census of 1678 was wildly out of date, but no better basis of calculations was provided by the revisions of 1715-22. All the adding-up was frustrated by an elusive population. Many individuals had died off in the wars, which was very annoying. Some had fled the country, or were being concealed by their landlords. Others were respectable people who objected to being re-classified as peasants.

The poll-tax of the last years of the reign replaced the previous direct taxes, and it was assigned exclusively to military expenditure. The initial rate of eighty kopeks per annum was reduced to seventy-four in 1724, and to a final seventy in 1725. The business of collecting the cash was one of the forces which planted the army so firmly as a prop of the civilian administration. In the normal course of things the troops went out on expedition three times a year to beat the taxes out of the peasants, and on occasion the visitations were harsher still, as when Colonel Strogov and his regiment descended on the province of Velikolutsk, and discovered 388 men who had not been entered in the census of 'souls':

He tortured and knouted a number of nobles [complained the *voevoda*], and one of them died. A further seven nobles were crammed into barrels, and one of them was thereby crushed to death; seventy-one peasants and other people were likewise tortured and beaten, and one of them died; fourteen peasants and other folks were belaboured with sticks. (Beskrovnyi, 1958, 116)

In the same way it was an accepted part of peacetime military duty to assist in the collection of the revenues of customs and excise, to supervise the sale of salt and alcohol, to guard bridges, and to patrol the streets and the countryside so as to maintain order. All of Russian life was in fact subjected to a high degree of authoritarian control. Until the second half of the century men of even the highest rank had to obtain passports to travel from one province to another, and Peter set an example by having authentic papers made out for himself. 'Thus at this day [in the 1730s] even ambassadors, and field-marshals at the head of their victorious armies, must have passports, and consequently all inferiors must submit to the same regulation' (Cook, 1770, I, 20).

The development of the Russian war industry must take some part in our story, even if the details have been recounted many times in biographies of Peter and histories of his country.

At the beginning of the new century Peter embarked on a determined attempt to free himself from the need to import foreign weapons and ammunition. He succeeded so well that by 1705 he was meeting the immediate requirements for artillery, and by 1713 he was said to own a total of no less than 13,000 pieces of ordnance of every description. The Swedes were already dropping behind in the production of iron, and the British were soon outstripped as well, for they had exhausted their Wealden forests, and they had yet to open the coal-based industries of the North. Reckoned in *puds* (at forty pounds apiece), the Russian output of iron stood at 120-130,000 in 1700, rising to 1,165,000 in 1725, and about 5,000,000 by 1750. The manufacture of muskets fell off sharply after the Great Northern War, but was boosted once more to meet the needs of Empress Anna's Turkish campaigns, reaching a peak of 25,000 in 1736 and again in 1738. However, in neither quality nor quantity did the Russian-made muskets entirely answer the demands of the army.

Under the impetus given by the Great Northern War and the creation of the regular forces, centres of industrial production were expanded or created across two areas of Russia. The northern region embraced St Petersburg and its neighbourhood, and the shores of lakes Ladoga and Onega to the east, where production was facilitated by the ores of Karelia and the abundant forests, and by the nearness of the establishments to the theatre of war and the bases of the new navy. The southern region was a broad one, and its plants were scattered from Moscow and the western tributaries of the Don and Volga to the Ural hills, with their ores of copper and high-grade iron, their vast forests, and their rivers which provided power and cheap transport. Altogether forty private and state factories were in operation across the Urals region by the middle of the century, producing artillery, ammunition, pig iron and some steel and copper.

Russia was almost entirely self-sufficient in ready-made gunpowder, though some of the raw materials were obtained only with some difficulty. Quantities of sulphur had to be purchased abroad, and in 1712 Peter ordered the governments of

Kazan, Azov and Kiev to increase their production of salpetre, which was the scarcest and dearest of the ingredients.

With a measure of state supervision, the great quantity of dealers and small workshops were able to satisfy the requirement for leather for boots, shoes, belts, cartridge pouches, saddles and the like. The first paper mills were, however, set up only from 1705, and it was not until the middle of the century, when thirteen establishments were at work, that Russia was able to meet the very heavy demands of paper for the military bureaucracy and for making up musket cartridges.

The same held true of the supply of woollen cloth for the uniforms, for the native textile manufactures were in their infancy, except for the production of canvas, and the wool from the Russian sheep was very coarse. Britain and Holland represented the chief suppliers in Peter's reign, but the Prussians took the leading place in the late 1720s and in the 1730s

after diverse attempts and stratagems, as the making two suits of clothes as one suit of the best Prussian cloth they could pick out, not wetted, the other suit of the worst English cloth they could find, wetted and rough dried in order to make it look very ordinary and coarse. (C. Rondeau, 7 October 1732, *SIRIO*, 1889, LXVI, 516)

The economic strain of the Petrine war effort was colossal, and the burden of taxation represented an embarrassing legacy for his immediate successors. The plans for internal administrative reform were abandoned as early as 1727, and the impossibility of paying full salaries to state servants led to the revival of the system of 'feeding', by which officials were expected to pay themselves from the resources at their disposal, with all the consequent openings for corruption and oppression.

The human base

It was inherently easier to hew the forests, to dig, smelt and fashion the metals than to create a powerful army of reliable troops, led by officers of courage and expertise. Peter's successes and failures in these last respects were to be to a great extent the measure of Russia's military performance in the eighteenth century.

Peter proceeded from drastic principles of amazing scope, embracing nothing less than compulsory lifelong service for the entire nobility, and for conscripted masses of the peasants. The machinery for conscription was in working order by 20 February 1705, when on the basis of admittedly incomplete statistics the first orderly levies went ahead, summoning one young man from every twenty peasant households. In the event 44,539 men were called to the colours, instead of the anticipated 40,000, which in itself went some way to make up the total of 131,319 regular levies who were raised between 1701 and 1709. Recruits continued to be raised from households until 1724, when 'souls' became the basis of calculations.

Although conscription was a striking manifestation of state power, unique in the Europe of the time, it held elements of compromise with the old order (see p. 13). Already in December 1700 Peter had responded to noble pressure, and rescinded a decree of 1697, which freed voluntary recruits from serfdom. Military service was therefore seen by the populace as a hateful continuation of subjection, with the added disadvantages of a high risk of death from typhus, malaria or wounds, and the near certainty of lifelong separation from home and village. Small wonder that so many families escaped across the borders, or that desertion was rife in the regiments.

It is the miracle of the Russian army that an unpromising stock like this should have engendered some of the best infantry in the world. In contrast, the origins of the officer corps told all too heavily on the quality of the leadership of the army. For such and such an appointment, the choice frequently lay between a foreigner of undoubted experience, but uncertain competence and loyalties, and a native Russian who added a lack of inclination to an all-too-obvious professional ignorance.

With the creation of the regular army at the

beginning of the century, many of the existing native officers who appeared on the books were found to be unsuitable for admission to the new regiments. Golovin was therefore ordered to draw up a list of the nobles who could be taken on as officers, which produced a first batch of 1,091 individuals. Veterans, soldiers of the Guard and other folk offered another resource, and Peter later decreed that 'all officers, who do not come from noble families, are to be given patents of nobility, and likewise their children and descendants are from now on to be regarded as noble' (Beskrovnyi, 1958, 168). With variations from year to year, native Russians accounted for about two-thirds of the Petrine officer corps.

The remaining third, the foreigners, were still indispensable for leading the army in modern warfare, which made for all kinds of tensions and resentments. A first manifesto of April 1700 was published throughout Europe, opening the Russian service to all but Jewish officers. Three further invitations were published between 1702 and 1705, of which the last stipulated that Peter would admit officers 'of good reputation and skill, who have reached their condition through military service in the field, and not just as a result of recommendation, winning ways or money' (Beskrovnyi, 1958, 170). Again in 1711 James Bruce was sent to look for likely candidates in German towns, 'as an educated, skilled sort of person, with a nice judgment where things and men are concerned' (Strukov, in Skalon, 1902-c.1911, VI, pt 1, bk 1, 103).

The first screening was normally carried out by the Russian agents abroad, who had authority to invite foreign officers to sign a 'letter of contract', which set out the rank and pay they would enjoy in the Russian service. A foreign captain, for example, was normally entitled to a pay of eighteen roubles per month, as opposed to fifteen for one born in Russia of foreign parents, and a mere twelve for a native Russian, which scarcely made for good relations between the nationalities.

Once they arrived in Russia, the foreigners were inspected and assigned by the War College, or its administrative ancestors. In fact the Russian authorities were by no means sure what qualities they ought to be looking for, in view of their grievous ignorance of how military affairs were run in the West. James Bruce liked to tell how an Austrian brigadier once came to Field-Marshal Sheremetev, asking to be made a Russian major-general. Sheremetev, 'conceiving that to be a step too much, told the gentleman he ought to be satisfied with being made first a lieutenant-general, ... and the marshal claimed a merit in having satisfied the foreigner so easily' (Bruce, 1782, 113).

7 Infantry officer, 1700-2. Green coat with red cuffs; red breeches; hat with gold lace; gorget bearing the St Andrew's cross; sash in the national colours (top to bottom) of red, white and blue (Viskovatov, 1844-56)

Assessments

When looking at Russian affairs, it is so easy to fix your attention on the patent inefficiencies and shortcomings that the magnitude of the achievement is liable to escape from view altogether. For a comprehensive estimate of what Peter did, it is worth quoting a letter which the French diplomat de Campredon addressed to Louis XV in 1723:

I must report to Your Majesty something of the boundless efforts which he has expended in so many directions. He has regulated his peoples, making them useful for the service of his state, and for exalting his glory to the highest possible degree. He has worked to drag his nobility up from the subhuman lassitude in which they were sunk, and qualify them to serve in his armies and navies, for which they harboured an invincible aversion until very recently. We have seen him perform the duties of drummer and carpenter, and rise gradually to the rank of general and admiral, sedulously observing at every step the obedience and subordination due to his superiors, and that discipline which he wished to be maintained in the two arms of his service. And so, through inconceivable labour and patience, he has managed to form some excellent military and naval officers, a body of splendid soldiers, an army of more than 100,000 regular troops, and a fleet of sixty vessels, including twenty of the line. Russia, whose very name was scarcely known, has now become the object of attention of the greater number of the powers of Europe, who solicit its friendship. (*SIRIO*, 1885, XLIX, 310-14)

The verdict of the native Russian depended on the circumstances of the writer and his distance from Peter's time. In Peter's own generation a small circle of men like Yakov Dolgorukov and Fedor Saltykov — widely travelled, and experienced in several departments of state — knew and fully appreciated the motives for what their sovereign was doing.

These sentiments by no means corresponded with the general mood of the Russian people and nobility. Among the common folk the hatred of the taxes and the conscription was accentuated by a number of specific and deeply felt grievances. Old Believer priests railed against Peter as the Antichrist, while the rank and file of the army resented any intrusion of Germanism. Private Shmulov alleged that Peter 'beats people with the knout', and 'smokes tobacco with Germans'. Another soldier, Oshivalov, grumbled that the 'German-style shoes have large heels and are heavy to wear, whereas the Russian boots were lighter' (Golikova, in Beskrovnyi, 1959a, 283).

The resentments of the other classes went to feed the xenophobic sentiments regarding the Western world which were already clearly evident in the seventeenth century. From the start the city of St Petersburg was the object of the anti-Western feelings. The place was disliked as a forced, artificial creation, a symbol of Peter's military ambitions, and the home of foreigners and a *parvenu* native nobility, in all of which it compared unfavourably with the dirty, cosy and thoroughly Russian Moscow. Edward Finch maintained that even the nobles who travelled abroad, and those who made up the court at St Petersburg, were still in their hearts:

downright errant old russ . . . there is not one of them who would not wish St. Petersburg at the bottom of the sea, and all the conquered provinces to the devil, so that they could but remove to Moscow. . . . Besides they are persuaded, that it would be much better for Russia in general to have nothing more to do with the affairs of Europe, than it formerly had, but confine itself to the defence of its own ancient territories strictly called so. . . . All these gentlemen by consequence are utter enemies to the foreigners in their service; for though they may find the use of them in time of war, yet would they have them all discarded the moment after a peace. (2 June 1741, *SIRIO*, 1894, XCI, 107-8)

Convictions of this kind were ineradicable. However, a noticeable amelioration of opinion in Peter's favour becomes evident as the eighteenth century progresses. In part it proceeded from the publication of Voltaire's *Histoire de la Russie sous*

Pierre le Grand (1763). The work brought on Voltaire's head the reproach of Frederick the Great of Prussia: 'Tell me, I beseech you, why you took it into your head to write about the doings of those Siberian wolves and bears? . . . I can scarcely live with the thought that they inhabit the same hemisphere as ourselves' (Rambaud, 1895, 346). Less prejudiced people awakened to the magnitude of Peter's achievements and the changes which had come over Russia, and Voltaire's words assumed the status of gospel in the West.

Within Russia a consideration of some weight was the devotion which some of Peter's successors felt towards his memory. Elizabeth Petrovna was always aware of her responsibilities as his daughter, while Catherine II, although the daughter of a Prussian commander, excelled her in demonstrations of almost filial piety towards the shade of the great man.

Finally a new object of xenophobic resentments was provided by the outright Prussianising tendencies of the reigns of Peter III and Paul I. The policies of Peter the Great seemed moderate and patriotic in comparison, and by 1802 a person like Semen Vorontsov was ready to rank Poltava along with Kunersdorf, Kagul and Izmail as a victory obtained under a truly Russian dispensation of military affairs: 'The institutions of Peter the Great are the best for our army. The decline of our army is the measure of our departure from their principles' ('Zapiski ... o Russkom Voiske...', *AKV*, 1870-95, X, 492).

Three The Age of Marshal Münnich 1725-41

The turmoils of 1725-30

Peter built so well that his army survived, shaken but intact, through years of political instability that would have overthrown a structure built on less firm foundations. The upsets were largely the fault of Peter himself, for by the time of his death in 1725 he had made no proper provision for the succession. Indeed he had killed off his own son Aleksei in 1718, and abolished the principle of primogeniture.

The person best placed to seize power was his second wife, the Empress Catherine, who had entered the royal circle as a prize of war (see p. 20). In her short reign Catherine I had to reduce the oppressive poll-tax, but otherwise she did what she could to run affairs as Peter would have wished. The projected Academy of Sciences became an accomplished fact, and on 21 May 1725 she instituted the Order of St Alexander Nevsky, which had been mooted by her late husband three years before.

When Catherine's own life was coming to its end in 1727, she arranged for the succession to pass to her twelve-year-old charge Peter, who was a grandson of Peter the Great by his first marriage. Menshikov was confident of securing his position in the new reign by marrying off his daughter to the young emperor. He had a further source of strength by his influence in the Guard. The political inclination of the Guards was in fact a weighty consideration in Russian political affairs of the time. The two regiments of Preobrazhenskii and Semenovskii had come into being as the nucleus of the regular army, and their commanders were men of the highest influence in the state. The ranks of NCOs and private Guardsmen, while still retaining an element of rough soldiery, were now being filled out with wealthy and idle young nobles who could fulfil their duty of rising from the lowest grades without the inconvenience of having to do real military service. The Guards, taken with the neighbouring line regiments which invariably followed their lead, made a mass of 30,000 troops which were concentrated around the capital.

Peter II was a restless and irresponsible lad, but he was able to strike at the over-mighty Menshikov at a moment when the Guardsmen were marching back to their quarters. Menshikov was deprived of his offices and honours, and exiled first to his estates, and then to Siberia.

Peter died in 1730 of a sudden infection, and for the second time in five years Russia was without a ruler. A cabal of magnates, dominated by the Golitsyn and Dolgorukov families, looked for a candidate whom they could dominate, and to this end they whisked up from the Baltic coast the pudgy figure of Anna, Duchess of Kurland, who was a niece of Peter the Great, and persuaded her to accept important limitations on her authority.

Anna very quickly rediscovered her bearings in Russia. With the counsel of a few well-disposed persons, she declared herself colonel of the

Preobrazhenskii Regiment, and regaled the Guardsmen with drinks. A little later a knot of the Guards broke into a meeting which Anna was holding with the principal magnates in Moscow, and she accepted from their hands a 'spontaneous' invitation to arm herself with all the powers of the traditional sovereign.

Anna duly conferred hereditary nobility on all the members of the grenadier company of the Preobrazhenskii, but also, showing a grasp of political realities, she established an additional regiment of foot guards, the Ismailovskii, so called after the village near Moscow where she was staying at the time (17 August 1730). The rank and file were formed of picked specimens of the Ukraine Land Militia, but Germans and other foreigners were heavily represented in the officer corps. A corresponding body of Horse Guards was founded on 31 December 'on the foot of the late King of Sweden's trabands' (C. Rondeau, 4 January 1731, *SIRIO*, 1889, LXVI, 272). Frederick William I of Prussia sent several of his officers and NCOs to introduce the Prussian drill, and Anna reciprocated by exporting batches of tall grenadiers to Potsdam as a present. It became clear that 'these two new regiments of Guards were raised so as to counterbalance the old ones, and hold the people in respect' (Manstein, 1860, I, 71). Anna was convinced that she must keep her subjects firmly pressed down, 'for if she did not, the russ were of such a nature, that they would dance on her head' (C. Rondeau, 4 January 1731, *SIRIO*, 1889, LXVI, 272).

There was certainly a great deal in the new order of things to excite the hatred and contempt of the native Russian. The capital moved back from Moscow (where it had resided in the last reign) to the detested St Petersburg, and the tone of court and society became German, and provincial German at that. Strangers claimed the important positions of power and scorned the Russians. We may cite the case of Prince Ludwig of Hessen-Homburg, a landless, ill-educated young boor, who was heaped with honours in Anna's Russia, and ultimately became Master General of the Ordnance. No less detested were the people who now counted almost as Russia's home-grown foreigners — the Baltic Germans of Livonia, which was legally part of Russia, and of Anna's own Kurland. Among the latter was numbered the favourite Ernst Johann Biron, who instituted a reign of terror among his potential enemies, and was held responsible for the fate of thousands of folk who disappeared without trace or were banished to Siberia.

However, there is reason to suppose that on balance the reign was one of good management and positive achievement. The person of the Empress Anna was not unimpressive, as the Edinburgh doctor, Cook, discovered. She was no great beauty, 'but had something so graceful and full of majesty, that it had a strange effect on me. I, at the same time, both revered and feared her' (Cook, 1770, I, 102). Then again, the rogues, charlatans and murderers were a minority among her foreign helpmates. External affairs were in the charge of the unselfish and wise Count Ostermann, who came from Westphalia. James Keith hailed from further afield, as a Jacobite who had fled from Scotland after the defeat of the Old Pretender at Sheriffmuir, and who took service in France and Spain before coming to Russia in 1728.

He kept excellent discipline in the army, yet the soldiers called and esteemed him as their father. He was never vainglorious, no high language did he ever utter; every expression was modest. But the word of command was resolution itself. (Cook, 1770, I, 451)

He was a lieutenant-general in 1734, and distinguished himself in the campaigns against the Turks and Swedes before an accumulation of frustrations caused him to resign in 1747. He was killed eleven years later as a Prussian field-marshal. 'He was in truth a man imbued with honourable instincts, and one whose modesty proceeded from a courteous disposition' (Nashchokin, 1842, 177).

The beloved Field-Marshal Peter Lacy was numbered among Keith's closest associates. He too was a supporter of the Jacobite cause, and left his native Ireland at the age of thirteen as an ensign in the army of King James II. After spells in the French and Austrian services he arrived in

Russia in the interesting year of 1700. He was reputed to have done great things in the Narva campaign, and to have set up the first grenadiers in the Russian service, and in any event he earned the distinction of being held in equally high regard by the three sovereigns Peter the Great, Anna and Elizabeth.

Lacy crowned his active military life by his triumphant campaign against the Swedes in 1742. He entered into prosperous semi-retirement as governor at Riga, after having served in thirty-one campaigns, three general battles, eighteen lesser encounters and eighteen sieges. Lacy sent considerable annual sums to the Bank of Amsterdam, or so people said, and he had the satisfaction of seeing his son Francis Maurice launched on a career in the Austrian service, in which he was to reach supreme command. 'This great good man' died at Riga on 19 April 1751. Cook reported that: 'All the citizens of Riga mourned for the loss of the late field-marshal, and tolled their bells eight days. The army were not behind them in expressing their grief; and I lamented his death with as much sincerity as is possible for a human breast' (Cook, 1770, II, 618, 622).

The doings of Keith, Lacy and the rest were chronicled by Christoph Hermann von Manstein, who was a deserving figure in his own right. He was described as a tireless soldier, and a humane and cultivated man. He knew and liked the Russian people and language, and had a fine command of German, Swedish, French, Italian and Latin.

However, Manstein's narratives are devoted above all to the deeds of Field-Marshal Burchard Christoph von Münnich, who was the dominating personality in Russian military affairs in the second quarter of the eighteenth century, who developed and completed in many respects the work of Peter the Great, and who laid some of the most important foundations on which the army was going to fight the Seven Years War.

Münnich was the eighteenth-century military adventurer *par excellence*. He was born in 1683 in Oldenburg, in the sodden, inhospitable north German plain. His father, who was a lieutenant-general, gave him a good educational grounding, and sent him to travel in France, where he was

8 Burchard Christoph Münnich

able to develop his taste for military engineering. As a young officer he was employed as an engineer by Prince Eugene of Savoy, and he embarked on a career in the armies of a succession of German princes. At the murderous battle of Malplaquet, in 1709, he was present as an officer in the Hessian service. Three years later he fell into the hands of the French at Denain, but he was able to put the experience to good use by taking the opportunity to strike up a friendship with the celebrated Archbishop Fénelon of Cambrai, a man whom he greatly admired.

The close of the War of the Spanish Succession put an end to the prospect of advancement in the West, and Münnich entered a not very satisfactory spell of employment in the army of King Augustus II of Poland, where he became a major-general.

Münnich was taken into the Russian service in February 1721. Peter was at first disconcerted by Münnich's dislike of strong drink, and his neat appearance, but he soon became entranced by the

German's technical expertise and ambitious projects — 'the work of my good Münnich does me good!' (Fabritsius, in Skalon 1902-c.1911, VII, pt 1, xxvii) — and he put him in charge of important works of civil engineering, like the Ladoga Canal, which had run into serious difficulties.

Münnich rose steadily in the military hierarchy in the restless years after Peter's death. On 23 May 1727 he was appointed *Ober-Direktor* of fortifications, which made him supreme in all matters of engineering. The veteran Huguenot de Goulon was disgusted, and left the corps altogether. The next prize was the artillery, which lay under the authority of the *General-Feldtseigmeister*, or Master General of the Ordnance. Münnich was at daggers drawn with the incumbent, the boastful and mercenary Johann Günter, but when that unpleasant gentleman died in 1729 he was able to take over the post himself. Finally under Anna came the rank of field-marshal and the presidency of the War College, which gave Münnich authority over the field army as well.

The forcefulness and activity of this remarkable man were expressed in his gleaming eyes and rock-like face, and are transmitted with almost undiminished impact across the centuries. 'Robust and active by temperament, he seemed to be a born general. He was absolutely tireless' (Manstein, 1860, II, 207). He did important things for the Russian army, but all the time his driving motive was pride, for which, according to the Prussian envoy, he was 'prepared to put everything at stake, and run the risk (as he admitted himself) of seeing his head parted from his body on the scaffold' (Mediger, 1952, 153). Indeed it very nearly came to that.

Early in the new reign Anna's advisers set in train the first systematic review of Russian military affairs in the eighteenth century. The matter was of some urgency, in view of the neglect and abuses of the last few years, and the burden of the poll-tax. A decree of 9 June 1730 established a Military Commission, which was to range over an extensive programme of fifteen points. On 14 March 1731 Münnich took over the management of the Commission in person. In the next year he added the full presidency of the War College, and in 1736 he centralised all military administration under the authority of that body.

Oddly enough, the dictator Münnich failed in probably the most central of his concerns, which was to save about 650,000 roubles out of an annual military expenditure of four million. He hoped to make considerable economies by reducing the army in peacetime to a special stripped-down establishment. However, the expected savings were not forthcoming, and the expenditure on the army actually rose to an annual five million roubles, three million of which was derived from the poll-tax.

Elsewhere Münnich's efforts were attended with more success. It is of interest to note that Münnich, the arch-German, went much further than Peter had dared in the work of Russifying the officer corps. We have seen how Peter established three rates of pay for his officers, of which the lowest went to the native-born Russian, but Münnich 'represented that the Russian officers could not live on such modest pay, and that it was unjust for the foreigners to be treated better than the natives' (Manstein, 1860, I, 87). Münnich remedied the anomaly by raising the pay of native officers, and reducing that of the foreigners, so that for each rank the reward became the same.

Münnich was more concerned with the proficiency and enthusiasm of the officer than with his origins. Foreigners were now admitted only with imperial consent and under strict conditions, and Münnich enforced professional standards throughout the corps as a whole, if necessary by subjecting officers to public humiliation. Another monument of Münnich's care was the military academy (Noble Land Cadet Corps), which he founded in July 1731 to provide a systematic military education for at least an element of the body of native officers.

Otherwise Münnich's dealings with the officer class reflected his principles of military economy, and the circumstances in which his sovereign Anna had come to the throne. In fact, after the death of Peter the Great every revolution in regime was accompanied by an advance in the independence and freedom of the service class. In Anna's time an initial decree of 17 March 1731 confirmed Peter's measure of 1714, abolishing the distinction between service and hereditary holding of noble estates, and thereby distanced the tenure of land from the duties of state service. The new military academy began to offer a path to a commission without even the nominal commitment to service in the ranks, and finally on 31 December 1736 the term of compulsory military service was limited to twenty-five years, and the noble father who had more than one son was given the right to select the individual who was to enter the army, leaving the others to manage the estate. Only sons were in any case exempt from military service.

Münnich levelled some radical criticisms at the way the army was recruited. He regretted the unpopularity of military service, which he attributed to the losses of the Great Northern War, and the misuse of soldiers as slave labour, and he complained that the enforced lifelong conscription was both inefficient and demoralising. Even Münnich was unable to dismantle such fundamental features of the Petrine structure, but it was within his power to alleviate at least the incidental miseries of military life. He insisted that recruits must be properly paid, fed and sheltered during the march to their regiments, and that, once they got there, they should be received and trained in an orderly manner. The pay of all troops was effectively increased in 1731, when Münnich did away with the deductions for clothing, and he made sure that the money was made over in regular monthly instalments. Corporal punishment was no more severe under Münnich's regime than in other periods (despite what some Russian historians have alleged). He promoted the public expressions of the Orthodox faith (even if he did not share it), and his concern for the humane treatment of sick, wounded and prisoners made a good impression on Russian and Turk alike.

Münnich had the satisfaction of seeing less than 3 per cent of the recruit levy of 1733 lost through desertion, and when his work was complete this phenomenon became 'something almost unknown in the Russian armies' (Manstein, 1860, I, 264).

Point eleven of the Commission's instructions had dealt with the need of enforcing uniform tactics among the regiments, 'since the diversity of drills could lead on occasion to considerable disorder and other evil consequences' (Gippius, in Skalon, 1902-c.1911, IV, pt 1, bk 2, sect. 3, 40). The consequent codes for line infantry, grenadiers and cavalry were already being circulated in manuscript in 1731. The flavour of the whole was decidedly German. The new uniforms too were unmistakably Prussian in inspiration, what with the slimmed-down coats, the powdered locks and long whip-like pigtails, and the brass-fronted grenadier caps of the grenadier companies. In the Seven Years War only the traditional green livery of the infantry rendered the troops distinguishable at first glance from the hated Prussians.

With some success, Münnich built up the effectives of the ordinary infantry, the 'fusiliers'. He increased the combatant strength of the company to 90 per cent, and disbanded the separate regiments of grenadiers, redistributing the men among the other regiments. Still greater numbers of troops were retrieved by doing away with the 'Persian Corps', which had been guarding the Caspian provinces that were stolen in the 1720s. The British ambassador reported that you could 'scarcely imagine the number of officers and soldiers that die in that hot country. A major in this service assured me that he and twenty-six other officers were sent there three years ago, and in two years they all died except himself' (C. Rondeau, 30 May 1730, *SIRIO*, 1889, LXVI, 49). The provinces were returned to Persia in 1734. The equivalent of about a dozen regiments returned to Russia, leaving the bones of perhaps 130,000 of their comrades who had died there from disease during the period of occupation.

Münnich was probably less well advised when he complicated the structure of the cavalry by introducing a new category of mounted troops, the cuirassiers. The Commission declared

The Russian army has never possessed any other category of horse . . . than dragoons. Several other armies, however, and especially that of Imperial Austria, own regiments of cuirassiers, which have proved more effective than other kinds against the Turks. . . . Since light cavalry regiments are incapable of withstanding regiments of heavy cavalry or cuirassiers with advantage, the Military Commission considers that, in the present time of peace, we should establish ten cuirassier regiments of this kind, mounted on German horses. (Baiov, 1906, I, 10)

The 'cuirassiers' in question were heavy, part-armoured men, riding powerful horses, and designed to deliver massive blows on the field of battle. The Russian dragoons seemed by comparison puny, half-bred creatures, too feeble when mounted to resist the cuirassiers in open combat, and presenting a clumsy imitation of infantry when fighting on foot.

The formation of the cuirassiers proceeded very slowly, and never approached the ambitious target which had been set by the Commission. The first of the breed appeared on 18 November 1731, when the Vyborg Dragoons were transformed into the Cuirassier Regiment Münnich. Two more regiments of dragoons were converted in 1732, and a fourth and final regiment underwent the process in 1740. The root of the problem was the shortage of native animals strong enough to bear the rider, together with all his gear and his twenty-three-pound breastplate.

The new regime actually had more luck with its light cavalry. Münnich reinforced Peter's regiment of Serbian hussars, and established new hussar companies of Balkan refugees and Georgian nobles. He was anxious to improve the proficiency of the Cossacks, whether for border defence or open warfare, and he was the creator of the regiment of Chuguevskii Cossacks, which became the most expert and reliable of all the Cossack bands of the middle decades of the eighteenth century. The main burden of guarding the Tartar borders rested, however, upon the Ukranian Land Militia, which Münnich expanded to 21,000 men, and on a line of ramparts, stockades and strongpoints extending across the steppes from the Dnieper to the Don.

Münnich was an engineer by origin, but he addressed himself to the affairs of the artillery with all the enthusiasm of the late convert. He had a programme of re-casting carried out by the reliable old Wilhelm de Hennin, and in the process he increased the proportion of light regimental artillery — the 3-pounders — to 25 per cent of the ordnance, while the ratio of Peter's favourite 8-pounder sank from 40 to 18 per cent. Münnich's intention was to endow the squares of Russian infantry with greater firepower against the Turks, and he was now able to equip every regiment with four such 3-pounders instead of the previous two.

In 1727 Münnich had taken over the combined management of the schools of engineering and artillery, where he increased the number of pupils and revised the syllabus. He circulated sets of manuscript *Instructional Articles* (1731) to the corps as a whole, and he sent trained men in eights at a time to teach the service of the regimental artillery. The Russians responded to the encouragement, and the gunners of this period are described as 'a most glorious body of men' (Cook, 1770, I, 41).

Münnich elevated his beloved engineers into a separate corps in 1728, and he arranged its affairs on the best Western models. His work in creating an independent, well-organised engineer corps was of lasting value, for it enabled this important branch of military affairs to survive the neglect of successive Masters General of the Ordnance, who were interested only in the artillery, in so far as they were interested in anything at all.

Münnich managed both the engineers and gunners in a despotic fashion, as chief of a 'Chancellery' of artillery and fortification. He ultimately yielded the post of Master General of the Ordnance to the loathsome Hessen-Homburg in 1735, and relinquished that of head of the Chancellery in the following year, but by then his authority had little to do with formal titles, and it remained intact until he fell in 1741.

Western excursions

If Peter the Great had accomplished a physical breakthrough to the Baltic, the Russian military enterprises of the 1730s and early 1740s represent a process of widening Russia's avenue to the West by means of an effective working alliance with imperial Austria. As a result, French interests were defeated three times over.

Poland, with its elective monarchy, had long been a scene of conflict between France and the two great empires of eastern Europe, and 1733 found Russian forces committed deep in Poland in support of the joint Austro-Russian candidate Augustus III. Small Russian detachments were campaigning against the French sympathisers all over the land, and 'never in this war did parties as small as three hundred Russians go a step out of their way to avoid three thousand Poles. They could rely on beating the Poles in every encounter' (Manstein, 1860, I, 132). The main concentration of 12,000 troops was, however, brought against the free city and fortress-port of Danzig, where a Polish garrison made a stand with the help of French advisers, and later with active French participation. Münnich impatiently snatched the direction of the siege from Lacy, promising energetic measures, but the operation proved to be slow and costly, and dragged on until Danzig submitted to King Augustus on 30 June 1734. Poland was to remain under a passably acquiescent regime for the next few decades, and offer a passage for most of the Russian armies which wished to march through the kingdom on their way to more distant theatres of war.

Anna's Austrian friends were meanwhile locked in combat with the French along the Rhine, a circumstance which invited Russian troops deeper into western Europe than ever before, and established a precedent for some very significant interventions later in the century.

The immediate Austrian request was for the assistance of 12,000 Russian troops on the Rhine. Anna was agreeable, and in a rare demonstration of military ardour the younger generation of high nobility pressed forward to volunteer their services. Lacy led a parent body of sixteen regiments through Poland to winter quarters in the Austrian province of Silesia, and from there a contingent of eight regiments, or 10-11,000 men, marched for the Rhine in the spring of 1735 under the command of Lieutenant-General Keith. 'Everybody was delighted and astonished by the good order and discipline which the troops maintained on the march and in their quarters' (Manstein, 1860, I, 133).

The Russians were too late to take part in hostilities before the Austrians and French concluded an armistice, but the expedition was in most respects a worthwhile enterprise, showing as it did the capacity of the Russians to intervene far afield on behalf of an ally, and reinforcing the demand of Anna to be treated with due respect. Keith made a point of insisting that the Austrians must refer to his sovereign by her full imperial title.

With the defeat of their party in Poland, the French turned in some despair to their old client state of Sweden as a last prop to shore up their collapsing interests against the Russian advance in Europe. The older generation in Sweden had had enough of wars and absolutism, but the French overtures met with a ready response among the aggressive elements in the young nobility, who helped to stampede Sweden into declaring war on Russia in the high summer of 1741. The Swedes hoped to profit by the political turmoils consequent upon the death of Empress Anna in 1740, and they were further encouraged by the reports of their ambassador Nolcken, who wrote that the Russian army had been ruined by its recent Turkish campaigns.

On the Russian side Münnich put the fortresses of the Gulf of Finland in a state of defence, and helped to rush the reinforcements which gave Field-Marshal Lacy a small but excellent army of some 26,000 men in Russian Karelia. Among the folk who arrived on the theatre was a body of Don Cossacks under the seventy-year-old brigadier Krasnoshchekov (Red Cheeks), who aroused wide comment by his determination to use the methods of the Turkish war to accomplish the physical destruction of the Swedish race.

The negligent Swedes had only about 8,000 troops in Finland at the time they declared war. Lacy was not the person to miss such an opportunity, and in a classic pre-emptive raid he crossed the border at the beginning of September 1741, and marched through forests, rocks and marshes to smash the Swedes outside Willmanstrand. Lacy stormed and razed the town, and returned with his booty across the border. The Swedish officer prisoners were treated with respect in the Russian noble houses until one Lieutenant-Colonel Vasaborg, 'a man with a small brain but a big mouth' (Manstein, 1860, II, 180), spoke disrespectfully of the Russian army, whereupon he and his companions were packed off to distant provinces.

The advent of Elizabeth as empress of Russia promised the Swedes a little respite, but it was clear that if the active war was resumed, it was going to be waged on terms fundamentally unfavourable to Sweden.

Münnich's Turkish war, 1735-9

While Europe was beginning to feel something of the strength of the new army, Russia embarked on the first of her great eighteenth-century Turkish campaigns, those experiences which were the most significant of all her schools of war, and formed the generals and the armies which were going to fight in later decades in Finland, Prussia, Holland, Italy and Switzerland.

The quarrel of the 1730s was engendered as much by pressures within Russia as by the provocations of the Turks. Certainly, the Crimean Tartars were as vexatious as ever. They repeatedly raided into Russian territory on slave-gathering expeditions, and by their forays towards the Caspian they threatened to cut off the Russians from Georgia. There were circles in Russia which were more than willing to take up the challenge. The usually pacific Ostermann was alarmed by reports that the activity of the renegade Pasha Bonneval betokened a modernisation of the Turkish army, and even the oldfashioned Moscow nobility could sympathise with a war that might smash the Tartars, and liberate the Orthodox peoples of the Balkans.

Münnich, as usual, was spurred on by ambition and vainglory. He was disappointed that he had been unable to revive Peter's excellent system of summer exercise camps, or to relieve the men completely from works of civilian labour. As a matter of principle he was therefore searching for a war against almost any enemy, just 'to give the troops opportunity to exercise at arms' (Mediger, 1952, 325). He began to warm in particular to the notion of the new crusade against the Turks, and on the eve of the campaign of 1736 he outlined to Biron his scheme for a four-year programme of conquest. The first campaign was to give the mastery of the steppes, after which the army would proceed in 1737 to secure the Crimea and the Sea of Azov; in 1738 the Russians were to move around the western side of the Black Sea to deliver the peoples of Moldavia and Wallachia, and 'in 1739 we shall raise the standards of Her Imperial Highness. Where? Why over Constantinople!' (Baiov, 1906, I, 199).

Münnich now had to come to terms with the peculiar demands of the southern theatre, and he addressed himself to the problem as a student of military affairs as well as an accomplished practical soldier. He had published an edition of Saint-Rémy's famous *Mémoires d'Artillerie* in 1732, and his well-illustrated biography of his old master Prince Eugene of Savoy was to be translated into Russian and published in 1740.

The most immediate problem was to gather information about the scene of forthcoming operations. Neither the Russians nor any other power had reliable maps of the area, and indeed the campaigns of Münnich and Lacy were to do much to advance Europe's knowledge of that corner of the world. In February 1738 the British ambassador wrote to London, concerning the Crimea, that

> as Field-Marshal Lacy has made a very curious map of those parts, and has been so good as to give me a copy of it, I take the liberty to send the same enclosed, for I fear without such a map, neither the King nor anybody else, will be able to know where the russ army is. (C. Rondeau, 7 February 1738, *SIRIO*, 1892, LXXX, 273)

For reconnaissance and other purposes Münnich would have liked to have made full use of the Cossacks, but he found that only 32,000 of the nominal force of 110,000 actually turned up on campaign, since the stay-at-homes were concerned with protecting their camels, cattle and sheep against Tartar raids, and because the Zaporozhian Cossacks and the Kalmyks from beyond the Volga 'wished to have themselves regarded not as Russian subjects, but only as friends and allies' (Vischer, 1938, 564-5). However, a small party of intelligent Cossacks was responsible for furnishing Münnich with his first useful information as to the best time of the year to cross the steppes. These people had been sent out in November 1735, and they reported that the best season to embark on campaign was in the spring

for at this time of year there will be no shortage of water, thanks to the recent snow and rain. Also the grass will be everywhere in full growth, and impossible for the enemy to burn, and the spring will allow you to take advantage of the winter wheat growing on the arable lands. (Baiov, 1906, I, 198)

Unfortunately, the spring in those parts all too soon gave way to the intense heat of high summer, which was likely to find the Russian armies short of wood and water, and toiling across the empty steppes. The eerie landscape was dotted with mounds, which some supposed to have been erected as landmarks, and others (more correctly) to be the tombs of Tartar chiefs. The nomads gave further evidence of their presence when they set fire to the seas of tall grass, which exploded into walls of flame and smoke and placed the Russians in physical danger, as well as denying pasture to their multitudes of horses and oxen. Every time the Russians made themselves a camp they had to fashion fire brooms, and dig a fire break around the perimeter. The Russians could alleviate some of their difficulties by marching alongside the clear waters of the Dnieper, but the cataracts made continuous navigation impossible for craft of any size, and in any case the army sooner or later had to abandon the river and cut across country to its final destination.

A vital, though negative, aim of the Russians was to do something to conquer, devastate or mask the Crimean peninsula and the adjacent mainland, with their strategic flanks at Azov to the east, and Ochakov to the west. The more positive ends of raising the Balkan Christians and perhaps even of reducing Constantinople itself drew the Russians around the western edge of the Black Sea, with its successive barriers of the Bug, the Dniester (with Khotin and Bendery), the Pruth and the Danube Delta (with Izmail and Kilia), and finally the great looping course of the upper Danube (with Rushchuk, Silistria and Braila).

The Turks could be expected to make a determined stand in their fortresses, bringing into play their lively garrisons and powerful artillery. In the open field the enemy were more dangerous still, for they compensated for their lack of discipline by their individual prowess and fanaticism, and by their masses of irregular cavalry, which lapped around the Russian armies and cut them off from communication with their homeland. What with the distances concerned, the featureless terrain, the isolation, uncertainties and dangers, a Russian expedition against the Turks partook more of the nature of a voyage into unknown seas than of a campaign against an army.

Münnich's method of war in the southern theatre evolved as a remarkable association of offensive strategy, defensive minor tactics, and an increasingly self-contained system of supply. He was convinced of the value of offensive operations, for 'the attack imbues the soldier with courage, and establishes respect for the attacker in the minds of the enemy. By remaining inactive, on the other hand, you lower the morale of your forces and cause them to lose hope' (Baiov, 1906, II, 301).

The last notion was explored in more detail in a *Disposition for Military Arrangements and Movements for a General Battle against the Turks*, a document which Villim Villimovich Fermor composed at Münnich's request in 1736, and which was circulated in the army. Femor and Münnich were well aware of what was at stake in open confrontation, since 'upon the issue of a general battle depends not only the outcome of the campaign and the whole war, but nothing less than the welfare of the state and the security of the throne' (Baiov, 1906, I, 54). This sentiment was common at the time, but whereas in the West it induced a strategic paralysis, the Russified Teutons, Femor and Münnich, were impelled in the opposite direction, thanks to their confidence in the ability of the army to outmatch the Turks through superior discipline, the capacity for rapid movement, and the delivery of accurate and heavy fire from artillery and muskets — 'on our side we should not evade battle. On the contrary, we should seek it out as circumstances permit, so as to defeat the enemy' (Baiov, 1906, I, 55).

Both the nature of the ground and of the enemy indicated an army formation in one or more great rectangles, which could move across country with the baggage in the centre. When the grass was green, the leading regiments 'could not make a step without having to push their way through the vigorous and tall grass, which was often damp. The soldiers soon went barefoot, which was the occasion of various maladies' (Warnery, 1770, 57). The rest followed over the trampled grass, forming a mass of men, animals and vehicles which astonished people like Roman Maksimovich Tsebrikov, when they experienced the phenomenon for the first time:

Trumpets and woodwind resound on every side. You are startled by the rattling of the regimental drums, while the terrible, majestic thunder of the kettledrums sends the blood coursing hotly through your veins. The huge assembly aroused in me musings on life and death, on the power of empires, and on their fall. (*RS*, 1895, LXXXIV, 152)

In Münnich's time boar spears and pikes accompanied the regiments by the cartload, to enable the Russians to confront the enemy cavalry with a bristling barrier of *chevaux de frise* and levelled pikes, but otherwise the Russians sought to break the Turks by weight of musketry and regimental guns, and even the officers and the NCOs were expected to arm themselves with muskets so as to augment the firepower. Fermor here makes a clear distinction between artificial parade ground drills, and genuine combat tactics — a difference rarely recognised by military historians. He maintained that an individual rank within a single platoon was the largest sub-unit which could be kept under effective control, and that the mass volleys of the drill square were unworkable in action, on account of the confusions consequent upon noise, smoke, broken ground and casualties among the officers.

Münnich might establish magazines of cereals for the war along the Dnieper and Don, and try to help himself out from local sources of supply, but when it came to crossing the steppes, the army had to carry along everything it might need, down to wood and water if needs be. The ratio of 'tail' to 'teeth' therefore reached almost twentieth-century proportions. Altogether it probably took about one waggon to keep two men in the field. Experiences like these did much to colour the habits of the Russians when they came to fight in the West.

The campaign of 1736 was a grandiose affair, designed to inaugurate Münnich's plan of conquest by a comprehensive assault on the Moslem strategic bridgehead on the northern side of the Black Sea. St Petersburg allowed Münnich considerable freedom as to his line of march, 'for, as he was on the spot, and most certainly the best judge, it was left to him to go which way he thought best' (C. Rondeau, 5 May 1736, *SIRIO*, 1891, LXXVI, 512). His 54,000 men followed the Dnieper from the Ukraine in five columns, then began to march in the classic oblong formation. The objective was to break into the Crimean peninsula over the isthmus of Perekop, which was barred by a massive old earthwork. Münnich subjected the lines to a bombardment, then on the night of 19 May he executed a movement in six columns against the western sector. The soldiers climbed the obstacle by dint of plunging their pikes and bayonets into the rampart, and they mastered the position at a cost of just thirty dead and 170 wounded. A little later a garrison of 2,554 surrendered the supporting fortress of Perekop.

After this splendid start there was little of permanent good to be done in the Crimea. Münnich seized a number of little Tartar towns, but the elusive enemy burnt the provisions and poisoned the wells, and by early September the Russians were back on the mainland, prostrated by sickness and the heat. No regiment could muster more than six hundred combatants.

Lacy had meanwhile brought a smaller force against the stronghold of Azov. His proceedings were characteristically systematic and economical, and he was rewarded by an explosion of the main Turkish powder magazine, which ravaged the

52 The Age of Marshal Münnich 1725-41

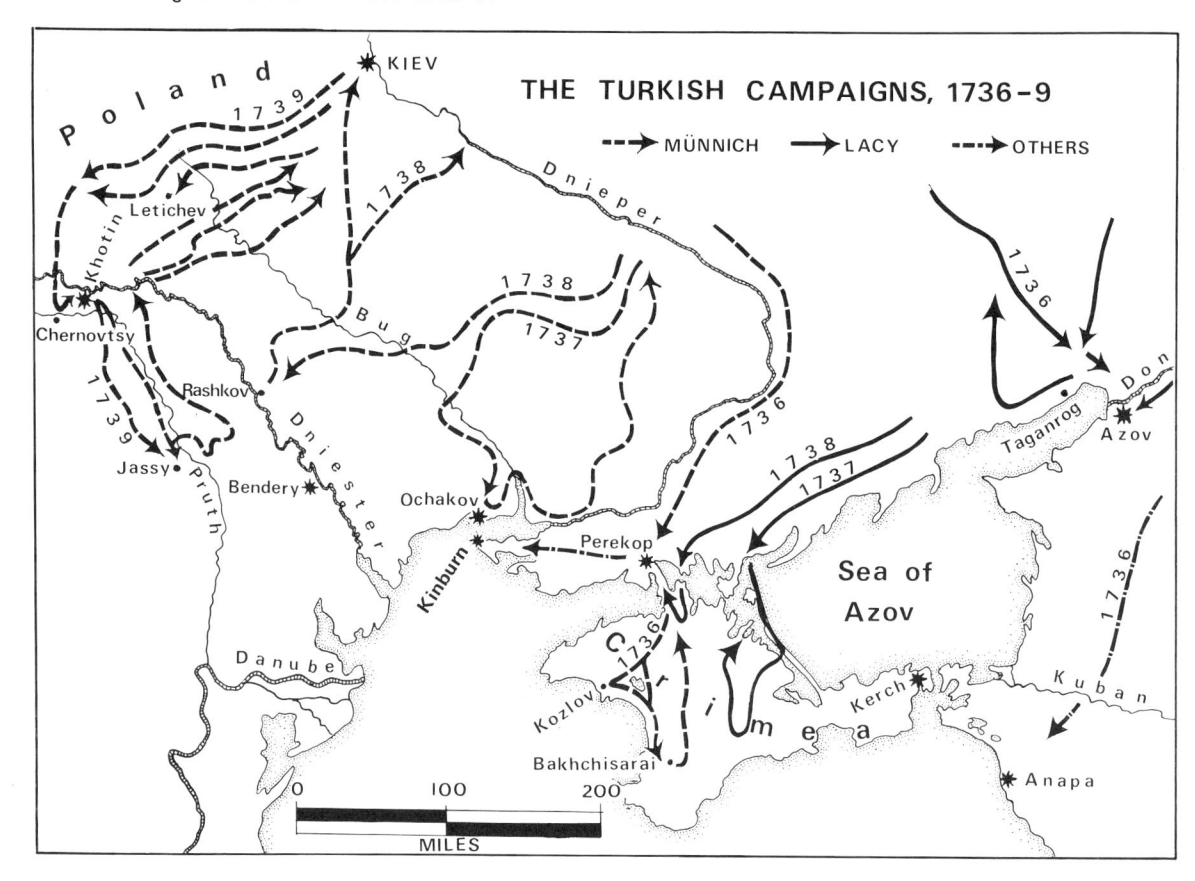

interior of the fortress. Azov capitulated on 1 July, and so Lacy had attained with the minimum expenditure of force an objective which had cost Peter the Great two campaigns.

In 1737 General Stoffeln successfully held Azov against a determined siege by 40,000 Turks. The Russian pikes on this occasion proved very useful in repelling the many furious storms, 'as the only weapons which were of any avail against the Turkish sabres' (Manstein, 1860, I, 293). Now it was Lacy's turn to attend to the Crimea, and this year and the next he led his army into the peninsula. Lacy was disappointed to find that his campaigns ended up as little more than extended raids, but the court was sympathetic to the difficulties he faced.

Münnich had an army of 70,000 men at his disposal for the campaign of 1737, and he undertook the westward shift which opened the second phase of his plan of war against the Turks. He was able to subsist for a time with the help of flatboats which brought provisions down the Dnieper, and 28,000 carts and 2,000 camels were at hand to support the move across the steppes to the Bug. He made the passage of the river at the end of June, only to find that 'Ochakov is farther from the Bug than is marked in the map' (C. Rondeau, 9 July 1737, *SIRIO*, 1892, LXXX, 165). The air of confusion and uncertainty continued through the campaign. Münnich needed to have Ochakov in his possession, to clear the way for a further advance, and obtain desperately needed supplies of water and firewood, and without waiting for his siege train to arrive he opened a generalised cannonade on the night of 12-13 July.

Whole streets were aflame, and so as to divert the Turks from putting out the fires, Münnich at once launched an assault in almost total ignorance of the nature of the defences. The Russians were beaten off in disorder. Next morning, however, the Turkish powder magazine blew up (as those establishments were prone to do), and the garrison indicated its wish to surrender. While the negotiations were going on a party of Don Cossacks fought their way into the town, and Münnich exploited the opportunity to throw in his regulars as well. Some 2,000 Turks escaped by water, and about 4,500 survived to surrender, but many of the townsfolk and garrison were cut down in cold blood.

After the fall of Ochakov, Münnich marched up and down the Bug. Any ambition to press on to the Dniester was thwarted by the Tartars, who burnt all the grass between the two rivers, and towards the end of August he headed back to the Ukraine. Manstein claims that during this campaign sickness alone had killed off 15,000 regulars, 5,000 Cossacks, and probably more than 20,000 peasant drivers and labourers.

Münnich's plan of aggrandisement was already dropping behind schedule, and the events of 1738 actually constituted a regression on the gains of the year before. Münnich set out with 108,000 men, and despite the huge size of the baggage train he chased the Turks with some energy all the way to the Dniester, where they lined the steep and rocky right bank. The Russian casualties were negligible in comparison with the havoc wreaked by the plague that was sweeping in from Moldavia and Wallachia, and Münnich was forced to turn back once more towards the Ukraine. The very air breathed of death, from the thousands of unburied corpses from the war, and in one spot the bodies of no less than 4,000 Tartars were lying in two soggy heaps, forcing everybody who passed that way to make a circuit of six miles. It proved impossible to maintain a garrison in pestilential Ochakov, which had already claimed 20,000 Russian lives, and so the place was razed and abandoned to the Turks.

In 1739 Russian strategy suddenly assumed a bolder aspect, for Ostermann persuaded Münnich and the empress's other advisers that the army must strike directly across Polish territory into the Balkans, where it could raise the local Christians and lend a more direct help to Russia's Austrian allies, who were faring very badly in their own campaigns against the Turks. The army of 65,000 troops set out from Kiev, and marching south-west it took a route comfortably distant from the Nogai steppes and the Black Sea lowlands. Münnich led the army across the Dniester well upstream, and on 28 August he evicted the Turkish army from its camp at Stavuchanakh, setting a precedent for many such vigorous undertakings later in the century. Nearby Khotin surrendered upon the first summons, and Münnich pressed into Moldavia, where the Christian nobles pledged their allegiance to Empress Anna. Just at that moment, when for the first time Russia appeared to have a footing in the Balkans, Münnich received news that the Austrians had left their allies in the lurch, and entered into humiliating terms of peace with the Turks at Belgrade.

Russia reached her own accommodation with the Turks in 1740. All the gains of the war were abandoned, save for an advance of the frontier into the barren steppes. The top corner of the Sea of Azov fell just within the ceded zone, though it afforded little profit to the Russians, since the fortifications of Azov were to be dismantled, and the Russians were not to be permitted to rebuild the naval arsenal at Taganrog. All of this offered precious little recompense for the thousands of men who had disappeared into the southern steppes. The armies had probably never amounted to more than 120,000 troops at any one time, yet they were said to have absorbed 50,000 reinforcements in 1738, and 100,000 in the following year: 'Though the Russians did not lose many men in battle, yet it cannot be denied, that they lost great numbers by fatigue, want of water, travelling through these scorching deserts, and by the plague' (Cook, 1770, I, 243).

Palace revolutions and the fall of Münnich, 1740-1

Empress Anna died on 28 October 1740. The leadership of the empire became the prize of contending factions, as represented by former favourites, some more-or-less remote scions of the imperial house, and finally and most importantly by the Guards, who acted in some ways as the unwitting conscience of Russia and put their weight behind the candidate who showed the most generosity and leadership. Russia underwent the process three times in the eighteenth century, almost as if a working-out of tensions was a necessary interval between one long reign and the next.

The sordid strife of Biron, Münnich and Ostermann inclined people more and more to look with favour on the undoubted claims of Princess Elizabeth Petrovna. She was an affable soul, she had a strong legal title to the throne, and she was the daughter of Peter the Great, whose once terrifying memory was already gilded with a certain nostalgia. Elizabeth cultivated the society of the Preobrazhenskii Regiment, to the scorn of her enemies, but it was with the help of a company of its soldiers that she seized power in St Petersburg on 25 November 1741.

A reckoning was soon presented to the servants of the old order. Münnich, Ostermann and others were tried, convicted and sentenced to death for an assortment of crimes. Münnich in particular was indicted for his dictatorial ways on campaign, when he had failed to consult his generals, and inflicted demeaning punishments on senior officers. On 29 January 1742 a cortege duly made its way to a crude plank scaffold standing in the wide square in front of the College Building. Ostermann was in the leading sledge, and he presented a pitiful sight, dressed in his old fox fur, and literally paralysed with terror. The civilians had grown long beards in their captivity, but 'the field marshal was shaved, well-dressed, and with as erect, intrepid and unconcerned a countenance, as if he had been at the head of an army or at a review' (E. Finch, *SIRIO*, 1894, XCI, 422). The executioner was already approaching Ostermann with an axe when a secretary came up and announced, 'God and the empress grant you your life.' Ostermann and all the others were banished to exile in the provinces. Münnich received the news with unaltered composure, but he was aware that his active public life was over.

The xenophobic historians of the later nineteenth century were fond of associating the name of Münnich with that of Biron and the other tyrannical Teutons who made the air of Anna's reign alien to native-born Russians. Among men of the field-marshal's own century, however, the talk was not just of Münnich's vaulting ambition, but of his military talents and his work in consolidating the legacy of Peter the Great. We may cite the favourable observations of the field-marshals Apraksin and Buturlin, the gunner lieutenant-general Tolstoi and the soldier and diplomat Semen Vorontsov. 'The name of Münnich shines brightly amid the memories of those gloomy times' (Wiegel, 1864-6, I, 14).

When the Russians prepared for the Seven Years War, it was in the papers of Münnich that Petr Shuvalov found the principles on which he designed his military reform (Zinzendorf, in Volz and Küntzel, 1899, 687). After the close of that struggle old Münnich was summoned back to court: 'He entered the hall clad in a soldier's greatcoat. But written on his face was the composure, pride and dignity of a commander-in-chief reviewing his army' (Lubyanovskii, 1872, 65).

Four   Elizabeth Petrovna 1741-1761/2

Elizabeth, daughter of Peter

In the middle of the eighteenth century Russia pursued an aggressive, Western-looking policy, and took on and beat the best of all the European armies, led by the finest soldier that the age had to show. In the process Russia ceased to be merely a formidable presence in the northern world, and advanced into the select ranks of first-class European powers. The wonder is that all this was achieved without the intervention of any individuals of heroic stature, and during the reign of a princess who abhorred conquests and bloodshed.

The clemency which Elizabeth extended to Münnich and Ostermann was the expression of one aspect of a most attractive personality. Foreign observers spoke with approval of her pleasant rounded figure, her blonde hair, her 'almost English face' with its high colour, and of her benevolent character. She banished the small-town German ways of the old regime from St Petersburg, and set a fashion for Frenchified luxury that was taken up with enthusiasm by the more open-minded of the nobility.

At the same time, people had certain reservations about Elizabeth's conduct of public affairs. She was notoriously 'a person of an amorous turn' (Richard, 1780, 16), and so the element of personal attraction weighed considerably in the choice of some of her servants. Important military men like Petr Shuvalov and Field-Marshal Buturlin owed their position directly to the inclinations of the empress. Officials, who had weighty business to conduct, testified that 'In the first years of her reign she was prepared to devote one hour a week

9 Elizabeth Petrovna

for sessions with her Chancellor. According as her tenure on the throne became more secure, she gave still freer rein to her bent for dissipation' (Zinzendorf, in Volz and Küntzel, 1899, 680). Important questions of state might languish three or four years before Elizabeth could be persuaded to take an interest in them, while routine matters were usually forgotten altogether. Only occasionally did Elizabeth bestir herself from her lethargy, bursting out with foul language and physical violence, and giving herself over to bouts of work, and this was when her pride was affronted, or when she felt herself or her country under threat.

The lack of leadership in public life did much to promote the rise of Count Aleksei Bestuzhev-Ryumin, who became her Chancellor, or foreign minister, in 1744. 'He was not without judgment', testified Manstein, 'and by dint of long routine he acquired a considerable knowledge of affairs, being very industrious. At the same time he was afflicted with a temperament that was haughty, debauched and treacherous' (1860, II, 222-3). Here was a notable exception to our rule concerning physical comeliness. Bestuzhev was equally hideous, whether his visage wore its habitual expression of sour discontent, or was split in a horrid grin, revealing toothless gums.

Elizabeth's guiding principles in the early years of her reign were to destroy the work of Anna's time, and rearrange affairs according to what she imagined to be the ideas of Peter the Great. The case of the drill regulations was typical. Elizabeth emphasised that the provisions were to be observed: 'in every respect according to the earlier code, which was in force during the lifetime of His Imperial Highness Peter the Great. This is to hold true for all regiments, without the slightest exception, and *the Prussian way is not to be followed*' (Beskrovnyi, 1957, 128). Since, however, the *Code of 1716* did not enter into tactical details, Peter Lacy had to supply the lack by composing a *Description of the Drill of an Infantry Regiment*, which was circulated in manuscript in 1746.

Although men like Lacy were absolutely indispensable, the foreigners as a whole became an easy target for the rampant xenophobia of those years. Officers were liable to be manhandled by their own troops, or by thugs in the streets, and at court they attracted the hostile glare of Bestuzhev. Nobody grieved much for the departure of some of the Germans, but the resignation of people like Keith was generally felt to be a severe loss.

Under the same dispensation, the unity of military affairs was destroyed for the sake of building up the authority of the Senate, which was not only restored on its Petrine foundations, but endowed with law-making powers, and permitted to carry the voice of the high nobility into the management of state affairs. The War College forfeited the supervision of all matters appertaining to supply, provisions, and the administration of the artillery and engineers, which were taken over by a number of bodies which answered to the Senate — namely a *Glavnyi Kommissariat*, a *Proviantskaya Kantselyarya*, and a *Kantselyarya Glavnoi Artillerii i Fortifikatsii*. It was typical that the post of Master General of the Ordnance was left unfilled between 1748 and 1756.

In the process, a number of vital functions of administration were forgotten almost entirely, particularly the ones relating to the supervision of accounts, and to the inspection of the regiments (so important for keeping up numbers and standards). Thus the army began to suffer arrears of pay, which was a significant detail, since Münnich had always been meticulous in the matter. The shortage of cash was accentuated by the extravagance of the court, and the creation of fifty new battalions in 1747, which brought the establishment of the regular army to 270,791 men. The government, therefore, had to raise the poll-tax and the price of monopoly products, and cast about for foreign subsidies. All of this provided a very uncertain base for the great military effort of the Seven Years War.

The reckoning with the Swedes, 1742-3

Encouraged by some irresponsible advice from the French, the Swedish government threw aside the chance of an accord with the new regime in Russia, and pressed for the return of all Karelia with Vyborg, which would have brought the Swedes once more within eighty miles of St Petersburg. Elizabeth was inclined towards conciliation and peace, but she was also the daughter of Peter the Great, and 'that great prince knew the importance of being a European power, and would rather have suffered a thousand deaths, than return again to be an Asiatic one, as his ancestors were' (E. Finch, 1 December 1741, *SIRIO*, 1894, XCIV, 350). Peace negotiations were broken off, and Elizabeth declared to the people of Finland that she would make their country into an independent state, and that it would serve as 'a barrier and division between the Russian and Swedish borders'.

In Field-Marshal Lacy Elizabeth had a commander who excelled in the rapid and economical style of campaigning that the situation demanded, and who knew the theatre of war from his experiences in 1741 (see p. 48). He crossed the borders of Swedish Finland on 24 June 1742, and drove his 25,000 men in a single column down the coast road, relying on his galley flotilla to keep him supplied. 'The main road offered the only practicable route, since rocks, woods and marshes stretched endlessly on either side' (Manstein, 1860, II, 250).

Lacy seized the advanced Swedish magazine at Fredrikshamn without opposition, and ignoring the instructions from the court he pressed over the River Kyumen in pursuit of the Swedes, who wanted to make good their escape at Åbo. Lacy learnt from some Finnish peasants of a circuitous track which Peter had cut through the same forests thirty years before, and a rapid march down this path brought him to the coast road just ahead of the Swedish army, which was consequently bottled up in Helsingfors and forced to capitulate.

For 1743 the Russian government decided to prosecute the war with vigour, and pile as many of their troops as possible on board the galleys for wide-ranging offensive operations. For this purpose the army was formed into two divisions, with Keith taking the lead. The Swedes feared for the safety of their mainland, and in the face of the amphibious threat they brought hostilities to an end by coming to terms at Åbo on 6 August 1743.

Bestuzhev was all for annexing the whole of Finland as a near-impenetrable obstacle against the Swedes. The other leading members of the government were, however, unwilling to press home the advantage, and they settled for an advance of the frontier sixty miles to the Kyumen, 'which river, as it traverses the whole country, is looked upon as a very necessary barrier to prevent the Swedes from attacking Russia on the side of Finland' (C. Wich, 26 August 1742, *SIRIO*, 1897, XCIX, 50).

The march to Germany, 1748

Long-term political considerations and the hope of financial gain drew the piggy eyes of Bestuzhev to the West, where the British and Dutch armies were being soundly beaten by the French in the last campaigns of the War of the Austrian Succession. Bestuzhev was genuinely anxious to do something to prop up the maritime powers, whom he saw as a necessary counterbalance to the Swedes and Prussians, but he also hoped that these rich but unlucky people would reciprocate by helping Russia in her financial straits. In 1747, therefore, a series of agreements bound the maritime powers to make over 2,250,000 roubles (£500,000) to Russia over a period of a year and a half, in return for which Russia was to maintain a corps in Livonia to hold the Prussians in check, and send another powerful force marching against the French.

Russia was treaty-bound to dispatch 30,000 troops to Germany, but in the event 37,000 actually set out, which was a deliberate measure of military over-insurance. The officer complement was assembled only with difficulty, and consisted half of native Russians, and half of the best of the remaining foreigners. Old Field-Marshal Lacy was the most obvious choice for supreme command, but Elizabeth could not bear to let him leave Russia, and the command of the columns was entrusted to people like Prince Vasilii Anikitich Repnin and Lieutenant-General Lieven, who were some of the best horses in the Russian stable. Cook describes the ensemble as 'a body of the most complete troops I ever saw, commanded by choice generals' (Cook, 1770, II, 568). Everything about the expedition indicates that the Russians were aware that their army was going to be on show before the world.

As the Russian corps emerged into Central Europe, it came under close scrutiny from Western military men and students of human affairs. The British commissary, Major-General Mordaunt, admired the soldierly air of the force, but he noticed that the Russians were:

behindhand with their neighbours in some particulars. Alertness seems the very soul of our [military] calling, and the Russian troops, appointed as they are, can never act with expedition. They always march in heavy, high-heeled boots, and each soldier carries a large cloak, or what is worse, it must go with the baggage. Their tents are made of a sort of sailcloth and consequently weighty, and to add to the weight all their tentpoles even go on the waggons. (9 June 1748, *SIRIO*, 1901, CX, 160)

Technically speaking, the Russians were acting as auxiliaries of the Austrians, who were allies of the British and Dutch, and the route took the Russian corps by way of the Austrian province of Moravia. Towards evening on 16 June the first regiments marched into Kremsier, with their cloaks slung over their shoulders like scarves, and they were greeted by the co-sovereigns of Austria, the Empress-Queen Maria Theresa and her consort, Emperor Francis Stephen. Over the following days the little army went through its evolutions under a burning sun, while the commanders dined with the two Imperial Majesties. An Austrian courtier noted that:

Repnin spoke excellent French and a little German. Lieven (as a Kurlander) spoke German as his native language, but Lopukhin needed an interpreter. Of the other generals and staff officers, who included some foreigners, most understood German, and they included in their ranks a very large number of extremely handsome and fine-mannered men.

For us Austrians, who were accustomed to the white uniform of our infantry and the diverse garb of our cavalry, the appearance of the Russians was odd, with all their infantry clad in green, and their cavalry in blue. The Kalmyks in particular . . . made a strong impression on people who had not seen visages of that kind before.

The Austrian military men concluded that, with the exception of a few regiments, the 'Russian forces fully lived up to their renown' (Khevenhüller-Metsch, 1907-72, II, 241-2).

While the Russians were marching through Germany, still well short of their goal, they learnt that their presence was unnecessary, for peace negotiations were already well advanced at Aix-la-Chapelle. Prince Repnin was one peaceful victim of the campaign, dying of an apoplectic stroke on 31 July. Otherwise, the losses on this long march were small, since the officers took good care of the health and discipline of their troops, and less than eight hundred of the men deserted during the outward and homeward trek of eight months.

Bestuzhev calmly retained the whole of the subsidy for Russia, which gave the Treasury a clear profit of nearly one million roubles, and he reported with satisfaction to Elizabeth:

The flames of war spread apace, as long as Your Imperial Majesty was content to be a spectator while the intrigues [of France and Prussia] tore Europe apart. Once, however, Your Imperial Majesty made clear Your desire to intervene with an impressive force, the face of European affairs immediately assumed a very different aspect . . . the Russian corps of observation advanced only as far as was needed to imbue the whole of Europe with a sense of the glory of the Imperial arms, and win for Your Majesty the flattering title of 'Peace-Giver of the Continent'. (Rambaud, 1895, 5)

Here was a clear and significant statement of the role of Russia as the resolver of muddled affairs in the West, a theme to which the rulers of that country were to return in later generations. More immediate precedents were set by the apparent winning of great political ends for the minimum expenditure of military force, and for the ease with which affairs had been directed from distant St Petersburg — all of which was going to colour Russia's intervention in the Seven Years War. At the same time some useful lessons had emerged, particularly concerning the relative backwardness of the Russians in matters of drill and supply, and the pressure from Colonel Zakhar Chernyshev and other young officers was to lead directly to the Military Commission of 1755 and the consequent reshaping of the army.

The approach to the Seven Years War — the Diplomatic Revolution and the rise of the Shuvalovs

When the Russians returned to Central Europe, it was by right of the sword, and to fight some of the bloodiest battles of the century. The enemy concerned was the new and most formidable power of Prussia under King Frederick II, the Great, and the man ultimately responsible for bringing the Russian and Prussian armies into conflict was Chancellor Bestuzhev, who detected a long-term threat to Russian interests in the character and ambitions of Old Fritz.

The Prussians were already intriguing in Sweden and Poland, and Bestuzhev feared that Frederick's schemes of aggrandisement might extend to Kurland (now virtually a Russian province) and Livonia. For ends such as this Frederick was likely to sacrifice every engagement. Bestuzhev was well informed of the state of his own army through his connections with Marshal Apraksin, and he echoed an old sentiment of Münnich to the effect that some kind of war was desirable on first principles, so as to afford the soldiers 'employment in their noble and proper calling, in which they can never be given sufficient practice' (Mediger, 1952, 325).

Bestuzhev submitted a detailed memorandum on the nature of the Prussian threat to the empress as early as September 1745. For one who was normally so pacific and unsystematic, Elizabeth over the following years began to warm to the scheme of the Prussian war with remarkable enthusiasm. She disapproved of Frederick as a man, as well as a potential enemy to Russia, and she was infuriated by the stories he was spreading about her manner of life.

The foundation of Russian foreign policy was the long-enduring alliance with Austria, with whom Russia shared common interests against Turkey and France, as expressed in a treaty of 1726. The Empress Maria Theresa actually surpassed Elizabeth in her loathing of Frederick, whom she regarded as the enemy of her dynasty and the robber of the rich Austrian province of Silesia, and this further bond was cemented in a defensive alliance of 2 June 1746. So as to lend weight to his dispositions, Bestuzhev held a heavy concentration of forces in the Baltic provinces, despite the high cost of provisions in that part of the world.

An imperial conference of 25 and 26 May 1753 constituted the most determined step so far towards achieving Bestuzhev's aggressive designs. Elizabeth and her ministers decided not merely to lend help to Russia's allies, if they came under attack by Prussia, but to take positive measures to reduce Prussia once more to the category of a minor principality. With such an ambition in mind, Russia was to maintain a corps of 60,000 regulars in Livonia, to gather a reserve force of another 60,000 troops, and to undertake a large overall increase in the establishment of the army:

As soon as our forces have attained the above-mentioned strength, we will be well-placed, both to make a diversion against Prussia, in case the King of Prussia attacks Hanover, and, if we find it necessary in the future, to take the initiative in declaring and opening the war against him. (Mediger, 1952, 456)

Bestuzhev's intelligence and consistency were no defence against a rival force that was gathering at court around the glamorous and ambitious Shuvalov clan. The three brothers Shuvalov (pronounced Shuvárluv) came from an old but poor noble stock, and they owed their collective place in the imperial confidence to the support which they gave Elizabeth in her revolution of 1741. The young and gentle Ivan Shuvalov was now the object of Elizabeth's most tender affections. Aleksandr Shuvalov, in contrast, had a firm control of the physical instruments of power in St Petersburg, as head of the police and the dreaded state tribunal of justice.

The Shuvalov who has the greatest relevance to our story is, however, Petr Ivanovich (1710-62), 'a man of enterprise and great thoughts' (Danilov, 1842, 80). He became an influential voice in the Senate (1744) and the new court conference, *generalanshef* (1751), Master General of the Ordnance (1756), and finally effective controller of the war machine and the national finances, and commander of the Livonian division.

His financial gifts by themselves made Petr precious to the state. The cost of maintaining the army in being rose from 5,428,108 roubles in 1749, to 6,683,096 in 1756, and to 7,924,749 in 1760, independently of the costs of the war and other additional expenses. Petr Shuvalov was unwilling to increase the poll-tax still further, but he hoped to meet the deficit by raising the indirect taxes, and by carrying through a profitable re-coinage by which the state called in the pieces of gold and silver, and issued a copper currency that was struck from the metal of obsolete guns. In 1756 Petr set up an 'Artillery Bank' to supervise the process, thereby anticipating the opening of the first public bank in 1772. So it was that financial affairs offered an exception to the habitual slow pace of Russian government. Petr Shuvalov did not neglect his own interests. His house was stuffed with documents relating not just to his public concerns, but to private enterprises like seal oil or mast timber, which gave him a personal income of an alleged 400,000 roubles a year.

As evidence of the impressive quality of Shuvalov's military thought, we may cite his projects for a Higher Military Department or School, which he advanced in various forms in 1753, in 1755 and finally, with the help of Lomonosov, in 1758. Shuvalov was convinced that a sound knowledge of the mechanics and principles of war must go towards the formation of the young officer, and that 'leadership is not enough' (Shmidt, in Beskrovnyi, 1969, 393). To provide this foundation, his Higher Military Department was to instruct the students in military writing, the paths of the transmission of orders, the means by which ammunition, clothing, pay and provisions reached the army, the laying-out of camps, and the conduct of marches and movements in the field. However, Shuvalov appreciated the dangers of a narrow professionalism. He believed it important 'to consider all the well-known battles and encounters, evaluating the mistakes which caused them to be lost, and exploring the action of artillery and its employment in battles and sieges'. Likewise, on Saturdays a professor was to discuss 'the present political affairs of Europe, and the armed forces of the European powers' (Shmidt, in Beskrovnyi, 1969, 400). These excellent proposals were put before the Senate, but they were lost to view in the turmoil of the later Seven Years War.

To begin with, Petr Shuvalov had opposed the Bestuzhev policy of military build-up and confrontation, but by 1755 he had seized the initia-

10 Petr Shuvalov

tive in the matter for himself, declaring 'the Prussians are certainly formidable people, and we will have to work night and day in order to draw level. But the most important thing is not to be afraid of them' (Zinzendorf, 1755, in Volz and Küntzel, 1899, 688).

The Shuvalov tribe was well placed to profit by any miscalculation on the part of Bestuzhev. The Chancellor offered an opening to his rivals through his obstinacy concerning the structure of the alliance, which he conceived in terms of an immutable grouping of Russia, Austria, the maritime powers, Hanover and Saxony. The Shuvalovs were bound by no such commitments.

Oddly enough, Bestuzhev failed to appreciate that the increase in Russia's own power might bring about a change in relations. This more than anything else was what concerned Frederick of Prussia, who in his fear of Russian intentions was willing to throw over his old French connection and make a deal with Hanover and Britain, as some kind of insurance and restraint in respect of the Russians. The consequent Prusso-British accord was expressed in the famous Convention of Westminster of 27 January 1756.

The Convention set in train two sequences of events. First, the French were appalled by the treachery of Frederick, their old ally, and the Austrian Chancellor Kaunitz at last managed to make some headway in his ambition to overthrow 'an ancient, deep-rooted prejudice' and win the French over to an active alliance with the two empires of eastern Europe. The question of true French interests in the affair has long been a matter of debate among historians, but there is little doubt that the weakening of the French position in the Baltic and the East helped significantly in the extension of Russian influence into Europe in the second half of the eighteenth century.

Second, the news of the betrayal by the British served as a catalyst within Russia. The 'system' of Bestuzhev lay in ruins, and in an explosion of rare energy Elizabeth worked with the Shuvalovs and the 'French' party of Vice-Chancellor M. Vorontsov to visit punishment on the head of the doubly perfidious Frederick. On 25 March 1756 an imperial conference resolved to make overtures to Austria concerning offensive action against Prussia, and to carry out a mobilisation of forces in the Baltic provinces. Over the next two months nearly 130,000 troops were alerted to execute the great design (see p. 73). Galleys and warships assembled at Riga and Revel, and spies and topographical experts began to sound out the land avenues to the west. Kaunitz wrote in some alarm to his representative in St Petersburg 'The Russians are pushing ahead with far too much speed and violence, before affairs are ripe. This could ruin everything' (Volz and Küntzel, 1899, 370). On 10 June the Russian government accordingly suspended the move to the frontiers.

It took a little time for the diplomats to catch up with all the warlike enthusiasm. The initial agreements revolved around the First Treaty of Versailles of 1 May 1756, which was a defensive agreement between the ancient enemies Austria and France. Frederick the Great sought to break the ring of his gathering enemies through military action, and in the autumn of 1756 he launched his splendid army into an invasion of the neutral state of Saxony, which had valuable resources and an important strategic position. Thus, in spite of all the provocations of the allies, Frederick had cast himself in the role of the bad man of Europe, which greatly assisted the diplomats in their work.

On 11 January 1757 Russia acceded to the First Treaty of Versailles, which made her for the first time an ally of France. Then, on 2 February, the Russians and their old Austrian friends concluded a Convention of St Petersburg, which was a programme for military co-operation against Frederick of Prussia, as disturber of the public peace. Austria and Russia accepted the common obligation to put 80,000 troops each into the field, while Austria promised to pay a subsidy of one million roubles per annum, and the Russians undertook to invade Prussian territory as soon as possible. Russia asked for no territorial gains, yet bound herself not to lay down arms until Maria Theresa was reinstated as mistress of Silesia and Glatz. These proposals had been made by the Austrian ambassador Esterhazy, and they were accepted *in toto* by the Russians. Articles five and eleven dealt with practical questions of military liaison. The armies were to help each other out with transport and supply, and they were to exchange military plenipotentiaries who would have a seat and voice in councils of war.

Although the Austrians had taken the initiative in tying the great Austro-Russo-French alliance together, the power of Russia had worked to decisive effect in the interesting events of 1755-6, and in the process of the Diplomatic Revolution as a whole:

The calculation of Russia's enormous military potential was the key to Maria Theresa's understanding of her role in European politics. The fear that dominated Frederick was his belief that his territory would soon be invaded by tens of thousands of Russian troops in the pay of Great Britain. It was that conviction which made him conclude the Convention of Westminster. (Kaplan, 1968, 125)

The approach to the Seven Years War — the rebuilding of the army

In a characteristically Russian style the War College entrusted the work of bringing the army up to the times to a special Military Commission. Yurii Lieven was one of the leading lights in the first board, which came together in November 1755, and worked out the establishment (size and composition) of the army, as well as putting together new codes for the infantry and cavalry, and defining the organisation of the grenadiers, regular cavalry and Cossacks. The sessions of 1756 and 1757 looked more to the management of rear services, camps and the like.

In 1755 Petr Shuvalov eagerly sought out the Austrian representatives in St Petersburg, so as to talk of the 'novel evolutions he had made in imitation of the Prussians' (Zinzendorf, in Volz and Küntzel, 1899, 711). These were expressed in the new infantry code, the *Opisanie Pekhotogo Polkovogo Stroyu*, which was published on 15 December 1755. The articles were composed by Shuvalov and his favourite, Colonel Zakhar Chernyshev of the St Petersburg Regiment, and they were what you might have expected of keen and professionally minded officers who had little or no experience of warfare. It is not unkind to say that the 1755 Code sought to out-Prussianise the Prussians through weight of fire, complexity of evolutions, and accuracy of execution. Almost every formation, movement or method of fire could be carried out in a variety of ways. Out of combat the line was one of four ranks, disposed at intervals of three paces, making a total depth of line of between ten and twelve paces. The intervals were closed up to deliver fire, with optional formations of three or four ranks; in the first instance only the first rank loaded and fired in the kneeling position, but in the case of the four-rank line, both the first and second ranks flopped to the ground in the same way.

As for the arrangement in width, the regimental adjutant made a tactical subdivision of the musketeers of the battalion into 'divisions' (usually four), half divisions, and platoons (at two to the half division). A grenadier company of six platoons stood on either flank of the battalion. As soon as the fire-fight began, a small reserve was to be formed from one platoon of the battalion of musketeers and two platoons from each company of the grenadiers, so as to cover the flanks, replace any losses, and reinforce weak points.

As was normal at the time, the men were expected to fire in massed volleys, which became an almost impossible ideal after a couple of minutes of combat. On top of this, Chernyshev and his friends worked out wonderful arrangements for rolling fire by Prussian-type platoons, whether standing (in the order 1, 3, 2, 4) or on the march, as well as by various combinations for the half divisions.

No less than four kinds of square are described for defence against cavalry, namely, the regimental square, the battalion square, the 'bent' square and the 'long' square. The regiments usually marched to the field in the standard mid-eighteenth-century open platoon column, which made it possible to deploy into line by the processional movement (see Duffy, *The Army of Frederick the Great*, London, 1974, 83-4), but the

1755 Code has some interesting things to say about the offensive use of columns by the battalion and the sub-units:

No formation may compare with the columns with respect to the strength and solidity they derive variously from their depth, facility of movement, striking-power, and the quality of speedy and dogged marching. Such columns may therefore be employed both to break the enemy front, and to withstand attack by cavalry. (Gippius, in Skalon, 1902-c.1911, IV, pt 1, bk 2, sect. 3, 56)

Here we may detect the influence of authorities like the Frenchman Folard.

The new infantry code was first applied by Petr Shuvalov to his Livonian division, and then, in the course of 1756, huge printed volumes went out to all the infantry regiments. Officers and men had to re-learn their trade from scratch, and the consequent confusions lasted into the war years, at least according to the Prussian spy Lambert:

The first rank always remains kneeling. They deliver fire very badly, and although deployment into line has been introduced into their service, the infantry regiment is scarcely capable of arranging a line in less than an hour, and even then the process is always attended with disorder. (*AKV*, 1870-95, VI, 481)

In this matter, as in almost everything else, people were willing to make an exception in favour of the elite of the Russian infantry, the grenadiers. Münnich had done away with the original regiments of grenadiers in the 1730s, but in 1742 Elizabeth (who liked big men on principle) revived them in the shape of forty-five companies of 130 grenadiers apiece, who were attached to the regiments of musketeers, 'as fine men, and as well exercised and appointed as ... in any part of Europe' (C. Wich, 10 April 1742, *SIRIO*, 1894, XCI, 456). On 30 March 1756 the third, or reserve, battalion of each infantry regiment was deprived of its grenadiers, and the troops went to form four complete regiments (numbered First, Second, Third, Fourth) which were accounted very fine, 'both in point of men and clothing' (Tielke, 1788, II, 29). Even Lambert conceded that 'The chief strength of their army lies in their regiments of grenadiers. The men are really tough and strong, if lacking in nimbleness and vivacity. The officers are likewise splendid men, though cast in the Russian mould' (*AKV*, 1870-95, VI, 48).

As for the horse, 'The whole activity and strength of the cavalry ... consists in the bravery of the men, in the good employment of the sword, in firm and compact formations, and in a ferocious impact delivered at a fast gallop' (Mikhnevich, in Skalon, 1902-c.1911, IV, pt 1, bk 1, 169). This passage from the new cavalry code of 1755 gives a clue to the nature of that clear, forceful and sensible document, altogether superior to the corresponding regulations for the infantry. The tactical unit of the cavalry was established as the squadron of about 150 men (138 in 1756), divided into two companies of two platoons each. By the end of 1757, for the sake of greater flexibility, the squadron had been reduced to forty-six three-rank files, and the company to twenty-three. The squadron column was the usual formation for movements on the battlefield, and the regiment deployed into line for combat by diagonal movement of the component squadrons from the centre. The troopers were now drawn up in a line three ranks deep, and upon the order to attack they moved forward at the trot; at four hundred paces from the enemy the trot gave way to a gallop, and this in turn broke into a wild *carrière* before the final impact. Fire from the saddle was positively discouraged, except in rare circumstances.

It was a pity that the appearance of the cavalry regulations was overtaken so soon by the two mobilisations for the Seven Years War, and by a very extensive reorganisation of the whole cavalry arm. Rumyantsev's cuirassiers and the mounted grenadiers at Riga put a lot of effort into learning the new ways, but the rest of the horse still carried out the rules of the 'Prussian Exercise' of 1731, which was one of the less happy products of Münnich's time.

A review of the cavalry was certainly an urgent necessity, and in the busy year of 1755 a Cavalry Reorganisation Commission was constituted with the aim of making the Russian horse not just equal, but superior to the cavalry of the other powers, 'since experience shows that unsupported infantry is incapable of beating an enemy who has effective cavalry at his disposal'. It was only too clear that the dragoons, the mainstay of the Russian regular cavalry, were 'completely unsuitable for mounted combat against the regular cavalry of other European armies' (Maslovskii, 1888-93, I, 317).

On 30 March 1756 Elizabeth approved a range of proposals from the Reorganisation Commission, relating to the doubling of the prices allowed for fodder, a raising of the sums paid for dragoon and hussar remounts, a closer supervision on the part of regimental officers of the quality of the remounts, the reduction of the regimental establishments to forty-six files per squadron, and the breaking of the near-monopoly of the dragoons in the regular cavalry. The last aim was to be achieved through increasing the number of regiments of cuirassiers, and by creating a new category of horse — the mounted grenadiers.

Three regiments of cuirassiers survived from the Münnich era. They were now reinforced by three more, those of Kazan, Novgorod and Astrakhan, which were simply conversions from the dragoons. Indeed, until late in the war they were still clad in their infantry-type coats of light blue, and rode light Russian horses that were quite unsuitable for the work of heavy cavalry. The veteran regiments were not in much better state, at least according to Captain Lambert, who saw two of them in November 1757. They had to make up their deficiencies in horseflesh by buying up carriage horses as they marched through the Baltic provinces, and

> They are very slow to form their squadrons, and they deliver the charge at nothing faster than the trot. When the order comes *Halt! Dress!* you might find twelve or more ranks piled up in one spot, while in other places there will be room for a whole platoon to drive through. On these occasions they open fire by entire ranks, but with such confusion that I still do not know what they really intended to do, for the whole regiment subsides into a heap, where many of the horses stumble and decant their riders from the saddle. (*AKV*, 1870-95, VI, 483)

Six further regiments of dragoons were transformed into mounted grenadiers, with rather more success. The Commission hoped for great things of them, for no other army had anything of the kind, and a Saxon officer testifies that the grenadiers were 'the flower of the dragoons', though almost as badly mounted as the rest (Tielke, 1788, II, 27). On the field of battle they were to be employed as an elite reserve, holding themselves ready to charge home with cold steel when they were most needed. On campaign, however, they were to consider the employment of their special attribute, the grenade, of which every man carried two in a pouch. It was thought likely that in East Prussia the main resistance would be offered by hussars and peasants in uniform, who might try to hold out in buildings or behind other cover. In such an event the grenadiers were to dismount and cast their grenades inside the strongpoint, where the explosions would work to devastating effect in the confined space.

The regiments of mounted grenadiers were accompanied by several carts with spare grenades, and like the new cuirassier regiments and the parent regiments of dragoons they were each supported by mounted artillery in the shape of two 3-pounders with horsed detachments.

The sad rump of eighteen regiments of dragoons still formed the basic stock of the regular cavalry. They came low in the order of priorities, and they arrived at the war with little training or sense of cohesion, having spent the last years scattered in penny packets along the Tartar and Polish borders.

Nobody attempted to make much provision for the Cossacks in time of peace, and not a great deal could be expected of the other element of light irregular cavalry, the hussars, even though the Serbian colonels Horvat, Deperadovich and Sevich had recently settled with thousands of their Orthodox compatriots under this name in New Serbia and Slavonic Serbia.

Even the more conscientious of the cavalry officers were overwhelmed by the untimely coincidence between this fundamental re-making of the cavalry and the arrival of the Seven Years

11 Cornet of cuirassiers, Seven Years War. Straw-coloured elkskin *collet* (short coat); straw-coloured waistcoat and breeches; 1731-model black cuirass. He carries a white (first squadron) standard. This uniform, almost identical to that of the Prussian cuirassiers, was introduced by Münnich (Viskovatov, 1844-56)

12 Dragoon, Seven Years War. Blue coat with red collar, cuffs and turn-backs; white, straw-coloured or blue waistcoat; white or straw-coloured breeches; hat with white border and white cockade (as with infantry); white or yellow belts; blue or red shabraque and holster covers (Viskovatov, 1844-56)

War. In the winter of 1756-7 we find Rumyantsev bombarding the colonels of his command with detailed and pointed rebukes and instructional letters, calling company commanders to account for negligence, and ordering physical punishments for cuirassiers who failed to keep their uniforms and weapons in a clean and tidy state.

The broken-backed double mobilisation of May and August 1756 was destructive enough in itself, and some of the best of the regiments were ruined by forced marches in the snowy spring of 1757. The full establishment of the regular cavalry stood at 39,546, yet for all his efforts Apraksin was able to muster only 7,000 troopers at the battle of Gross-Jägersdorf. The cavalry therefore remained the weakest of the Russian arms in the Seven Years War, despite all the care which had gone into its formation.

The management of the technical branches engaged Petr Shuvalov more immediately, and his concern was evident even before he was appointed Master General of the Ordnance in 1756. Already in October 1755 the Austrian diplomat Zinzendorf wrote that in the field of artillery the Russians 'have made some astonishing advances which they are trying to keep secret' (Volz and Küntzel, 1899, 687). On 31 May of the next year came Shuvalov's Master Generalship, and in September he took under his wing the *Oruzhennaya Kantselyariya*, which was responsible for manufacturing the artillery. 'Upon the count's assuming control of the artillery, many projects saw the light of day, both sensible and useless, principally because the count was an inventor himself, and accordingly asked all the officers what devices they might have to show him' (Danilov, 1842, 81). Ingenious folk like the technicians Martinov and Danilov were close to his heart, but he reposed his principal confidence in the excellent Major-General Kornelii Bogdanovich Borozdin (1708-73), who helped him to work out his regulations for the artillery. In 1757 Borozdin went off to the wars to take command of the field artillery, and he distinguished himself at Zorndorf, Paltzig, and above all at Kunersdorf. He was so badly shot up in the process that he had to return to Shuvalov's side at St Petersburg.

The new Master General had a variety of measures for keeping people up to their work. He issued appropriate codes to the branches of the artillery, and in the summer of 1756 the gunners held a series of long exercise camps, where they learnt to build up the speed and accuracy of their fire. Within the artillery-engineer administration (reunited in the 1740s) Shuvalov drew up a detailed code for the conduct of business, and he began to sound out how his staff actually spent their time. It transpired that in the eighteen months from June 1756 to November 1757 the veteran Engineer General Hannibal reported for only seventeen days at his office; ninety-three further days were allegedly spent on duty elsewhere, and Hannibal gave out that for the rest of the time he was unwell. The paperwork was in arrears by literally thousands of documents, and the blackamoor was ultimately forced to retire in 1759.

In virtue of the Artillery Establishment of 11 January 1757 and subsequent ordinances the artillery of the Seven Years War comprised four major formations, each commanded by its own general, namely:

1 the Field Artillery, which was made up of:
(a) a regiment of field artillery proper, with medium and light pieces (208 by 1759), destined to form massed batteries;
(b) a Regimental Artillery Regiment, with seventy-six commands of gunners, and 456 3-pounder cannon and light coehorn mortars. Every infantry regiment was allotted between two and four pieces of each type, while every regiment of horse had a 3-pounder cannon and one or two coehorns;
2 the artillery of the Observation Corps, with 408 pieces (twenty-four 3-pounders and 384 coehorns);
3 the specialised artillery of the Secret Howitzer Corps;
4 the siege artillery of three parks, those at St Petersburg, Kiev and Belgorod. The only train which actually appeared on the theatre of war was a park of sixteen 18- and 24-pounders, seven heavy mortars and fifty coehorns, which was contributed

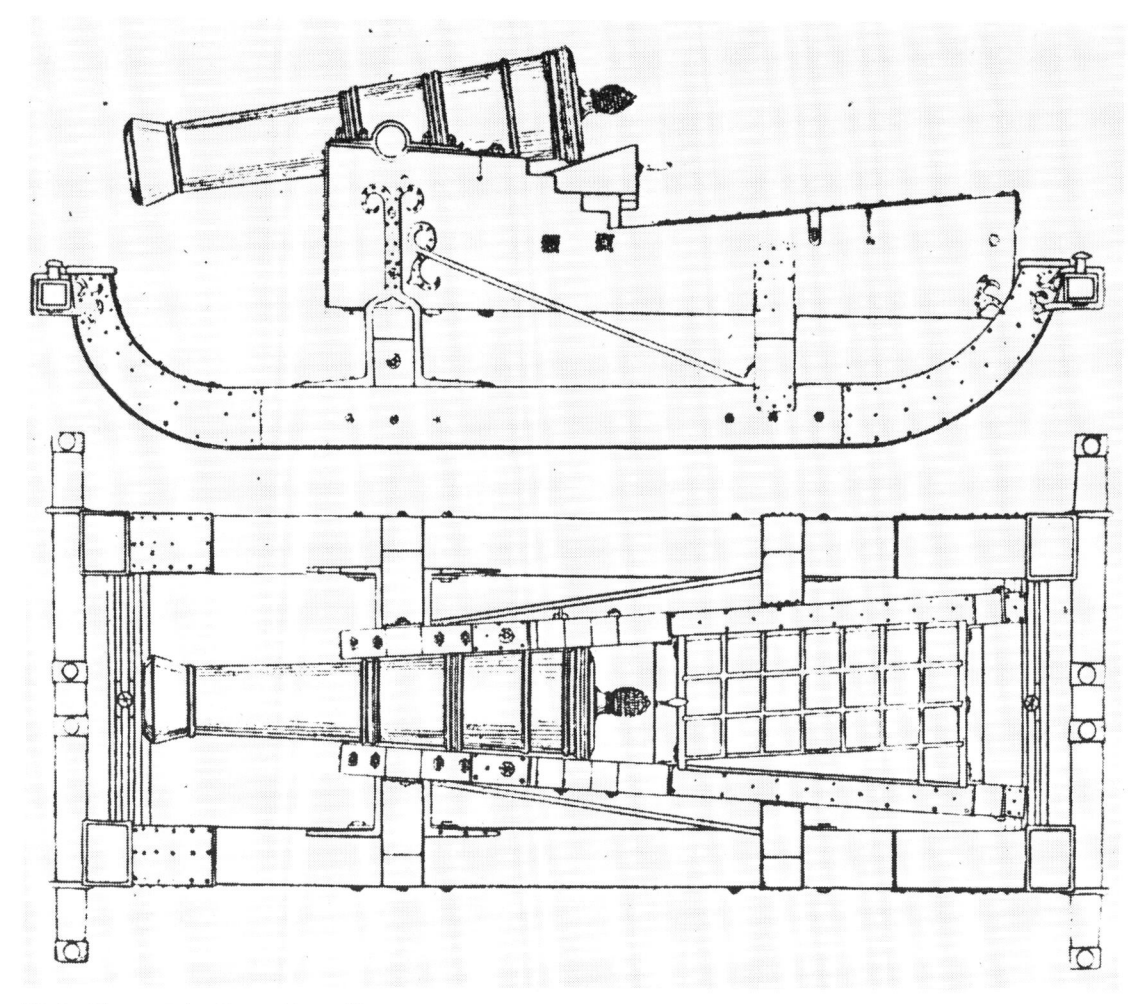

13 Artillery of the Seven Years War: cannon on sledge for winter campaigning

by the St Petersburg park. The pieces were landed at Libau in 1757, and were later moved to Königsberg. Here they stayed idle, thanks to the indecision of the Conference at St Petersburg, and the burden of land transport, which would have demanded 12,000 horses and ruined the economy of East Prussia. The rest of the artillery was moved by a Field Artillery Train of 2,052 personnel and 4,461 horses, which was put on a permanent footing in 1757.

So far we have been describing conventional artillery which approximated closely to the ordnance of other lands, to wit:

Cannon: 3- (two horses), 6- (seven horses), 8- (nine horses), 12- (fifteen horses), 18- and 24-pounders;
Howitzers: half-*pud* (at forty pounds to the *pud*) (seven horses), one-*pud* (fifteen horses);
Mortars: 6-pounder coehorn, 2-*pud*, 5-*pud*, 9-*pud*.

The lighter cannon were each accompanied into the field by ammunition carts carrying 120 round-shot and thirty rounds of canister. The barrels of all pieces were rather weighty by Western standards of the 1750s, and the carriages were of clumsy and rude manufacture, and indeed were often made by the regiments themselves.

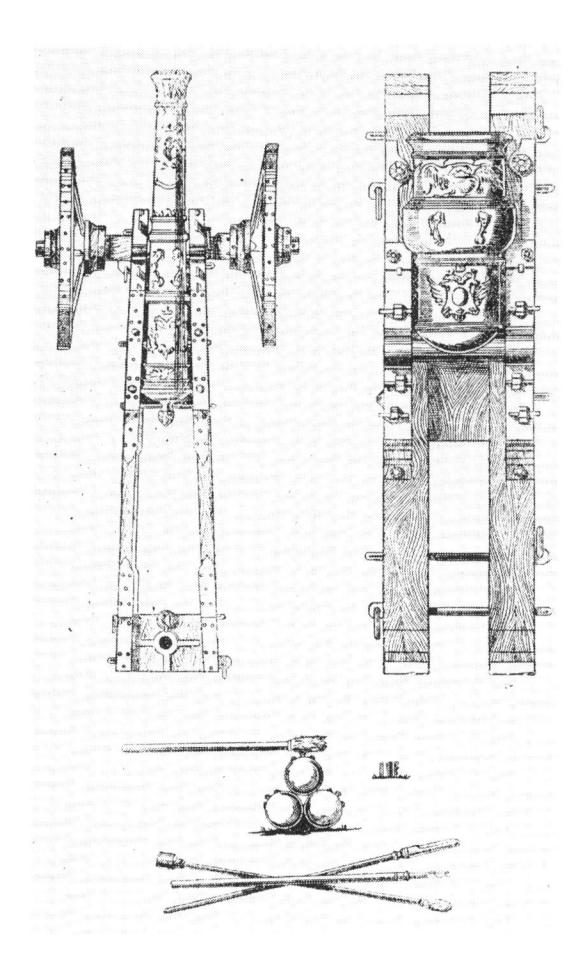

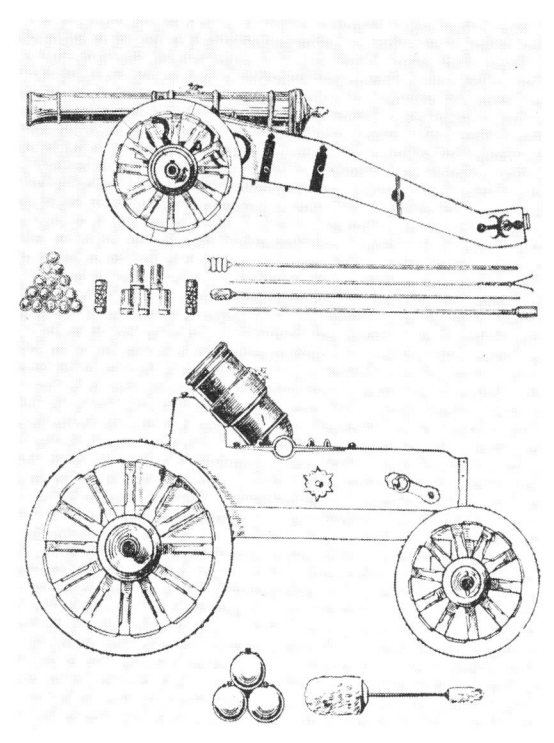

14 Artillery of the Seven Years War: 24-pounder cannon (left) and 5-*pud* mortar (right)
15 Artillery of the Seven Years War: 24-pounder cannon (top) and 5-*pud* mortar (bottom) (side view)

Seized by an access of what the eighteenth-century would have called 'enthusiasm', Shuvalov went on to develop a series of pieces that were intended to dazzle the world through their technical brilliance and originality. These were of three types:

1 The *Bliznyatki* were tiny field mortars, cast two-and-two together, designed by the artillery officer Mikhail Vasilevich Danilov after he had read Saint-Rémy's *Mémoires d'Artillerie*. Great quantities were sent to the army in 1757, but they were soon discarded as useless.

2 The *Secret Howitzer* was a still more eccentric piece which owed its genesis directly to Shuvalov.

He wished to become Master General of the Ordnance, and so, even before he attained this post, he devised a certain howitzer with a bore that was not round, but oval... Since the piece scattered its small shot widely, it was called the 'secret howitzer', and nobody was allowed to see the muzzle, which was shielded by a copper lid, which in turn was fastened with a lock. (Danilov, 1842, 80-1)

The secret howitzer looked normal enough at first sight, and attracted attention only through its spindly wheels, and (in some pieces at least) the fairly advanced feature of screw elevation. The barrel was eighteen calibres long, and conventionally round in exterior diameter, but if you got close

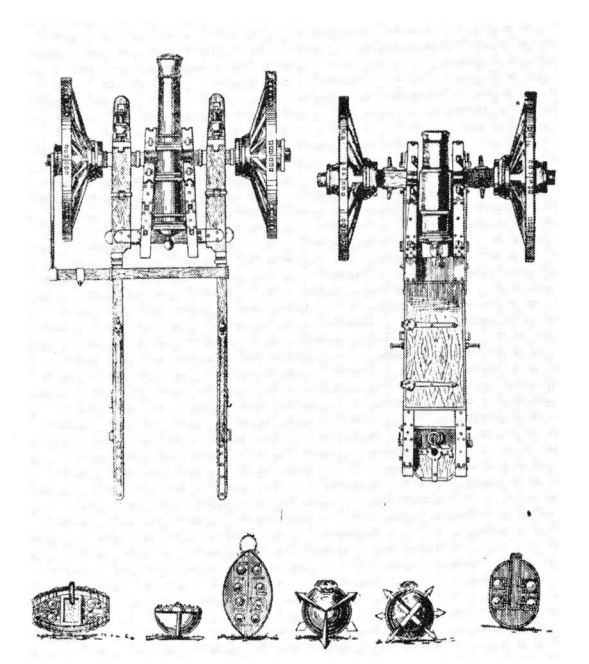

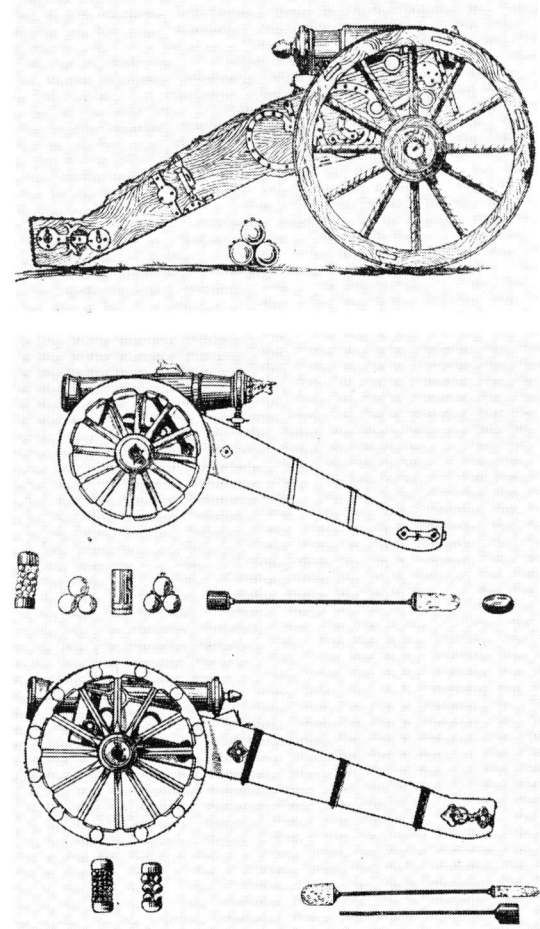

16 Artillery of the Seven Years War: light field gun (left). Note the tiny coehorn mortars set on the brackets of the carriage. Conventional half-*pud* howitzer (right)

17 Artillery of the Seven Years War: side view of the conventional half-*pud* howitzer

18 Artillery of the Seven Years War: half-*pud* unicorn (top) and half-*pud* Shuvalov secret howitzer (bottom)

enough to see the muzzle you at once noted that the bore was markedly flattened along the horizontal plane, with a width equal to a 24-pounder, but a height equivalent only to a 3-pounder. The intention was to discharge a shower of deadly canister parallel with the ground at about the height of a man.

The propelling charges, the packages of shot, and the specially-designed shells were all of oval shape to match. The powder charge came in two weights — one of five pounds for normal ranges, and six pounds for longer ranges — and it was wrapped in a flannel bag. The charge was first positioned in the bore in a hollow cylinder of tin, and then pushed home with the rammer. 'Their loading is ... so troublesome and slow, that an active cavalry is in upon them before they can be loaded a second time, which was the case at Zorndorf, where seventeen of them were lost' (Tielke, 1788, II, 39-40). The round *par excellence* of the secret howitzer was the canister. The package of 168 2-ounce lead balls spewed out to three hundred paces, and that of forty-eight 7-ounce lead balls carried up to six hundred. It was probably the latter round that de la Messelière saw demonstrated in winter quarters in 1757-8, when he was informed that at six hundred paces the secret howitzer could shower a zone equivalent to the frontage of a battalion (Messelière, 1803, 116). The grape ranged up to 1,200 paces, and was made of an agglomeration of 3-pounder balls which separated on leaving the

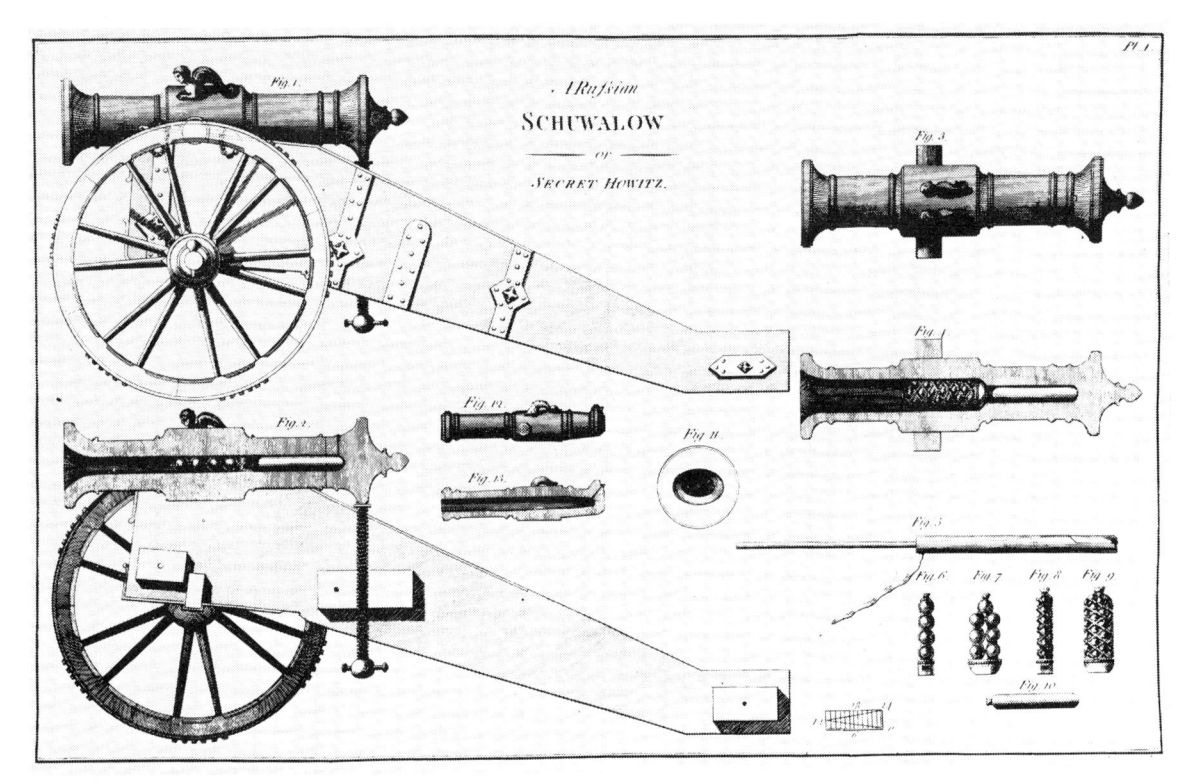

19 Details of the Shuvalov secret howitzer. Figs 12 and 13 (centre) show the barrel of the unicorn

muzzle. Illuminating rounds and shell were also provided, though the shape must have made for a very erratic performance.

A first casting of about seventy secret howitzers was made before the war, and a Secret Howitzer Corps of three specially sworn-in companies was assigned to their service. A few of the pieces appeared in an experimental way at Gross-Jägersdorf, and then on a larger scale with the Observation Corps at Zorndorf in 1758. In the following year Shuvalov overruled the protests of Fermor and distributed 181 pieces among the regiments as a replacement for 3-pounder cannon. It was generally felt that the performance of the secret howitzer did not live up to expectations, though one of Frederick's officers describes it as a formidable weapon, capable of sweeping away a whole platoon with a single round (Prittwitz, 1935, 233). It seems to have disappeared from the inventories in the 1780s.

3   The *Unicorn*, the last and most significant of the new pieces, owed its name (*odinorog*) to the unicorn device of the Shuvalov coat of arms, which was reproduced in the design of the dolphins (carrying lugs) cast into the top of the barrel. Danilov says that the distinctive feature of the new weapon was the conical chamber 'which gave it long range ... it proceeded from a chance invention made by Martinov and myself, and we must say in its favour that it was far more useful than the secret howitzer, and is now found of great utility in the army and fleet' (Danilov, 1842, 82). Every feature of the design was carried through with a curious logic, which came from the principle that the unicorn was an exact compromise between the cannon, the howitzer and the mortar. Thus the length of the barrel was determined as nine or ten calibres, and the weight of the propelling charge to that of the missile was fixed at 1:5, as a mean between the heaviest charge for a cannon (half the weight of the shot) and the

lightest charge for a mortar (one-tenth of the weight of the bomb).

The unicorn looked like a stubby cannon, and was at once identifiable by a curious constriction of the barrel towards the breech, corresponding to the shape of the chamber inside. The lightest member of the family was an 8-pounder, which appeared in the spring of 1757. Shuvalov claimed that it was equally successful at firing an 8-pound shell, six little 1-pound shells (up to two-thirds of a mile), a fifty-ball round of canister (up to 360 paces), and a fire ball with which he claimed to have set a building ablaze at 420 paces. Eight men were sufficient to manhandle the carriage (which broke down into two pieces) and the wheels, and another two men could carry the barrel with ease on a stretcher. Otherwise the weapon was drawn by two horses. The heavier unicorns ran as follows: quarter-*pud* (three horses), half-*pud* (five horses), 1-*pud* (six horses), 2-*pud* (twelve horses). Shuvalov probably hoped that the unicorn would ultimately replace all the conventional artillery. The lighter pieces up to the half-*pud* assumed the role of regimental and field artillery, though it was soon found that the barrels were too light for the weight of charge (the original forty-*pud* barrel of the 1-*pud* was accordingly changed for a new version weighing 139 *puds*, and the propelling charge reduced from eight pounds to seven). Shuvalov claimed in addition that the whole range of unicorns was useful for siege work, whether laying down area fire in bombardments, or firing directly at ramparts.

The unicorns first appeared in quantity in 1758, when thirty-eight pieces were delivered to the Secret Howitzer Corps, which was renamed the 'Bombardier Corps' and reconstituted into thirty-five detachments, each equipped with two secret howitzers and a unicorn. In the same year Rumyantsev obtained some half-*pud* unicorns for his command of cavalry, and at the beginning of 1759 a further 105 unicorns were at hand to effect a partial replacement of the conventional pieces of the field (medium) artillery.

The unicorn met with a very mixed reception in service. The Austrians asked for the loan of a fully-manned battery of the novel pieces, which reached the testing grounds near Vienna after a very slow journey, and carried out a demonstration shoot on 7 August 1759. Four secret howitzers and two half-*pud* unicorns were sent on to the army of Field-Marshal Daun, but the Austrians were acting only out of politeness, for they concluded that the effective range of the pieces was too short, and the carriages unduly heavy. The train began its long homeward trek on 23 February 1760.

In the Russian army, the Saxon volunteer Tielke reached much the same conclusions (Tielke, 1788, II, 38). The misgivings were shared by commanders like Fermor, and towards the end of 1759 Shuvalov was infuriated by reports that people were saying that his new guns were inferior to the conventional artillery. The War College arranged a shoot-off at Marienwerder in January 1760, which failed to give Shuvalov the vindication he required, and at his insistence the Senate issued a decree of 16 February 1761, explaining that although the tests were unsatisfactory, they demonstrated that 'all the pieces of the new invention were considerably better than the old ones which were compared with them' (Maslovskii, 1888-93, III, 173).

On balance, Shuvalov's interpretation was probably the correct one. The monstrous 2-*pud* unicorn was dropped from the inventory soon after Shuvalov's death in 1762, but the lighter unicorns answered a genuine need for a mobile and versatile artillery, and remained in service until the second half of the nineteenth century.

We have dealt at some length on the work of Shuvalov for the ordnance, for his pieces owed nothing to Western precedents (except for the ill-fated *Bliznyatki*) and they added greatly to the efficacy of the Russian army in the Seven Years War, giving it a killing-power and solidity that compensated for the failings of the cavalry and the Russians' general lack of mobility. The impetus which Shuvalov gave to the Russian artillery was never entirely lost, and surviving every catastrophe and change of regime the tradition of professionalism and inventiveness became the foundation of the terrifying potential of the modern Soviet ordnance.

Russia was about to embark on its first major war in the west for more than a generation, and its fitness to take on a redoubtable enemy like the Prussians was inevitably the subject of much speculation. At first sight the size of the army seemed to correspond to the huge resources of manpower. On paper no less than 437,823 men stood ready to spring to arms to execute Elizabeth's will. These consisted of:

  15,000 grenadiers
145,000 fusiliers
  36,680 cuirassiers and dragoons
    7,000 hussars
  12,937 personnel of the Artillery and
             Engineering Corps
  74,548 troops of the Garrison Army
  27,758 Land Militia
  44,500 Cossacks
  74,400 Asiatic tribesmen

The numbers contract remarkably upon closer examination. The Garrison Army and most of the Land Militia did not come into the reckoning for offensive operations, and nobody expected the hussars, Cossacks or Asiatics to put more than a small proportion of their complements into the field. The shortfall in horses told heavily against the regular cavalry, and against the mobility of the army as a whole. Moreover, the ambitions of Petr Shuvalov deducted considerably from the strength of the forces at the disposal of the field commanders. Not content with managing the artillery, he desired to have a private army under his control. For a little time the command of the division in Livonia satisfied his craving, and he was reported to be strict in managing its affairs. In 1756, however, the troops in Livonia went to form the field army, and so Shuvalov persuaded Elizabeth to let him set up a special 'Observation Corps', drawn partly from recruits, and partly from men of the Land Militia and the unmobilised regiments. The Corps was amply endowed with regimental and field artillery, and especially the secret howitzers and unicorns, and the body was made up of one super-large regiment of grenadiers and five corresponding regiments of musketeers, with a nominal establishment of 30,000 men. This expensive anomaly was re-incorporated in the army only half-way through the war.

The problems of raising an effective field force were compounded by the peculiar circumstances of the double mobilisation of 1756. The first mobilisation in April and May was halted in June, out of political considerations (see p. 61). The movement to the west was resumed in August, but came to an end of its own accord within a few weeks, thanks to the deficiencies in the magazines, the lack of horses for the cavalry and the transport train, and the small numbers and low morale of the recruits. When the army finally set off for war in May 1757 it numbered just 72,000 infantry, 7,000 regular cavalry and 16,000 Cossacks.

The Austrian observer Zinzendorf was impressed by the warlike ambitions of Zakhar Chernyshev and some of the other young officers, but he was disturbed by the thought that

Russia has engaged in no regular war, in the proper sense of the term, since the time of Peter the Great. The siege of Danzig in the Polish war hardly comes into the reckoning. The campaigns against the Turks, or rather against the Tartars, had substance only in the gazettes. The Swedish expedition was over in a moment. Hence the Russians have had no opportunity to form their generals. (Volz and Küntzel, 1899, 701)

The programme of military reform had some remarkable things to its credit, but it was undertaken only on the eve of the war, far too late to catch up with the headlong rush of the bellicose foreign policy, and it never addressed itself to matters of fundamental importance like the structure of military administration, or the means of organising supply in a western theatre under operational conditions.

As commander of the field army at the beginning of the war, Field-Marshal Stepan Fedorovich Apraksin (1702-58) did not himself inspire boundless confidence. He derived undoubted political power from his positions as President of the War College and *General-Kriegskommissar*, and from his extraordinarily wide net of liaisons, extending in the one direction to his patron Bestuzhev, and in others to the 'young court' of Grand Prince

20 Stepan Fedorovich Apraksin

Peter and Princess Catherine, and to Petr Shuvalov (who was carrying on an affair with his daughter). When, however, foreigners came to look for a warrior, they discovered instead the 'snuff box general' who could produce a *tabatière* for every day of the year, and had a wardrobe stuffed with hundreds of costly clothes. He was 'a man of most impressive stature, prodigious in his size and girth' (Messelière, 1803, 113). In practical matters he leaned very heavily on Major-General Ivan Ivanovich Weymarn, who was a former staff officer of Keith's, and on the old *Generalanshef* Yurii Lieven.

Frederick of Prussia lived in fear of any Russian intervention in Western affairs, yet he was strangely willing to lend credence to anything that people had to tell him about Russian extravagance, corruption and muddle. Such reports had come from the diplomats Vockerodt and Mardefeld, and from his bosom friend Winterfeld, who had seen the Russian army in 1741, when it was still in a bad way after the Turkish war. Keith's experience of the army was more recent, but when, shortly before the Seven Years War, he ventured some words in praise of the Russian troops, Frederick rejoined 'the Muscovites are a heap of barbarians. Any well-disciplined troops will make short work of them' (Retzow, 1802, I, 182-3).

The first invasion of East Prussia and the battle of Gross-Jägersdorf, 1757

As we have seen, Frederick the Great opened the Seven Years War in the south by invading Saxony, but the winter of 1756-7 found the Russian infantry still accumulating in crowded and dirty quarters in Livonia, and the wretched cavalry trailing up from the interior of Russia. In February 1757 the government heard with despair that Apraksin was still unable to march.

Ready or not, the Russians were galvanised by the news that their Austrian allies had been defeated by Frederick at Prague, and finally towards the end of May 1757 the green columns set out from the Dvina in a generally westerly direction. The commands of Apraksin and Rumyantsev reached the Viliya opposite Kovno in the middle of June, but in the absence of a bridge the whole force had to be ferried across the river on two boats — the consequence of 'the dire disorder and terrible confusion which dominates everything that relates to the Russian army' (quoted in Frisch, 1919, 28). Eleven thousand men had already fallen sick, and the difficulties of supply were augmented when the army could no longer avail itself of the facility of transport on the Viliya and Niemen, but had to strike across the marshes and woods of Polish Lithuania, losing contact with the chains of magazines that stretched back to the Russian Baltic provinces and the Ukraine.

A spell of rain gave way to a period of intense heat that was to last through the summer, and return in almost every campaigning season of the Seven Years War. Weymarn writes that the result was a greater mortality still, for 'the ordinary soldier is tormented with heat under his covering of sweat and dust, and common experience shows that no force or punishment is capable of preventing him from drinking hard and long of the stinking, foul and muddy water, and letting it pour over his body' (Weymarn, 1794, 26-7).

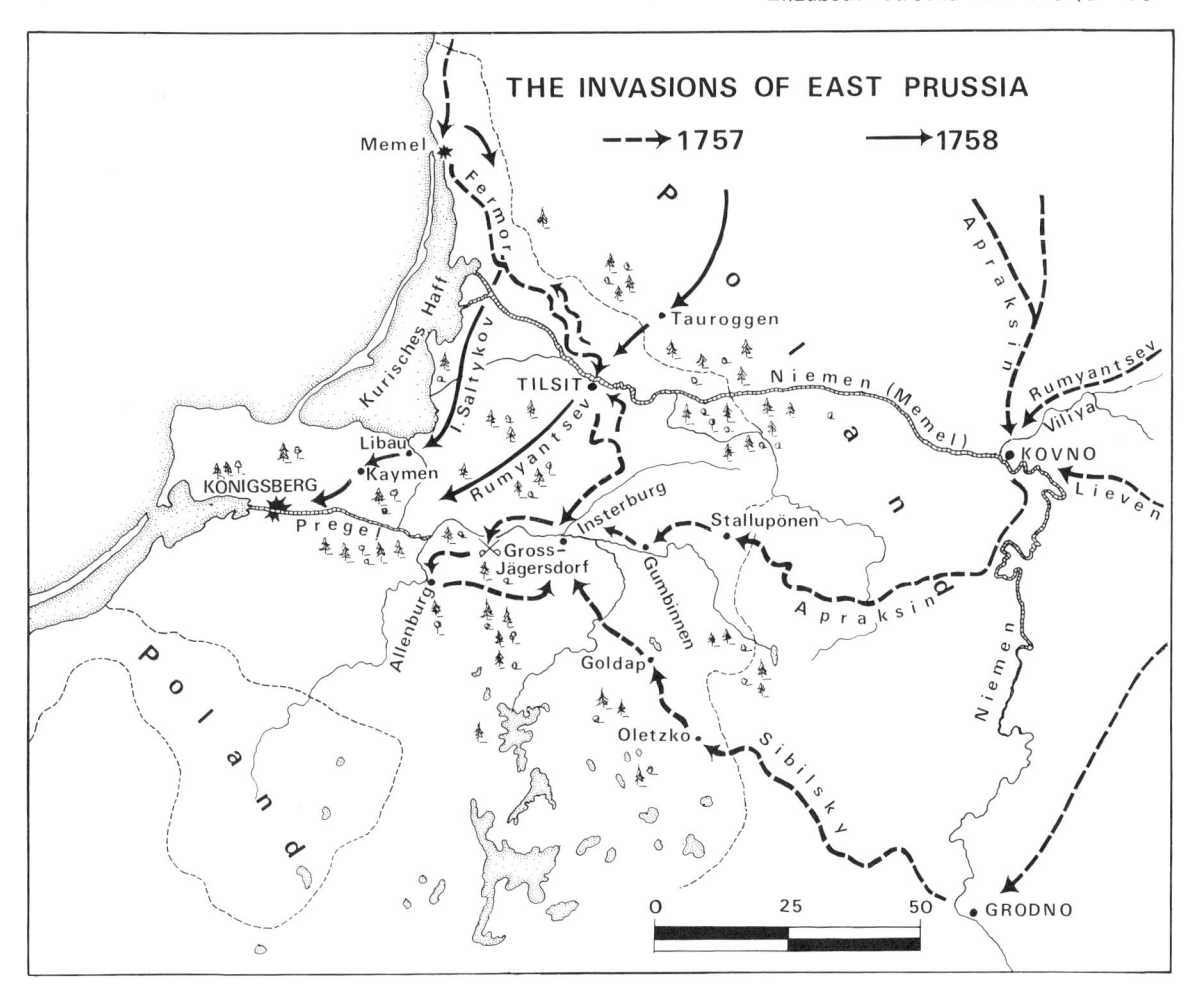

The strategic objective was to reduce the sizeable enemy province of East Prussia, which was weakly held by Field-Marshal Lehwaldt with 32,000 troops and militia, and conveniently isolated by the 'Polish corridor' from the rest of the King of Prussia's states. In August 1757 the Russian host at last crossed into Prussian territory, and the cavalry began to spread out. Like the soldiers described in Solzhenitsyn's *1914*, the Russians of 1757 gazed in wonder at the almost inhuman cleanliness of the landscape and the villages. Apraksin sought to maintain good order, but the Cossacks gave a lead in rapacity and vandalism to even the best regiments of the army. The movement as a whole resembled an emigration of nomadic barbarians. Apraksin never bothered to sound the way ahead, and in this example the generals followed him religiously. All of this was to have dire consequences for the outcome of the campaign, and for the West's impression of the Russian army in the Seven Years War.

At Kovno Apraksin had been joined by two southerly columns, and at Insterburg he was met by the light corps of Sibilsky, and the 16,000-strong detachment of Fermor, who had reduced the little port of Memel after a brief bombardment. Finally, by the last week of August the movement coalesced into a single thrust north of

76 Elizabeth Petrovna 1741-1761/2

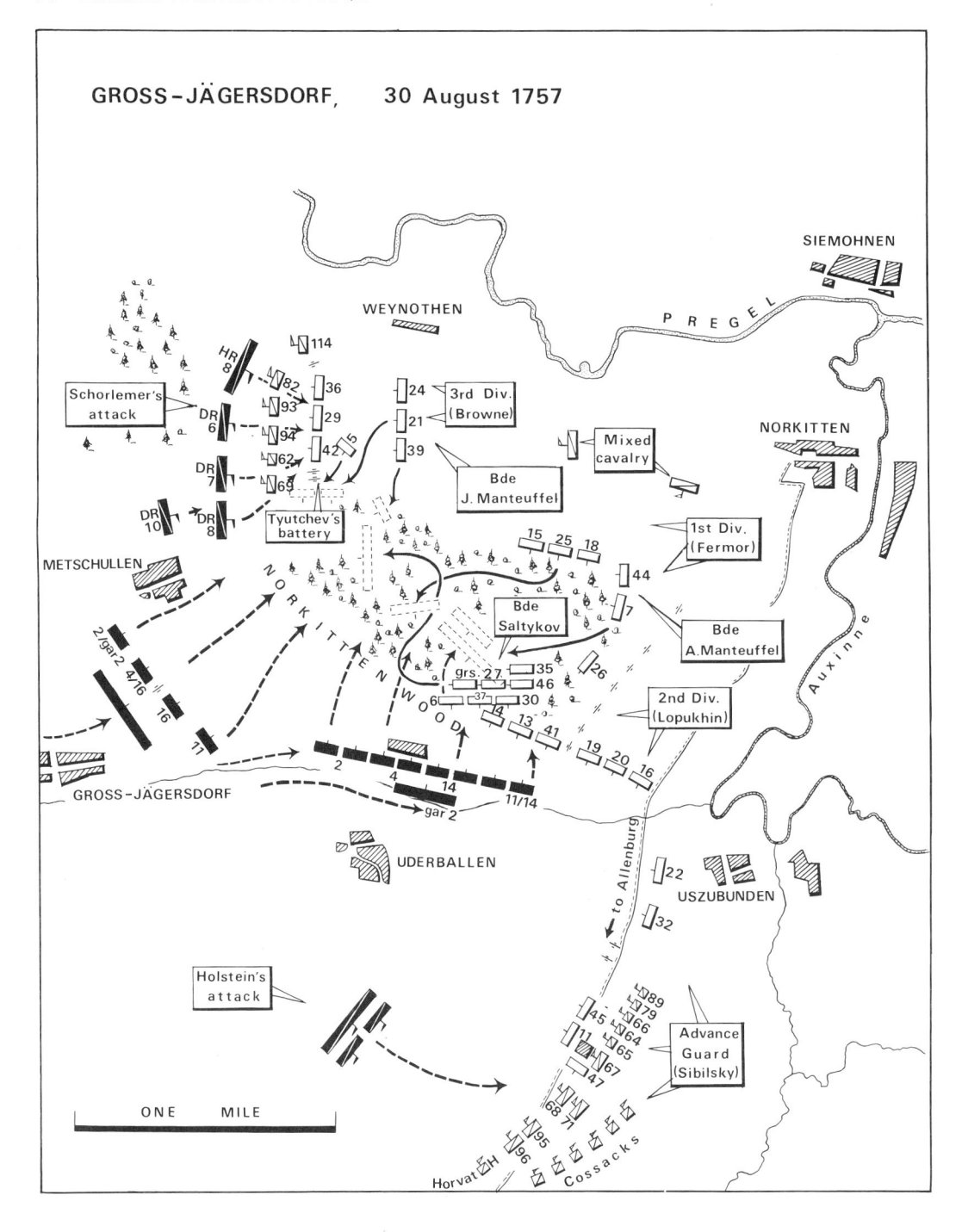

GROSS-JÄGERSDORF, 30 August 1757

SIEMOHNEN
PREGEL
WEYNOTHEN
NORKITTEN
Schorlemer's attack
3rd Div. (Browne)
Mixed cavalry
Bde J. Manteuffel
1st Div. (Fermor)
Tyutchev's battery
METSCHULLEN
NORKITTEN WOOD
Bde Saltykov
Bde A. Manteuffel
2nd Div. (Lopukhin)
Auxinne
GROSS-JÄGERSDORF
gar 2
UDERBALLEN
to Allenburg
USZUBUNDEN
Holstein's attack
Advance Guard (Sibilsky)
ONE MILE
Horvat   Cossacks

KEY TO THE SEVEN YEARS WAR BATTLE MAPS

Heights are given in metres.

- Russian infantry regiment
- Russian cavalry regiment
- Austrian infantry regiment
- Austrian cavalry regiment
- Prussian infantry regiment
- Prussian cavalry regiment

For identification of individual Austrian and Prussian regiments, please see the codes in *The Army of Maria Theresa* (London, David & Charles, 1977) and *The Army of Frederick the Great* (London, David & Charles, 1974). For the sake of clarity, Russian regiments are numbered here according to order of seniority at the time of the Seven Years War.

Guard
1 Preobrazhenskii
2 Semenovskii
3 Ismailovskii
4 Horse Guards

Infantry
5 First Grenadiers
6 Second Grenadiers
7 Third Grenadiers
8 Fourth Grenadiers
9 Ingermanlandskii
10 Astrakhanskii
11 Butyrskii
12 First Moskovskii
13 Second Moskovskii
14 Kievskii
15 Troitskii
16 St Peterburgskii
17 Vladimirskii
18 Novgorodskii
19 Shlyushelburgskii
20 Kazanskii
21 Sibirskii
22 Pskovskii
23 Smolenskii
24 Azovskii
25 Voronezhskii
26 Nizhegorodskii
27 Chernigovskii
28 Ryazanskii
29 Suzdalskii
30 Rostovskii
31 Velikolutskii
32 Arkhangelgorodskii
33 Yaroslavskii
34 Permskii
35 Vyatskii
36 Vologdskii

37 Narvskii
38 Tobolskii
39 Nevskii
40 Koporskii
41 Vyborgskii
42 Uglinskii
43 Kegsgolmskii
44 Ladozhskii
45 Belozerskii
46 Muromskii
47 Apsheronskii
48 Shirvanskii
49 Kabardinskii
50 Nasheburgskii
51 Nizovskii
52 Kuraskii
53 Tenginskii
54 Navaginskii

Observation Corps
55 First Grenadiers (of Observation Corps)
56 First Musketeers
57 Second Musketeers
58 Third Musketeers
59 Fourth Musketeers
60 Fifth Musketeers

Cuirassiers
61 Lifeguards
62 Heir Apparent
63 Third Cuirassiers
64 Kievskii
65 Novotroitskii
66 Kazanskii

Mounted Grenadiers
67 Kargopolskii
68 Narvskii

69 Rizhskii (Riga)
70 St Peterburgskii
71 Ryazanskii
72 Astrakhanskii

Dragoons
73 Moskovskii
74 Troitskii
75 Vladimirskii
76 Novgorodskii
77 Sibirskii
78 Pskovskii
79 Tverskii
80 Permskii
81 Vyatskii
82 Nizhegorodskii
83 Rostovskii
84 Arkhangelgorodskii
85 Azovskii
86 Ingermanlandskii
87 Vologdskii
88 Yamburgskii
89 Tobolskii
90 Revelskii
91 Olonetskii
92 Lutskii

Hussars
93 Serbian
94 Hungarian
95 Gruzinskii
96 Moldavian
97 Wallachian
98 Slobodskii
99 Macedonian
100 Yellow
101 Hussar regiments of New Serbia
102 Hussar regiments of Slavonic Serbia

Irregulars
103 Don Cossacks
104 Yaik (Ural River) Cossacks
105 Grebhinskii Cossacks
106 Terek Cossacks
107 Semenieskii Cossacks
108 Volga Cossacks
109 Orenburg Cossacks
110 Slobodskii Cossacks
111 Little Russian Cossacks
112 Zaporozhian Cossacks
113 Baptised Stavropol Kalmyks
114 Chuguevskii Cossacks
115 Astrakhan Cossacks
116 Azov Cossacks
117 Bakhmut Cossacks

the Masurian Lakes in the direction of the provincial capital of Königsberg. Apraksin was disturbed to learn that an enemy army under Lehwaldt was somewhere in the offing, but the Prussians were decidedly inferior in numbers, and the constant daily false alarms from the Cossacks had succeeded in breeding attitudes of 'false security and contempt for the enemy' (Weymarn, 1794, 95). The 29th of August found the army short of fodder, and moving irresolutely just south of the Pregel in a terrain of marshy streams and stands of dense woodland. There was precious little space to draw up the regiments in order, if it came to a fight, and the ailing *Generalanshef* Yurii Lieven urged Apraksin to hold the troops overnight in a precautionary battle position in the clearing of Gross-Jägersdorf. *Generalanshef* George Browne supported this opinion 'with his usual violence and impetuosity' (Weymarn, 1794, 90). Apraksin rejected these good ideas, and under the influence of Fermor he brought the army back for the night to the site of the last camp, where the troops could eat and rest. The army slept well. Early on 30 August

a purple glow suffused the horizon, fortelling a splendid day. The mist had set in heavily before dawn, but now it began to thin out, and the air became clear and transparent. The sun, rising above the hills, had already lit the whole horizon when the sonorous signal of cannon fire broke our sweet slumbers, and set the whole army in movement. (Bolotov, 1870-3, I, 517)

At about four in the morning the army got once more to its feet and began to shuffle around the east flank of the wood of Norkitten, with the leading elements striking south in the direction of Allenburg and a region of temptingly untouched pastures and barns.

Sibilsky got successfully under way with an advance guard of 10,000 men (4,000 cavalry and fifteen battalions of infantry). The main body was supposed to follow in two parallel columns, but in fact the appointed right-hand column (the First Division, under Fermor) was still sorting itself out behind the wood of Norkitten, and the stout and comfortable *Generalanshef* Vasilii Lopukhin emerged alone into the clearing with his Second Division. By the scheme of things the Second Division was supposed to stand in the rearward line in any engagement, and Lopukhin had been forced to yield up his field artillery to the advance guard and the First Division. He retained only his regimental artillery and a complement of secret howitzers, and Fermor told him that even these were unnecessary, 'since your force is tucked away as securely behind the First Division as if you were sitting in your mother's lap' (Weymarn, 1794, 93). A Third Division under George Browne was to follow up behind and cover the general baggage of the army.

Such was the state of affairs when the little Prussian army erupted into the scene from the west. Lehwaldt had just 24,700 men to pit against the mass of 55,000 Russians, but he threw his force into the attack in unthinking obedience to King Frederick's orders (for a résumé of forces and casualties in the battles of the Seven Years War see the author's *Army of Frederick the Great*, Newton Abbot, 1974, 234-5).

The first effective Russian response was probably made by a battery of field artillery which Major Tyutchev brought to a height near the western salient of the Norkitten Wood, in the path of the leading Prussian cavalry under Lieutenant-General Schorlemer. The gallant Tyutchev usefully delayed the enemy until Fermor unaccountably ordered the guns off the position. Now everything depended on how quickly the Russians could transform their straggling line of march into a coherent battle frontage.

On the right, or northern, flank Browne and his Third Division tried to cover the ground from the Pregel to the western part of the Norkitten Wood. On the right centre Fermor's First Division sought to hold the southern edge of the wood and reach out to the right flank of the Second Division. Lopukhin (Second Division) and Sibilsky (advance guard) in turn were strung along the Allenburg road, and trying to form a line facing westwards over the Gross-Jägersdorf clearing. The process was attended with some confusion, thanks to the way the troops became entangled with the divisional baggage trains. Andrei Timofeevich Bolotov was a company commander in the advance guard, and he witnessed how the advent of the enemy reduced the columns to chaos. The commanders had no experience of this sort of thing, and never had Bolotov seen them:

in such a state of bewilderment as at that moment. One of the officers was galloping around distractedly, his face ashen grey, and shrieking, and shouting out meaningless orders. A second officer concentrated on bringing up the carts, and was swearing at the drivers and beating them. . . . Another, having got hold of some regiment or other, forced a path with it through the baggage, smashing through the drivers and carts, without having any idea where he was taking his men. (Bolotov, 1870-3, I, 520-1)

The two Russian wings were soon battling to hold their ground against determined attacks of Prussian cavalry. On the northern sector Schorlemer brought a powerful concentration of thirty squadrons against the Russian right, scattering a hastily formed screen of horse, and threatening the infantry brigade of Leontev. This first thrust was parried by the quick reactions of the local Russian commanders. Lieutenant-General Matvei Lieven made the First Grenadier Regiment turn about and hasten from its place in the First Division, while Browne brought up the brigade of Major-General Johann Manteuffel (the Nevskii and Sibirskii Regiments) from his own second line. The Prussian cavalry were driven off, and with the further help of Major-General Rumyantsev, who advanced his brigade from the reserve, Browne went on to clear the Norkitten Wood of the left wing of the Prussian infantry. All the time the Russian artillery worked to great effect, whether lobbing shells at the Prussian cavalry in the open ground, or clearing the infantry from thickets with blasts of canister.

In the Gross-Jägersdorf clearing the Russian centre and southern flank had preoccupations of their own, for twenty Prussian squadrons under the Duke of Holstein were coming through Uderballen with amazing speed. The Russian response was probably concerted between Sibilsky and hetman Serebryakov of the Don Cossacks. At any rate the Cossacks put on a very convincing demonstration of headlong flight, and drew the Prussians on to and through the regiments of Sibilsky's infantry and against his heavy guns. Many Prussians were shot down, many fled, and 'the survivors were caught like rats in a trap when the infantry closed its lines again, and they were cut down to the last man by the Russian horse' (Bolotov, 1870-3, I, 532).

Towards six in the morning the main body of the Prussian infantry arrived on the scene, and pressed home a very dangerous attack against the First and Second Divisions as they tried to shake themselves out into some kind of order on the southern flank of the Norkitten Wood. Bolotov followed the Prussian move from his vantage point to the south, and he gives us something very rare in eighteenth-century military literature — an impression of a battle as seen by a spectator. He watched with his heart in his mouth as the Prussians advanced in superb order, stopped to deliver a salvo, and then, reloading on the march, fired two more volleys at successively closer ranges. Bolotov and his friends could not understand why the Russian infantry remained so silent and passive:

'This time', we exclaimed, 'it must all be up — they must all have been killed'. The words were still on our lips when . . . our muskets and cannon replied, certainly not by salvoes — in fact in great disorder — but shooting with considerably greater speed than the enemy. From this moment the Prussians too ceased to fire by volleys. The firing on both sides continued without a break, and we were unable to distinguish the enemy fusillade from ours. Only the cannon shot could be made out, and in particular the discharges of the secret Shuvalov howitzers, which could be detected by the peculiar sound and dark smoke.

Only the extremities of the two battling lines were to be seen through the smoke, but:

Our army was ranged immobile for the whole duration of the combat, with the first rank kneeling and sitting. The Prussian line appeared to be in ceaseless movement. It would advance a few paces, then retire again, but all the time fighting with no less courage and steadfastness than our own men.... Behind the two lines we could discern a great number of people on various occupations. An officer was racing about on horseback, bearing, no doubt, some important order — then suddenly he was shot, and flew headlong to the ground. An individual fled from the ranks, but, overwhelmed by wounds, he could not keep his feet, and collapsed. Dead and wounded were being carried back, while ammunition and reinforcements came up in the opposite direction. (Bolotov, 1870-3, I, 527-8)

Quartermaster-General Weymarn could not take such a detached view of affairs, for he was standing with the Second Division. He confirms that the first three salvoes of Prussian musketry caused little execution, 'but the fourth enemy volley worked to deadly effect, and our men responded with a fire of considerable violence, with every lad firing at the instant he had finished loading, without awaiting the orders of his officer' (Weymarn, 1794, 198). The Russians, however, had no field guns (see p. 78) with which to counter the Prussian artillery, and the Second Grenadier Regiment was driven back into the wood, which threatened the collapse of the centre. Fortunately the Narvskii Regiment stood its ground, and victorious cries spread along the line.

Wherever the shouting came from, it had the good effect of restoring the countenance of the Second Grenadiers, who advanced anew against the enemy. The Narvskii Regiment meanwhile pushed forward with levelled bayonets under a continuous fire. Most of its officers had already been killed or wounded, and its formation dissolved so completely that you could make out neither rank nor file. (Weymarn, 1794, 200)

The crisis of the battle was over, but the intensity of the fighting on this sector is betrayed by the casualties among the Russian commanders. Weymarn, Yurii Lieven and Major-General Villebois were wounded, while Lopukhin was hit by three musket balls, and fell dying into the hands of a Prussian *Feldwebel*, who relieved him of his order of St Alexander Nevsky.

The offensive effort of the Prussians was spent, and the bluecoats melted away into the smoke of the battle and the burning villages, leaving some 4,000 men on the field alongside still greater quantities of dead and wounded Russians. The Prussian dead were stripped with miraculous speed by the Russian camp followers, who left them with only the wooden blocks from the cartridge pouches, and the rounds themselves, wrapped in blue paper.

Sibilsky took off in pursuit with three regiments of mounted grenadiers and some Cossacks, but he had no infantry with him (for reasons which have never been properly explained), and he had no means of stopping the Prussians from re-crossing the Pregel and making good their escape. Probably the Russians were more disorganised by their victory than the Prussians had been by their defeat. The ammunition carts for the infantry and artillery had been left uselessly in the rear, with their teams unhitched, and even the most devoted troops were sagging in depleted ranks in a state of total exhaustion.

Russia's first stand-up battle with the Prussian army had been completely unsought. Tielke remarked:

In the battle of Gross-Jägersdorf the Russians had neither time nor opportunity to form a square, and yet they did extremely well. It is very certain, that if these people, who are brave in the extreme, had better regulations respecting their baggage, provisions etc., and were equal to the Prussians in manoeuvring, which may possibly be the case some time or other, it would be very difficult for any army to withstand them. (Tielke, 1788, II, 171)

As the Russians were then little known [wrote Lloyd], 'tis no wonder the Prussian general should think his troops superior to theirs, and therefore did not think it necessary to oppose anything but infantry to infantry, and cavalry against cavalry. But experience has proved, that the Russian infantry is far superior to any in Europe; and, as their cavalry is not so good as other nations, reason dictates, that a mixed order of battle alone can conquer them. (Lloyd, 1781, I, 145-6)

We might add that the Russian artillery had shown a clear superiority over the Prussian, while the divisional and brigade commanders gave evidence of initiative and a spirit of mutual support in this desperate scramble of an encounter battle.

Having moved to within scarcely thirty miles of Königsberg, Apraksin shocked every person of good will by taking the decision to retreat. The army straggled back through autumn rains to winter quarters behind Memel, nearly breaking up in the process. Talk of treason was rife among the officers, while in France the government feared that Apraksin had taken the 'first step towards the disintegration of a system so well begun' (Oliva, 1964, 82). Apraksin was ordered back to St Petersburg to undergo investigation, and the revelation that he had been in touch with the 'young court' leant colour to the reports that he had been counting on the early death of Elizabeth. Bestuzhev was caught up in the ruin of his protégé and was exiled to his estates. Apraksin himself escaped further earthly punishment by dying of an apoplectic seizure.

Fermor's command, and the occupation of East Prussia, 1758

The departure of Apraksin delivered the leadership to the most un-Russian of all the commanders in the war, Cavalry General Villim Villimovich Fermor (1702-71). He was a Baltic Lutheran of German and Scots ancestry, who in his younger days enjoyed the patronage of Münnich and had a certain name as a designer of imperial buildings and parks. He owed his present command to the fact that he was the one man of undoubted technical competence who happened to be with the army. As 'a very regular sober man' (G. Riniking, 27 December 1757, PRO SPF91/65), Fermor was happiest in the company of his German officers, but he was treated with disdain by the noisy Irishman Browne and the majority of the Russians, which only served to accentuate his heremetical tendencies. All this, of course, was relative to Russian standards. Otherwise his habits were luxurious in the extreme:

The baggage and its escorting columns always went ahead, with Count Fermor's tent and other effects, which were borne on camels. Then came the train of the commander-in-chief. And how did *he* travel? — well, first of all we encounter the commander's escort, namely two thousand Cossacks and Kalmyks, riding in splendid order. Then follow a company of cuirassiers with kettledrums, keeping up an incessant din like the rest of the music. Behind the music ride two adjutants, and finally come Fermor in person and his party of generals, followed by a numberless host of retainers under the escort of several thousand Cossacks. (Täge, *RA*, 1864, II, 286)

Fermor spent the nights in his tent, so as to set an example of hard living to the rest of the army. This was no great ordeal, since the shelter in question was a massive Turkish affair of dazzling white cloth, which was draped over a lattice framework. The interior was hung with blue and white brocade, and provided a suitable ambience for the count's ponderous feasting, when he and his guests dined off silver plate, and drank deep from gilded cups.

Few people, however, gave proper credit to Fermor's grasp of military realities. His comments on tactics were invariably interesting, and he brought some order to the matter of supply by insisting that the commissariat officials must be physically present on the theatre of war, and by sending home the more useless of the Cossacks and tribal Asiatics, retaining only the Don and Chuguevskii Cossacks, the hussars and five hundred Volga Kalmyks. The ordinary soldiers benefited greatly from Fermor's solicitude. Their loads were lightened, they were allowed to dispense with the pigtail and hair powder, and they were given warm shoes, ample sheepskin jackets and lined bonnets.

Fermor's talents showed to the best advantage in his opportunistic and well-calculated winter campaign of early 1758, when he made good the unfinished business from the year before, and moved the army back into East Prussia. Lehwaldt was conveniently away in the west facing the Swedes, who had joined the great coalition, and Fermor was so confident of the outcome that he did not even bother to take his artillery along with him. The style of the operation was altogether different from that of Apraksin's horde of 1757. The 72,000 men were divided into five columns, and moving with remarkable speed they covered the 125-odd miles to Königsberg in between six and nine days of January snow.

The people of East Prussia were treated with sedulous regard, and instead of fire and sword the Russians bore proclamations from Empress Elizabeth which apologised for the ravages of the last campaign. At Marienwerder, at the start of the next campaign, the Lutheran pastor Täge and his flock awoke one morning to find the town full of Cossacks and Kalmyks,

proceeding down the streets with their long beards and grim faces, and armed with bows and arrows and other weapons. The sight was at once alarming and majestic. They rode through the town in silence and good order ... and we were actually less afraid of the Cossacks than of some of the other armies we had seen pass through Marienwerder. They gave us not the slightest cause for complaint, since they were maintained in exemplary discipline. (Täge, *RA*, 1864, II, 276)

Täge himself was summoned to Fermor's presence, and told that he was to go campaigning with the Russians as a regimental chaplain.

The Russian occupation of East Prussia is a little-known episode of the Seven Years War, but it was fraught with all kinds of social, cultural, strategic and political significance. The Russians knew that they were on parade before Europe, and they clearly regarded their dominion in East Prussia as a test of their civilisation as much as of their power. Slipping easily and unobtrusively into the seat of government, they confirmed the functionaries of the province and of the 'Imperial Russian City' of Königsberg in their authority, and they changed the official Prussian gazette into a Russian one, bearing the double eagle, and given to boasting of the 'exquisite taste which is the distinguishing feature of the rich and costly uniforms of the Russian officers'. Indeed, one of the natives of Königsberg was willing to ascribe the arrival of prosperity and fine manners in that city to the coming of the nominal enemy (Scheffner, 1823, 67). The young Aleksandr Romanovich Vorontsov happened to pass through Königsberg on the way to his studies in France, and he was surprised to see the Fincks, the Dönhoffs and many others of the leading nobility present in the place, and 'they all seemed quiet and happy under our domination' (*AKV*, 1870-95, V, 39). The stiff and provincial Prussian aristocrats were introduced by the Russians to the Western fashions of masquerades, Frenchified small-talk, and the drinking of tea and punch, and in the relaxed atmosphere they even learnt to enjoy the company of the Prussian middle classes and of their own womenfolk, who had hitherto been excluded from high society. In their turn the Russian officers attended the public sessions of Königsberg University, where they could hear lectures from luminaries like Immanuel Kant, the mathematician and philosopher.

Sixteen Russian subjects actually enrolled at the university during the war, and they afterwards rose to eminence in public and academic life in their homeland (see Amburger, 1961, 220).

Away in Berlin there gradually collected a number of Russian officer prisoners on parole — gentlemen like Zakhar Chernyshev (later exchanged) 'whom you might have almost taken for a young Frenchman, from his lively, restless and elegant ways' (Lehndorff, 1910-13, I, 194). Chernyshev and his companions wrought havoc among the Prussian ladies, and in 1759 one witty soul posted a notice on the arcade of the royal *Schloss*, detailing the names of all the females who had thus succumbed. The city commandant made things worse by having the placard torn down almost immediately, which left the entire female society of Berlin under suspicion.

In fact the Russo-Prussian interchange could be defined as one of social amenity for intellectual challenge. The Western Enlightenment worked to devastating effect on the beliefs of someone like Andrei Bolotov, who had bidden a thankful farewell to campaigning, and taken up a post as translator to the Russian governor of Königsberg. He had been brought up in the closed world of Orthodoxy, and his childhood faith was no proof against the rationalism he encountered among the more free-thinking Prussians. It took the sage words of a Prussian pastor to restore his trust in divine verities.

In the harsher world of international politics, foreign governments were alarmed to see how well the Russians were settling down in their conquest. Frederick the Great was all the more outraged because he derived his royal title from there, being technically 'King in Prussia' (i.e. East Prussia), and because the land was the spiritual home of his nobility. Russia's allies harboured reservations of their own. Elizabeth had at first envisaged the seizure of East Prussia as a temporary affair, designed to win her certain advantages at the peace, but in proportion as she, her generals and her ministers gained confidence in the power of Russian arms, they made bold to claim possession of East Prussia by right of conquest as a full belligerent. The Austrians tried to make the Russians abate their claim, and at Versailles the Duc de Choiseul wrote to his representative in St Petersburg that 'it would be contrary to our political interests in the north to give East Prussia to Russia. This would make Russia the mistress of the Baltic. Fears of such an event are pronounced in Sweden and Denmark, our true allies' (Oliva, 1964, 150).

Paradoxically, the very success of their occupation of East Prussia restrainted the Russians from deriving full benefit from their conquest. The Russian governor, Lieutenant-General Nikolai Korff, set himself against any attempt to tap the physical resources of the province, or to raise recruits there, for like Petr Shuvalov, Chancellor Vorontsov and the German-Russian generals he was anxious to avoid any possible accusation of 'barbarism'. Only on 25 January 1761 were orders sent from St Petersburg to Field-Marshal Buturlin, telling him that Russia might after all have to face up to the relinquishment of East Prussia, and that the considerations which caused it to be spared no longer applied. Even then the Russians treated the land in a far more gentlemanly fashion than Frederick behaved in his conquest of the electorate of Saxony.

Again the Russians were far too restrained in the matter of the free city and fortress-port of Danzig, which stood in the 'Polish corridor' beside the Vistula delta. The possession of Königsberg certainly gave the Russians a useful place to land provisions and equipment, but the unrestricted use of Danzig would have been more valuable still, offering them a strategic flank towards Prussian Pomerania, as well as the means of turning the Vistula into a base of supplies. The citizens and magistracy were German, and they made little secret of their support for Old Fritz. They refused a Russian garrison, they permitted the Russians to land cargoes only in small and grudging amounts, and finally in the autumn of 1759 Shuvalov proposed to punish the place by subjecting it to a bombardment. The Russians, however, held back out of consideration for their Saxon, Austrian and French friends, who were unwilling to countenance any infringement of the rights and neutrality of Danzig and Poland in the matter. Elizabeth could not refrain from drawing a comparison with the way the French had made free with Frankfurt-am-Main, nominally the most privileged city of the German empire.

The march to Zorndorf, 1758

East Prussia was a comprehensible, manageable objective compared with the main body of the Prussian state, which reached across the great north European plain from the sandy Baltic coastlands of Pomerania to the ranges of wooded hills where Prussian Silesia adjoined the Austrian provinces of Moravia and Bohemia. The lowlands were traversed by a series of river lines which mostly trended from the south-east to the north-west, which was a direction calculated to be of little use to the Russian communications. More annoying still the greatest river of all, the Oder, lay almost completely within Prussian territory, and was studded with a series of strongholds – Breslau, Glogau, Cüstrin, and the fortress-port of Stettin – which gave it the character of a

THE CENTRAL THEATRE

CAMPAIGN OF 1758

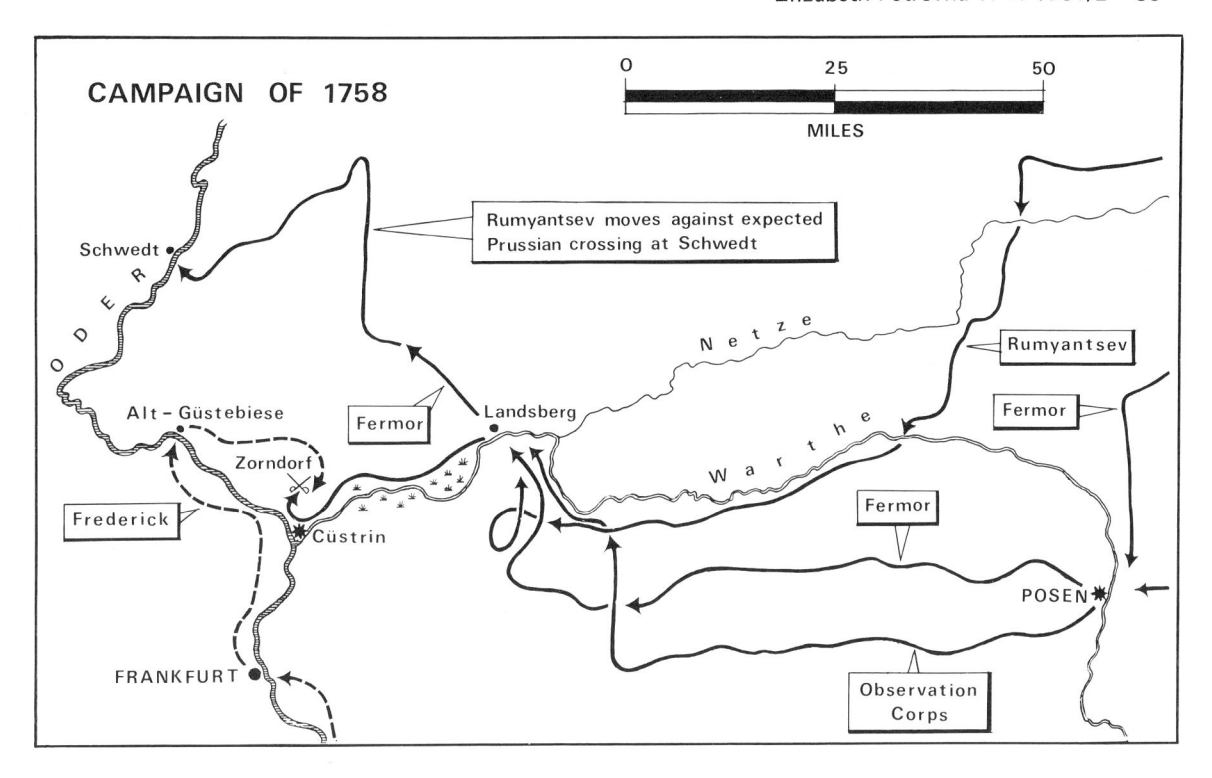

powerful transverse barrier. From the point of view of the Russians the most interesting stretch of this river was the central one between Frankfurt-an-der-Oder and Cüstrin, for it owned direct communication by way of the Warthe to the Russian depot of Posen in Poland, and it lay closest to Berlin and the heartland of the Prussian state. Unfortunately some unkind god decreed that this axis of advance must stand at an equally unfavourable distance from support on either flank — whether from the seaborne supplies and the allied Swedes on their right, or the Austrians on their left, skulking in the border hills with Saxony and Bohemia. Frederick of Prussia and his hard-marching army were able to exploit to the full all the consequent uncertainties of the alliance.

At the start of the campaigning season of 1758 Frederick caught the Austrians at a disadvantage, when he pushed into Moravia and threatened Vienna itself. In these circumstances no set plan of joint operations was worked out, beyond a general desire to see the Russians march west and act by way of diversion in favour of the hard-pressed whitecoats.

In the spring the Russian army began a straggling, disjointed march across western Poland. Fermor had been forced to get under way before all his arrangements were complete, and to a casual eye, at least, the Russians seemed to revert to some of the worst habits of 1757. Fermor led the main body on the central axis from Posen. The troops marched in one or two massive columns, and although precious little was known about the theatre of war or the location of the enemy, Fermor scarcely bothered to scout the ground. The baggage trailed behind, at least as long as ever, and when the army entered enemy territory the Cossacks began to behave in the bad old style. Fermor called the Cossack leader, Démicoud, to account, but that gentleman was able to prove that matters were beyond his control. Démicoud (or Demiku) often told his friends that he 'considered it as the greatest misfortune to have Cossacks under his command' (Tielke, 1788, II, 78).

In the middle of August Fermor's progress came to a halt in front of the fortress of Cüstrin on the Oder. The place was small and not particularly strong, but the Prussian general Dohna was able to feed in reinforcements and supplies from the far bank of the river, and Fermor had no siege artillery with which to batter down the walls. Since it was important to conserve the solid shot for combat in the field, Fermor was reduced to employing the explosive shells of the howitzers and unicorns in a generalised bombardment of the town. The fortifications remained undamaged, and the episode added to the unfortunate impression given by the Russian army at this time, as an organisation that was at once murderous and blundering.

The Russians were plainly doing little good at Cüstrin, but 'Count Fermor did not wish to hear anything about crossing the Oder, saying that he could not take such a step without a specific order from the court' (Prince Charles of Saxony, *AKV*, 1870-95, IV, 16). Fermor was therefore stranded in a static position with a disintegrating army. The infantry were worn out with having to stand guard in the trenches, and their effective numbers were reduced still further because so many men had to be set to work to grind flour and bake bread. Likewise, the cavalry had to go foraging far afield, because the grass of the locality was soon eaten up. The Observation Corps had still to arrive in the offing, and Rumyantsev was sent with a precious 11,854 men (eight regiments of infantry, eleven squadrons of cavalry, eleven field pieces) to guard a possible crossing point of the Oder downstream at Schwedt.

The detachment of Rumyantsev was occasioned by the news that King Frederick of Prussia had left his main army behind in the south in Silesia and was hastening against the Russians with a compact striking force. On 21 August Frederick reached Dohna at Cüstrin, and his hussars brought him twelve captured Cossacks, the first he had ever seen. The king examined them attentively, then exclaimed: 'Just look at the kind of scum I have to fight!' (Archenholtz, 1840, I, 164). Fermor sent Rumyantsev orders to hold Schwedt at all costs, to prevent the enemy reaching the 'Russian' side of the Oder, but in the event Frederick cast a pontoon bridge over the river at Alt-Güstebiese, between the two Russian forces, and his army completed its crossing by three in the morning of 23 August.

Still ignorant of whether he was dealing with a detached corps or a royal army, Fermor decamped on 24 August and marched his troops some six miles north-east to confront the Prussians somewhere beyond the village of Zorndorf. The generals were left in ignorance of his intentions, and so they were to remain.

Prince Charles of Saxony had proposed that the Russians should draw themselves up on the high ground near Gross-Cammin. Fermor said he would fall in with the suggestion, but instead he merely deposited the main baggage in a fortified *Wagenburg* by the village, and pushed the army into a potentially disastrous position in a marshy hollow that was intersected with watercourses, and overlooked by higher ground on all sides. Rumyantsev was lost beyond recall well down the Oder, but as some compensation Browne arrived with 9,000 or so men of the Observation Corps and took up position on Fermor's right or eastern flank, giving the Russians a total of about 43,000 men, or, in other words, a paper superiority of 6,000 troops over the enemy. In fact the advantage of the Russians in infantry was balanced by the fragmentation in command and position, and by the overwhelming weight of the Prussians in heavy cavalry (10,500 troopers as against 3,282).

Almost simultaneously with the arrival of the Observation Corps the Prussian army bore down from the north. The Russian hussars had sent in no reports of any value, and so Frederick was allowed to prosecute an overnight outflanking march which took him on an easterly circuit to an advantageous position overlooking the rear of the Russians. This horrid sight forced the Russians to undertake a total change of front to the south in the early morning of the 25th. The second line now became the first, the right wing became the left, and vice versa, and the troops now stood with their backs to the Mietzel stream, which threatened to become an embarrassment in the case of a defeat. Inside the wings, the infantry

ZORNDORF: Prussian turning movement

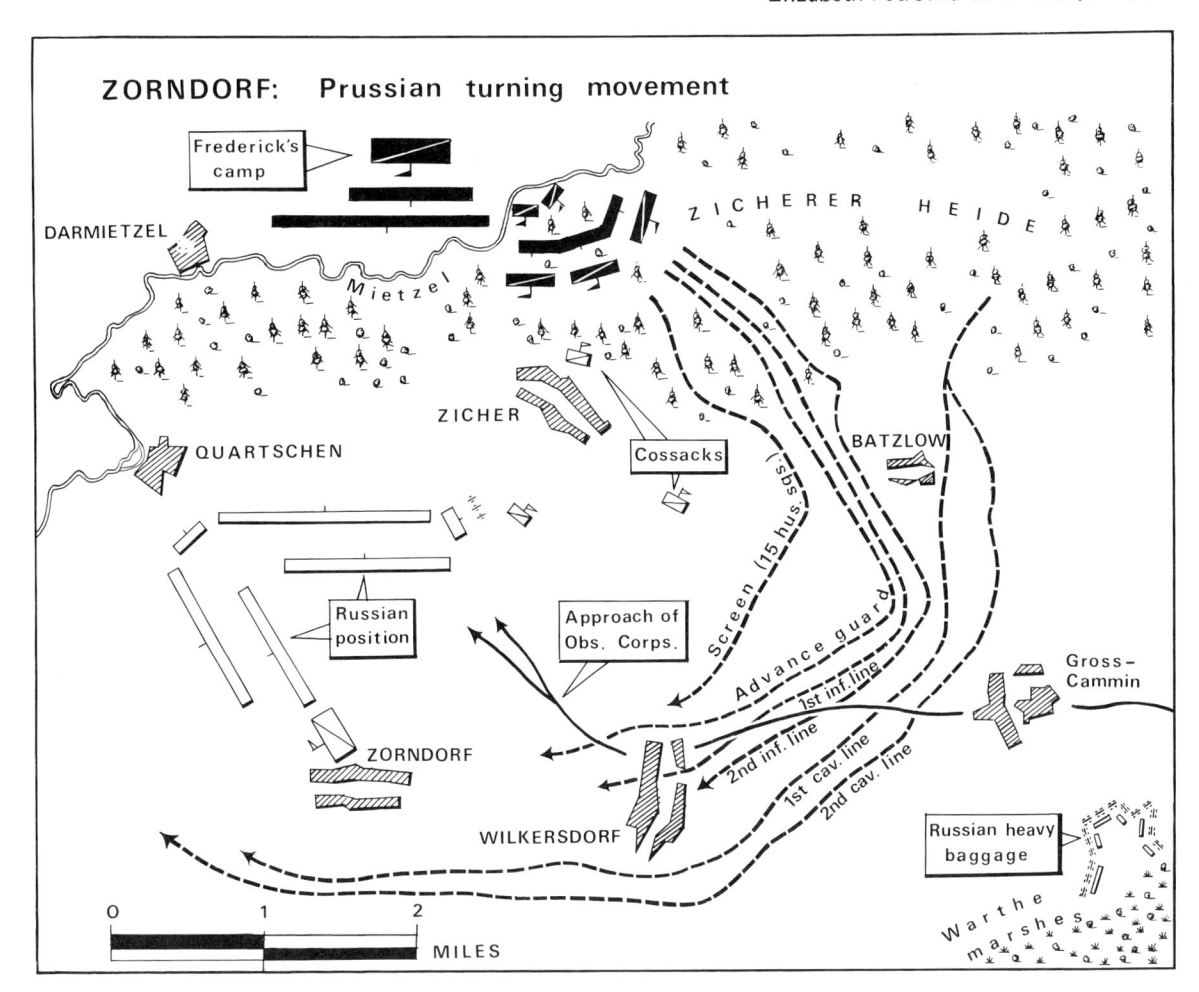

countermarched by regiments, so as to restore an element of the original order of battle, and on the new right flank the dragoons and Cossacks changed places.

Fermor and the main army were now properly designated the right wing, and they occupied the western side of the field up to the doubtful flank protection of the marshy Zabern hollow. Browne's Observation Corps constituted the left wing and extended to the village of Zicher. The position of the Russian infantry was scarcely one and a half miles in breadth, and the troops were packed together line upon line with the light baggage in the centre.

A beautiful starlit night gave way to the last dawn that many of the combatants were to know. The Cossacks proceeded to open the great battle of 25 August in characteristic style by setting fire to the abandoned village of Zorndorf. The Prussians hesitated to feed their artillery ammunition carts through the blazing streets, but in compensation the smoke blew into the faces of the Russians, along with the dust raised by the thousands of feet and hooves. Among his new Russian comrades the exhausted Pastor Täge had slept until he was awakened by a cry of 'The Prussians are coming!'

The sun was already shining brightly. We leapt on our horses, and from the top of a ridge I saw the Prussian army as it marched towards us. Their weapons flashed in the sun, and the spectacle was frightening,... Never shall I forget the silent, majestic approach of the Prussian army. I only wish that my readers could imagine to themselves in all its immediacy that splendid but alarming moment when the Prussian array suddenly deployed into a thin, staggered line of battle.... Then the menacing beat of the Prussian drums carried to our ears. For a time their woodwind was inaudible, but as the Prussians approached we could hear the oboes playing the well-known hymn *Ich bin ja, Herr, in deiner Macht!* I cannot express what I felt at that instant, but I do not think that people will consider it odd when I say that never since in the course of my long life have I heard that tune without experiencing the utmost emotion. (Täge, *RA*, 1864, II, 295-6)

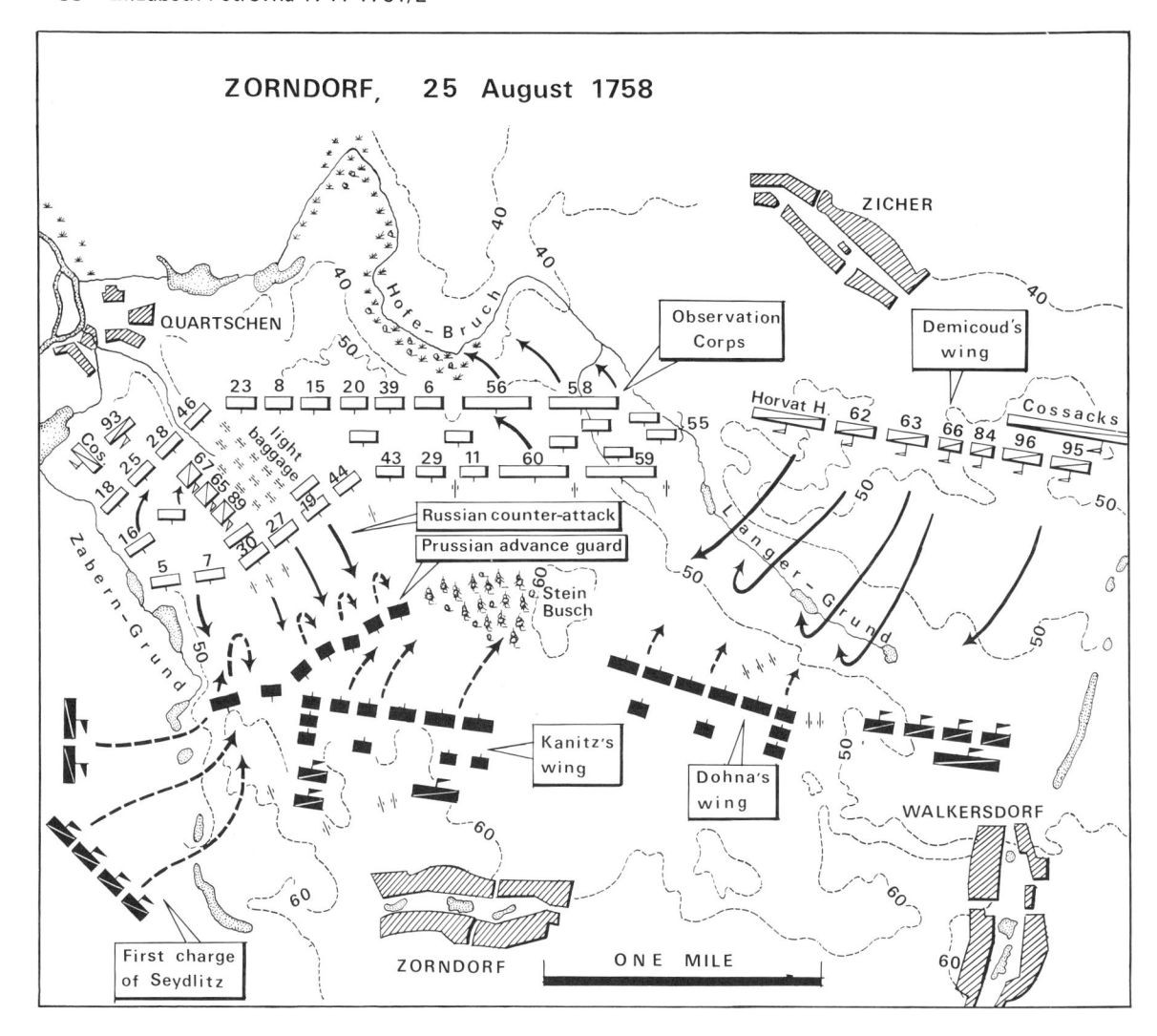

The respite came to an end when the Prussians arranged their heavy guns on the heights north of Zorndorf, and opened fire against the densely packed masses of the Russian right wing below. The 18- and 24-pounders fired showers of grape at short range, and the solid shot operated to probably greater effect still. 'It was scarcely surprising that a single enemy cannon ball should have killed or wounded forty-eight men when it hit one of our regiments of grenadiers' (Bolotov, 1870-3, I, 784). Tielke exclaims that:

the extraordinary steadiness and intrepidity of the Russians on this occasion is not to be described; it surpassed everything that one has heard of the bravest troops. Although the Prussian balls mowed down whole ranks, yet not a man discovered any symptoms of unsteadiness, or inclination to give way, and the openings in the first line were instantly filled up from the second, or the reserve. (Tielke, 1788, II, 180-1)

The Russian artillery offered a spirited reply, but could only inflict insignificant damage on the more thinly spread Prussian lines.

After two hours of cannonade the main Prussian attack declared itself in a concerted move against the badly shot-up Russian right wing. At eleven in the morning an advance guard of eight picked battalions strode boldly ahead, followed in a more tentative manner by the main body of the Prussian left wing which lost its bearings in the smoke and began to veer off to its right. Finally the redoubtable Lieutenant-General Seydlitz was at hand with thirty-six squadrons to close up the flank and seek targets of opportunity.

The unsupported enemy advance guard was met by a devastating fire of musketry and artillery from Fermor's main army, and the Prussians had already lost about one-third of their numbers when they came under a flank attack from the first line of the right wing of the Russian cavalry. The wretched Prussian infantrymen had memories of a similar experience at the hands of the Austrians at Kolin in the year before, and they collapsed and fled. The Russian cavalry was in its turn overthrown by Seydlitz, who carried on in the direction of Fermor's infantry, who were soon caught up in the exciting events. The first line of greencoats had executed a more or less spontaneous advance to cries of *Ura!*, but the movement staggered to a halt after two or three hundred paces under the double ordeal of being fired on by its own second line in all the confusion, and then receiving the attack of Seydlitz. Now it was the turn of the Russian infantry to scatter. Only the First and Second Grenadier Regiments held out as coherent units, enabling a few other knots of heroes to stand their ground with levelled bayonets and save the fugitives from complete destruction.

The rest of the Prussian army collided piecemeal with the Russian host over the following hours. Having missed its way at the beginning of the battle, the main body of the Prussian left under Lieutenant-General Kanitz buried itself in the multiple lines of the Russian centre, which gave rise to a battle of extraordinary ferocity. Fermor was nowhere to be found at this critical moment. It was later given out that he had been bruised or lightly wounded, but Prince Charles of Saxony records that at two in the afternoon he met the commanding general:

who was making off with a great quantity of hussars and Cossacks. He called out to St. André (the Austrian liaison officer) 'General St. André, I shall try to get through to Schwedt!', and then he disappeared from my sight, on account of the dust raised by the swarms of men who were fleeing with him. (*AKV*, 1870-95, IV, 120)

At about the same time the Prussian right or eastern wing under General Dohna began to bear down on the hitherto unengaged Observation Corps, and the events on the western wing were here reproduced in a curiously similar sequence. Démicoud with the left wing of Russian cavalry responded to the threat by launching some lively attacks against the open Prussian flank. Dohna's troops wilted, but Seydlitz restored the day when he came hastening up all the way from the far side of the field and rushed a powerful force of cavalry into the action. The Prussian infantry now began to push in earnest, and the Observation Corps was bent back at an angle until it came to a disorderly stand amid the trees and marshes of the Hofe-Bruch. Zakhar Chernyshev fell into the hands of the enemy at this dangerous stage of the proceedings, and George Browne was severely wounded.

This very long-drawn-out battle had by now escaped the control of the generals, and it was prolonged into the evening by the frenzy of the troops. The Russian army had collapsed into an irregular square around the light baggage. Many of the horses were maddened by the incessant whistle and smack of the Prussian shot and shell, and plunged through the ranks dragging their carts behind them. Other waggons were plundered by the infantry of the Observation Corps, and:

the confusion in the Russian army was much increased by the soldiers getting possession of several casks of brandy, of which the Russians always carry a great quantity with their baggage. It was to no purpose that the officers broke the casks in pieces, for the men threw themselves on the ground, and drank the liquor out of the dust: this made them quite mad and ungovernable. (Tielke, 1788, II, 185)

In the rear the Prussian cavalry had a free hand at Quartschen, where they seized the money chest of the Observation Corps, but the suicidal resistance of the Russian gunners helped to maintain a semblance of cohesion around the perimeter. Speaking of the Russians, an enemy officer testifies that:

these warriors offered the Prussians the vision of a kind of battle they had never seen before . . . even a shot through the body was often not sufficient to bring them to the ground. The Prussians were therefore left with no alternative but to hack down anyone who refused to give way. (Archenholtz, 1840, I, 167)

As the sun was setting a final outburst of Russian fire showered the Prussian ranks so thickly that it seemed as if they were being pelted with peas, and the ground was left littered with bullets.

This bloody day's work cost the enemy 355 officers and 12,442 men, or nearly one-third of their complement:

The battle ruined the East Prussian infantry, . . . and since then the regiments of that region have been worthless. Mass desertion set in among the soldiers who had left their wives and children in East Prussia, or who had some property or goods there, not least because the Russians promised to leave them at peace in their homes, and exempt them from military service. (Warnery, 1788, 276)

Modern Russian estimates put Fermor's own losses at more than 6,000 killed or captured, and nearly 12,000 wounded, together with 53,000 roubles in the money chests. Also, 'to the great annoyance of Count Shuvalov at that time, the Prussians captured some of his secret howitzers in that battle — the pieces which had those muzzles that even his own Russians had not been allowed to see' (Danilov, 1842, 110).

The indecisive slaughter of 25 August 1758 has gone down as the archetypal Russian battle of the eighteenth century. 'Since the invention of gunpowder, no battle has been fought which could equal this for duration, obstinacy, and the uncommon proofs of valour displayed on each side' (Tielke, 1788, II, 194). The enemy and the whole of Europe were made aware for the first time of the power of elemental resistance possessed by Russian infantrymen and gunners. Afterwards Old Fritz affected to despise the Russians for their performance in the battle, but he let slip a number of expressions which indicated how close he had come to disaster. Speaking of the achievement of his right wing, and especially the regiments of Forcade and Prinz von Preussen, he declared: 'These regiments and General Seydlitz were my salvation!'

In contrast with the steadfast performance of most of the troops, the Russian higher management of the battle inspires very little respect. There was no attempt to deny Frederick the crossing of the Mietzel, or to obstruct his consequent progress around the Russian flank and rear on to the higher ground at Zorndorf. The chosen field was not only low-lying but uncommonly cramped, which prevented the local commanders from acting with the freedom they had shown at Gross-Jägersdorf. The outnumbered cavalry showed great enterprise and courage, and the infantry as a whole fought extremely well, though the Observation Corps with its untried regiments showed less discipline and steadiness than the veterans on the right. The disbandment of this private army could not long be postponed. 'From the beginning, as far as its organisation was concerned, it was an abortion' (Maslovskii, 1888-93, II, 202). Petr Shuvalov suffered a further disappointment when he evaluated the performance of the artillery. Many of the gun detachments fought on until they were physically annihilated, but they were often reduced to these sore straits simply because the rest of the army did not give them the support they needed — whether tactical cover for the field batteries, or infantrymen to help to serve the regimental pieces.

In his first relations concerning the 'unfortunate affair' at Zorndorf, Fermor wrote to Elizabeth that the poor discipline of the army had prevented him from 'attaining such a complete victory over the enemy as was desirable' (Korobkov, 1940, 186). In response, the Conference furnished him with a notorious manifesto, which Fermor distributed to every company of the army for public reading on two days of every week. After uttering some dry words in praise of the courage of the soldiers, the document accused the army as a whole of drunken rioting (which in fact occured only in the Observation Corps), and of breaking into the money chests (which was the doing of the Prussian cavalry). Every soldier was physically searched for the plundered coins, even in the division of Rumyantsev, which had not taken part in the battle. The episode reflects badly on the sense of man-management of Fermor and the Russian bureaucracy. On the subject of this offending manifesto, with its convoluted style, an historian observes that:

nothing gives a clearer indication of the length of the road which Elizabeth's Russia still had to travel before it deserved the title of 'European'. While the Russian armies were already capable of taking on the army of Frederick in battle, Elizabeth's pen-pushers (and indeed the Empress herself) remained on the intellectual and literary level of the logothetes of Byzantium. (Rambaud, 1895, 198)

Fermor's own role in the affair underwent a searching investigation by Lieutenant-General Kostyurin (a brother-in-law of Aleksandr Shuvalov), who was sent by the Conference to make enquiries in the army. He completed his report in April 1759, and detailed all the failings of the campaign — the miscalculations concerning the siege of Cüstrin, the failure to prevent Frederick from crossing the Oder, the omission to occupy the little hills on the south of the field, and the charge that 'all the generals declare that they received no orders during the battle, or in fact any instructions at all, apart from a *Disposition* that was issued several days beforehand' (*AKV*, 1870-95, VII, 355).

Both armies were too exhausted to renew the battle after the bloodbath of 25 August, and the outcome of the campaign now depended on the respective power of the Prussians and Russians to outlast one another on the theatre of war.

Frederick had to march away to face the Austrians, leaving Dohna with just 17,000 men in the east. From St Petersburg the Conference urged Fermor to do something to exploit this state of affairs, and at headquarters Prince Charles of Saxony begged him at least to reoccupy the field of Zorndorf, as a matter of honour. Instead, Fermor remained inactive at Landsberg on the Warthe, until the difficulties of supply became so acute that he had to retreat to winter quarters behind the Vistula.

As the city of Danzig still refused free access to the Russians, the only hope of retrieving something in return for the great effort of 1758 was to capture the useful little port of Colberg, as George Browne had urged some time before. Colberg stood at the mouth of the Persante, on a long and otherwise featureless stretch of the sandy Pomeranian coast, and with this place in their possession the Russians might have been able to maintain themselves through the winter in enemy territory, instead of having to fall back deep into Poland.

When Fermor told off General Palmenbach to attend to Colberg the season was already far advanced, and 'the enterprise became an operation which was monumentally bad in execution and consequences' (Bangert, 1971, 363-4). The supporting squadron kept so far off shore that its fire had no effect. The land forces had no map of the fortress, and no proper siege artillery, and they were so short of ammunition that they had to wait for the Prussians to fire, so that they could pick up the cannon balls and shoot them back. The siege corps finally decamped on 1 November, and 'thus ended a siege, which may justly be called too serious for a joke, and too trifling for earnest' (Tielke, 1788, II, 361).

The Russian army in the early Seven Years War

The bare narrative of events gives only passing clues as to the nature of the Russians' performance in their first three campaigns against the leading army of the West.

In the first place the character of the war direction helps to make sense of much that would otherwise be inexplicable. Empress Elizabeth Petrovna never altered in her antagonism towards Frederick of Prussia, but through her temperament and physical constitution she could lend only fitful support to the prosecution of the war. Her distrust of her servants encouraged her to throw together irreconcilable enemies in the various departments of state, as Maria Theresa of Austria was quick to notice. Her sensitive humanity was another disqualification for high command. The news of Gross-Jägersdorf, for instance, was enough to disquiet her conscience for weeks.

Most disturbing of all, the empress was liable to throw herself into such excesses of social pleasure and religious enthusiasm as to leave her in a state of physical and mental prostration, and arouse fears of her death. Elizabeth lived on in sluggish acquiescence in the fact that she would be succeeded by a man who was an admirer of Old Fritz and a declared enemy of the war. This was her nephew Grand Prince Peter, who had been snatched from his beloved duchy of Holstein-Gottorp, and put through a thoroughly unconvincing course of Russification as the heir apparent. His wife was the intelligent and dominating German lady Catherine (born Sophie of Anhalt-Zerbst), who spent her time in political and amorous intrigues, and was the soul of the 'young court'. Field-Marshal Apraksin was not the only military man who was probably unwilling to compromise himself in the eyes of the new generation through an over-enthusiastic conduct of the war against the Prussians.

The Russian state was therefore deprived of the kind of personal guidance that was given elsewhere by the King of Prussia or (in a different style) by Maria Theresa. The virtual abdication of the empress, therefore, left the management of the war in the hands of an institution, the Conference at the Imperial Court (*Konferentsiya pri Vysochaishem Dvore*).

Since the late 1740s the chancellor, Bestuzhev, had been in the habit of calling together officials for meetings on inter-departmental affairs, but in February 1756 the approach of the war persuaded him to put the thing on a more formal basis. The immediate objective, he announced, was to alleviate the 'grievous state' of the commanding officer in the field, by providing him with a unified source of political, military and administrative support. The Austrian ambassador, Esterhazy,

21 Grand Prince Peter and Catherine, leaders of the 'young court'

took an important part in the formation of the body, and arranged for the once-weekly proceedings to be summed up in a paper and put before Elizabeth for her decision.

The Conference first came together on 25 March 1756. Bestuzhev sat as the first president, and the regular membership comprised such important men as Apraksin (in his capacity as President of the War College), Count Mikhail Bestuzhev (President of the Admiralty College), the Vice-Chancellor M. Vorontsov, and Petr Shuvalov and his brother, the mighty Aleksandr. Elizabeth herself was spurred into taking an interest in public affairs, though in later years she did not bother to so much as inform herself of what the Conference was doing in her name.

At the highest level of its work, the Conference resolved fundamental questions of state policy. On successively less exalted planes it sent operational orders to commanders in the field, it directed trade and all matters of military supply (down to the purchase of Kalmyk caftans), and it intervened to make or break the careers of quite lowly officers.

The Conference has been accused of all the vices of the Austrian *Hofkriegsrath* (itself a widely misunderstood institution). There was something evidently absurd in the principle of a committee of amateurs seeking to dictate the operations of a general who might be 650 miles distant by eighteenth-century roads. The detail was certainly badly managed. The renderings of foreign documents were clumsy and obscure, thanks to the incompetence of the translators, and in the summer of 1758 Fermor was in the receipt of four contradictory sets of orders in the space of a month.

These manifest shortcomings can sometimes conceal the fact that no other source of authority had the will to address itself to the important things that the Conference set out to do. The War College and the Admiralty College proved slow and obstructive in their dealings with the commanders, as Bestuzhev had foreseen, and the College of External Affairs attempted to manage foreign policy as a private domain. It is easy to imagine the Conference as a body of bureaucrats, which put artificial restraints on some wild-eyed Suvorov of a commander, who was dying of mortification because he was not allowed to get to grips with the enemy. However, the Seven Years War general was more typically a soul like Fermor, who invoked St Petersburg as cover for his own irresolution, and thus the Conference was often in the position of having to urge some positive course of action which the commander was disinclined to take, whether assuming the offensive against Lehwaldt or Dohna, or resorting to the drastic method of requisition to obtain his supplies.

The determination of grand strategy rested above all upon the connection with Austria, since the French had renounced any direct interest in the eastern theatre, and the allied Swedish army was a shadow of its former self and very disinclined to venture beyond the bounds of Swedish Pomerania. By the middle of the war the allies had arrived at some remarkably astute assessments of the strengths and weaknesses of their enemy. The Conference told the Russian representatives with the Austrian headquarters in 1759 that while Frederick of Prussia was a practitioner of the offensive *à outrance*, there was now evidence to show that he was easily downcast if events did not conform with his expectations (Thilo von Trotha, 1888, 23). The Austrian major-general, Tillier, told the Russians with equal sagacity that Frederick's advantages could be traced to his central position, and his strategy of concentrating his forces against one enemy at a time (16 January 1759, *AKV*, 1870-95, CI, 393-4). The Russians and Austrians concluded that Frederick was not fundamentally unbeatable, and that the best means to bring him down was to act with concerted forces. The physical means of liaison were at hand in abundance. A message could be got from one commander to the other in about a week through couriers or lancer-post, and each army had a representative in attendance at the other's headquarters.

With all these considerations in mind, how was it possible for the Russians and Austrians to let Frederick escape destruction? In part the failure proceeded from the forces which drew the allies aside from the natural theatre of joint operations on the lower middle Oder and in Brandenburg. The Russians felt that they could not ignore their northern flank, whether to secure their territorial expansion along the Baltic coastline, or to safeguard against a counter-offensive from Pomerania. The Austrian concern with the Oder theatre was liable to decline once they had a footing in Silesia, they were uncomfortable in the open plains, and their dynastic interests all the time attracted them westwards, in the direction of Saxony and the rest of the German empire.

For most of the war, therefore, the Austrians thought of the Russian action in terms of indirect relief, counterweight and diversion. One exception relates to the interesting idea of incorporating a Russian auxiliary corps in the Austrian army, which would have given Maria Theresa a useful accession of force, while enabling a cadre of Russian officers to profit by the instruction and example of the Austrians. The Austrians wished to see George Browne take command of the corps, for he was an active commander, related to some of Austria's own Irishmen. They also knew and trusted Zakhar Chernyshev, and would have liked to have him appointed as an assistant. Russia steadfastly rejected the whole scheme, as an infringement of her status as a full *puissance belligérante*.

The two Austrian triumphs of the middle of the war, at Hochkirch in 1758 and Maxen in 1759, came very late in the season, when the Russians had already left the scene of the campaign. The Russians' own cycle of operations was of no great use to the Austrians. It used to open with a series of discussions at the Conference, which rarely reached any concrete understanding with the allies by the time the army straggled on to the theatre of war. Some great blow would be struck against the Prussians in July or August, and then in the late autumn the Russians began the long march back to the Vistula.

The indecisive outcome of so much effort had a great deal to do with the question of supply, which the Conference defined as the 'first and principal' question in a war against Prussia. The Russians were aware that they had no experience of sustaining an army during a heavily contested campaign in a Western theatre. There were no Russian-born contractors of any expertise, no regulations or routine, little geographical or statistical knowledge of the Oder country, and a wholly inadequate staff in the departments of the *General-Kriegskommissar* (which saw to supplies and transportation), and the *General-Proviantmeister* (which obtained the foodstuffs). These last two functionaries actually remained at St Petersburg until Fermor hauled them up nearer the army (see p. 81). All of these difficulties were compounded by the desire to spare East Prussia for political reasons, and the need to have regard for the prickly sensibilities of the Polish nobility. Thus the Conference wished to pay for everything in cash, so as to shame Frederick for his brutal exactions in Saxony.

Much of the Russian system of supply evolved upon conventional lines. Broadly speaking, an eighteenth-century army needed three main types of commodities:

1 clothing, artillery, ammunition and other items of military hardware, which almost invariably had to come all the way from the home base;
2 grain and flour for the men, and perhaps also some beef cattle, which were usually obtained nearer the theatre of war;
3 fodder for the horses, which in view of its bulk had to be sought on the scene of operations.

All possible use was made of river transport – the Niemen for the operations against East Prussia, and then the Vistula and the Warthe for the later campaigns. Posen on the Warthe became the focal point for the whole war, receiving supplies from Russia and Poland, and dispatching boats and carts to the field army. Provisions for man and beast were obtained for preference by way of contract or direct purchase from the locality, since the Russians still shrank from forcible exactions. On the immediate scene of operations, however, all armies of the time found that their calculations were dominated by the need to keep their animals alive. While a field battle remained the supreme test of an army's fighting qualities, the outcome of the campaign was more likely to depend on an army's ability to sustain itself on the contested ground (see the author's *The Wild Goose and the Eagle. A Life of Marshal von Browne 1705-1757*, London, 1964). The very fact of remaining in a single locality was enough to exhaust the barns and the grazing, hence the urgent need to move on Allenburg in 1757 (see p. 78). While the Austrians were able to wage an effective war for territorial control with their hussars and Croats, the Russians proved their own worst enemies in this kind of warfare, for their Cossacks chased the peasants away and wasted the resources of the country.

The Russians resorted to a number of expedients to help themselves along. The artillery and baggage horses were turned out to graze during halts on the march, while the cavalrymen were sent to mow hay and gather fodder, which menial tasks reduced their combat strength still further. Most characteristic of all, the Russians reverted to some of the habits of their Turkish wars, and hauled around with them a vast train of carts which held cereals and even fodder for twelve days' consumption or more, giving them a certain independence of the neighbourhood, though at a heavy cost to their mobility.

In happy contrast to the state of affairs obtaining in Austria, the Russian war effort experienced few limitations through lack of economic backing, even towards the end of the war. The Russian finances were innocent of debts or credit, and although the army experienced some shortfalls in pay, the despotic power of the government was sufficient to exact what was usually needed in cash and commodities from the Russian people.

However, a fundamental shortcoming in logistical support resulted from the failure of the Conference and the high command to consider the war in terms of more than one campaign at a time. Henry Lloyd pointed out that the Russians could have usefully planted magazines at the East Prussian port of Memel, after Fermor conquered it in 1757:

The want of this precaution, both this and all the following campaigns, rendered their victories useless. They made war, and always will, in all probability, like the Tartars. They will overrun a country, ravage and destroy it, and so leave it; because they can never, according to the method they now follow, make a solid and lasting conquest.... Their own light troops, and the want of a solid plan of operations, will one day ruin their army. (Lloyd, 1781, I, 146)

Later in the war, instead of just sending armies to glorious battles, it might have been better to pursue a strategy of industrious advantages, and brought up the siege train to batter the Oder fortresses, as well as making better use of the neglected fleet to mount a proper expedition against Colberg. The Russians could then have spent their winters in enemy territory, something that they consistently failed to do, as the Marquis da Silva indicated (Silva, 1778, 41).

We now turn to the instruments of Russian warmaking. The lack of good generals was always a weighty factor in allied calculations. Already in 1756 Esterhazy wrote that the Austrians must give 'due consideration to the fact that they do not have one capable general who is up to commanding the Russian army' (to Maria Theresa, 22 April 1756, Volz and Küntzel, 1899, 319). The successive leaders were certainly more notable for their political connections than outstanding military talent. Apraksin was a favourite of Bestuzhev, just as Fermor was a client of Vice-Chancellor Vorontsov and the 'French' party. The honest Saltykov was appointed at the urging of Austria, while Buturlin owed his position directly to the empress. Men such as these were accustomed to return to St Petersburg in wintertime as much to test their standing in the court circle as to prepare for the coming campaign. The outstanding middle-ranking generals, Browne and Golitsyn, lacked the necessary influence and seniority for the top command, and the same disqualifications applied with still greater force to Chernyshev, Rumyantsev, Villebois and Volkonskii, who were to become famous in the reign of Catherine the Great.

All grades of generals were given to insubordination, tale-telling and quarrelling of a most damaging kind. Petr Shuvalov fell out with Fermor, after the latter's rude comments on the new artillery. Fermor was at daggers drawn with Rumyantsev, and Rumyantsev in turn was seen to enter into an undignified quarrel with Golitsyn over the possession of a couple of stolen geese.

Some people were beyond all control. From St Petersburg Petr Shuvalov managed the Observation Corps as a private army, and insisted that its field commander must render his reports direct to him, and not to the War College. Then again, the 'flying corps' of light troops operated as an independent entity under its successive chiefs Sibilsky (1757), Démicoud (1758-9) and Totleben (1759-61). They felt only distantly answerable to the commander-in-chief, and their indifferent performance in the pursuit detracted considerably from the worth of hard-won victories like Gross-Jägersdorf and Kunersdorf.

If the staffs had been properly organised, they could have acted as a restraint on the childish ways of the generals. Excellent men such as Weymarn and Stoffeln held the post of quartermaster-general at times during the war, but they were overwhelmed by a mass of unrelated detail which produced more paperwork than 'in ten German armies taken together' (Lambert, *AKV*, 1870-95, VI, 492). Weymarn explained that his work involved negotiating with the Polish magnates, selecting and staking out camp sites, interrogating Prussian prisoners and deserters, arranging supply in enemy land, and composing a journal of operations that was written out first in German, and then translated into Russian, all of which left him with very little time to consider the future course of the campaign. The same extravagance prevailed at every kind of headquarters. After Count Hordt, a Swedish mercenary, was taken prisoner after Kunersdorf, he was brought to dine with Totleben and found him in the company of a host of adjutants and half a dozen clerks. 'It is well known', he commented, 'that Russian generals invariably drag along with them a whole office staff in their suite' (Hordt, 1805, 40).

While the military bureaucracy swelled to an inordinate degree, the ranks of the line officers were heavily depleted by the war. By 1759 Fermor estimated the shortfall at more than 422 officers of all grades. The Conference released a number of NCOs of the Guard and pupils of the Cadet Corps, which went a little way to meet the deficiency, but promotion for the ordinary soldier remained almost unknown. Also, the Russians were not disposed to look benevolently on the foreign gentry who took advantage of their need, and streamed out to the army, drawn variously by curiosity, love of adventure or hope of distinction. The highest-born of this tribe was Prince Charles of Saxony, who was given a magnificent send-off to the wars at St Petersburg, and repaid his hosts by commenting adversely on every aspect of Fermor's generalship.

The rank and file appeared on the theatre of war in numbers that were startlingly small, in proportion to the extent of the Russian empire. In September 1759 Montalembert wrote to Paris that the last campaigns showed that the Russians could put no more than 40,000 effectives into the field (Montalembert, 1777, II, 87), yet since 1755 a total of 231,644 men had been called to the colours. These had been through the standard procedure of the conscription of a proportion of the 'souls', or taxable male population, in the ten governments of Great Russia (1:135 in 1756, 1:194 in 1757, 1:116 in 1758, 1:128 in 1759). However, the process operated so slowly that the recruits raised through the levy of 1 October 1756 only reached the regiments over a period extending from the summer of 1757 until the beginning of 1758. Many others had died or fallen sick on the march, and the chaos and suffering reached such proportions that the third battalions of the infantry regiments were eventually told off to remain in the rear, where they were to act as centres for reception, training and reconvalescence. The Garrison Army (see p. 35) was supposed to provide a first-line reserve for the field forces, but this too failed to meet the demands of the war, thanks to its poor discipline and material condition. When Petr Shuvalov formed his Observation Corps in 1756, he was disappointed to find that he could raise only 7 or 8,000 good quality men from this source.

An Austrian officer wrote in November 1757 of the horrid sight of the sick, who were 'stretched out on the grass without tents or covering....

22 Fusilier and sergeant of infantry, Seven Years War. Green coat with red collar and cuffs and brass buttons; red waistcoat; red breeches; black gaiters (red in the Apsheronskii Regiment, in honour of the bloody day of Kunersdorf); hat with yellow lace (Viskovatov, 1844-56)

What kind of an impression must this make on their comrades?' (Rambaud, 1895, 53). By this time men were dying at the rate of fifty a day, and the healthy troops were far outnumbered by the sick, yet the director of medical services was living in fine style at Riga, and downing oysters by the score at his dinners with Apraksin.

Such troops who survived the marches and the diseases were all too often diverted to drive or escort the vast quantity of baggage carts, and 'the consequence of all this is, that on the day of battle full a fourth part of the fighting men are absent' (Tielke, 1788, II, 32). The general baggage (transport train) of the army carried the reserves of ammunition, and provisions for sometimes as much as one month. On the battlefield it was leaguered up into a defensible *Wagenburg*, like the one that was left at Gross-Cammin on the day of Zorndorf. On the move, it was inserted somewhere behind the marching columns.

The regimental baggage was if possible more burdensome still. The regulation allowance of transport for the infantry regiment stood at two hundred two-horse train and baggage carts, fourteen two-horse carts for the musket ammunition, and two two-horse ammunition carts for each of the four 3-pounders. As for the cavalrymen, they had 'no bags or portmanteaux; but all their baggage, of which they carry a great deal, and more than the infantry, is loaded on waggons' (Tielke, 1788, II, 20). Everything possible was thrown on to the carts, down to the hats of the troopers, and the coats of the infantry in summertime, as well as intrinsically heavy items like the tent poles and *chevaux de frise*. In addition every *artel*, or mess, of the troops had its jealously guarded cart, driven by one of the men, and each officer was entitled to a private train of ten or more vehicles — a limit that was often surpassed many times over. 'No matter how much I try to reduce my train', wrote Apraksin, 'I cannot get by with less than 250 draught horses, in addition to the riding horses, of which I cannot possibly have less than thirty' (17 April 1757, *SIRIO*, 1872, IX, 465). The sutlers, or private dealers, swelled the mass still further. Since the regimental and private baggage was so intimately intermingled with the units, it was almost impossible to sort it into proper order in the event of an enemy attack, with consequences that were evident at Gross-Jägersdorf and Zorndorf.

All of this harked back to the practice of the Turkish wars, and was reinforced by the experience of having to march across the sandy heaths of the new theatre of operations. Fermor appears to have conceded defeat, after his first ambitions to reduce the train. Lieutenant-General Kostyurin interviewed him at length on the subject on 14 March 1759, and reported to the Conference:

You may imagine the difficulty that is experienced in feeding such a mass of animals. Also, when the baggage is constituted on this scale, great numbers of men must be detached to guard it, if the enemy is in the offing or intends to give battle. Count Fermor has certainly given consideration to these matters, but he remains absolutely convinced that such an establishment is necessary to feed the men of his army. (*AKV*, 1870-95, VII, 357)

For these reasons the marching formations of the Russians in the early Seven Years War did not differ in kind from the monstrous oblongs of Münnich. On the way to Cüstrin in 1758 Prince Charles of Saxony affected surprise to see the army blundering forward in two massive columns, giving 'evidence of very little training in the various military movements and evolutions, which they carry out by the whole army in entire corps, as events and circumstances dictate' (*AKV*, 1870-95, IV, 114). As quartermaster-general of Apraksin's army the year before, Weymarn conceded the advantages of movement by small columns, but he maintained that such a formation was impracticable, because of the general ignorance of the theatre of war. In this respect the Cossacks did far more harm than good, for they spread false alarms, and forced the local populations to scamper off to the woods. The same inflexibility was evident in the choice of camps, for the army arranged itself on no set principles, and 'usually occupied sites of the most disadvantageous kind in hollows, making no attempt to exploit low outlying hills of the kind which always

23 Infantry officers, Seven Years War. Green coat with red collar and cuffs; red waistcost; green breeches; black leather waist pouch with brass plate; yellow and black sash; silver gorget. The musket replaced the officers' spontoon in Münnich's time (Viskovatov, 1844-56)

prove so useful' (Prince Charles of Saxony, *AKV*, 1870-95, IV, 122).

Gross-Jägersdorf was an untidy encounter battle, fought out and decided as a series of local combats. For Russian notions on the management of a large-scale action we therefore have to turn to the reports of observers, and evidence like Fermor's *General Disposition for Battle with the Enemy* (14 July 1758), and the details of the clash at Zorndorf which shortly followed it. According to the English captain Lambert, the Russians were confident that their *chevaux de frise* would make their infantry invulnerable to cavalry, which helps to account for the fact that they disposed all their own cavalry in Western style, on either flank. The two main lines of battle stood between three and five hundred paces apart, with an intermediate force of infantry (what Buturlin called 'regimental reserves') stationed between. The regimental artillery was deployed immediately in front of its various parent units, while the batteries of field artillery took up station before the flanks of the army according to the dictates of the brigade commanders. The rearward line of the army was to reinforce the first only upon specific command, 'for otherwise the losses cannot be made good again from the reserves positioned between the two lines' (Fermor, in Maslovskii, 1893, II, 129). On basic tactical principles, Fermor declared in 1758 that

> Everybody is aware that in the last campaign both the Prussian infantry and cavalry launched themselves recklessly into the attack, and opened fire before they came within range. Consequently ... we must meet them with a brave demeanour, and pay due regard to the effect of our artillery. Then you must open fire by platoons at the command of the officers, aiming at the enemy soldiers' middles. When the Prussians come nearer still you employ divisional fire, and continue the fight with the bayonet until, through the help of God and the courage of the Russian army, the enemy are beaten and chased away. (Fermor, in Maslovskii, 1893, II, 344)

In the first two battles of the war the Russian

24 Grenadier of a regiment of musketeers, Seven Years War. The mitre cap with the plate and leather neck guard was introduced in 1756. The brass plate bears the regimental badge (Viskovatov, 1844-56)

infantry more than surpassed every expectation. Their brothers in the regular cavalry fought with dash at Zorndorf, but they were still suffering from the reorganisation that had been so unwisely undertaken on the eve of the war, from their lack of training, and from a grievous shortage of horses.

25 Captain of a regiment of grenadiers, Seven Years War (Viskovatov, 1844-56)

26 Cuirassier on dismounted sentry duty, Seven Years War. Uniform as in 11, except for 1¼ inch wide border to *collet* (Viskovatov, 1844-56)

Rumyantsev wrote to the War College early in 1759 that the only way to remedy the last failing was to make the squadron commanders personally responsible for the selection and welfare of the mounts.

Rumyantsev himself had done excellent work as a trainer of horse, and with the regular cavalry so far behindhand, he did his best to make the regiments of hussars as adept in the Code of 1755 as in their own irregular style of combat. Four regiments of hussars actually reached the army (the Serbian, the Hungarian, the Moldavian and the Georgian [Gruzinskii]). However, they proved to be a poor investment, despite Rumyantsev's efforts, for they were as incompetent as the Cossacks, while costing far more.

The Cossacks themselves failed dismally at almost every task they were set. On the march they devastated the countryside and terrorised the population, with dire consequences for the supply and intelligence of the army, and yet they failed to provide an effective tactical screen. Prince Charles of Saxony saw them in 1758, and claims 'they proceed a little way in front of the advance guard, moving very sluggishly at that, and they do not attempt to reconnoitre to the side of the route, which means that the army could well be exposed to an unexpected enemy attack on the march.' If the camps were badly chosen in the first place, 'the Cossacks are in no position to render any service in this respect. They have no officer with the understanding or capacity to render reports detailing the position or strength of the enemy army' (*AKV*, 1870-95, IV, 114, 122; see also Lambert, *ibid*., VI, 486).

The Cossacks' undoubted skills at evasion were mostly practised at the expense of their own commanders:

The Cossacks, in general, when they go out upon party, lead a horse, on which they get when the one they are mounted upon is tired; thus they will go ten or twelve German miles in one excursion, plunder and burn one or two villages, and be in the camp again almost before they are missed (Tielke, 1788, II, 78).

The feigned retreat and subsequent counter-attack at Gross-Jägersdorf was the one notable feat of arms to their credit, but before the next great battle they had once more largely escaped from control. After Zorndorf they became almost totally unmanageable, because so many had dispersed during the action. The Dnieper Cossacks were generally recognised to be the worst of the lot, while the people from the Don were of higher intrinsic worth, but managed by poorish officers. The Ukranian variety was more tractable and better-organised, but the men were of limited military value, and they never recovered from the hardships of the campaign of 1757.

Although the Russian artillery still lacked a certain ensemble, it already commanded wide respect on account of the power of its ordnance, and the devotion and skill with which the detachments served their pieces. Prussian officers like Retzow and Prittwitz were struck by the suicidal dedication of these gunners in the great battles, and even Lambert found some good words to say about the prominent artillery commander Lieutenant-General Tolstoi. It was unfortunate that the heavy siege train languished at Königsberg,

27 Artilleryman, Seven Years War. Red coat with black collar, cuffs and turnbacks; red waistcoat; red breeches; brass-fronted box and priming flask (Viskovatov, 1844-56)

while the Russians sought to take fortresses like Cüstrin and Colberg by field artillery alone. These attacks were very perfunctory indeed, by the standards of siege operations in the West.

While the Russians performed with valour and credit in the open field, they were losing very heavily to Frederick in a war of another nature. The Prussian veteran, Archenholtz, draws attention to the peculiar importance of 'public relations' at this time:

Never had there been a war in which so many battles were fought. No less remarkable was the great quantity of official pronouncements that were published during this period of general distress. The great monarchs were anxious to justify their strange doings in the eyes of all the world, and even win the approval of such people whose opinions they could easily have ignored. Such was the victory of 'Enlightenment', which at that time was beginning to radiate its beneficial beams over Europe. (Archenholtz, 1840, I, 95-6)

We may speculate that the propagandists had in mind such targets as British political opinion, and neutral bankers and contractors, as well as a public which followed the events of the wars with much closer interest than most commentators on the eighteenth century are prepared to admit.

A particularly damaging document was in circulation in 1758 — an alleged *Lettre d'un Voyageur*, which was composed at Riga on 8 November 1757. The author enumerated the shortcomings of the Russian army in scathing terms, describing the generally poor state of the infantry, the parlous condition of the cavalry, and the limited capacity of nearly all the generals. The Russian resident, Simolin, forwarded a copy of the paper from Augsburg on 12 August 1758: 'Thoroughly contemptible in all respects, this letter is nothing but a tissue of accusations and false charges, intended to detract from the quality of our army and the ability of our commanders' (*AKV*, 1870-95, VI, 478). At the instructions of the Vice-Chancellor, Fermor identified and arrested the author, who turned out to be the English captain Lambert, who was acting as a Prussian spy and publicist.

As the war went on, the Prussian propaganda concentrated on atrocity stories. Ortmann published long accounts from East Prussia and the Neumark, detailing the Russian misdeeds at great length. The poetaster Gleim took up the theme in *Der Grenadier und die Kriegsmuse nach der Niederlage der Russen bei Zorndorf* (March 1759), where he described how the Russians, 'more ravenous than an army of locusts', worked their way through the blessed land of Brandenburg, reducing it to an image of their native steppes. Likewise, after the occupation of Berlin in 1760, Frederick got Finckenstein to compose a *Kurze Anzeige*, indicting the Russians for their barbaric behaviour.

The Russian response was confined to private outrage and the sending of diplomatic notes. The foreign public was left in general ignorance of episodes like the brutal Prussian exactions in Saxony, while in the Russian homeland the character of the enemy was transmitted merely through the medium of fantastic folk tales, in which the 'cruel king' Frederick repeatedly escaped his just deserts by assuming the various forms of blue pigeon, grey cat, falcon, crow, duck or fish.

Thus the Frederickian version of the Russian behaviour in the Seven Years War has come down to modern times unchallenged, and has succeeded brilliantly in distorting the West's perception of the eighteenth-century Russian army. The atrocities were in fact confined to the Cossacks, and to occasional failings on the part of the regulars. As a general rule, wrote the Saxon Tielke, the 'Russian regular troops yield to none in Europe in point of exact discipline, and perhaps surpass, in this respect, most armies' (Tielke, 1788, II, 16). There is a good deal of evidence to support this contention. The Russians behaved impeccably during their long tenure of East Prussia, and their eventual departure was seen with some regret. After the action at Paltzig, in 1759, General Petr Ivanovich Panin wrote to his brother Nikita how even the Russian wounded were concerned to drag the Prussian casualties to a place of safety. One of the Prussian injured in that encounter was Lieutenant Lemcke, who testified that the Russian officers treated the Prussian wounded with the greatest generosity and kindness, and gave each of them a Russian soldier as an attendant. 'I had a good old lad, who looked after me most attentively and served me day and night. I only regretted that I could not speak with him' (Lemcke, 1909, 39-40). The more cultivated Russian officers were distressed to learn that the celebrated poet Major Kleist had died in their hands, after he had been struck down by a canister ball at Kunersdorf, and maltreated by the Cossacks. The Russian officers joined the dons of Frankfurt University in the funeral train, and one of them laid his own sword on the coffin.

In their private memoirs, the Prussian military men spoke of the prowess of the Russians with respect, and after Zorndorf the open-minded Seydlitz did not hesitate to take Frederick up on his disparaging remarks about the enemy. Indeed, Old Fritz's pretended contempt seemed to grow in proportion to his increasing comprehension of the Russian fighting-power.

Saltykov's command, 1759

The Russian army slowly gathered its strength for what was to be its most glorious campaign of the war:

The season of Lent arrived. Skylarks climbed to the sky, and flowers and plants appeared in the fields. The soldiers cleaned their weapons, while the officers arranged their accounts and fitted out their vehicles. Everybody put themselves in readiness, awaiting the order to advance. (Täge, RA, 1864, II, 308)

The provision magazines at Dirschau, Elbing, Marienwerder, Kulm and Graudenz were filled by 20 March, and the British diplomat Keith was already aware of an accelerating pace in the war:

I see no appearances here that seem any ways to tend towards peace. On the contrary, the military preparations go on with vigour. Four hundred thousand roubles have been ordered for General Shuvalov's new corps, of which several regiments have lately passed through this city [St Petersburg] on their way to the army, and recruits are pouring in from all quarters daily. (2 February 1759, PRO, SPF91/67)

Lieutenant-General Kostyurin reported to the Conference that:

the entire army of Her Imperial Highness, from the highest commanders to the lowliest soldiers, is imbued with an invincible courage. We may expect a correspondingly good performance in action, when the army is provided with its needs. (14 April 1759, AKV, 1870-95, VII, 356)

What was still lacking was confidence in the top leadership. Keith noted that Fermor was 'disagreeable to, and despised by, the troops. And it is added, that the uneasiness of his situation has drawn him into a state of habitual drinking, which, if true, must lessen him still more in their eye' (29 May 1759, PRO, SPF91/67). In his assessment of the state of the army, Kostyurin reported that 'most people are discontented, if they do not actually complain, and in their conversation many of the generals and officers remarked that they would like to be commanded by a Russian' (AKV, 1870-95, VII, 356).

Fermor was still considered indispensable to the army on account of his technical competence, but he had to abdicate the leadership in favour of General Petr Semenovich Saltykov (1698-1772), who in his sixties was still the least known of the senior commanders.

He is a gentleman of family and very fair character [noted Keith], but has had very little experience as a soldier, for having passed his younger days at court, and being made a chamberlain, which in this country gives the title and the rank of a major-general, he took that opportunity of entering into the army, and accordingly served in that character in the last campaign of the Swedish War under Marshal Lacy, which was the only occasion he ever had of learning his trade. He afterwards commanded in the Ukraine, but in the time of profound peace. (29 May 1759, PRO, SP 91/67)

When the Russian military bureaucrats turned out to see Saltykov arrive at Königsberg, they were disappointed to find an insignificant, greying figure, walking through the streets in a plain white militia coat. Opinions of Saltykov could only improve. Some of the officers remained aloof, but the army began to warm to his concern for its welfare, and his comfortable and systematic way of life. He was good at joking with the soldiers, he had the eccentric habit of checking the reliability of information by going to see things for himself, and he even maintained that something might be made of the Cossacks, with proper direction.

Paltzig (Kay) and the second march to the Oder, 1759

Plans of campaign were already being revolved at St Petersburg. To begin with the Russians thought in terms of devoting the effort to the reduction of Stettin. This would certainly have accorded with the desires of the French, who feared any more positive moves on the part of Russia, but the scheme was overtaken by an initiative of the Austrians, who for the first time in this war showed themselves willing to bring about an interaction of the two imperial armies in the Prussian heartland. Vienna desisted from its long-standing demand for a Russian auxiliary corps, and instead agreed with the Russians as to the strength of the two main armies, the selection of a common objective on the middle Oder, and the choice of 25 June as the day the forces were to set out – the Austrians from Bohemia, and the Russians from Poland. The other theatres of war were for the time being regarded as subsidiary. An army of Austrians and troops of the German empire was to attend to affairs in Saxony, while the Russians would gather a corps for an eventual siege of Colberg.

The Russian army assembled at Posen in a strength of 60,000 men, including Cossacks, and under its untried leader it set off across the plain for the middle Oder. The main Prussian army under Frederick had occupations elsewhere, but the command of the Oder was disputed by the combative if rather stupid Lieutenant-General Wedel, who had a corps of 28,000 men in position at Züllichau.

Declining the obvious challenge, Saltykov sidestepped with notable adroitness on the night of 22-23 July, and brought his army around the north of Wedel's force to a blocking position at Paltzig, which threatened the Prussian communications with Crossen. In the early morning of the 23rd the huge clouds of dust told the Prussians that Saltykov was on the move, and a few hours later they knew that they would have to improvise some kind of attack if they wished to restore their lifeline.

Saltykov gave further proof of his professionalism in the way he set out his army to receive the Prussians. The broad and swampy Eichmühlen-Fliess afforded him a good frontal barrier, and the troops were arranged in two main lines in a well-articulated fashion on the higher ground on the west bank. The left was teased out rather thinly to face an almost impassable stretch of the stream,

28 Petr Semenovich Saltykov

CAMPAIGN OF 1759

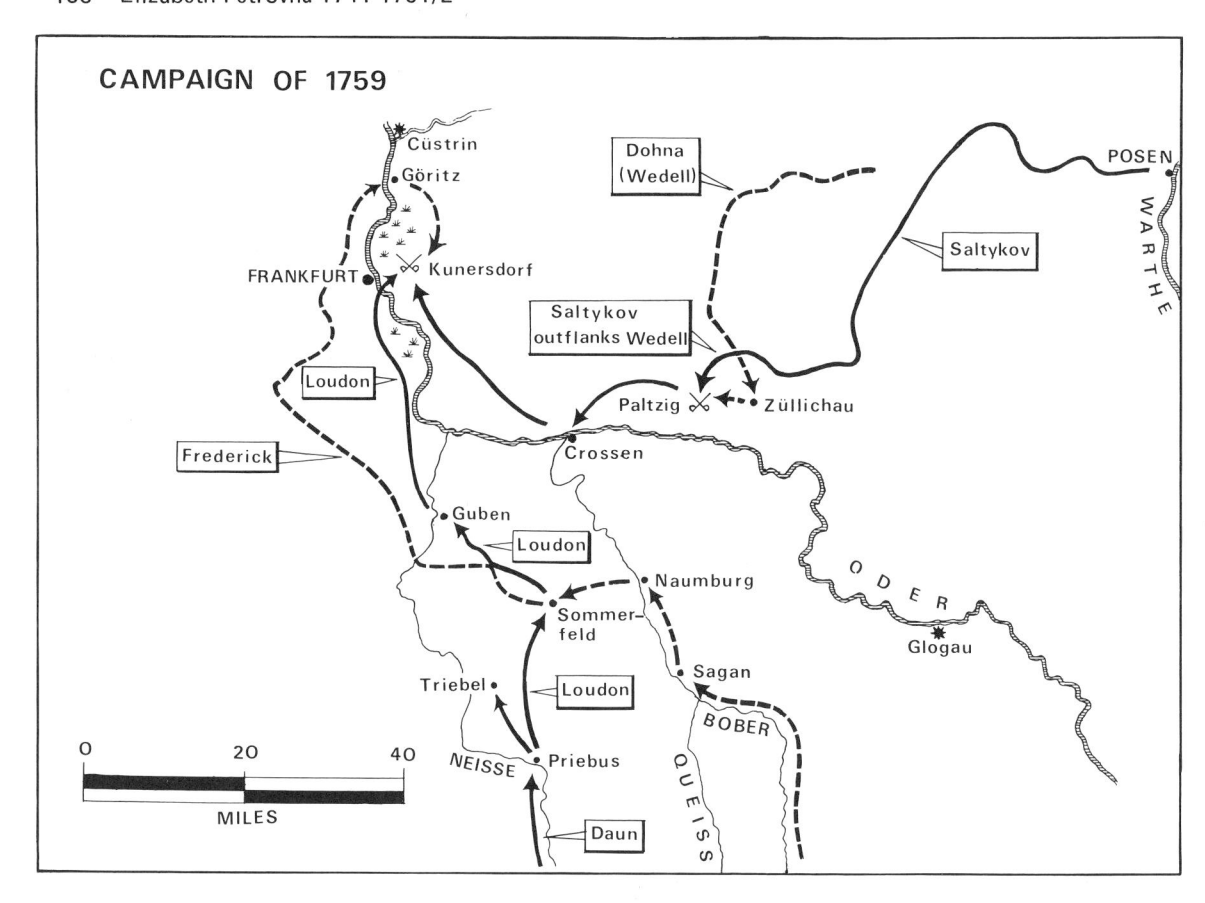

but the right was disposed in depth in a zone of sandstone hillocks behind Heidemühl, and Saltykov retained the capacity to move further troops to this sector as occasion might demand. Eight batteries of field artillery were planted in hastily constructed entrenchments (the first the Russians had ever built in this war), and those on the right were artfully sited on some commanding knolls between the two lines.

Wedel moved to the attack at four on the extremely hot afternoon of 23 July. He had at first calculated on making the assault on a broad frontage, but the difficulty of passing the Eichmühlen-Fliess eventually compelled the Prussians to advance by divisions across the single stretch between Heidemühl and Glogsen and up the ridge that led to the Russian right. The generals Manteuffel, Hülsen, Kanitz and Wobersnow each had their commands smashed in turn. Saltykov responded to the pressure by interleaving his cavalry with lines of infantry, and bringing up two regiments of musketeers from his left wing. A useful force of cavalry (three regiments of regulars, three of hussars, and the Don and Chuguevskii Cossacks) had already been summoned up from the east of Paltzig, and was hovering around the Crossen road.

These balanced dispositions were enough to repulse not only the frontal assaults, but also a dangerous move by four regiments of Prussian cuirassiers, which worked their way across the swampy ground beyond the Russian right, and managed to drive some way into the flank before they were shot up by the rearward batteries of field artillery, and forced back by the Russian cavalry.

All those who were present at this action have

PALTZIG, 23 July 1759

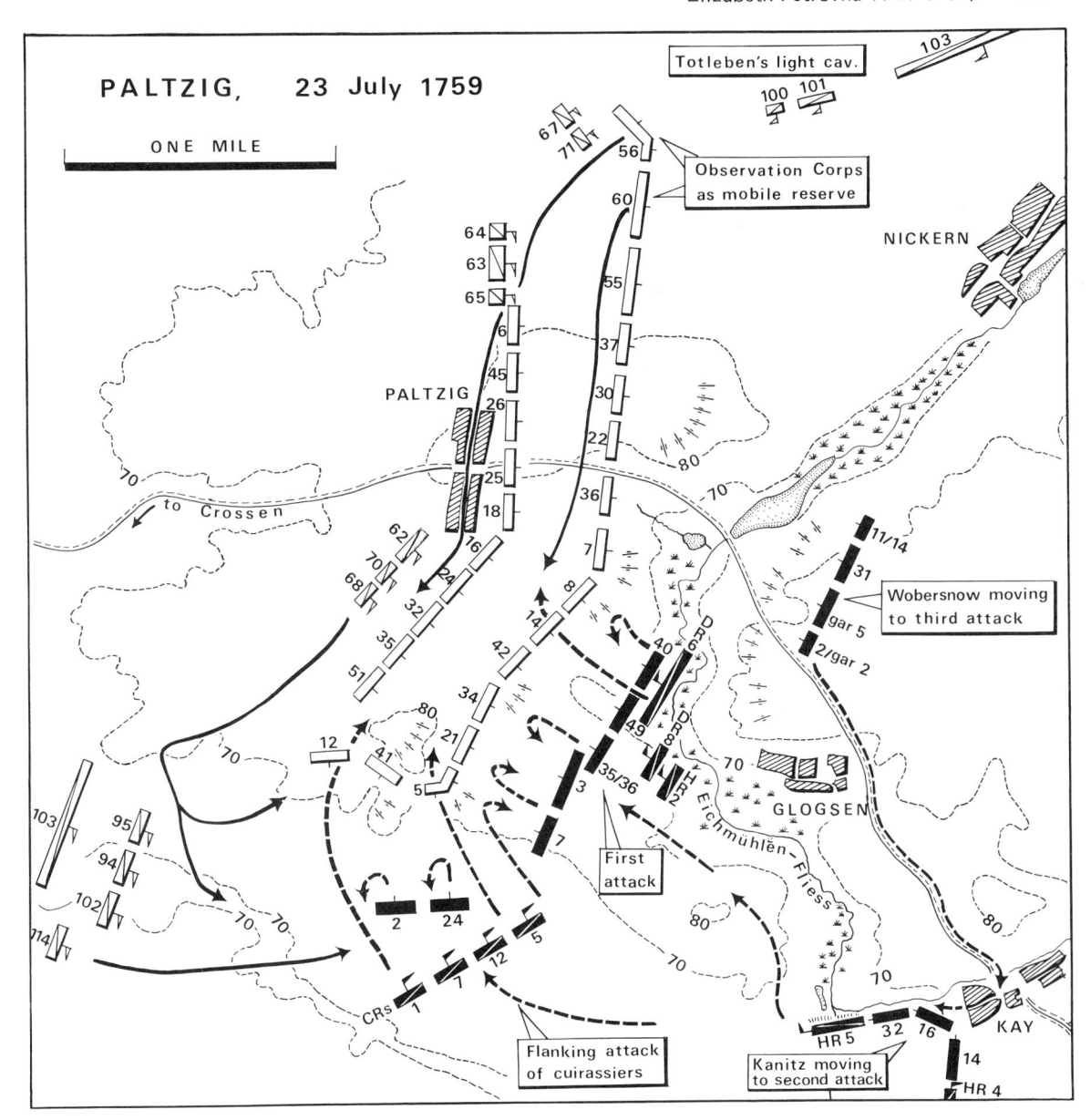

testified that no battle had so far proceeded in such an orderly fashion. Nowhere was there the slightest disorder on either side during the whole continuance of the combat, and so the victory may be attributed above all to the superiority of our force, to the advantage of a well-chosen position, and to the good effect of our unicorns and Shuvalov howitzers. (Bolotov, 1870-3, I, 907)

This destructive little battle ended at about eight in the evening, with up to 8,000 Prussians left on the field, and the rest in full retreat. Saltykov lost about 4,700 in dead and wounded out of the 40,500 or so men he had in the action. 'The whole army drew encouragement from its victory over the enemy, and began to repose greater trust in its elderly leader. Saltykov had been fortunate enough to enjoy the love of his soldiers from the time he first arrived, but now they positively adored him' (Bolotov, 1870-3, I, 907). On the day after the action Wedel withdrew across the Oder, abandoning the east bank to the Russians. Saltykov moved to Crossen, and on 1 August he occupied the city of Frankfurt-an-der-Oder with a combined force of all arms.

Kunersdorf, 1759

Now that he had fought his way so manfully to the Oder, Saltykov had every right to expect that the Austrians would live up to their part of the bargain and come to join him for the campaign in the centre of the Prussian state. In June the main Austrian army marched down from the Bohemian hills into Silesia, but it moved only very ponderously across the plain in the direction of the Russians, and finally came to a halt about fifty miles short of Saltykov and on the 'wrong', or western side of the Oder. The Austrian commander, Field-Marshal Daun, was temperamentally unsuited for wide-ranging offensive operations in the open field, and he displayed little interest in joining the Russians, or even keeping Saltykov *au fait* with what was going on. The Austrians had promised to take over the supply of the Russians, if they crossed to the west bank, but there was no sign of Daun making any active preparations to that end.

Finally, as a compromise strategy, Lieutenant-General Loudon crossed to the Russian bank with a corps of some 24,000 Austrian troops. Embarrassingly enough, Loudon had just lost his supply train to the Prussians, and once he arrived among his allies he had to go begging for rations for his men. He was one of the best of the younger generation of Austrian generals, and far more enterprising than Daun, but he at first found it by no means easy to strike up a friendly relationship with Saltykov, whom he described as 'all too evidently a fundamentally evil man, in whom it is impossible to repose any trust' (Bangert, 1971, 277). On his side, Saltykov was an old-fashioned Muscovite who did not believe his translators, and had no German with which he could communicate with Loudon.

The Russians and the Austrian fragment were still stranded uselessly on the east bank when their time of grace elapsed, and King Frederick arrived on the scene with an army of 50,000 troops. Saltykov's watch along the Oder was uncharacteristically lax, and Frederick was able to bridge and ford the river a short distance below Frankfurt. Just as had happened last year in the campaign of Zorndorf, the Russians were left to face a royal army without support from their allies.

Saltykov had a combined army of about 52,000 infantry and 12,000 cavalry under his command. Rather than undergo the danger of coming under attack on the march, he dug himself in along a low ridge extending in a north-easterly direction from Frankfurt. At six thousand paces the position was considerably longer than the one at Zorndorf, though much more shallow. The fortifications were dug from the sandy soil, and formed curtains and angular redans around most of the position, with batteries of field artillery positioned on especially vital sectors. Two such strongpoints were to figure prominently in the story of the battle of Kunersdorf — the central battery on the Grosser-Spitzberg hill, which was defended by seventeen Russian regiments under the command of Rumyantsev, and the outlying fortifications on the north-eastern salient on the Mühl-Berge, which were separated from the main position by the hollow of the Kuh-Grund. The Russian infantry regiments were largely committed to the defence of the perimeter, but the cavalry and the Austrians were held ready as a reserve of intervention.

Frederick made a distant and uninformative reconnaissance of the bristling position from the north-east, and reached the false conclusion that the south-eastern, or further side was unprotected, and therefore vulnerable to his favourite device of the flanking attack. Oddly enough the Russians assumed that they would be assailed along this sector all the time, for they had not anticipated that Frederick might cross the Oder in their rear. At two in the morning of 12 August 1759 the Prussian columns were set in motion. While a diversionary force under Lieutenant-

KUNERSDORF, 12 August 1759:
First positions

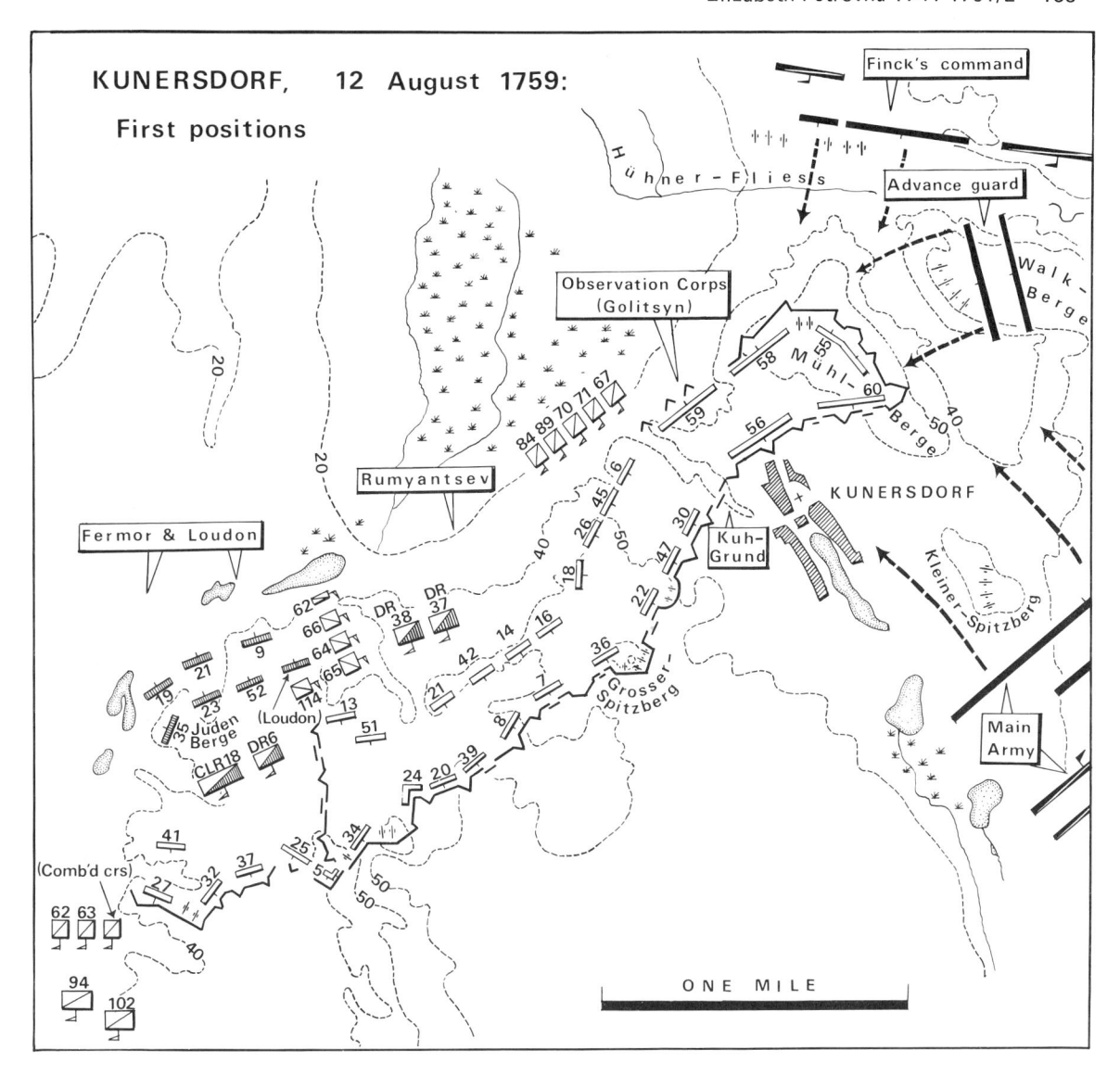

General Finck picked its way across a marshy heath and made directly for the northern front, Frederick led the main army on a wide circuit through a tract of woods, and finally emerged opposite the supposedly open allied 'rear' towards the end of a brilliant morning. Old Fritz could now see that his calculations had gone astray, but by this time his army was irrevocably committed to the attack.

The Mühl-Berge salient took the first impact of the Prussian onset. The unfortunate regiments of the Observation Corps wilted under a concerted pounding from a wide arc of Prussian guns, and they gave way under the assault which followed. Saltykov moved up the twelve elite companies of Austrian grenadiers in support, but they were unable to stay the flight of the Russians across the Kuh-Grund.

Having carried the Mühl-Berge, the Prussian advance guard put in the first of a series of attacks

KUNERSDORF:

The defence of the Kuh-Grund

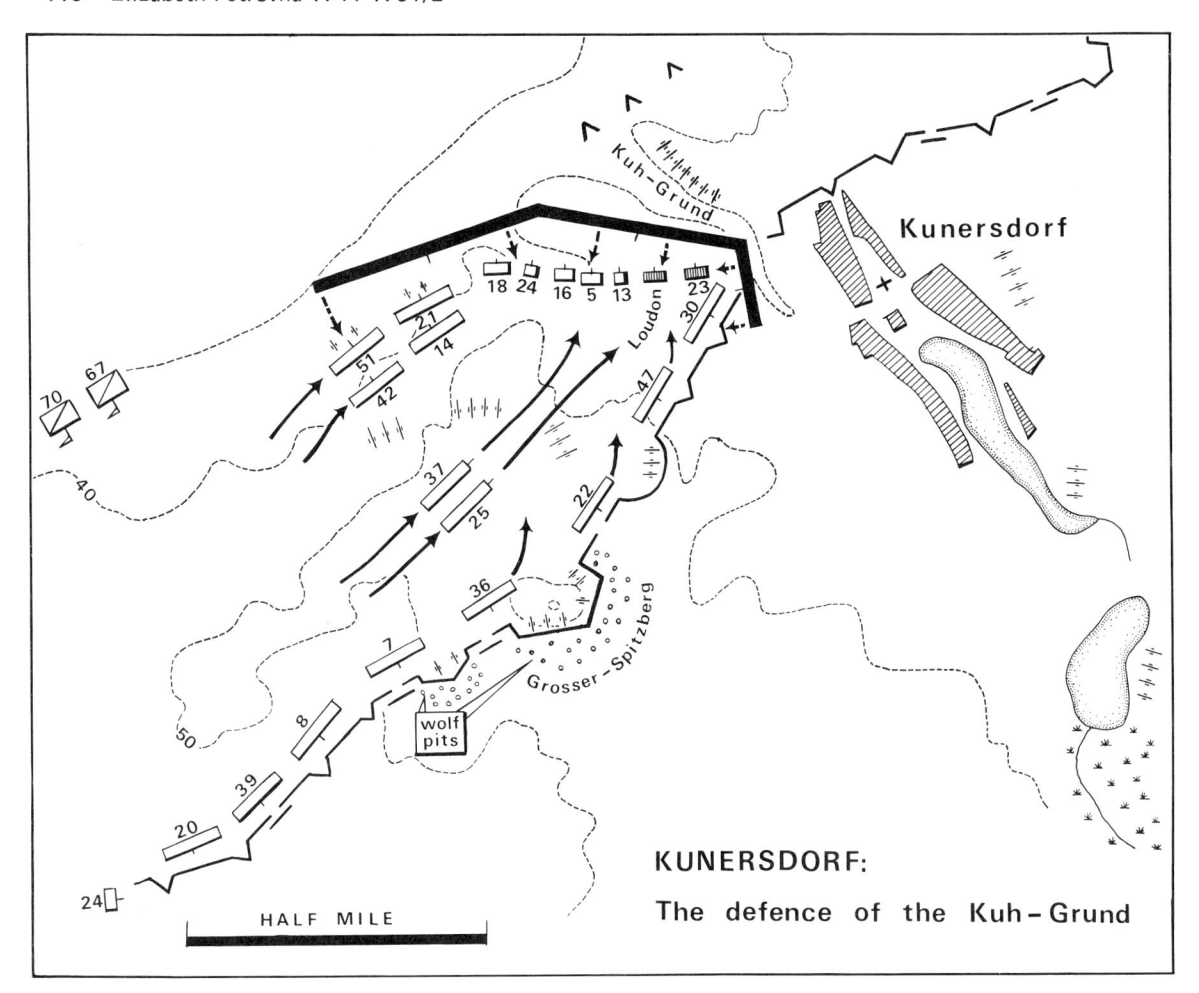

against the main position behind. The corps of Finck closed in from the north, while Frederick's main army occupied the smoking ruins of Kunersdorf village and began to climb the southern slopes. The Russians were taken on three sides, with the salient facing the Kuh-Grund coming under the heaviest pressure.

Saltykov brought up the Austrian regiment of Baden-Baden to support its brothers in the grenadiers, as well as General Panin with the Russian regiments of the second line, but for the rest he was:

in such a state of perturbation and despair that he dismounted, fell to his knees, raised his hands and with tears in his eyes beseeched the Almighty to assist him in this extremity of misfortune, and save his men from total ruin. Who knows? This prayer, offered by a virtuous old man in all the purity of his mind and heart, may well have carried to Heaven. In any event the face of affairs changed almost instantly, and there ensued a sequence of events which nobody could have conceived or imagined. (Bolotov, 1870-3, I, 917)

By the middle of the afternoon the infantry battle had become a standing fire fight, and the Russians were 'jammed eighty or one hundred men deep, forming a disorderly mob on an eminence. But this mob was protected by fifty cannon, which rained down a hail of canister' (Archenholtz, 1840, I, 255).

KUNERSDORF: Victory

HALF MILE

Prussian infantry in flight

KUNERSDORF

Repulse of Schorlemer Drags

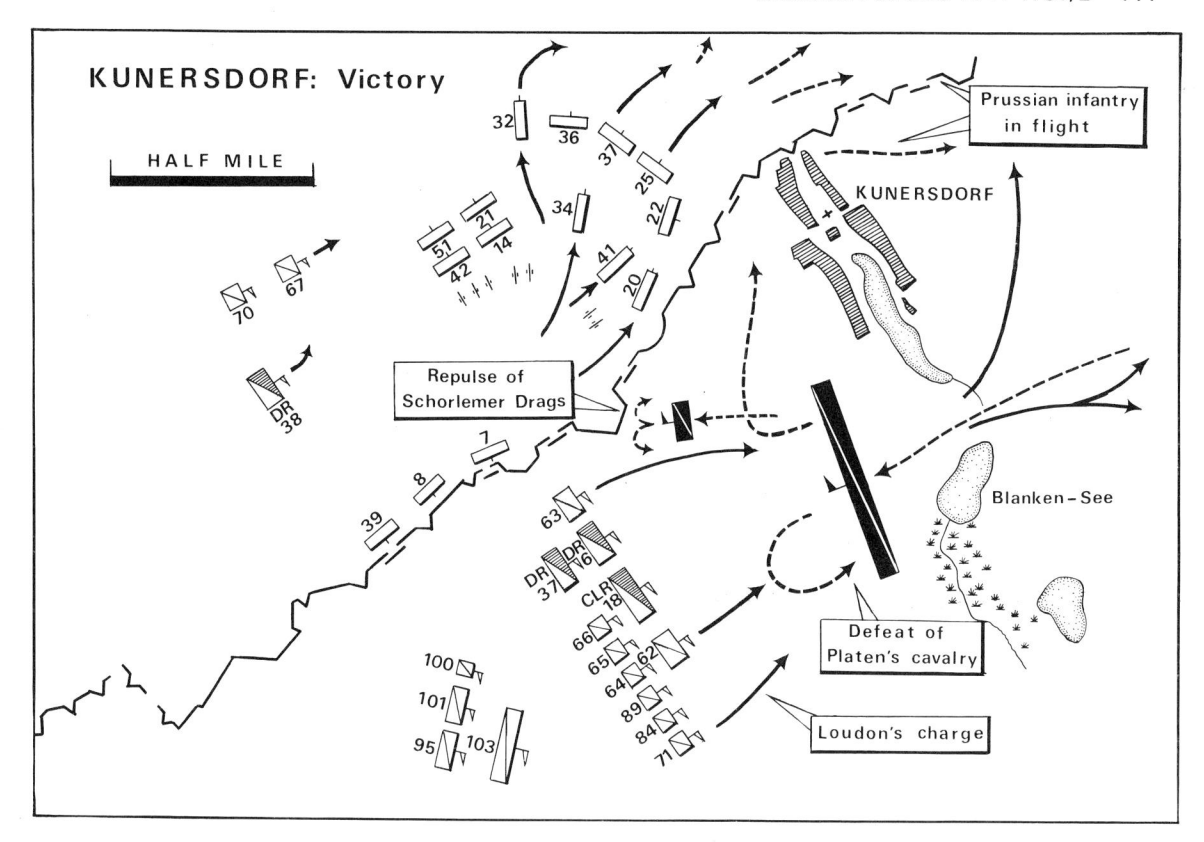

Blanken-See

Defeat of Platen's cavalry

Loudon's charge

With the Prussian infantry making so little progress beyond the Kuh-Grund, Lieutenant-General Platen began to feed the cavalry across the line of ponds by Kunersdorf and threaten the southern flank of Saltykov's position. However, the five squadrons of the Schorlemer Dragoons were destroyed by the fire from the Grosser-Spitzberg, and before the rest of the Prussian horse could assemble it was hit in the left flank by a series of attacks by the united Russo-Austrian cavalry, which had been brought together by Loudon. The Prussians fled through the passages between the ponds, or made a circuit to the north of Kunersdorf and plunged into their own infantry. The Prussian foot soldiers had been on their feet now for sixteen hours or more, they had seen thousands of their comrades killed at their sides, and towards six on this burning afternoon they gave way *en masse*. A mob of men were caught on the Mühl-Berge and massacred by the Russian bayonets and secret howitzers, while a last reserve of two squadrons of the Leib-Cuirassiers was overwhelmed by the Chuguevskii Cossacks, who captured their commander and a standard. The king himself was saved only through the courage of *Rittmeister* Prittwitz and one hundred escorting hussars.

Loudon set off to chase the Prussian cavalry, while Totleben with the light troops was sent in pursuit of the main body. The Russians were feeble in the way they exploited their successes, but even so the enemy loss amounted to about 19,000 men, and Frederick by his own admission was for a time left with just 3,000 formed troops.

Considering the calibre of the enemy and the scale of the combat, the battle of Kunersdorf ranks as the greatest Russian feat of arms of the eighteenth century. In Vienna Empress Maria Theresa was genuinely horrified by the slaughter of the Russian soldiery, but she consoled herself with the thought that Frederick would no longer be able to use the strategic potentialities of the

Oder for splitting the allied armies. The French were, however, not pleased at all, for they were weary of the war, and feared the westward expansion of Russia. Nothing could have been less welcome to them than the new confidence of their Russian allies, who declared with daunting enthusiasm in October that they were prepared to continue the fight for several more campaigns, and would demand East Prussia at the eventual peace.

Saltykov and his army had every reason to congratulate themselves. The battle had been won through a combination of static defences, massed batteries and mobile reserves. Moreover, Saltykov and Loudon had worked together with complete freedom — the Austrian infantry and guns had fallen naturally under Russian direction, while Loudon commanded the joint cavalry with as much authority as a Russian general. Saltykov wrote in his relation that the victory was an example to the world of the 'unity and harmony of allied forces'. As an historical document Saltykov's account of the battle was clear and accurate, and supported by detailed maps for the benefit of the Conference, and it confirms the impression that he was one of the very few people who ever had a grasp of the terrain and of the sequence of events. Frederick was never able to sort out what really happened.

Elizabeth had a special medal issued to all those who had taken part in the battle, and elevated Saltykov to the rank of field-marshal. The empress wrote to him that Frederick might have been able to find excuses for the maulings the Prussians had received at Zorndorf and Paltzig, but the great day of Kunersdorf must have shown him that he could not overthrow the Russian army even when he had significant advantages. Instead of following the sequence through to what we might think was a natural conclusion, Elizabeth ends by explaining to Saltykov that big battles were irrelevant and risky. Frederick knew very well, she wrote, that the Russians would always fall back again to the Vistula in the autumn, whatever victories they had gained in the campaign. Also, a general action was to be shunned as a matter of principle, for battles were becoming 'more bloody and hard-fought' (Rambaud, 1895, 290).

Now that the main Prussian army was for the time being eliminated from the strategic map, there seemed to be no good reason why the Russians and Austrians should not have joined forces and advanced to the capture of nearby Berlin. Frederick called their failure to do so the 'Miracle of the House of Brandenburg'. It was, in fact, the product of slowness and lack of goodwill on the part of Daun, and the unwillingness of the Russians to put themselves out any further for the allied cause, after two pitched battles which had cost them nearly one-third of their effectives, namely the 4,700 at Paltzig, and another 19,000 at Kunersdorf.

Saltykov was persuaded to bring his army to the west bank of the Oder four days after his great victory. Daun took over the supply of the Russians on this side of the river, but he wished to postpone any further operations until the city of Dresden had been captured and secured by the force of Austrians and Imperial Germans acting in Saxony. Saltykov was in despair:

We had it in our power to terminate the war, by imposing a peace or finishing the thing off in some other kind of way ... the [Prussian] royal family sought refuge in Magdeburg, and Berlin was expecting from one day to the next to act as host to us or the Austrians. (21 September 1759, *SIRIO*, 1872, IX, 491)

The project of uniting the armies was abandoned on 15 September. Over the next few weeks Daun led his Austrians away to Saxony in the west, while the Russians made an unconvincing lunge upriver against the fortress of Glogau. Vienna trusted that the Russians could still salvage something from the year's work by settling down for the winter in quarters along the Oder. On 29 November Saltykov instead embarked on the march all the way back to winter quarters on the Vistula, thus returning a poor reward for all the sacrifices of this glorious campaign.

The collapse of Saltykov, 1760

Russia faced the campaigning season of 1760 with

CAMPAIGNS OF 1760 AND 1761

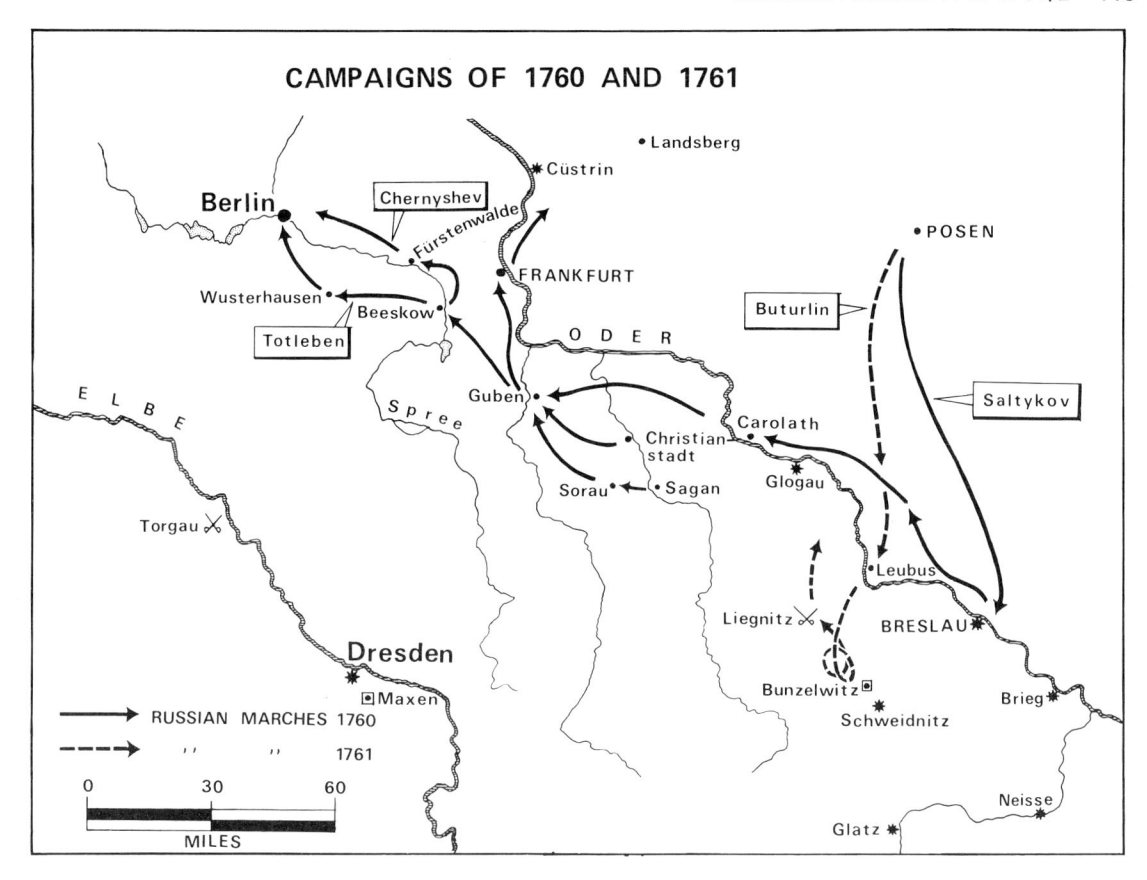

a reasonably well-found field army of about 60,000 men. Saltykov at first projected a campaign conceived purely in Russian interests, designed to open up the Baltic coastline by reducing Colberg or some other port. The scheme was, however, rejected by the Conference on 30 March, for St Petersburg genuinely desired to make another trial of co-operation with the Austrians, and substituted a plan for an advance in several columns to the middle Oder between Glogau and Crossen, there to establish *points d'appui* for eventual winter quarters. General Totleben was meanwhile to operate with the flying corps in Pomerania. Somewhat later an amended plan directed the march further upstream against the Silesian capital of Breslau, where the army could act in closer proximity to the Austrians. Altogether it was possible to heap up 375,000 allied troops against Frederick's 200,000 Prussians. Various details gave the allies further cause for encouragement. General Loudon was assigned to command the Austrian force in Silesia, and Saltykov 'expressed public satisfaction concerning the appointment of this fine general, which augments the hope that the two sides will offer each other the most energetic assistance' (Count Brühl, 4 June 1760, Eelking, 1854, 16). For their part the Austrians were glad to hear that Saltykov had been ordered by his government to heed all the directions that were relayed to him from Vienna through the medium of the Austrian deputies.

This time it was the Austrians who took the initiative. Loudon irrupted into Silesia, and on 23 June he defeated and captured the Prussian general Fouqué at the road junction at Landeshut. Another important strategic point, the border fortress of Glatz, was taken on 26 July. Unfortunately Loudon did not have the physical means of reducing the city of Breslau, which would have been the most valuable prize of all.

The Russian army lurched into motion only on 26 July, and although Chernyshev hastened ahead with an advance guard of 25,000 men, the Austrians were already at grips with the King of Prussia. On 15 August Chernyshev listened impotently to the sounds of battle from Liegnitz, where Frederick was beating off a badly co-ordinated Austrian attack on his position.

The Russians spent the next weeks in useless marching and counter-marching. The provisions promised by the Austrians had not materialised, and the Russians had no siege artillery with which to reduce Glogau, which would have given them a firm footing in the theatre. These disappointments accentuated a malaise which had gripped the Russian army for some time. Saltykov felt miserably tired and unwell, and Chernyshev had to write to St Petersburg that he had virtually abdicated the command, and that the army was sinking into disorder.

On 12 September Saltykov was compelled to resign in favour of Fermor, in the capacity of acting commander. Fermor could not be admitted to the permanent command, in view of his unpopularity, but the Conference hoped that he would serve well enough for immediate purposes.

The Berlin raid, 1760

Fermor's first mandate was to give effect to a remarkably enterprising scheme which had first been suggested by Montalembert, the French representative at Russian headquarters. This envisaged nothing less than a kind of commando raid writ large, in the form of a joint Austro-Russian descent on Berlin, the capital of Prussia. Montalembert rightly calculated that this blow would compel Frederick to hasten towards the threatened city, and so break up his concentration in Silesia. For this purpose the Austrians told off Lieutenant-General Lacy (son of the Russian field-marshal Peter) with a force of 18,000 Austrians and bitterly anti-Prussian Saxons. On the Russian side Major-General Totleben was to lead the way with an advance guard of 5,600 men (three regiments of hussars, three of Cossacks, two of mounted grenadiers; four battalions of foot grenadiers, and fifteen guns), while Lieutenant-General Chernyshev came pounding up behind with a main body of 12,000 (seven infantry regiments and some cavalry).

Totleben set out on 26 September, and prosecuted a march by way of Sagan, Sorau, Guben, Beeskow, and Wusterhausen, which he reached on 2 October. On that day Chernyshev arrived at Fürstenwalde, having taken the route Christianstadt – Sommerfeld – Guben – Beeskow. The Russians arrived in dribs and drabs outside Berlin, almost simultaneously with three small contingents of Prussian reinforcements which rushed in through the gates. On 3 October Totleben's Cossacks reconnoitred the defences, to the consternation of the citizens, and his main force was up later in the day. Chernyshev's troops streamed in between 5 and 7 October. On the last of these days Lacy arrived with his Austrians and Saxons, and by 8 October allied troops to the number of 37,000 were arranged around Berlin on both banks of the Spree. The Prussian garrison amounted to no more than 14,000 men, in spite of the reinforcements, and the allies prepared to deliver an assault at seven on the morning of 9 October. According to Chernyshev it was 'impossible to describe the impatience and greed with which the army awaited this attack. Expectation was written on every countenance' (Korobkov, 1940, 128).

Very early on the 9th, two Prussian commands slipped away from the city, and at four in the morning Totleben on his own authority allowed very generous terms of capitulation to the commandant, von Rochow. Chernyshev did what he could to remedy the damage. The Brandenburg and Halle gates were delivered up to the Austrians, with the promise that 50,000 thalers would be set aside for them from the 'contributions', while Panin managed to overhaul the Prussian troops on the way to Spandau, and eliminated 3,300 of them in the process.

This episode, like the events which followed, is possibly explicable by reference to the character of Totleben. He was notorious as an 'ignorant braggart' (Ligne, 1795-1811, XVI, 42), entirely typical of the contemporary tribe of 'worthless self-made gentlemen, devoid of honour and feeling, unprincipled and bold' (Totleben, 1762, II, 5). Count Totleben came from a Thuringian family, and he had seen service in the Saxon, Prussian and Dutch armies before he came to Russia early in the Seven Years War, allegedly drawn by the prospect of fresh employment. Palmenbach praised his activity in the 1758 siege of Colberg, which helped to secure him the rank of major-general in the Russian service, and Apraksin and Fermor gave him the money and facilities to raise a corps of light troops in the conquered provinces and St Petersburg. Totleben's clownish escapades gave rise to a host of stories, and nobody paid much attention to a warning which was dispatched by the Russian resident in Danzig, who had heard from Hamburg that this individual's loyalty was suspect.

Now at Berlin the wilder elements among the Austrian and Saxon forces gave full vent to their hatred of things Prussian. The Russian regulars in contrast behaved with scrupulous concern for private property, as we might have expected from their exemplary conduct in East Prussia, but there at first seemed no explanation for the excessive regard for the wealth of the community and state. Totleben was under orders to exact the greatest possible contribution from the municipality, and destroy all the war industries and objects of military significance. Instead he almost immediately abated the initial demand for four million thalers to one of one-and-a-half million, payable in instalments. Totleben was persuaded to spare the gold and silver factory and the *Splitgerber und Daum* bronze foundry as private property, and instead of confiscating the weapons held by the citizens *en masse*, he arranged to have a few hundred old firearms delivered up at a designated spot. The pieces were thrown into the Spree and promptly fished out afterwards.

Only 62,000 thalers are said to have been confiscated from the state treasury, and historians are in disagreement as to the real amount of damage inflicted on the archives, the clothing factories, the Mint and the Arsenal (see Grosser Generalstab, 1890-1914, pt 3, XIII, 267; Korobkov, 1940, 284). At any rate, many of the Russians were furious at the leniency, and under some pressure Totleben agreed to blow up the powder mill — an operation that was carried out so clumsily that fifteen Russians were killed in the explosion.

The Austrian and Saxon diplomats would have liked to have seen the allies plant themselves for the winter around Berlin. However, the expedition had been conceived only as a short-term raid, and Frederick was likely to arrive in the neighbourhood in considerable force. The Russians and Austrians accordingly evacuated Berlin on the night of 11 October and on the following day, and they made for their parent armies with some speed. Chernyshev reached Frankfurt on the 13th, and Totleben arrived on the 14th.

The only other event of note was staged on the Pomeranian coast, where a desultory siege of Colberg was broken by the Prussians in September. This disappointment did not detract from the glory of having lorded it in the enemy capital for a few giddy days. Confidence and self-satisfaction were evident in the St Petersburg cabinet, and the Vice-Chancellor, Vorontsov, who was normally so sensitive to French feelings, remarked to a French diplomat that Poland was 'a poor country, which, within the next fifty years, ought to be divided among its neighbours' (Oliva, 1964, 179). The more than generous conduct of the army produced in Voltaire's words 'a more favourable impression in Berlin than all the operas of Metastasio', and the operations had been conducted so economically that after a campaign spent in enemy territory the army ended with only 131 combat deaths, and a complement of manpower that was more than 9,000 over strength.

While it would be unhistorical to condemn these feeble proceedings from a neo-Clausewitzian viewpoint, there were some Russians at the time who felt that they ought to have exploited the advantages of 1760 with more resolution. On 6 November the Prussian merchant Gotzkowsky reached Fermor's headquarters and delivered a request to reduce the outstanding instalments of Berlin's contribution still further. Gotzkowsky relates that Fermor turned down the plea, reminding him that the Russian demands were moderation itself, compared with the ones which

Frederick had made on the merchants of Leipzig, and 'some of the generals, who were present at this conversation, declared that if they had been in charge of this expedition, they would have dealt with us in a very different manner' (Gotzkowsky, 1768-9, I, 64).

Buturlin's command, 1760-1

By December 1760 the Russian field army of 83,000 men had almost completely forsaken the Prussian heartland, and was drawing up winter quarters along the Vistula and in East Prussia. Its generally excellent condition reflected not just an easy campaign, but something of an administrative triumph on the part of its new commander, Aleksandr B. Buturlin. To all appearances this gentleman's accomplishments were more modest still than those of the self-effacing Saltykov. Tales were current concerning his noisy, night-long drinking orgies, and people were willing at the most to allow Buturlin a certain talent for survival. He had begun his career as one of Peter's 'batmen', and was bound to the great man's daughter Elizabeth by ties of lifelong friendship.

Opinions began to change in Buturlin's favour when he got to work on the army in the autumn of 1760, armed with a severe instruction from the empress. While he carried out a reduction of the baggage of all ranks, he filled the magazines with requisitions and purchases from the people of East Prussia, clothed and armed the troops from the convoys that were coming through from the homeland, and exchanged the broken-down horses for good remounts. At the close of 1760 the Conference presented an eulogy of Buturlin's efforts to the empress, and one month later the Marquis de l'Hôpital testified that the army was 'in a splendid state' (Rambaud, 1895, 338).

Totleben's treason, 1761

The Conference based the planning for 1761 on the sensible principle that 'the diminution in the King of Prussia's strength is only temporary, and of such a character that unless advantage can be taken of it, he will build up his force to a still greater degree than before' (Korobkov, 1940, 291). Under the influence of Buturlin, the Conference directed the main army along the familiar axis towards the middle Oder, from where it could reach out to an army of 70,000 whitecoats under Loudon, who was now the Russians' favourite Austrian general. At the same time there lingered a hankering after Saltykov's plan for an offensive in Russian interests through Pomerania to the fortress-port of Colberg. Totleben was therefore to inaugurate a secondary operation in this direction with his flying corps, which was reinforced by a brigade of infantry to a strength of 14,000.

Totleben's troops scampered over Pomerania in the early weeks of 1761, and he actually began a distant blockade of Colberg before he was driven back by superior Prussian forces in the middle of February. Thereafter, Totleben's conduct became less and less explicable except in terms of treasonable correspondence with the enemy. He was finally arrested at the end of June, when confidential documents were discovered in one of the boots of his go-between, the Silesian merchant Isaac Sabatky. Totleben was court-martialled and sentenced to death in 1763, but his good luck did not desert him even in these dire straits. The sentence was commuted to one of exile, and he was able to return to the Russian service after an interval of six years.

The capture of Colberg and Schweidnitz, 1761

The operations on the Baltic theatre languished until early September, when a detached corps descended on Colberg under the command of Lieutenant-General Rumyantsev, one of the ablest of the younger generation of Russian leaders. Frederick had been given ample warning by Totleben of the threat to this vital port, which enabled him to strengthen the defences, and bring the garrison of the fortress and the adjacent entrenched camp to 16,000 men. In addition, a force of Prussian cavalry under Platen executed a destructive raid on the great magazines at Posen, and carried on to the hinterland of Colberg, where he hovered in Rumyantsev's rear and constantly threatened to break through to the relief. Rumyantsev's own command was reinforced to 20,000 troops, and finally to 35,000 by the end of November.

For these reasons Rumyantsev's attack on Colberg resembled a miniature campaign rather than a regular siege. The Russian squadron under Admiral Polyanskii lent effective inshore support until the onset of bad weather compelled the ships to return to Revel. Rumyantsev was therefore reduced to his own resources, and he kept his force in being through organising a systematic programme of requisitions from the locality. Two battalions of jaegers (the first of the kind in the Russian army) operated to good effect in the broken country, and General Berg proved to be a more than adequate replacement for Totleben as commander of the light horse. Colberg finally surrendered on 16 December, after most of the defenders had broken out. The enemy field forces withdrew into Mecklenburg after a clash with Berg's cavalry four days later, and all Prussian Pomerania was left in the hands of the Russians.

On the main, or southern theatre, Buturlin's army moved into Silesia to a strength of 50,000 men. By the second half of August the force was across the Oder and acting jointly with Loudon's 70,000 Austrians. For the first time in this war the Russians and Austrians had met in a spirit of whole-hearted co-operation, and over a period of three weeks they stood within reasonable distance of attaining the goal for which their sovereigns had gone to war. Frederick and his 55,000 troops stood at a disadvantage of more than two to one, and they were hemmed into a small tract of land in southern Silesia, where they dug themselves into an entrenched camp at Bunzelwitz, and lived off convoys of precious supplies from the powerful new fortress of Schweidnitz. All the armies were suffering equally from exhaustion and thirst in one of the hottest of those torrid summers of the Seven Years War.

The same question of supplies, and especially fodder, was the consideration which finally compelled the allies to break up their concentration of force. The assault on the Prussian position was three times postponed, and finally abandoned in early September, when Loudon appeared at the Russian headquarters and announced that the lack of forage must force the two armies to draw apart. As an earnest of co-operation, however, the Austrian corps of Beck (eight hundred infantry and forty squadrons) came to Buturlin, while the 20,000-strong corps of Chernyshev (twenty battalions and three regiments of cavalry) went to the Austrians.

Buturlin fell prey to pitiful irresolution, once he was separated from the vital influence of Loudon. The Conference urged him to strike once more at Berlin, but his nerves were shaken by the news of Platen's circuit in his rear, and after assembling a series of councils of war he made back to quarters on the lower Vistula.

Only Chernyshev was left to uphold the honour of Russian arms on the main theatre of war. Loudon was not the man to be disheartened by the departure of most of his allies, and when he heard that Frederick was once more manoeuvring in the open field, he took the opportunity to pounce on the fortress of Schweidnitz, where Old Fritz had left a small garrison. On the early morning of 1 October the allies marched to the assault to the number of twenty battalions of Austrians and eight companies of fine Russian grenadiers. While the Austrians assailed the Galgenfort, the leading Russian grenadiers threw themselves into the narrow ditch of the Bogenfort in a human wave, which enabled their comrades to march over the bodies and carry the parapet behind. The Russians were said to have been fired by drink, but when they reached the ramparts of Schweidnitz town they remained in perfect order, and not a single grenadier left the ranks to plunder the houses. Under the influence of this blow Frederick abandoned southern Silesia and recoiled to Breslau.

Though barren of 'decisive battles', the campaign of 1761 significantly altered the strategic map of Europe in favour of the alliance. Just as the reduction of Colberg gave the Russians a firm footing in Pomerania, and an advanced landing point for seaborne supplies, so the storming of Schweidnitz afforded the Austrians an open door into Silesia. Frederick's two flanks therefore crumbled away, and in the winter he learnt that a new government had come into power in Britain, and was declining to renew the subsidy to Prussia. Under the weight of this accumulation of misfortunes, Frederick wrote to Finckenstein on 6 January 1762, instructing him to prepare for negotiations to save the remnants of the Prussian monarchy.

The Russian army in the later Seven Years War

The nature of intensive and prolonged wars is to drive forward the military art in an almost geometrical rate of progress, so that the struggle in the final years may share more in common with the next conflict, albeit lying decades in the future, than with the first campaigns of the original war in question. These comments apply with particular force to the Russian army of the Seven Years War.

More than in later ages, armies in the eighteenth century needed the stimulus of actual warfare in order to spring into life — rather like blood dripping on Dracula's ashes. Hence the repeated appeals of commanders to their sovereigns to commit the troops to war, almost *any* war, in order to keep the forces *en haleine*. In peacetime the men were usually in poor physical condition, and schooled in tactics which were of little relevance to real combat. By the same token the officers were devoid of the experience of moving large formations, and they lacked the guidance of anything but regulations of the most routine kind. It was accepted that commanders would give directions of a more relevant nature on the actual theatre of war.

A military historian most sagely remarks that:

Between 1748 and the outbreak of the Seven Years War in 1756 we seem to step from one era to another. When we read of the operations of the latter war, we seem at last to be dealing with modern times, to be reading about officers who ... are living in a world where the ideas which still affect us are beginning to germinate. The Industrial Revolution and *les droits de l'homme* are only just around the corner. The Age of Methodicism is passing. The Age of Reason is in its high summer (Young, 1970, 49).

In this war we gain an impression of some interesting advances in the expertise of the various belligerents. The British acquired a formidable amphibious striking power. On the Continent the armies learnt to operate in semi-independent formations, as witness the Austrians at Hochkirch in 1758, the French at Bergen in the following year, and the Prussians at Burkersdorf in 1762. However, the relative advance of the Russians was the most striking of all, because their programme of military reform had begun so late, and because they needed time to learn the conditions of warfare in a Western theatre. Whereas the Austrian effort fell away after 1760, and the French and Prussians approached exhaustion, the Russian army continued to increase in combat effectiveness and strength (to more than 100,000 in 1761).

The improvement of the Russian army could be seen in many particulars. Fermor had the sensible idea of grouping the regiments together into permanent divisions and corps. Nothing came of the project, but as some compensation the army underwent a number of beneficial reorganisations. The third battalions of the infantry regiments had been left behind in East Prussia towards the end of 1757 as a measure of desperation, consequent on their parlous state. Later in the war, however, these units came to be seen as a most useful device for receiving and training up recruits, and Buturlin gave a proper organisation to these 'supply' battalions, and to the corresponding 'supply' squadrons of the cavalry regiments. This excellent system was abandoned after the war, much to the regret of Rumyantsev. A further useful measure was the break-up of the Observation Corps, after the battering at Zorndorf and Kunersdorf, and its re-constitution in 1760 as three regiments of artillery (see p. 121).

As the war went on, Elizabeth and the Conference were increasingly concerned to see their commanders tighten up the discipline of the army, while assuming more initiative and responsibility in operational matters. The empress wrote to Buturlin on 28 September 1760 'We cannot at the present moment prescribe your operations, since time is short, and you are on the spot, and better placed to see and direct everything' (*AKV*, 1870-95, VII, 442). When the Conference intervened in Buturlin's proceedings in the next campaign, it was to chide him for holding so many councils of war, and urge him into offensive operations. The Conference deserves credit for working out plans of campaign more speedily than earlier in the war, while their application on the theatre of operations was facilitated by the relatively genial relations which now obtained between the Russian and Austrian commanders.

Following the strictures of Kostyurin and Elizabeth, the baggage of the army showed some diminution of the monstrous trains of 1757 and 1758. The abandonment of the *chevaux de frise* and the advent of a new canvas pontoon afforded some alleviation, and it was hoped to reduce the official baggage still further by restricting the infantry regiment to ninety-six carts, and the cavalry regiment to fifty-five. Scales of private baggage were also stipulated, if not exactly adhered to.

In the distant days of 1757 Apraksin had transported his supplies bodily with the army, just as if he had been campaigning in the steppes. Over the following years the Russians, however, felt their way towards more flexible means of subsistence. First of all, Fermor brought the chief supply officials closer to the army (see p. 81), and then in the last campaigns the Russians began to exploit the resources of the theatre of war in an energetic way. This was a policy especially associated with Vasilii Suvorov, who became the new *General-Proviantmeister*, and who replaced Korff as governor of East Prussia in September 1761. The regiments were allowed considerable freedom to collect grain on their own account, while supplies for the army as a whole were raised by compulsory exactions in East Prussia and even on occasion in neutral Poland, and assembled by contractors in magazines along the Vistula. By the end of 1760 Buturlin calculated that the requisitions in East Prussia had already saved Russia four hundred thousand roubles.

Transport animals were so scarce that seven thousand oxen were brought from the Ukraine to enable the army to retreat from Pomerania to Posen in the late autumn of 1760. Horses were therefore rounded up in the Neumark and Pomerania to help to make up for the deficiencies, and in East Prussia Vasilii Suvorov made the population form a transport train of two thousand horses, with which they had to deliver up their quotas of provisions at assigned spots.

The new means of subsistence were applied with notable success by Rumyantsev in his Colberg campaign of 1761. He raised the supplies in the first instance by a scheme of orderly requisitions, then forwarded the foodstuffs to his corps by means of a chain of provision magazines which were planted along the principal roads and waterways.

Greater vigilance may be detected at all levels. In 1759 Rumyantsev furnished the commandant of the Vistula fortress of Thorn with a comprehensive set of instructions, telling him to subject all travellers 'save well-known noblemen of substance' (24 May 1759, Rumyantsev, 1953-9, I, 241) to narrow questioning, and set out his own spies in places of public resort. Two years later Rumyantsev provided the final evidence which put an end to the treacherous career of Totleben. While the cuirassiers were retained with the main body of the army, the light cavalry ranged afield with increasing confidence, in the knowledge that if needs be they could bring into play their muskets and carbines, and their complement of mobile unicorns. It was a pity that the flying corps remained so long under the command of Totleben, who gave way to Berg only in the final campaign.

Saltykov was the first to see some potential in the Cossacks, who for most of the war had been regarded as an unmitigated curse. Saltykov's patrols failed him badly during Frederick's passage of the Oder before Kunersdorf, but the Russians were not to be caught off their guard so embarrassingly again. Seven thousand of the Don Cossacks were available by the second half of 1760, and they were used in large formations backed up by artillery, and not dispersed in penny packets among the divisions as before. Good leadership from regular officers and firm support from dragoons helped to improve the performance of the Cossacks still further, and the Prussian cavalryman Warnery reckoned that 'the Cossacks present a very dangerous enemy for the Prussian hussars, on account of their speed as much as because of their numbers' (Warnery, 1788, 313).

Developments like these helped the main Russian army to move across the theatre of operations with more freedom than before, as was evident in Saltykov's advance from Posen to Paltzig in 1759. The regiments now marched by divisions in separate columns, instead of in a single mass, and the daily rate of march increased from four or five miles to a respectable ten. Detached corps could press on with still greater speed when necessary, as when Panin hastened to Chernyshev at Berlin in 1760, and Dolgorukov marched to join Rumyanstev at Colberg in 1761.

If the congealed heap of regiments and baggage at Zorndorf represented the nadir of Russian battle tactics, the later actions show the Russians feeding unengaged units to threatened points with impressive skill, as happened with the regiments of the left wing at Paltzig, and of the right at Kunersdorf. It became a rule to form a third line of all arms as a general reserve. Paltzig likewise represents the first occasion in the war that the Russians had resort to fortifications on the battlefield. Works of this kind became one of the keys to victory at Kunersdorf in 1759, and from that time both infantry and cavalry regiments were furnished with entrenching tools which they carried around on carts.

Fermor's *General Disposition* of 14 July 1758 (see p. 100) remained the general guide for the management of battle, though in 1761 Buturlin added a number of points which were derived from the experience of the more recent campaigns. He was concerned in particular to endow the battle formations with depth. The third line, or reserve, was to be stationed 150 paces to the rear. No less importantly, 'the practice of the enemy offers clear proof that they direct their main attack against the flanks of the army, and not the centre. We must therefore do everything we can to fortify and strengthen the flanks.' Certain brigades were to be earmarked for this purpose in advance, so that they would know exactly where to go when they were called upon. On the level of minor tactics,

since the enemy usually open fire first, and launch a lively attack, we should counter by sparing our men and cartridges, and seek to anticipate the enemy fire by opening up with our artillery at a suitable range, and especially when they begin to deploy in our presence. (Maslovskii, 1888-93, II, 347)

All of this relates to the standard linear tactics of the eighteenth century. However, in his little campaign around Colberg in 1761 Rumyantsev showed that he was ready to explore new avenues of thought with as much enthusiasm as some of the pioneers who were appearing in France and Germany. In accordance with an instruction of 24 June, the corps was trained to move across country in columns of various sizes and patterns, but more particularly in regimental column of 'divisions' (see p. 62), and by a two-regimental square formation of four battalions, which could face to front or flank as occasion demanded. Rumyantsev envisaged his columns as compact, defensible formations, which could march and deploy into line with speed and convenience. However, despite what Soviet historians have written on the subject, we are still very far from the notion of employing columns as a formation with which to deliver attacks with cold steel.

For some time now Rumyantsev had been meditating how to form bodies of light troops. Lambert met him at Riga in 1757, and 'frequently chatted with him about the service of light infantry, in which matter he was a complete imitator of Brigadier Turpin de Crissé'* (*AKV*, 1870-95, VI, 490). The final spur came with the impending operation against Colberg, and the need to match the Prussian jaegers and free battalions. On 18 August 1761 he told Second Major Ivan Ivanovich Meller-Zakomelskii of his decision to set up a force of 1,040 light infantry. These were to be arranged in two battalions of five companies each. The troops were to be drawn as far as

* Author of *Essai sur l'Art de Guerre*, Paris 1754.

possible from men who had been hunters in civilian life, and who had lived together in the same regiments. Their equipment was to be light, though for the sake of self-sufficiency they were to carry provisions for three days in their knapsacks. This command was to act in co-ordination with Berg's cavalry, and its mode of operation was so alien to the mentality of the times that Rumyantsev had to spell out the tactics very specifically, instructing Meller-Zakomelskii that he was to employ the men in woods, villages, ravines and similar broken terrain where they could take advantage of the ground.

In the later years of the war the Cossacks were largely purged of their old vices, as we have seen, while the performance of the regular cavalry shows a sustained and impressive improvement, first evident in the counter-attacks at Zorndorf, and culminating in the victorious hammer-blow at Kunersdorf.

Artillery pieces of the new invention continued to reach the army throughout the war, and by 1760 the Russians owned a powerful and balanced park of artillery, comprising:

1 field artillery: 218 cannon, 224 unicorns, 168 howitzers
2 regimental artillery: 175 cannon, 21 unicorns
3 siege train: 210 cannon, 1 howitzer, 35 unicorns, 117 mortars.

However, the events at Zorndorf brought home to Shuvalov and others that the artillery stood in as much need of reorganisation as of new hardware. The first reforms were undertaken in 1759, and they received a new impetus from January 1760, when Major-General Aleksandr Glebov assumed command of the artillery of the field army, and Colonel Tyutchev (the hero of Gross-Jägersdorf) took the regimental artillery in hand.

The field artillery was arranged in four administrative brigades, which were in turn divided into tactical batteries of very unequal size. The largest batteries amounted to as many as twenty-four cannon and unicorns, and were to be found to the number of three along the front of the first line of the army. The batteries of the second line had each about nine pieces, and in addition to supporting the first line they had the very important task of preventing the enemy from penetrating between the lines from the flanks. Such an arrangement of artillery in depth proved most effective at Paltzig in 1759. So as to provide a final resource of firepower and ammunition, Glebov made provision for a 'reserve' artillery of field pieces and ammunition carts. The reserve artillery moved separately from the army on the march, lest it should get in the way of the columns, and on the battlefield it was held ready to intervene in the case of necessity. Glebov made his reserve park the subject of a very detailed instruction, which remained in force into the second half of the nineteenth century.

Glebov likewise penned a useful *Verordnung* on the relations between the field artillery and the officers of the line. At the highest level the chief of the field artillery answered directly to the commander-in-chief. By the same principle, the other artillery officers accepted the directions of the local senior officers of the field army, while remaining under the obligation to report to the chief of the field artillery.

At Zorndorf the total complement of professional gunners stood at 1,576 men. This paltry establishment had serious consequences, for the artillery was always dependent on the infantry to some degree to serve as well as protect the pieces. On this bloody day of battle the infantrymen found more pressing occupations, and the artillery suffered so badly that on 29 April 1759 Petr Shuvalov asked Fermor to set up three special artillery regiments, which could provide the necessary support. Little could be done until Shuvalov's beloved Observation Corps was disbanded in 1760, releasing 14,000 men who were reassigned by Tyutchev in May of that year to three full Artillery Regiments, which were formed on the plan of 1759.

Hard experience also helped to determine the tactical handling of the artillery. At Zorndorf the ammunition carts had been stationed close behind the parent pieces, which brought with it crowding, confusion and a series of devastating explosions. From 1759, therefore, just one cart accompanied the relevant pieces at a distance of thirty paces, while all the rest were kept under cover at fifty paces. Glebov expected the heavy pieces of the first line to open fire at about 1,700 paces. The lighter field pieces and the regimental artillery added their voices at just over 900. At 600 paces or less most of the pieces changed their loads from roundshot to canister, though the 8-pounder unicorns and the 3-pounder cannon were to reserve their canister until 160. Glebov adds:

When our infantry and cavalry undertake an attack, the artillery must cease to fire with canister, so as not to hurt our own men, but instead cast shells over their heads, so as to damage the enemy reserves and deter them from joining their forward troops. (Maslovskii, 1888-93, III, 173)

This must be one of the earliest provisions ever made for indirect fire on the battlefield.

The cumulative effect of the labours of Shuvalov and his associates was most impressive, and matched in its own time only by the achievement of Prince Liechtenstein in Austria. In the process the Russian artillery lost the last traces of the *Streltsy* guild, and emerged as a professional and self-sufficient arm of the Russian military power.

The death of Elizabeth, 1761-2

Only the death of Russia's sovereign was capable of setting at naught the magnificent work of her soldiers. Early in December 1761 the Austrian ambassador Mercy reported scenes of indescribable panic in St Petersburg, consequent on a dangerous turn in Elizabeth's health. As the empress became weaker, Mercy pressed Vorontsov to exact from Grand Prince Peter, the heir apparent, a formal promise that he would hold to the alliance. So valiant on the battlefield, the Russians were contemptibly craven at court, and Vorontsov took to his bed rather than have to face Peter. After long agonies, Elizabeth died between three and four in the afternoon of 6 January (new style date) 1762, leaving the memory of perhaps the most beloved of the rulers of Russia.

Peter III and the great betrayal, 1762

Shortly after Elizabeth's death, Princess Dashkova saw the Semenovskii and Ismailovskii regiments pass beneath her windows to render homage to the new sovereign. The soldiers 'appeared sad and downcast. They were all talking at the same time, but in a murmuring undertone, a suppressed and sinister muttering that was so disturbing and tense that I wished myself a hundred leagues away' (*AKV*, 1870-95, XXI, 35).

Almost every gloomy prediction was confirmed in the brief but extraordinarily damaging reign of Emperor Peter III. With the Third Reich behind us, we can see Peter more clearly than ever as an object lesson in the fascination which the trappings of Prussian militarism can exercise over people of weak mind. Peter's leanings were evident

29 Peter III. He is wearing the gorget of the two senior regiments of the Guard, with the commemoration of Narva, 1700

30 Peter III and his suite

from his early days as Prince Ulrich of Schleswig-Holstein. He constituted his corps of troops in the likeness of the Prussian army, and he brought the menagerie with him when he came to Russia.

As if his features were not sufficiently repugnant and grotesque, he planted on his head a tricorn with a vertical forepeak, like that of his model, the King of Prussia. However he resembled Frederick to about the same degree as an orang-utan resembles a human being.
(D'Eon, 1837, I, 127)

We could scarcely expect an energetic prosecution of the war from a man who could refer to Frederick as *der König, mein Herr*. Old Fritz now played up his part to perfection, awarding Peter the order of the Black Eagle, and reducing him to gibbering joy when he made him a Prussian lieutenant-general.

As the new sovereign, Peter did much the kind of thing that was expected of him. He invited back old Münnich from his long exile, he sought to introduce uniforms of skimpy Prussian cut, and he renamed the regiments after their colonels, which was another Prussian fashion.

Far more shocking was the extent to which Peter worked out his fantasies in the world of statecraft. Each step seemed more extreme than the last — first an armistice agreement with the Prussians on 16 March 1762, then a treaty of peace on 2 May, and active steps to evacuate East Prussia, when no conceivable power could have got the Russians out, if Peter had ordered them to stay. Most intolerable of all, Peter commanded Rumyantsev to prepare an army for war against Denmark, as Holstein's dynastic rival, and he put Chernyshev's corps of 20,000 troops at the disposal of Frederick in Silesia. The Austrians therefore found themselves outnumbered in their last campaign of the war, and some of Chernyshev's Cossacks actually raided across the border into Bohemia.

Such proceedings outraged many thinking military men. The Guards knew that Peter spoke of them as 'Janissaries', and they feared for their place in the new order, while many of the active officers could not live with the idea of ranging themselves alongside the Prussians. The resentment was channelled and directed by that most unlikely of patriots, Peter's German wife Catherine (see p. 92). Just like Elizabeth twenty years before, Catherine was assiduous in building up a military power base in St Petersburg, and drawing useful men to herself through her physical charms and the justice of her cause.

The Semenovskii Guards came over to Catherine, and so did the Ismailovskiis under their lieutenant-colonel, Count Kiril Razumovskii. Finally, with 14,000 troops on her side, Catherine was able to force the virtual abdication of her husband on 8 July 1762. He was killed shortly afterwards in a drunken brawl.

The new empress temporarily countermanded the evacuation of East Prussia, and put Chernyshev on his guard against Frederick in Silesia. It was, however, impossible for Catherine to renew the war, for her country was in need of rest and consolidation, and her allies were fading fast. On 6 August 1762 the people of Königsberg were told that East Prussia once more stood at the disposal of its king, and the Russian columns began their long eastward march.

The place of the Seven Years War

'In this bloody war the Russian army won great glory, advancing considerably in the estimation of all peoples' (Saikin, 1818, 7).

The intervention of Russia represents her supreme military effort in the eighteenth century, and though barren in immediately tangible results, it advanced her well on her way to the West.

Viewed in one perspective, the Russian military achievement represents the culmination of the work of Peter the Great and Münnich, and the fitful inspirations of the generation of the 1750s. Not many people would quarrel with the judgment that:

The Russian army, for all the inadequacies of its organisation, and despite the perfidy and treason of some of its commanders, and ultimately of the emperor in person, nevertheless showed itself the most victorious of the allied forces. Even the action at Zorndorf was an indecisive battle, rather than a victory for Frederick. The Russian soldiers gave Europe a model of valour and endurance, and if the flag they raised over Königsberg was finally pulled down ... Europe was forced to see that the rise of Russia to the status of a great power was no longer to be withstood. Russia's place and role in the circle of European states was consolidated. (Korobkov, 1940, 328)

Almost alone among the belligerents, Russia at the end of the war gave the impression of total invulnerability, and the sense of having something mighty in reserve for the rest of the century. Thanks largely to the presence which had been established by Elizabeth, her successor Catherine was able to advance Russia's borders deep into Poland and the Middle East, and become the arbiter of the quarrels of Western Europe. Frederick of Prussia assiduously avoided the occasion of any further conflict, and in 1769 he described Russia to his brother Prince Henry as 'a terrible power, which in a century will make all Europe tremble' (Rambaud, 1895, 11).

Considerations like these have weighed heavily with strategists, statesmen and historians, but they were not so evident to many Russians of the time, who felt themselves cheated of an adequate return for all their sacrifices. Chernyshev urged some compensation in Poland, by pushing the frontiers to the Dvina and Dnieper at the next change of throne in that benighted country. The response of Princess Dashkova was no less heartfelt. Travelling to the west in the winter of 1769-70 she put up at the *Russia Hotel* in Danzig, which was the resort of all people of distinction, and in the principal public room she found two paintings of battle scenes from the Seven Years War, full of victorious Prussians, and heaps of dead, dying or crawling Russians. She enlisted the help of two Russian diplomatic officials, who went out to buy oil colours in blue, green, red and white:

After dining we barricaded the door, so that nobody could surprise us at our work. Then I and these two gentlemen, who were expert with the brush, repainted the uniforms of the troops, so that the Prussians, the alleged victors in the two battles, became Russians, whereas the beaten troops were rigged out like Prussians. We passed the entire night in this occupation. (*AKV*, 1870-95, XXI, 128)

Five   The Russian Soldier

Origins and recruitment

We break the thread of our narrative to devote a little attention to some questions of wider significance. Many famous armed forces have had one salient characteristic which has seized the imagination of the commentators — the leadership of a great commander, perhaps, or the existence of an officer corps of peculiar pride and pretensions. However, the authorities leave us in no doubt that, alone among armies, the Russian has commanded attention over the centuries through the outstanding quality of its rank and file.

He is the finest soldier in the world [declared the émigré Count Langeron]. He is as abstemious as the Spaniard, as enduring as a Bohemian, as full of national pride as an Englishman, and as susceptible to impulse and inspiration as French, Walloons or Hungarians. He combines all the qualities which go to make a good soldier and a hero. (*RS*, 1895, LXXXIII, 199-200)

Our Russian paragons of military virtue prove to be oddly elusive, when we try to determine their numbers. Out of the vast geographical extent of the Russian empire, only certain areas came into the reckoning for human resources, and in particular the historic heartland of Great Russia, where the taxable males amounted by the middle of the century to only about seven million. Just 3.3 per cent of the Russian male population was to be found in military service in the 1760s, and only 3.1 per cent in the 1790s.

The system of compulsory military service certainly produced vast phantom armies, which existed on paper to a strength of 200,000 men at the beginning of the century, and more than 400,000 at the end. However, very little convincing detail ever came to light from official sources, and informed observers put the effectives a good deal lower. Manstein reckoned that in the Turkish and Swedish wars of the 1730s and 1740s the number of the combatants in the various Russian armies never reached more than 100,000 together (Manstein, 1860, II, 366-7), while at the end of the reign of Catherine II, Langeron rated the regular forces at 140,000 infantry, 30,000 cavalry and 8,000 gunners. Coming down to individual operations, we note that no more than about 60,000 troops took the field in the campaigns of Peter I, or the great battles of the Seven Years War. Suvorov had 16,000 effectives at the storm of Praga in 1794, and only about 20,000 men on his Swiss campaign of 1799.

Patently 'in all the armies of Europe, there obtains a huge difference between the forces which exist on paper and those which actually appear under arms. But nowhere does this discrepancy reach such proportions as in Russia' (Langeron, *RS*, 1895, LXXXIII, 197). For a start we have to strike off the garrison regiments, the Land Militia, and the unmobilised masses of the Cossacks and Asiatics. This leaves the rump of the regular field regiments, which in their turn had to set aside thousands of men to drive and escort the carts and tend to the officers' needs, as well as losing many more to the civil administration, which employed them on police and tax-collecting duties. Long-dead heroes might remain on the regimental books for years on end, to the benefit of the company commander or the colonel, and when the fiction became difficult to sustain, it was the custom to write the ghosts off as casualties in the first battle of the next war, which consequently appeared in the official lists as a bloodbath.

To the outright casualties we have to add the many more men who were lost on forced marches of a thousand or more miles across the vast expanse of Russia. Once the process of destruction was begun, the losses progressed at a geometrical rate, for the survivors had to cover for all the duties of their defunct comrades. Writing of the First Grenadiers, Semen Vorontsov explains that 'during all the years I commanded a regiment, I never had more than eight hundred men under arms out of an establishment of 1,360, even though my regiment was always the best up to strength of the army' ('Zapiski', 1802, *AKV*, 1870-95, X, 479).

In the middle of the century we encounter the first notions as to the proportions and distribution of the armies. As regards the positioning of the regiments, Peter the Great, Münnich and even Petr Shuvalov seem to have been guided above all by considerations of economy, but for strategic reasons Bestuzhev and Apraksin wished to hold a powerful concentration against the Prussians and Swedes in the comparatively barren Baltic provinces, even though provisions were more expensive there. From 1746, therefore, forty regiments of infantry were stationed in the north, as opposed to a mere six in the interior of Russia.

The debate was widened by Catherine's Military Commission of 1763-4, which declared that:

the strength of the army consists not in great numbers, but in the upholding of good discipline, the quality of the training, sound maintenance, firm loyalty, but most basic of all, the existence of common language, religion, customs and blood. (Beskrovnyi, 1958, 307)

The foot soldiers were defined as the repository of firepower, which was the most important element in tactics, and so the infantry were to stand to the cavalry in the ratio of two to one. The Commission also mentioned that the army must be disposed in such a way as to provide for the defence of the land against all likely enemies, which gave rise to some interesting memoranda over the following years. In 1777, soon after the Pugachev rebellion, Rumyantsev penned the most stimulating of these essays, a comprehensive set of *Thoughts Concerning the Composition of the Army*. He asked the government to provide for the needs of 'internal peace', as well as to evaluate the threat to 'external security' according to the extent of the country and the nature of the potential enemies. He therefore proposed a balanced disposition of forces between:

1 a coastal army in the Baltic provinces and Finland;
2 a Ukranian army in the Ukraine proper and White Russia;
3 an army on the Volga, to keep an eye on the Turks;
4 a reserve army in central European Russia.

In one perspective Rumyantsev's paper (which was never taken up) would have helped to resolve the old conflict between the Western and Eastern commitment (see p. 6), by institutionalising the differences between the two. In another it embodied the military, political and geographical considerations that were going to shape the 'theatre' concept, so powerful in later Russian military history.

Calculations of this kind were based on the system of compulsory military service, which was established in 1705 and maintained throughout the century. Münnich set himself against the principle, as did Potemkin later in the century, but the facility of voluntary enlistment was extended only in very exceptional cases. The scheme of things scarcely permitted otherwise. The peasants lost more and more of their freedom with almost every decade of the eighteenth century, and the

31 Russian infantry of the later eighteenth century. Probably a more accurate representation than the stiff and gloomy figures of Viskovatov. Note the medals worn by the musketeer on the left

lords rightly feared that the serfs would desert them in droves for the relative attractions of the army, if they were ever given the chance. The state was willing to placate the nobility in this respect, for the advantage of employing willing recruits was offset by the administrative difficulties of having to make provision for volunteers. Service was literally lifelong in the first half of the century, and afterwards defined as twenty-five years, which for most individuals probably amounted to the same thing. Sick leave was granted grudgingly, and under the most exact conditions. We have the case of one of Peter's dragoons, Fedor Durakov, who collected a bullet wound in his right temple, another on his left cheek, a sword gash in the hand and three more on his head. The state allowed this hero a temporary release from service, on condition that he submitted himself for re-examination no later than twelve months hence, on pain of death.

Manpower was summoned for the army (and in smaller numbers for the fleet) from the product of proportional levies on the liable male population. This grew nearly three-fold in the course of the century (5,528,742 in 1722; 6,643,335 in 1743; 7,363,348 in 1761; 14,532,200 at the end of the century). Altogether seventy-three levies were raised between 1705 and 1802. The heaviest recruiting of all fell in the middle years of the Great Northern War, when between 1705 and 1715 40,000 males were raised annually, many of them being lads of fifteen or sixteen. Anna's Turkish wars also made considerable calls on manpower, but Elizabeth's peacetime army was so fully up to strength than no conscripts were summoned between 1749 and 1754. However, 231,644 men were called up between 1754 and 1759 for the confrontation with Prussia, and Catherine's first Turkish venture weighed so heavily on the population from 1768 as to account for some of the support for Pugachev's rebellion. The frightened government raised no levies in 1774 or 1775, which was anyway the beginning of a period of external peace, and took in only small numbers between 1776 and 1781.

The priests were exempted altogether and a series of local and occupational concessions permitted many merchants, manufacturers, freeholders and the like to furnish substitutes or buy exemptions, which effectively reduced the product of each levy by up to ten per cent. The populations outside Great Russia escaped entirely until 1776, when an obligation of fifteen years' service was imposed on Little Russia, the Baltic provinces, and the *odnodvortsy* (freeholders) of southern central Russia (at least according to Mikhnevich, in Skalon 1902-c.1911, IV, pt 1, bk 1, sect. 1, p. 191. Madariaga enters Little Russia as 1773, and the Baltic provinces as 1783).

Almost every year the machinery of conscription was set in motion on the grandest possible scale by the Senate and the War College, which worked out the deficiencies in manpower from the army returns, and raised the appropriate numbers simultaneously throughout all the liable 'governments'. The system was clumsy and inconvenient, as Petr Shuvalov pointed out in a memorandum of August 1757 (*AKV*, 1870-95, VII, 428-9).

At the local level, the inspection and assembling of recruits was managed by appointed functionaries — originally by appointed *voevodas* and officials of the governments (from 1711), then by military officers (from 1732), and finally by local authorities working under the eye of regimental officers and senior officers appointed by the War College (from 1757). These people were concerned to see that the recruits met the specified requirements for age (usually from seventeen or twenty to thirty-five) and height (usually at least five feet two inches), and that they were in prime physical condition. The soldier needed a good set of teeth to bite open his musket cartridges, and a full complement of digits to hold the stock and press the trigger. This was why the country abounded with gap-toothed *muzhiks* and ones who had been careless enough to lose their fingers. (The availability of conscript manpower permits the same principle of narrow physical selectivity to be applied today by the Soviet Army, which chooses little men to crew its tanks.)

Certain regional characteristics became evident as the geographical basis of recruiting was widened in the course of the eighteenth century. The people of Little Russia and the southern 'free provinces' provided the regular army with its best natural horsemen. These folk had something of the spirit and liveliness of the Poles, and Rumyantsev thought it significant that in that part of the world 'every peasant has a saddle, and rides around on his horse, which he loves, manages and tends to perfection'. Semen Vorontsov was in agreement, and said that he could invoke the whole army to 'bear out the assertion that none of our regiments of cuirassier or carabiniers may be compared with the hussars recruited from provinces like Kharkov, Akhtyrka, Izyum or Sumy'.

The people of Great Russia were of a heavier cast, and their tendency towards high cheekbones and slit eyes betrayed an ancient mixture of Finno-Ugric blood. Here the horse was degraded to a draught animal, and when the peasant returned from his fields he led his plough-horse by hand, rather than risk a ride. 'If, however, the Little Russians are incomparably superior as horsemen to the Great Russians, the latter are beyond doubt the finest infantry in the world' (Vorontsov, 'Zapiski', 1802, *AKV*, 1870-95, X, 480). Langeron notes that among this race 'the Siberians are the best-looking and the strongest, but the men raised from around Moscow are the most intelligent' (*RS*, 1895, LXXXIII, 150). Vorontsov regretted that towards the end of the century this excellent stock of infantry was diluted by the recruiting of Finns and Estonians, who were fit to be employed only as batmen or drivers.

The officials at the collecting stations had no concern with the initial rounding-up of the recruits, which distressing business was left to the landowners and their stewards, and the choice of the village communes. With the end of voluntary enlistment, military service came to be seen as a sentence of exile and death. Russian rural life certainly had its sordid aspects, which caused a traveller to exclaim that 'to pass to leeward of a Russian peasant is really so terrible an event that I always avoid it if possible' (Reginald Heber, in M. S. Anderson, 1958, 95). However, the existence of many peasants was far removed from a state of brutish misery:

They enjoy good bread, frequent meals of meat and fish, good beer and spirits, as well as garden produce in considerable quantity if no great variety. A warm sheepskin, and a small but well-heated house gives them ample protection against the cold. (Wonzel, 1783, 21)

A certain tension was therefore evident when the landowner had to raise his quota of recruits:

If among his peasants or servants there is an incorrigible thief, then he will send him. In the absence of a thief, he will dispatch a drunkard or an idler. Finally if his peasants are made up only of honourable men (which is almost impossible), he will consign the feeblest person he can find. (Langeron, *RS*, 1895, LXXXIII, 148)

The last that the friends and relations were likely to see of the recruit was a scarcely recognisable being, who was shaven and shorn, and stumbling at the end of a chain. Nobody dared to rescue or shelter him in this state, and his acquaintances saw him off 'as if it was his funeral, with tears, lamentations and songs, the purport of which is that they shall never see him more' (Parkinson, 1971, 103).

Except possibly for the trans-Atlantic passage of the negro slaves, it is difficult to think of a collective ordeal in the eighteenth century which compares with the march of Russian recruits to their regiments. Peter the Great's immediate concern was to prevent the men from escaping from the fate that was determined for them, hence the notorious if short-lived 'branding decree' of 1712. It soon became clear that the losses from desertion were far exceeded by those resulting from cold, starvation and exhaustion. Almost every reign therefore saw the publication of sets of rules, designed to regulate the movement, rations and quartering of the recruits, and the way they were received in the regiments. The Petrine ordinances of 1713 and 1719 were succeeded by those of Münnich in 1734, and these in turn by Elizabeth's recruiting codes of 1757, which became the foundation of Catherine's *General Establishment* of 1766, which remained in force until 1802. Nothing was capable of improving the recruit's lot, except perhaps the attention of a Münnich or the temporary expedient of the 'supply battalions' in the later Seven Years War. In the 1770s Rumyantsev was shocked by the pitiable sight and deplorable waste of the recruits who straggled through to his army on the Turkish theatre, only to die from the first fatigues of military duty. Twenty years later Langeron could still put the mortality of every recruit levy at fifty per cent.

For such recruits as survived this experience, the initiation into regimental life was probably managed with a little more sense and humanity as the century wore on. A final sorting-out of men according to arm and regiment was undertaken when they reached their destination, and the recruit was assigned as soon as possible to *artel* and company, where his training was taken in hand by designated officers and NCOs. Commanders like Rumyantsev introduced systematic programmes of instruction, beginning with the perfection of the individual, and the various private and public regulations emphasised the need for positive motivation in the process of transforming peasant into soldier (*Instruction for Cavalry Colonels*, January 1760; Major-General Bibikov's *Instructions for Infantry Colonels*, November 1764; Semen Vorontsov's *Instructions for Company Commanders*, January 1774).

The life and spirit of the Russian soldier

It requires an impossibly great effort of the historical imagination to recreate the mentality of the eighteenth-century Russian soldier, so alien to the thought-processes of Western man. While seeming to endure so much with bovine apathy, he maintained a self-sufficiency of body and mind that were beyond the ability of his masters to crush, just as they defy our feeble investigations.

Like his counterpart in foreign armies, no Russian soldier ever made his fortune from his pay. The rate for a Petrine infantryman was eleven roubles a year, which was handsome in itself, but soon reduced to about half that sum by the heavy deductions made for the cost of clothing, equipment and cleaning materials. In 1731 Münnich gave the private a full nine roubles free of deductions. Early in Catherine's reign, however, the generals reckoned that this liberality was encouraging 'drunkenness and various disorders' (Klugin, *VS*, 1861, XX, no. 7, 86), and reduced the emolument to seven roubles fifty kopeks.

The young soldier soon became aware of compensations that could not be measured in cash. In the reigns of Peter I and Catherine II the soldiers were likely to spend the summer months in strenuous exercise camps, but each September they settled down for eight months of reasonable plenty in billets among the civilian population. Every regiment was assigned a town or a zone of villages for its quarters. The officers liked to set themselves up like little princes in country mansions, while individual soldiers requisitioned the resources of up to four houses at a time. On the whole the troops treated the peasants of Great Russia with more regard than elsewhere, but even here it was possible for the householders to return to the little villages around Moscow after the great manoeuvres of 1799, and find their homes 'wrecked and plundered as completely as if in the time of the Nogai Tartar raids' (Turgenev, *RS*, 1885, XLVIII, 77).

We learn from a few stray references that a number of the soldiers of the marching regiments were married, and that the wives accompanied the menfolk on campaign, where they made themselves generally useful by washing the soldiers' linen and other services. Something which approached a normal family life was possible in the garrison regiments, for here the husband had a settled abode, and the opportunity to follow a spare-time civilian trade. The offspring received a good basic education in the famous Russian 'garrison schools', the first of which were founded by Peter in 1721. The number was augmented by Münnich in 1732, and again through the incorporation of the 'counting schools' in 1744. Four thousand pupils were entered on the books by 1765, and 16,500 by the time Paul I established a unified system in 1798. Already in the 1730s a garrison school was established in principle in every garrison town, and open to all the children of the garrison and the marching regiments of the locality. The instruction was in the hands of NCOs, who taught the lads reading, writing, arithmetic, and sometimes also the art of playing on the drum and fife.

It is of some significance to note that the first Russian national civilian schools were opened in 1786. Indeed, in Central and Eastern Europe the advance of education owed less to the vapourings of Rousseau than to the state's need for minor functionaries and NCOs. The 'genuine' Russian NCOs (as opposed to the officer candidates) were usually of excellent standard, thanks to the large number of literates, and a commitment to the military life which often proceeded from childhood.

Even the unmarried soldiers had the support of a family of sorts in the shape of the *artel*, an ancient, sacred and uniquely Russian institution. It is best described as a little community of soldiers, organised on the basis of about four to every company, and run by veteran corporals who were designated *artelchiki* by election of the men. Signifying far more than the German *Kameradschaft*, the *artel* had roots deep in Russian village society, with its peasant meetings and sense of joint enterprise. 'Looking at our soldiers' way of life, we notice something of the same phenomenon. We discover that the Russian soldiers too have a peculiar form of shared possession, and similar communal assemblies' (Klugin, *VS*, 1867, XX, no. 7, 82).

The *artel* received all the tangible assets of the soldiers — spare pay, plunder, and the proceeds from the sale of the civilian clothes of the recruits and of the effects of dead soldiers. The monies were used to buy meat and vegetables, as well as the horses and carts necessary to transport them. Considerable sums of money were often lodged in the *artels*, and hard-up Russian officers and regimental commanders would go cap in hand to the soldiers to request a loan. An officer could commit no more disgraceful offence than to fail to pay back an advance from this source. Suvorov cashiered one of his colonels who had offended in this respect, and gave out the reason as simple military incompetence, so as to conceal the crime.

The self-sufficiency of the troops was further promoted by their habits of eating — 'no soldier is easier to feed than the Russian' (Silva, 1778, 53). The rations were distributed by the company captain, at a daily rate of a little salt and a couple of pounds of rye or barley, which came either as flour, or as grain which the soldiers ground for themselves in their little hand mills. Vegetables, meat and everything else were provided from the soldiers' own resources.

Flour for up to ten days was usually carried in the company transport, and the basic diet of bread and water permitted the Russians to launch expeditions with the minimum of preparation, which was useful when campaigning in the sandy Mark of Brandenburg, and vital when it was a question of outmarching the French of the Revolution. When opportunity offered, the soldiers excavated a hole to serve as an oven. The cavity was heated to a high temperature with firewood, after which the ashes were raked out and cakes of dough inserted to bake. The blackened pieces of *sukhare* were then retrieved from the hole, and either cut into lumps the size of walnuts, or put in to bake a second time.

This biscuit, if one may call it so, looks like the burnt mortar that comes out of an oven, and it requires good teeth, and better gums to chew it, which latter often bleed in the operation. They seldom, however, eat it without bruising it, and making it into a porridge, with boiling water, salt, and a spoonful of flour (Tielke, 1788, II, 99).

When cabbages were available, they were chopped up and cooked with lard into a kind of sauerkraut called *shchi*, which was lightly fermented and eaten as a soup with great quantities of water. *Kasha* was a glistening, greyish-brown preparation of buckwheat, which to Western tastes reeked of a rancid poverty, but was eaten with relish by the Russians.

The soldiers' requirements in drink were equally modest, since, with a few lapses from grace, their habits stood in marked contrast to the drunkenness of civilian society. For most of the time they were content with water, though they liked to brew up fermenting flour and the remains of their biscuit in earthen pots, producing a yellowish small beer that went by the name of *kvas*, 'which they prefer to ordinary water, though it tastes disgustingly to anyone who is not used to it' (Masson, 1859, 328).

Many of the soldiers renounced meat altogether, during the season of the Lenten fast, and the Prince de Ligne saw 'religious fanatics who preferred to die rather than take a meat broth' (Ligne, 1890, 73). Peter had to compel the soldiers to eat flesh by force, while Apraksin persuaded the Synod to dispense his army from the fast when on campaign.

Marching with his regiment to the Crimea in 1783, Pishchevich admired the tirelessness and resource of these folk. He noted how the Russian soldier:

manages to appear all neat and prepared for the next march, after a whole day on his feet. At the end of each day's progress, if he is not required to perform sentry duty or look after the horses, he at once betakes himself to the river, where he washes his small clothes. These are still not dry when a mighty voice summons him back to drill in the ranks. Nothing is more agreeable than to pass through a camp site, and watch as the soldiers pitch their tents with miraculous speed amid the steppes, and then get down to their various occupations (Pishchevich, 1885, 36).

The more acute observers resisted the temptation to regard the Russian soldiers as superhuman. Speaking from long experience, Manstein detailed the hardships consequent upon the religious fasts, the endless marching of the Turkish campaigns and the almost total lack of medical care, which combined to kill off the soldiers through scurvy, malaria, dysentery and other maladies (Manstein, 1860, I, 265). Another formidable indictment comes from the Duc de Richelieu, who saw the Russian army in the campaign of 1790, and remarked on 'the little attention which is generally paid to the care of the men — a neglect which is as impolitic as it is barbaric, when you bear in mind that the population is pretty small in relation to the great size of the land' (*SIRIO*, 1886, LIV, 162). Richelieu attributed these wasteful ways to the facility of raising fresh recruits through conscription. Then again, in 1799 the Russian prisoners of the French were amazed at the good treatment they received in the hospitals, and at the skill of the French physicians and surgeons, so unlike their own butchers, who were liable to carry out every surgical procedure with a single blunt knife.

It is notoriously difficult to evaluate the severity of the discipline of a military institution. If our attention is drawn by punishments of a spectacular and barbaric nature, we can easily overlook the small currency of blows and torments which have been meted out in every army known to history. Severe corporal punishments have been linked in Russian historical folklore with the rule of Empress Anna and her Germans. In fact the native Russians were as ferocious as any Teuton. The disciplinary code of Peter the Great is associated with the sound of crunching bones and the stink of roasted flesh, and while the death penalty was effectively abandoned by his daughter Elizabeth, the result was to add to the severity of the allegedly non-corporal punishments. The ordeal of the gauntlet was liable to result in the death of the victim, after about eight runs, while a single stroke of the knout, a long whip of untanned elkskin, could crack a spine or spill out intestines on the ground. Rumyantsev brought a tradition of severity into the reign of Catherine the Great, which was perpetuated by individual monsters of cruelty into the 1790s. Potemkin alone sought to ameliorate the barbarities as a matter of principle, with the full support of Catherine and her laws.

It would certainly be difficult to maintain that Russian discipline was more draconian *per se* than the codes that were enforced, for instance, in the British Navy, or the army of Frederick the Great. Where, however, Russian punishments probably differed in kind from those of the West, was in their casual nature. On parade the NCOs belaboured individuals with hundreds of little blows of a stick at a time, delivered with a flicking motion that was compared with that of a valet beating dust from his master's clothes. In contrast, the Austrians awarded punishment only after a formal court martial, and then fifty of their blows were enough to consign the man to hospital. Captain Gryazev explained that the difference 'proceeds from the fact that the foreign armies are composed of freemen, and ours of serfs. The first kind of person must be treated with some circumspection, whereas our men are long-enduring and docile' (Orlov, 1898, 161).

More demeaning than some of the outright punishments was the practice of treating soldiers as the merest chattels of their officers. These gentry were accustomed to hauling off the men as the impulse took them to serve as orderlies and servants, or to perform unpaid labour in the regimental workshops or on private estates. Some of the worst instances of cruelty were associated with the generals and regimental commanders who trained up troupes of musicians and acrobats for the delectation of themselves and their guests. Langeron claims that these sadists were quite happy to see nine men die under the stick for every one who survived to give an accomplished performance.

Coercion ought to have been unnecessary, for the Russian soldiers had an inborn love of music, and 'it is by no means unusual to hear them sing for five or six hours at a stretch without the slightest break' (Richelieu, *SIRIO*, 1886, LIV, 161). Every company had some jolly men who were pleased to cavort in front of the troops on the march, and lead the singing, and Langeron himself experienced no difficulty in summoning up a choir of up to three hundred soldiers to grace festivities.

We can only admire the courage of those soldiers who entered protests and petitions against the more outrageous of their commanders. In the early part of the century the plaintiffs were actually questioned under torture (which was Peter's way of discouraging litigation), and if their story failed to stand up they were themselves liable to be sent to the scaffold or the galleys. Some of the malcontents made common cause with peasant or tribal rebels, as happened in 1705-6, in 1707-8, and during the last great uprising of 1773-5, when 240 NCOs and men of the First Saratov Fusilier Regiment embraced the cause of Pugachev. Many more troops simply deserted, hoping to escape across the borders or melt into the civilian community. Desertion was already evident in the first months of Peter's new army, and it reached massive proportions in the years from 1705, when the nation began to feel the full rigours of conscription. In the autumn of 1707, for example, desertion left the twenty-three dragoon regiments on the Vistula with 8,000 men out of an establishment of 23,000. In 1710 20,000 recruits from Moscow alone deserted on the march to their units. Draconian decrees against desertion were published in 1705, but they worked to no better effect than the amnesty which followed in 1711.

Few detailed researches have been pursued in the desertion in the post-Petrine period, though it seems to have fallen off considerably in the 1730s. The dismal phenomenon made a reappearance in the reign of Catherine the Great, as a response to the tyrannical conduct of the colonels. Semen Vorontsov claims that he encountered 'thousands of our brave compatriots serving in the Prussian and Austrian armies, and people who have been to Sweden assure me that they have seen more than two thousand Russians in the ranks of the Swedish army at Stockholm and Gothenburg' ('Zapiski', 1802, *AKV*, 1870-95, X, 472).

Alongside these indictments it is only fair to set the many instances of leadership of a more enlightened kind. Fair and considerate treatment could go some way towards winning over the Russian soldier, as Bolotov discovered when he was training his company in the 1750s. Two decades later Vorontsov told the officers of his regiment, '*it is harmful and indecent when a soldier comes to hate his musket. This can happen all too easily, if he is beaten during instruction, and sees his weapon only as the instrument of his torture*' ('Instruktsiya Rotnym Komandiram' 17 January 1774, *VS*, 1871, LXXII, no. 11). Potemkin set his face against all cruelty, and purged the officers who maltreated the men. Emperor Paul was no less attentive in this regard, though he has been given precious little credit for it by the Russians.

It was, however, still more important for the senior commander to be aware that the soldiers expected him to be immediately accessible as a friend. Saltykov, Rumyantsev and Suvorov had the gift of exchanging jocular repartee with the troops, who responded by composing little songs in their honour. Conversely the men were affronted if the general showed himself unaccountably ignorant of their names and circumstances. The lenient Potemkin never established fully cordial relations with his troops, nor did his contemporary Count Panin,

who was considerably more indulgent towards the soldiers than Count Rumyantsev, but was much less loved by them than the latter . . . simply because he did not talk with the other ranks. Inhibited by a reserved and austere character, he believed that he could gain the affection of his troops and of mankind in general through just and honourable conduct alone, regarding any other means of winning the soldiers' regard as useless and downright ignoble. (Strandmann, *RS*, 1882, XXXV, 317)

When both generosity and encouragement failed, the Russian officer was left with no alternative but to set a personal example: 'in this army rash bravery is much respected, and, if an officer wishes for the esteem of his troops, he must expose himself with them in a manner that would be esteemed absurd in any other army' (Tielke, 1788, II, 133). Langeron noted how at the bloody storms of Ochakov and Izmail the officer casualties were one-third heavier in proportion than those of the rank and file.

The distribution of decorations was another positive strain in Russian military leadership. At a time when recognition for private soldiers was almost unknown in the West, Peter the Great gave out silver medals *en masse* to the regiments which had taken part in his victories. This good custom was followed by Elizabeth and Potemkin. The veterans sported the decorations proudly in their buttonholes, and it never occurred to them to sell the medals for cash, even when they might be starving in enemy captivity.

Semen Vorontsov observed that the reputation of the individual regiments was known throughout the army, and jealously guarded over the decades. The Astrakhanskii and Ingermanlandskii regiments, for example, earned a glorious name in the wars of Peter the Great, while the First Grenadiers had distinguished themselves at Gross-Jägersdorf and again at Kunersdorf. Vorontsov believed that his officers had the duty of inculcating such traditions as a matter of policy, but in fact they can have been carried on only by the soldiers themselves, for individual companies knew up to three or four captains in a single year, while the whole corps of regimental officers usually changed with the arrival of a new colonel. Out of necessity Peter the Great made and re-made regiments after the bloody battles of the Great Northern War. Thus seven regiments went into the melting pot after the action at Fraustadt in 1707, and they emerged as one. Catherine herself was no great respecter of tradition. She casually allowed the Butyrskii Regiment to be absorbed in the Kuban Jaeger Corps, thus extinguishing the oldest regiment in the army, which had its roots in the time of the *Streltsy*. Conversely, she created an instant elite when she formed ten regiments of grenadiers from the villagers of the monastic estates.

Here we have an indication of the curious malleability of the Russian soldiers, who rapidly became the masters of whatever calling they were told to pursue. Masson, admittedly a hostile witness, asserts that the colonel of the Moscow Grenadiers did not even bother to find out the peacetime trades of his recruits, because he knew how easily they could be re-fashioned for their new life. Thus the Russian regiment became:

a nursery for every kind of art and craft. The low pay of the ordinary soldiers makes it vital for them to stretch their imagination, and make themselves self-sufficient in every respect. They become their own bakers, brewers, butchers, tailors, cobblers, perruquiers, locksmiths, wheelwrights, saddlers, blacksmiths, carpenters, masons, coppersmiths, musicians and painters — in other words, any occupation which comes to mind. Nowhere in the world are there people who are so resourceful. (Wonzel, 1783, 183)

Surprisingly enough, the same nation gave evidence of an ineradicable vein of slavish

32 Grenadier, period of Catherine the Great (Viskovatov, 1844-56)

stupidity. An order, once given, was liable to be executed to the letter:

During a naval battle with the Swedes, a galley sank with several of our Guards officers on board. The commander of the neighbouring galley called out to his men 'Save the officers of the Guards!' One of these unfortunates stretched his hand from the water and called for help. A soldier, before he would consent to haul him out, asked him 'Do you belong to the Guards?' Incapable of making a reply, the officer sank beneath the surface and drowned. (Masson, 1859, 181)

Many Westerners were forced to the conclusion that the Russians must ultimately be guided by force. 'It is scarcely possible for a people to be as fitted for slavery as the Muscovites. They are so corrupt by nature that they will do nothing of their own free will, but must be driven by hard and cruel blows' (Stiessius, 1706, 197). Manstein cites the action of Münnich in reducing one of his major-generals to an ordinary dragoon in the militia:

It might seem a fairly steep punishment for a single instance of cowardice, or rather a lack of expertise in working out an effective plan. But this kind of thing is absolutely essential in Russia, where good treatment makes less impression than severity. They have become accustomed to acting only under duress. Indeed, you can hardly give a set of orders to an officer without adding a whole chapter of threats, which you will put into execution if he falls short. (Manstein, 1860, I, 177)

There was something passive in the very endurance which the Russians showed in battle — 'taken as individuals the Russians are gentle, even timorous. But massed in battalions they manifest a herd-like cohesion which makes them redoubtable, and sometimes unbeatable' (Masson, 1859, 343). It had already been noted that in the wars of the later seventeenth century:

they are lively and ferocious in their first onset, like the Poles and Turks. When, however, they cannot at once break through the enemy ranks, they come crashing back, and let themselves be hacked down by their victors . . . without offering resistance or asking for quarter. (Stiessius, 1706, 204)

Hence the words of Frederick, to the effect that it was not enough to kill Russians in action, for you still had to knock them to the ground. Hence also the Russian soldiers' saying: 'The Turks are tumbling like ninepins, but through the grace of God our men stand firm, though headless.'

The force which resolved every contradiction, and distinguished Russian soldiers from all others in Europe, came from the circumstance that they formed a purely national body of troops, bound together by a belief in a national God. The service of this deity had not much to do with morals, but a great deal to do with the hatred of foreigners, and the performance of rituals of a kind which were calculated to bind all classes of Russian society. At St Petersburg, at the end of the Easter Sunday service, the archbishop's announcement of the risen Christ was the signal for all the men and women present to exchange Easter eggs and kisses. 'These last ceremonies are reckoned so essential, and are so strictly adhered to, that if a common soldier were to meet the empress, and offer an egg, declaring his belief, he would have the honour of an imperial kiss' (Cook, 1770, I, 49).

As the century wore on, the soldiers lost their trust in some of the beliefs that had sustained them in earlier times, like the one which imagined that a man killed in battle came to life on the third day, free and happy in his native village. A great deal still remained, for the Russian God kept his watch over the armies and 'Suvorov, more than anybody else, had a blind faith in this Divinity, and more than anybody else he fostered His cult.' On the field of Zürich, after the battle of 1799, 'there was hardly one of the mortally-wounded Russians who had not clutched at the image of the patron saint which he wore about his neck, and pressed it to his lips before drawing his last breath' (Masson, 1859, 351, 365).

Six   The Russian Officer

The native officer

For most of us terms like 'the Russian officer' or 'the Russian aristocrat' have connotations of dissolute young wastrels, who were freed of care and responsibility by the labour of thousands of serfs, who spent their evenings throwing vodka glasses against the wall, and who finally subsided into unconsciousness among a wreckage of gilded furniture. Patient scholars have shown that the ability, let alone any inclination to lead this kind of life was restricted to a very small proportion of the folk who had the right to call themselves nobility. The highest and proudest Muscovite aristocracy entered the eighteenth century as a tight group of 137 families, which owned a disproportionate share of the 360,000 peasant households, and whose names have become familiar to us as leaders of the army and the state. The Golitsyns were masters of the fate of 7,860 peasant families, and they were rivalled by the Saltykovs, who had an establishment of 7,758. Lesser potentates like the Dolgorukovs, the Sheremetevs, the Golovins and the Volkonskiis still had a clear pre-eminence over all but the wealthiest of the mass of 3,264 noble families which comprised the *dvoryane*, or Middle Service Class of lesser gentry.

The old Muscovite families maintained their relative dominance during the vast expansion of the nobility which ensued in the eighteenth century. While the formal title of 'boyar' died out with Field-Marshal Ivan Trubetskoi in 1750, it was still possible towards the end of the century to point to grandees who maintained the old standards. In Count Ivan Ivanovich Saltykov:

you could see the type of the old boyar, though one who had already become accustomed to European ways. His style of living was grand rather than whimsical. He owned a large but well-dressed train of servants, expensive carriages, and fine, splendidly-harnessed horses. A very large number of people, if not absolutely everybody, had the right to sit at his abundant and tasteful table. His manners, though simple, always bore the imprint of precedence and authority. (Wiegel, 1864-6, I, pt 1, 97)

Prince Nikolai Vasilevich Repnin was described in almost identical terms (Lubyanovskii, 1872, 166-7).

In modern academic circles few subjects are capable of arousing as much rancour as the question of the status of a nation's gentry — whether in a given period they were rising or falling, and who indeed could be classified as gentry at all. Here we give only very broad indications of the people who lost or gained in the eighteenth century after Peter gave definition to the social system, and bent it to the purposes of the state.

At the lower end of the social scale, immobile elements like the freeholders and the very poor squirearchy found themselves subject to conscription and the poll-tax of 1724, and therefore hardly distinguishable from state peasants. The middle class, or rather the town-dwellers, almost doubled in number between 1652 and 1722, and by their taxes they enabled Peter to rebuild the army and government on modern lines. These townsmen too were parcelled and categorised, being classified in 1720 respectively as 'irregular' manual workers, or the 'regular' professional men, merchants and smaller dealers.

Moving up the scale, Peter sought to raise up a privileged but dedicated mass of military men and bureaucrats, whose status would stand in direct relationship to their service to the sovereign. Peter introduced Western military ranks at the beginning of his reign, and a corresponding civilian hierarchy appeared in 1709. Finally, in 1722, the famous Table of Ranks matched a system of fourteen equal grades of military, bureaucratic and court service — a classification so fundamental that it endured until 1917. As we might have expected, the magnates of ancient stock gravitated effortlessly to the highest ranks. At the same time, lesser folk were fired by the prospect now held out to them of climbing to position and honour through state service — an ambition that led to a great increase in the Middle Service Class of lesser gentry (since commissioned rank now brought nobility), and provided the Russian army with most of its officers.

Whether grandees or parvenus, Peter's nobility was supposed to earn its privileges in a very hard way. The names of the male children were entered on official rolls at the age of sixteen, and all save the only sons were assigned to lifelong service to the state — about two-thirds in the army or fleet, and the remainder in the civilian administration. Decrees of 1714 and 1723 bound all young nobles to undergo courses of education, and such lads as were destined for the army were told in addition to undergo a period of service in the Guards. Peter thereby intended to put an end to the scandal of the well-connected young men who appeared as officers, yet were 'either ignorant of the fundamentals of soldiering, or if they have served in the army, have done so only for show and for a matter of weeks or months' (Beskrovnyi, 1958, 169).

No such compulsion was exercised in respect of the newly conquered provinces of Estonia and Livonia. The Baltic Germans were hungry and warlike folk, very much like their cousins the Prussians, and though they were allowed the choice of their manner of life, many of them presented themselves to the army of their own accord.

Over the decades the iron simplicities of Peter's dispensation were gradually eroded. 1736 brought the limitation of the term of service to twenty-five years, and in 1762 Peter III wrought the most fundamental change of all, when on 18 February his decree *Concerning the Granting of Freedom and Liberty to the Entire Russian Nobility* allowed his officers to retire at will from the service. The peasants hoped that they too might benefit from the break in the chain of obligation, and their later disillusionment did much to account for the support which some of them gave to Pugachev's uprising. Catherine did not attempt to reinstate the old social contract, for mass conscription of the nobility had been a crude and indiscriminate means of enlisting officers, and in any case the social and economic advantages of a military career offered sufficient inducement in their own right. By a decree of 1785 she confirmed the nobles' right to freedom from service, except for a primordial duty in 'necessary' time of war, as defined by the sovereign.

The gentry numbered 108,000 males in 1782 (including those of the Ukraine), and by the end of the century a mass of possibly as many as one million people of both sexes had pretensions to nobility. The word 'pretensions' is here used with some care, for if princes and the like abounded, it was only because the absence of effective primogeniture divided up patrimonies of title and land equally among the males of every generation, a process which reduced many of the nobles to the status of little more than free peasants. Holdings of land and serfs were, in any event, widely scattered, and changed hands very frequently among these restless folk.

Clearly, for a great number of the nobles the concessions outlined above signified very little, for state service continued to offer the only prospect of escape from the soil, if not immediate fortune. Pishchevich recalls that as a young officer he was so poor that on the Crimean expedition of 1783 he had to sit with his soldiers and share the *kasha* from their kettle:

The soldiers imagined that I was doing this out of special affection, and liked me all the more on this account. I must avow to my discredit that at the beginning I was ashamed to sit among them ... conceiving it shameful to show familiarity with the kind of men whom the supercilious nobility call, I do not know by what right, the 'dark people'. (Pishchevich, 1885, 38)

Wiegel (Vigel) declares with some exaggeration that in contrast to the state of affairs in western Europe,

in our country the path to glory, rank and riches is open to people of every condition. To the Russians there is something very attractive in the idea of a new name winning great eminence and general renown, and in the very contrast between low birth, and the high position which lucky or able men can attain. We consider it ludicrous when men who are devoid of personal merit like to boast about their ancestors.

He conceded, however, that grandees who did not give themselves airs could win 'new claims on our respect', and that the Russian nobility as a whole possessed something unique in Europe — 'the right of owning people of their own race' (Wiegel, 1864-6, I, 97).

The constant recruitment of fresh faces into the nobility was not to the taste of the aristocrats who were already firmly entrenched. The conservatives had a second line of defence in the process of admitting a new officer to the regiment, which demanded the assent of the community of the regimental officers. Such agreement was not always forthcoming from the military caste in later years, and on 18 May 1788 Catherine found it advisable to give fresh encouragement to the commoners to present themselves for admission to the officer corps, and thus to the nobility. On his side, Potemkin offered commissions on a sliding scale of rank for people who brought appropriate numbers of settlers to New Russia. Thus Semen Vorontsov could write in 1792 that peasant officers were infecting half the army at a time when all Europe was threatened by the overthrow of the established order. Among many frightening instances he knew 'the case of one of Count Skavronskii's laqueys, who thirteen years ago served me at table in Italy, and whom I encountered three years later as an officer'. Two thousand sons of merchants had entered the Guards as NCOs, and were procured officer places in the army *en masse*, and 'so at a stroke they and their issue are as noble as the Pozharskois and the Sheremetevs. Can you wonder if the nobility is despised in Russia?' (7 November 1792, *AKV*, 1870-95, IX, 270).

It is possible to piece together a fairly representative picture of the kind of influences which shaped the Russian officers. Generally speaking, the native flavour was strongest in their earliest years. Again and again the veterans harked back to a childhood spent in the surroundings of a smallish country estate, remote from the modern elegance of St Petersburg. Andrei Bolotov (born 1738) recalls the bare rooms of his house, furnished with simple tables and benches, and lined with dark wooden walls hung with pictures of saints. Many of the womenfolk were also constructed in the old Russian style, like Bolotov's mother, or the doting grandmother of Lev Nikolaevich Engelhardt (born 1766), who called him after a son killed in the Seven Years War, and let him run around in a peasant shirt and bare feet. 'Physically my education resembled the system outlined by Rousseau. But I know that my grandmother was not only ignorant of that work, but had a very uncertain acquaintance with Russian grammar itself' (Engelhardt, 1868, 3).

The family home was likely to be found in or near a small provincial town such as Penza formed in the 1760s:

Penza at that time consisted of ten or so not particularly large wooden-built seignorial mansions, and a few hundred huts of the ordinary people, many of which were roofed with thatch and had wattle walls. ... The only architectural adornment was the principal church, which was built of stone ... a certain Mikhail Ilich Martinov was the owner of one thousand souls, and was more hospitable and lavish than the rest of the nobles. He had ... a set of silver spoons, which he set before the more important guests, leaving the others to manage with spoons of pewter. (Wiegel, 1864-6, I, 21-2)

The occasional passage of great people and great events left a deep impression in these simple communities. In the southern provinces the triumphal progress of Potemkin and Catherine was treasured in the memory of many individuals. Older traditions spoke of the march of the Swedes and King Charles, 'gaunt, pale and ugly' (Lubyanovskii, 1872, 9). At Revel on the Baltic the twelve-year-old Waldemar Löwenstern was fortunate enough to witness the sea fight in which Admiral Chichagov destroyed the Swedish fleet of the Duke of Södermanland on 2 May 1790. Count Bobrovskii whisked the lad off in a boat to the battery at the entrance to the harbour.

He was decked out in the magnificent uniform of the Horseguards, in which he was a captain, and so nobody thought of preventing us from landing at the battery. I followed at his heels with unaffected youthful joy. Swedish cannon shot came in our direction, and the whistle they made, as they passed over our heads, put me in a transport of delight. Some of the shot crashed into the side of the old wooden battery, and I noticed that the people around me did not share my happy mood. Some of the old warriors turned positively pale (Löwenstern, *RS*, 1900, CIII, no. 3, 268-9).

Further acquaintance with the outside world was likely to come from an attentive father and a small but good domestic library, such as the one in the Suvorov household. Tutors, governors and literate NCOs were often hired to inculcate the first rudiments of knowledge, and some of the arts and accomplishments of a gentleman. Many young folk were then sent to perfect their education in provincial noble schools, like the Kharkov College or the Revel Ritterakademie, or in boarding schools (*pansions*) such as Ellert's hard-driving establishment in Smolensk. The Russians seemed to have taken readily to the French language, though German became something of an ordeal in the second half of the century, when it lost its place as an important medium of administration and culture. Some people entertained the suspicion that the available foreign tutors were not always the best of their trade, and that something provincial still hung around the culture of St Petersburg itself. Even by the middle of the century, Westerners noted the icons on the walls of gilded ballrooms, the fleas and bugs in the furnishings, the collections of monstrosities in the St Petersburg Academy of Sciences (opened 1724), and the hint of cabbage and sewerage in the air.

In the earlier period Peter was probably right to hold that a direct acquaintance with the Western world was almost indispensable for men who were to be responsible public servants. He sent batches of promising young men abroad in 1690 and again from 1700 to 1705. However, as the eighteenth century progressed, the drive to travel in foreign parts lost something of its force. Large establishments of education were now opening in Russia, and in particular the various military and naval academies, while St Petersburg began to take wholeheartedly to the rococo culture of France, and the secular spirit spread to the provinces. At the same time, observers harboured doubts as to the wisdom of letting young Russians roam abroad, with their wealth, their ignorance and their strong passions. They seemed to learn little, and they reverted to the worst of their old habits when they returned home. In 1717 the tutor Petr Fedorov had to report to Field-Marshal Anikita Repnin on the sorry state of his two sons, who had gone to join Prince Eugene's army before Belgrade:

They are living in the utmost misery on this campaign. The two princes left great debts behind them when they set out from Vienna. When they were still there, they maintained two French companions at their own cost, and this pair led them into great losses. Now that they have arrived at the theatre of war, one of the Frenchmen has robbed your two children and gone over to the Turks, taking with him . . . a horse of Prince Vasilii Anikitich, and from Prince Yurii a saddle, a pair of pistols . . . a sword, a sword knot embroidered in gold, and a pair of breeches. (Strukov, in Skalon, 1902-c.1911, VI, bk 1, pt 1, p. 200)

Some young folk of a more responsible kind contrived to benefit from life among the foreigners. It is significant that two of the greatest military men of the third quarter of the century had youthful experiences in Russian embassies in foreign countries — Petr Rumyantsev in Berlin, and Zakhar Chernyshev in Vienna. Rumyantsev actually enlisted in the Prussian army before he was hauled back to Russia. Chernyshev, more fortunate, was able to return to Austria as Russia's military deputy, and he took part in Field-Marshal Daun's victory at Kolin in 1757.

In Russia the fledgling officer's introduction to military life was almost invariably attended with ludicrous circumstances. Peter desired potential leaders to go through service in the ranks, as we have seen, and in 1736 Anna stipulated that such young noblemen as were destined for the army had to sign themselves up with regiments as 'supernumerary soldiers' at the age of thirteen. The idea was a superficially attractive one, but like all experiments of the kind it resulted in hypocrisy and evasion. The case of Lev Engelhardt was typical. His father secured him a cadetship in the hussar regiment of the wealthy Colonel Drevich, and he later remembered his 'infantile joy when I dressed up in my hussar uniform, and how I was more delighted still when I could play with the sabre and its sabretache' (Engelhardt, 1868, 6). Over the following years Engelhardt passed rapidly through the Ellert and Shklov colleges and the Preobrazhenskii Regiment, and he did a spell of duty as an aide to Prince Potemkin, but his military education proper began only at the age of twenty, when he was taken on as a supernumerary ensign in a marching regiment.

All of this helped to postpone the young officers' first serious break with their families, which in many cases occurred when the summons came to serve on campaign. Engelhardt's father told him 'I would rather hear that you had been killed, than that you had brought shame on yourself', whereupon they shed a few manly tears and parted (1868, 68). Adrian Denisov relates an almost identical ritual, and Tolstoy reproduces the scene for Prince Andrei's farewell to his father in *War and Peace.*

At leisure moments Engelhardt put himself through a course of self-education in fortification and engineering, 'preparing myself to serve with distinction and qualify myself for suitable employment when the occasion might arise' (1868, 95). Engelhardt's bookish concerns were shared by many other members of the officer corps, or at least the ones who bothered to write their memoirs. Löwenstern was categorised as a 'pedant' by his young acquaintances, while Pishchevich claims that by his fifteenth year he was 'already familiar with all the great commanders, and the history of their campaigns was always before my eyes. I preferred Prince Eugene above all. . . . I spent much of every night with a book in my hands' (Pishchevich, 1885, 14). Even the ape-like Aleksei Arakcheev assembled a library of 11,000 volumes, while Rumyantsev, 'whenever he was recovering from the labours of his campaigns, showed the same thirst for knowledge as in his youth. If he heard anybody praising his deeds, he would point to his books and say: "there are my teachers!" ' (Saikin, 1818, 67).

A much more detached approach to their profession was shown by those officers who kept their names on the rolls of the Guard Regiments for any length of time. The Guards had entered the century as the hard core of Peter's new regular army, and distinguished themselves at Narva when the rest of the regiments had earned the contempt of Europe. In later years, however, their concerns lay far from the battlefield, for 'through the many changes in régime the Guard regiments had to some degree acquired the habit of overturning the government by force' (Wonzel, 1783, 47). The successors of Peter the Great sought to direct the Guard, not by cutting down on its numbers or influence, but by adding new units which they hoped would be devoted to their interests, like Anna's Ismailovskii Regiment of 1730. Elizabeth

33 Officer of the *Leibkompagnie*, formed by Elizabeth from her adherents in the Preobrazhenskii Regiment. Black cap with yellow metal decoration and white plume (Viskovatov, 1844-56)

34 NCO and officer of the Chevalier Garde, 1764-96. Full court dress of blue surcoat edged with gold; red coat edged with gold with blue turn-backs and silver lace on sleeves; polished white metal helmet with ostrich plumes (Viskovatov, 1844-56)

showed the greatest consideration for the feelings of the Guards, after the part they had played in her accession, and she never called on them to take the field in the Seven Years War. Catherine the Great was no less beholden to the Guards, and in her reign the bloodless glory of this splendid body reached its apogee. Closest in every sense to the person of the sovereign was the one hundred-strong company of Chevalier Gardes, composed entirely of men of noble blood.

None of this prepared the Guard for the rude affronts it received at the hands of Paul I, who stuffed it with officers of low birth, and augmented it with a battalion of jaegers, a regiment of hussars and a regiment of Cossacks, so creating the balanced corps which went to war against Napoleon.

The social pretensions of the Guard soon matched its political ones, for it offered facilities to the sons of the higher aristocracy to fulfil their obligation of service in the ranks in a most agreeable way. The sprigs of the nobility were entered on the books on the day of birth, and by the age of fifteen or sixteen or earlier they were doing nominal duty as supernumerary sergeants, to the number of a thousand or more in each regiment. The young gentlemen of the Moscow or provincial nobility scarcely bothered to report for service at all, while the St Petersburgers or exceptionally enthusiastic folk could always find servants or substitutes to clean muskets or take over annoying spells of duty on guard. It was pleasing to know that a rank in the Guards was one grade higher than the equivalent rank elsewhere in the army, and that the difference jumped to two ranks if the Guardsman chose to transfer to a marching regiment. Langeron cites the case of the Siberian Grenadier Regiment, which had lost eight of its captains in the bloody storm of Praga in 1794. The surviving lieutenants began to dream of promotion, after ten years of service, but they had to give way to eight sergeants from the Guard, who became captains in their place, probably without having seen a private soldier in their lives. By the 1790s, therefore, ex-Guardsmen account for between forty and fifty per cent of the regimental commanders, and very many of the field officers.

Throughout our period, only a small proportion of the leaders of the army followed a formal course of military education. Things had promised well in the early years of the new army, when Peter was inspired to set up a number of useful establishments on the Western model. Such were the School of Mathematics and Navigation (1701), the two Moscow artillery schools (1701 and 1712) and the two engineering academies (Moscow, 1712-24 and St Petersburg, 1719).

However, the life in the technical schools was of an exacting kind, which of itself was calculated to limit the interest of the nobility. Clothing came to the pupils free, but most of them had to lodge in private houses, where they lived in conditions of near-starvation. These wretches had to turn out of bed at six in the morning, and they pursued courses of instruction until six in the evening. Mikhail Vasilevich Danilov was admitted to the St Petersburg artillery school in 1740, and he explains that the noble pupils were divided into three classes, according to specialisation. He himself was admitted to the first class, or the 'School of Draftsmanship', where in addition to technical drawing he 'also executed some paintings and other works, including landscapes and portraits in oils. Many officers came to the school to see what I had done, and the compliments of these spectators ... increased the application and bent I had for my art.' The quality of instruction was extraordinarily diverse: 'The director of the school was Captain Günter, an obliging and quiet sort of man, who was one of the foremost experts of the time, and who brought good proportion to the design of the whole artillery' (Danilov, 1842, 58). At the other end of the scale stood brutes like the drunken and quarrelsome *Styk-Yunker* Alabushev, who committed no less than three murders before he was finally disgraced.

At the end of three or so years of study, the products of the technical schools became variously NCOs, tradesmen or clerks in the corps of gunners or engineers, from where a few ultimately rose to become senior generals.

As we might have expected, technical education formed one of the first objects of attention for Petr Shuvalov, after he became Master General of the Ordnance in 1756. He combined the artillery and engineering academies, with an establishment of 135 pupils, and he widened the syllabus to embrace civil architecture, Latin and French, dancing and painting. The facilities of the academy included a printing shop, a hospital, a gallery of fortress models, and a small library where the cadets could read foreign publications. Shuvalov selected the instructing staff, and he often attended the teaching periods in person.

At the beginning of her reign Catherine the Great approved a code for the management of the Shuvalov establishment, and renamed it the 'Artillery and Engineering Noble Cadet Corps'. The year 1783 saw some important developments. The engineer and artillery elements once more went their way as independent schools, but in compensation the reorganised artillery academy was increased to admit 400 pupils, and it entered one of the most prosperous periods of its existence under a new director, General P. I. Melissino. This ingenious Greek maintained the broad educational ideals of Shuvalov, and his pupils were to be largely responsible for carrying through the important artillery reforms of the Napoleonic era.

While the beginnings of technical education

may be traced to the earliest years of the new Russian army, the notion of forming young men for the field arms was not taken up until the reign of Anna. The immediate inspiration came from a project of Count P. I. Yaguzhinskii, who, as ambassador in Berlin, had become acquainted with the famous Prussian corps of cadets. Yaguzhinskii's scheme of 1730 was given practical form by Münnich, and on 17 February 1732 the Noble Cadet Corps (1742 renamed the Noble Land Cadet Corps, *Sukhoputnyi Shlyakhetskii Korpus*) admitted its first pupils. The full corps of 360 cadets was lodged in the spacious Menshikov Palace in St Petersburg, and the fledglings pursued a wide course of military and polite education for five or six years from the age of about ten. Münnich turned to Potsdam for inspiration on the practical side, for he believed that French military methods were falling out of date, and 'the King of Prussia sent a number of officers and NCOs to help in setting up the corps, and instructing the young pupils in the Prussian drill' (Manstein, 1860, I, 85).

Bearing in mind the difficulty of procuring adequate education at home, and their ambition to compare in knowledge with the Germans who held the foremost positions at that time, the better nobility and even the greatest magnates were only too glad to have the opportunity to place their children in the Noble Land Cadet Corps. (Wiegel, 1864-6, I, 14)

Anna was delighted with the almost immediate success of the Cadet Corps, and she sent it a white colour with the Imperial arms, exclaiming that 'from these brave sons I will be able to furnish my regiments with able officers' (Anon., 1792, 1).

The first graduates (who must have been fairly elderly) sallied forth in 1734 to the number of eleven. Seventy-eight more appeared in 1736, and from then until the end of the Seven Years War the yearly average remained at about fifty-five. Nearly one-fifth of these entered the civilian service, and the rest were assigned to the army as NCOs, ensigns, second lieutenants or lieutenants. If these numbers were capable of supplying only a tiny proportion of the needs of that large army,

35 Officer of the Cadet Corps, 1732-42 (Viskovatov, 1844-56)

they represented 'almost all the great public servants who were to be one of the glories of the reign of Catherine II' (Wiegel, 1864-6, I, 14).

Experience shows that the very title of 'military academy' is a notorious contradiction in terms, and that over the years many establishments of the kind oscillate between the respective extremes of the military university, and the blood-and-bayonets trade school, without finding a place of equilibrium. The movement to one side or the other has less to do with the merits of the case than the ambitions of the men who happen to be in charge at the time. In Russia in the middle decades of the eighteenth century the civilian ideals gained a clear ascendancy. From the beginning the Cadet Corps was a stranger to the harsh regimes of the other academies, and under Elizabeth the range of activities was such as to fit a young gentleman for almost any station in life. Before the Seven Years War some of the cadets came together in a Company of Lovers of Russian Literature, where they read out and discussed poems of their own composition. Aleksandr Petrovich Sumarokov, one of the graduates of the corps, was impelled by the resonance of Racine's tragedies to compose a native counterpart, *Khorev* (1747), which the company rendered with such distinction that they were invited to deliver a performance on the court stage on 8 January 1750. The piece was repeated many times, and led ultimately to the formation of an imperial Russian Theatre, where Russian plays replaced the French- and German-language dramas which up to then had dominated the Russian stage.

The sense of identity was further promoted by the lively feud which the cadets maintained with the Guards, who lived on the southern side of the Neva,

the effects whereof are sometimes very terrible, and numbers are killed on both sides. The Guards are all accoutered with broadswords, the cadets with small tucks. If the Guard soldier gets one blow, the cadet is no more. But very frequently the cadet shuns the blow, and before the Guard soldier can be ready to give another, the cadet runs him through. (Cook, 1770, I, 42)

From the first, Catherine the Great showed a lively interest in the progress of the corps. In August 1762, just two months after her accession, she increased the establishment of cadets to six hundred, and three years later she appointed the civilian 'lieutenant-general' Betzkoi as head, with the commission to carry out a radical transformation. Betzkoi and his sovereign were led by the writings of Locke, Montaigne, Fénelon and Montesquieu to the conviction that enlightened schooling had the power to 'inculcate proper behaviour and a love of industry, and to confer, by a new education, a new mode of life'. These words are taken from the code which Betzkoi gave to the corps in 1766. Declaring his intention to introduce the cadets to their studies 'as if to an agreeable field, adorned with flowers' (Petrov, in Skalon, 1902-c.1911, X, 35), he had the children taken into the corps as early as five or six, so as to separate them from the harmful influence of their families. In fact the whole is permeated by that mixture of sentimentality and coercion which became the essence of the socialist ideal.

Altogether the instruction in the Betzkoi period embraced nineteen subjects of general education, in addition to foreign languages, three specialised military subjects (the art of war, fortification and artillery) and nine extra-curricular classes of an artistic nature. The encyclopaedic character of the education accorded well with the philosophic mood of the 1760s, but it was incapable of inculcating a core of solid knowledge.

A chill air began to blow through the corps when the humane old director Count Friedrich of Anhalt-Bernburg died in 1794, and was succeeded by Mikhail Kutuzov. 'Count Anhalt treated you like children', Kutuzov announced to the cadets, 'but I shall deal with you like soldiers.' The instruction under the new regime was brisk and practical, and it was driven home with the stick. One of the cadets was so shattered by the experience that he threw himself from an upper gallery to his death on the stone floor below.

Finally in 1800 Paul renamed the establishment the First Cadet Corps, and reconstituted the engineer academy as a corresponding Second Cadet Corps. Military education as a whole lay in the hands of Grand Prince Constantine, who appointed German instructors who could be relied upon to inculcate high standards of drill and bearing. Everything else was neglected, and the products of the corps arrived at their regiments as fourteen- or fifteen-year-old ignoramuses.

It was probably fortunate that the Noble Land Cadet Corps, which underwent such extremes of regime, was complemented by a number of smaller establishments which stood in a roughly similar relation to the corps as do the Virginia Military Institute or the Charleston Citadel to West Point. One of the most celebrated of the kind was the Greek Cadet Corps (1775-96), which contributed altogether about one hundred officers to the army, and gave an excellent military and general education both to the Russian nobility and to the young Greek refugees for whose sake it was founded.

Another deserving institution was the private Shklov Cadet Corps, which began life in 1778 as a diversion for the eccentric Major-General S. G. Zorich on his estates in Livonia and White Russia. By 1800 the Shklov Corps had produced a total of 470 officers, who followed a balanced and enjoyable course lasting up to eight years or more. Lev Engelhardt passed just one year at the place, but he remembered how Shklov was packed with

human beings from every kind of family, position and nation. Many of them were relations of Zorich, or his colleagues from the time he served as a major in an hussar regiment, and they lived totally at his expense. The rest of the staff and the other officers were people like gamblers and adventurers of every kind who had no other shelter, or French, Italians, Germans, Serbians, Greeks, Moldavians and other assorted foreigners – altogether a motley rabble. At Shklov were staged balls, masquerades, carousels and fireworks, and sometimes Zorich's cadets used to carry out military evolutions, or go boating in sloops. (Engelhardt, 1868, 29-30)

Foreign officers

The eighteenth century was the age *par excellence* of the cosmopolitan officer, but in Russia the dependence on aliens went far beyond the norm in other services, for in neither quantity or competence was the native nobility capable of supplying the higher leadership which the army required. The resentments were correspondingly acute. If Manstein claimed that the Russians needed plenty of foreign officers, 'because the soldiers repose more confidence in them than in the officers of their own nation', he also had to admit that among the Westerners were 'the most useless throw-outs from the rest of Europe' (Manstein, 1860, I, 298; II, 366). Military tourists and sightseers were a kind of humanity which came in for some particularly harsh words. Fermor detested this breed of 'volunteer', and in the next generation the Prince de Ligne had to warn Potemkin against the host of charlatans who passed themselves off as military men. 'Do we stand in need of so many foreign officers?' asked General Rzhevskii. 'It is displeasing to see ... servants, merchants and teachers assuming the guise of Russian staff officers, which demeans the service, and occasions injustice to many meritorious natives' (*RA*, 1879, XVII, pt 1, 362).

As we might have expected, foreigners took many leading places in the army of Peter the Great, who stood in urgent need of Western expertise, and again in the Germanising period of Empress Anna. The climate of Elizabeth's Russia was by no means so welcoming to foreign interlopers. All the same, at the first siege of Colberg in 1758 we encounter a Berg in charge of the infantry, a Vermeulen leading the cavalry, an Ettinger directing the engineers, a Felkers managing the artillery, and the whole standing under the command of General Palmenbach – all Germans or Russo-German Balts. Meanwhile, the volunteer (or spy) Totleben was making himself busy and useful.

Under Catherine, native Russians took most of the leading places in the command of armies and in the imperial favour. However, a warm reception was still extended to people of foreign birth and ancestry, if they had something useful to contribute to the state. Such a person was Major-General Friedrich Wilhelm Bauer, who re-founded the general staff in 1770 (see p. 166). Teutonic experts of the same kind included the Westphalian Jakob Pfister, who was Quartermaster-General in the later Turkish campaigns, and the enterprising 'Ivan Ivanovich' Meller-Zakomelskii, who became acting Master General of the Ordnance in 1783.

A certain eccentricity becomes evident in some of the foreigners towards the end of the long reign. We note people like the Livonian-Irishman Boris Petrovich Lacy, who was a devotee of *rostbif* and *plum-pudding* (Lubyanovskii, 1872, 155), and used councils of war as an opportunity to catch up on his sleep. His contemporary, the colossal Danish-born cavalry general Numsen, was something of a natural curiosity, for his head had absorbed a canister shot in the Seven Years War, without apparent trace. He hauled his massive bulk over the ground on crutches, and his breastplate was so capacious that one of his sprightly young officers found it would float on water like a boat.

Entirely characteristic of this generation was Friedrich of Anhalt-Bernburg (see p. 144), who was a veteran of the Prussian and Saxon armies, and entered the Russian service as lieutenant-general in 1783. Shortly afterwards he prevailed on Lev Engelhardt to introduce him to a post of Russian grenadiers.

Arriving at the location, he began to chat with each grenadier in turn. He had learnt a sequence of questions by heart, and he reiterated them in a comical German accent: 'Are you well, my friend, and what is your name? What town are you from? Are you married? Do you have any children? How many sons do you have? How many daughters?' Even when the soldier announced that he was unmarried, the count followed his catalogue through from beginning to end, and then seized each man by the hand. There was one grenadier who concluded that Anhalt wished to test his strength. He in his turn gripped the count so firmly that he was almost reduced to tears, and only broke free with some difficulty. (Engelhardt, 1868, 62)

At times it almost seemed that there was something in the Russian air which infected the Westerners with some of the most abandoned habits of their hosts. Peter's close associates Lefort and Villebois gave themselves up to riotous drunkenness, while the statesman Ostermann lived in conditions of more-than-Slavonic squalor. The generals Rosen and Löwendahl brought a reputation of Muscovite barbarity to the sieges they conducted when they returned to the West (Derry, 1689; Bergen-op-Zoom, 1747), and there was something pathetic in the last years of Manstein, who was rejected in his native Russia as a foreigner, yet appeared to the Prussians as a hideous, ill-mannered Asiatic.

The Slavonic Russians made no fundamental distinction between outright foreigners from Germany and the home-grown breed of aliens, the Germanic Baltic upper classes of the conquered provinces in the north. The German element in the officer corps was very significant indeed, to judge by the evidence of the list of officers prepared for Catherine II in the early years of her reign (Lebedev, 1898). Here we find a grand total of 402 active senior officers (from field-marshal down to second major inclusive), from which we may derive the figures in the table, which are to be treated with the caution with which all sensible people approach statistics. Our 'foreigners' comprise not only Poles, Danes, Swedes, French, Hungarians, Serbs, and an occasional Scot, but probably also a few Germans whose names have been mangled beyond recognition by the Russian clerks. Even the older 'Russian' nobility, with thoroughly Russified names, was of very diverse provenance, as Amburger (1966) has pointed out.
Thus we can say that Germans and Balts represented well over one-third of the officers of field rank. Russians are perhaps unexpectedly dominant in the staff, though this is in the period before the Bauer reforms. From the distribution of titles, it appears that the Russian nobles disliked regimental soldiering at a lowly level, though they congregated at the rank of colonel, which probably represented an agreeable combination of material reward and lack of higher responsibility.

It is worth mentioning that inside the cavalry,

Rank	Total	Native Russians (%)	Balts and Germans (%)	Foreigners (%)
All ranks	402	58.7	31.3	10.0
Field-marshal	3	100.0	None	None
Generalanshef	16	56.2	37.5	6.2
Lt.-general	11	36.3	45.4	18.1
Maj.-general	48	47.9	37.5	14.5
Staff	14	64.2	21.4	14.2
Colonels	82	63.4	29.2	7.3
(Colonels of horse)	33	63.6	30.3	6.0
(Colonels of foot)	49	63.2	28.5	8.1
Lt.-colonels	81	60.4	28.3	11.1
(Lt.-colonels of horse)	32	56.2	31.2	12.5
(Lt.-colonels of foot)	49	63.2	26.5	10.2
First majors	76	65.7	28.9	5.2
(First majors of horse)	30	66.6	26.6	6.6
(First majors of foot)	46	65.2	30.4	4.2
Second majors	71	52.1	35.2	12.6
(Second majors of horse)	26	50.0	42.3	7.6
(Second majors of foot)	45	53.3	31.1	15.5

however, some of the regiments from the Baltic provinces appear to have been run entirely by Germans, to wit the Tverskii Carabiniers, and the Olonetskii, Vyborgskii, Ladozhskii and Shlyushelburgskii Dragoons. This corresponds with the anecdotal evidence of Pishchevich, who came from Saratov to the Narvskii Carabiniers in 1794, and found the regiment stuffed with Livonian and Kurland Balts:

In the whole regiment there were no more than five Russian officers. Thus I had left one German colony on the Volga, only to find myself in another, in which the pedantic etiquette so beloved of that nation was observed to the highest degree. They regarded it as a great offence to call somebody by surname without the German honorific 'von'. Although I cannot abide this nation, I was forced to adapt myself to all the trifles which they cultivate with such industry, and so I rapidly earned their good opinion, as well as adding the German 'von' to the Serbian 'Pishchevich'. (Pishchevich, 1885, 187)

It is curious to find some officers with German names who did all they could to distance themselves from their Teutonic forbears. Lev Engelhardt conceived a loathing for the German language, after his Jesuit tutor beat him every month for the slow progress he made in it. More remarkable still, F. F. Wiegel (Vigel), the son of a German favourite of Peter III, used to thank God for the integrity of his 'Russian' character. He wrote bitterly of the Germans of the newly acquired Baltic provinces, who had been confirmed in their privileges by Peter the Great: 'We all know how they repaid us at the time of Biron, these conquered tyrants of ours. Under Catherine II things proceeded differently, and a *rapprochement* became possible, but upon her death they once more distanced themselves from us' (Wiegel, 1864-6, I, 83).

Promotion and reward

The Russian nobility laboured under a seemingly appalling obligation of service to the state, which in theory doomed every suitable lad to serve in the ranks from his early teens. We have noted how easily and widely the letter of the law was circumvented. With any contrivance at all, a noble youth could be whisked through the ranks of NCOs while he remained at home, or performed only the most nominal service in the Guards. The best-connected of all were able to continue their painless ascent by becoming aides-de-camp to the sovereign (Catherine had two or three hundred of them), or joining the hangers-on who clustered about great men like Potemkin or Suvorov. If this last resort was not available, then in the corrupt atmosphere of Catherine's later years it was easy for rich noblemen to buy themselves promotion by paying set fees to Lieutenant-Colonel Stavitskii of the War College.

Enjoying the protection of his uncle, the powerful Count Benckendorff, it was possible for the sixteen-year-old Waldemar Löwenstern to be admitted as orderly to Count Nikolai Saltykov, the later prince and field-marshal. 'This appointment was exceedingly flattering to my self-esteem, since the post gave me the right to wear spurs, which was claimed by only four officers in my regiment.' Two more very rapid promotions followed, and at seventeen our young hero was a captain in the Ukranian light horse:

My uniform was of Prussian blue, with red cuffs and silver buttons and aglets. It was run up in twenty-four hours, permitting me to appear at the court ball of 1 January [1795]. I had the good fortune to be able to present my congratulations to the Empress, who graciously extended her hand for me to kiss. (Löwenstern, *RS*, 1900, CIII, no. 3, 270, 274)

The actual award of the commission in a regiment was effected after a cursory test, and the affirmation of the body of the officers of the unit. Thereafter the rise of the young man was supposed to be determined by seniority, and by the writ of the War College, which in this matter ran throughout the army. In fact the College fell so hopelessly behind in its paperwork that it was quite possible for individual regiments to be left for a long time without effective command, yet carry on their books up to two or three colonels and thirty supernumerary majors. Zinzendorf noted another inconvenience, 'namely that advancement is effected not in the branch of service, but in the army as a whole. At every promotion they therefore pass to a new regiment. They never get to know their men, and their men never know them' (Volz and Küntzel, 1899, 702). Such transferences were also carried out between arms as diverse as the cavalry and the engineers. The arrival of a fresh regimental commander in any event occasioned an involuntary exodus, for the newcomer brought his own officers with him, and evicted the sitting tenants. Langeron knew of officers who had served in fifteen regiments, and been expelled from each in turn. None of this made for a high degree of military commitment or expertise.

It is perhaps useful to enumerate the scale of the junior and middle ranks of the corps; namely:

Praporshchik	=	ensign
Podporuchik	=	second lieutenant
Poruchik	=	lieutenant
Kapitan	=	captain
Major (second and first)	=	major
Polkovnik	=	colonel
Brigadir	=	brigadier

The promotion to first major was a step of some moment:

Till a person arrives to the rank of premier major, which is the first commission signed by the empress, he is regarded as nothing. A captain even is regarded as nothing. But once having obtained the rank of premier major, he is considered on the road to preferment: he is looked upon as a gentleman. (Parkinson, 1971, 168)

However, the Russian officer first tasted the delights of arbitrary power when he became colonel and received a regiment of his own. 'The colonel was the despot of his regiment. Companies, and the business of administration and economy — all lay at his disposal' (Masson, 1859, 81). While the *Code of 1716* endowed the colonel with considerable powers, he was in some degree answerable not only to the very strict governmental fiscal authorities, but to the body of the officers of the regiment. These restraints were weakened by the codes and instructions of 1763, 1764 and 1766, which emphasised the wide powers of the colonel as the bearer of the honour and glory of his regiment. The unchecked abuse of these freedoms drew down the criticisms of soberminded officers like Rumyantsev, Rzhevskii and Langeron. Semen Vorontsov went so far as to claim that the new dispensations represented the first decisive break with the military system of Peter the Great:

I saw for myself how in less than seven years the colonels set about exploiting the liberty which had been so unwisely extended to them, in order

36 Generals of Catherine the Great, From left to right: *generalanshef*, lieutenant-general, major-general. Green coat with red collar and gold lace; red waistcoat with gold lace; red breeches; hat with gold border, white cockade and white feathers (Viskovatov, 1844-56)

150 The Russian Officer

37 Kiril Razumovskii

to perpetuate scandalous abuses which tended to their own profit. The crown was plundered with inconceivable effrontery, while the soldiers were inhumanly deprived of what little money was theirs by right. ('Zapiski', 1802, *AKV*, 1870-95, X, 472)

Brigadiers retained the proprietorship of their regiments, with all the agreeable appurtenances, but their assignment to the actual command of brigades hung entirely on the arbitrary will of the divisional commander. 'Those among the generals who have neither protection nor status, they send to Siberia, Orenburg, the Caucasus and places like that ... the favourites, on the other hand, serve in Moscow, St. Petersburg and so on' (Langeron, *RS*, 1895, LXXXIII, 146).

In ascending order the ranks of general officers ran:

Major-General	=	major-general
General Poruchik	=	lieutenant-general
Generalanshef	=	full general
General Feldmarshal	=	field-marshal

The supreme title of *Generalissimus* was bestowed just twice in the century — on Peter's favourite Menshikov, and on Suvorov after the campaign of 1799.

Westerners were astonished at the ease with which outright civilians were clad in the dignity of Russian officers. Laqueys, perruquiers, riding instructors, cooks and the like were frequently made into sergeants, and ultimately commissioned, while at more exalted levels the workings of Peter's *Table of Ranks* suddenly catapulted some peaceable denizen of office or ante-chamber into important military command. Only the Russian army could have witnessed a career like that of Kiril Razumovskii (brother of the favourite), who was born to a family of Ukranian Cossacks. He took a prominent part in the revolution which brought Catherine to the throne in 1762, and she rewarded him with further military honours. He once went to Berlin, where Frederick is reported to have asked him:
'Have you ever commanded an army?'
'No, I am only a civilian general.'
'I see. We don't have anybody like that here' (Helbig, 1917, 206).

Russian sovereigns and commanders had an impressive variety of devices at their disposal when they wished to encourage their subordinates. Peter set an inspiring example when he showered his armies with commemorative medals, chains, cash and promotions, and when he instituted the first of a new generation of orders of chivalry, designed to reward military valour, after the model of the French Order of Saint-Louis of 1693. This was the St Andrew (enamelled dark blue St Andrew's cross, on broad light blue ribbon and cordon), which was created in 1698, and bestowed on officers who had distinguished themselves in the Turkish war and the suppression of the *Streltsy*. In 1725 the widowed Catherine I brought a scheme of Peter's to fruition when she founded the second great order of the time, the St Alexander Nevsky (red enamelled cross formy on bright red ribbon and cordon).

Catherine the Great felt the need to reward the soldiers of her own age with a new military order in four grades, the St George, which was instituted in 1769 at the beginning of her first Turkish war. The badge was a gold cross formy enamelled in gold and white, and the cordon and ribbon were of orange with three black stripes. The order was conceived in the spirit of the famous Theresian Military Order of Austria, and it carried with it emoluments amounting to the equivalent of £8,000 a year, 'a very noble benefaction and a very useful in a service where the establishment is so low with respect to pay, and the expenses officers are exposed to are so high' (Lord Cathcart, 30 July 1770, PRO, SPF 91/85). Finally, Emperor Paul I introduced to Russia two orders which celebrated his ancestry and ambitions, namely the Schleswig Order of St Anne, and the Order of St John of Jerusalem. There was always an element of the arbitrary in the distribution of Russian decorations. Engelhardt was wryly amused to have put in years of unrewarded campaigning against the Turks and Poles, and then receive the last two orders simply because he happened to please the emperor at a review near Kazan in 1798.

The generosity of Russian sovereigns was

38 Cavalry officer, after 1769, probably a carabinier. Coat of light greenish blue with red collar and lapels and gold shoulder strap. He is wearing the St George

39 Infantry officer, period of Catherine the Great. Dark green coat with red collar and lapels. He wears the red cross of the St Alexander Nevsky, with red ribbon and red cordon

further expressed in the granting of promotions, golden presentation swords, pensions, estates and serfs. It was possible for the Cossack leader Thedor Petrovich Denisov to inherit a little plot with five peasant households, yet receive such bounty from Catherine as to end his days with 7,000 peasants, two diamond-studded sabres, the title of count, the rank of full general of cavalry, and the orders of St Alexander Nevsky, the St George second class, and the Prussian Black Eagle.

Peter the Great had insisted that officers who were no longer fit for field service had to transfer to garrison regiments, or go to the provinces to instruct recruits. These dreary prospects were banished by Peter III, who introduced the opportunity of voluntary retirement, which officers often chose to embrace at the rank of major:

The Russians are so fond of the country life, particularly as it gives them an opportunity of acting the despot, and tyrannising over their peasants, that almost all of them who have estates, quit the army and navy as soon as they can, and retire into the country. (Anon., c.1787, 11)

Between East and West, the character of the Russian officer

When they voyaged to Russia, or watched Russian armies as they marched into western Europe,

40 General of the 7th Jaeger Corps, 1797-1801 (Viskovatov, 1844-56)

foreign observers gained some inkling of the forces that were contending for the mastery of the Russian character in the eighteenth century:

There can exist ... striking differences between individual officers of the same regiment. While you may observe a considerable degree of education, elegance and polish among certain groups, you can be equally surprised by the total absence of those qualities among others. (Masson, 1859, 438)

It was tempting to give unqualified approbation to every advance which brought the service nobility closer to the standards of culture and behaviour observed among the superior classes in the West. Already in the 1740s and 1750s the censorious Austrians formed a favourable impression of their counterparts in the army of Empress Elizabeth, and, in its turn, the series of Russian military forays to the West 'having occasioned the gentry to travel, it has in some measure opened their ideas, and given them more relish for polite arts' (Richard, 1780, 32).

Occasionally the more perceptive Westerners began to wonder whether the transformations were complete, or, *per se*, desirable. Those who knew Russia best used to value the domestic virtues of the conservative nobility, or even, like Manstein, find a great deal to admire in the Russian peasants, the 'dark people' of the vast countryside.

Certain traits among the officers impressed themselves with particular force. Observers noted a childish innocence that was evident in the most surprising quarters. They saw also that some individuals, less happily, combined the cruelty of a child with all the despotic power which lay at the disposal of Russian commanders. Langeron believed that Catherine's Turkish wars exercised a brutalising effect, and he drew attention to the case of *Generalanshef* Mikhail Kamenskii, whose

talents were marred by one of the most frightful characters that has ever disfigured mankind. His ferocity was positively tigerish, and on drill manoeuvres he was seen to bite his soldiers, tearing away their flesh with his teeth. (Langeron, *RS*, 1895, LXXXIII, 160; see also Ségur, 1824-6, III, 62-3)

Münnich compiled some telling descriptions of the generals who served under him in the 1730s. Amongst others, he categorised Aleksandr Ivanovich Rumyantsev (legal father of the celebrated field-marshal) as brave and intelligent, but

also fond of his enjoyments, being given to downing a goblet of wine in the mornings and another at noon. He gambles until late in the night, and gets up late the next day. He is polite in the extreme, when he is sober, but most brutal, and most unbridled in his language when he has had too much to drink. (Vischer, 1938, 552)

Indeed Westerners could never accustom themselves to the contrast between the Russian soldier, so frugal and hard-living, and the sybaritic officer of the same nation.

You will probably find a number of things quite unbelievable [observed Langeron]. A Russian officer will never undertake a journey on horseback, but only in a carriage. He cannot contemplate travelling as much as ten versts without having his bed brought with him. He finds champagne and English beer quite indispensable. Finally he is quite incapable of wearing his own sword, but must have it carried with him by an orderly. (*RS*, 1895, LXXXIII, 189)

Orders of dress were a matter of individual whim.

Strict prohibitions forbade officers' wives from accompanying their menfolk into the field. They did so anyway, under a variety of guises, and Masson makes the point that famous generals like Ivan Saltykov were terrorised by their ladies. Whether sanctioned or not, sexual congress was pursued with the same ardour and brutality that is evident in Russia today.

The Russian officers' capacity for alcoholic consumption was huge (Langeron rated it at almost three times the Prussian), and the studious Pishchevich was often a witness of the 'quarrels and other unpleasantnesses which frequently ensue among people whose reason has been clouded by alcoholic vapours' (Pishchevich, 1885, 40). However, drunkenness almost certainly worked less destructively on mind and fortune than the inordinate addiction to cards, which was noted by Lambert in the 1750s, and again by Wiegel and Langeron in the 1790s. Furious play set in as soon as the officers received their pay, and 'when they have run out of money, they continue to gamble on their pledged word, making over their houses, their porcelain, their carriages, their shirts' (Langeron, *RS*, 1895, LXXXIII, 188-9).

The corruptibility of public men in Russia was notorious and extreme. Zinzendorf attributed the phenomenon to the physical impossibility of effective government, which rendered all decrees ultimately dependent upon 'the good will of subordinates' (1755, Volz and Küntzel, 1899, 705). When safeguards were introduced, they only made the evil worse, for their effect was to incorporate the skulduggery into the system of administration. Every year the regiments chose from their midst personnel to do duty as treasurers and commissaries, yet Langeron could urge with the greatest passion that 'of all the thieves spread over the face of the earth, these functionaries are the most impudent and the most foul' (*RS*, 1895, LXXXIII, 162). Likewise, every officer of the regiment was expected to sign his name twice yearly to attest to the correctness of the thirteen books of regimental administration, and he almost invariably continued to do so even when he knew that the accounts had been systematically falsified by the regimental commander. An individual might object,

but what happens to this poor officer, simply because he does not wish to violate his conscience or his oath? Having been thrown out of his regiment ... he betakes himself to another, clutching a bad personal report, and there he finds exactly the same state of affairs as in his original regiment. (Rzhevskii, *RA*, 1879, XVII, pt 1, 361)

While no part of Europe was a stranger to human fallibility, visitors to Russian encountered habits and assumptions that brought home to them how radically concepts of honour in that land differed from the values obtaining in the West. In fact the Russian officer was almost entirely void of those ideals of corporate pride and knightly values which were an attribute of aristocracy as it was known elsewhere in Europe. A proclivity to theft was not considered particularly reprehensible or demeaning, for it was to be found at all levels of society: 'It sometimes happens that in the apartments of the court, accessible only to authorised personnel and superior officers, your briefcase can be lifted with as much facility as at a public fair' (Masson, 1859, 174). Trickery at cards was dismissed as a joke, where it would have led to a duel in the West.

Just as undignified, in Western eyes, was the almost Asiatic subservience which subordinates were accustomed to display in front of their masters. Field-Marshal Nikolai Vasilevich Repnin was noted for the consideration he showed to his suite, and yet Masson claims that:

The Russian Officer 155

misconduct, a measure which would have been considered subversive of discipline in most Western armies. Oddly enough, the same code of conduct permitted a junior officer to present himself before a senior and ask for promotion and decorations, shamelessly detailing his own merits.

Throughout our period the bleak Western ideal of a glorious 'death for the fatherland' remained largely alien to the Russian mentality. In Peter's early days, when the nation went to war, the last of the feudal cavalry used to buckle on their swords

> with hearts full of dismay.... Nor do they consider it any disgrace to purchase at great cost the permission to live sluggishly at home, and deprecate the perils of war. Nay, they go to the length of contending that some Germans of chivalrous mould must be demented when they strive and labour and entreat to be allowed to follow the army into the field, and into all the very manifest dangers that attend military service. (Korb, 1863, I, 141-2; see also Mediger, 1952, 110, 115)

In later years the sentiments of the younger, superficially Westernised nobility were not different in kind. In the Seven Years War Bolotov showed a typical reluctance at the prospect of returning to active service with his regiment, and 'being exposed to daily fatigues and dangers' after a spell of agreeable office work. Catherine's first military adventure, the Turkish war of 1768-74, caused consternation in the same circles, and when young Count Semen Vorontsov volunteered to join the field army at the outbreak of war, he was told that he was the only person to have done so, and that four hundred other officers had already asked to resign. The French envoy, Sabatier de Cabres, asserted how at the end of the first campaign the gilded youth abandoned the service *en masse*, and came streaming back to St Petersburg.

> The foreign volunteers, who saw them on this occasion, talk of them with the utmost scorn. The Prussians have been chewing their finger nails with mortification, and say they feel like dying from shame for having been ever beaten by such a vile rabble. (*SIRIO*, 1913, CXLIII, 68)

41 Nikolai Vasilevich Repnin. Sober, grave and circumspect — a model of magnificence in the old boyar style

people at Berlin were astonished to see how Repnin used to go for a walk, all decked out in his orders, and proceeding gravely in solitary state, while his nephew Prince Volkonskii, several aides-de-camp and the mystic Thielmann, his secretary, followed several paces behind. Every time Repnin turned to say a word, the members of his suite came to a halt like a platoon of soldiers, removing their hats as one man. (Masson, 1859, 149)

Things had been worse in the first half of the century when public servants lived under an arbitrary authority that was capable of depriving generals and ministers of state of their positions and fortune in an instant. Even in Napoleonic times officers could be reduced to the ranks for

The last sentence opens the possibility that Sabatier was not the most astute of observers, for the contemptible Russians had indeed beaten the Prussians, and they were shortly going to do the same to the Turks. Alexandre Langeron knew the Russian army much better, and elaborated its shortcomings in much more detail, yet he was driven to the conclusion that all the corruption, irresponsibility and professional ignorance did not fundamentally matter, given the endurance of the Russian soldier, and his masters' dedication to an infantile but workable concept of what war was about.

All their principles of war come down to their bayonets and their Cossacks. Indeed, with the exception of Rumyantsev, Kamenskii, Igelström and Prozorovskii, I am not aware of a single general of Russian origin who is not imbued with these extraordinary ideas. And, after all, they could be right. They put these notions into practice, and all their enterprises have been crowned with success. (*RS*, 1895, LXXXIII, 195)

Seven The Cossacks

Cossack origins and types

It is perhaps worth trying to lend some identity, definition and character to those almost legendary sons of the southern rivers and plains, the Cossacks, who went so far to shape Western thinking on the Russians and their army.

Although the origins of the name 'Cossack' are still obscure, the term came to be applied in early modern times to the peoples who migrated to the middle and lower reaches of the great rivers in order to escape from the depredations of Lithuanians or Mongols, or from feudal or state oppression. By the eighteenth century the Cossacks existed in three main groupings. Moving from west to east, we encounter first the somewhat colourless Little Russian Cossacks of the Ukraine, deficient alike in the Cossack virtues and vices, then the picturesque and reprehensible

42 Hussar of the Slobodskaya Ukraine, Seven Years War. Russian hussars were frequently recruited from the same stock as the Cossacks, but were organised and uniformed on the model of the Hungarian light horse. The gear of this Slobodskii Hussar comprises: white *mirliton* cap; dolman, barrel sash and pants, all in light purple with white decoration; white pelisse with black edging, light purple buttonholes and brass buttons; white sabretache and shabraque with light purple edges (Viskovatov, 1844-56)

Zaporozhians, and lastly the formidable warriors of the Don.

The first of these folk, the Little Russians, originally owned strong links with Poland, whose flanks in the Ukraine (*Ukraina*, lit. 'border') they helped to protect against the Turks. In point of religion, however, they had more in common with the Orthodox Russians, and in the period of unrest from 1640 the Ukrainian Cossacks transferred their support to the Muscovite tsar. Under the patronage of Aleksei Mikhailovich, parties of these folk moved east and formed little settlements at Kharkov, Sumy, Akhtyrka and other locations in the area of Belgorod. They became known as the Cossacks of the Slobodskaya Ukraine.

Over the following decades the Little Russians underwent taming and 'registration', and were given a characteristic form of military and political organisation by regiments, by *sotnyas* (of 200-930 serving Cossacks) and by *kurens* (or thirty-five to forty). The main body of settled territorial Cossacks (*gorodovye kazaki*) formed ten large regiments under *starshinas*. They lived with their families from their own resources, and upon the call of the tsar and their *hetman*, or chief, they were bound to report for military service with appropriate provisions and clothing. Each of the regiments comprised infantry and mounted men, with the cavalry predominating. A body of 'hired' Cossacks was maintained on low salaries, and was organised on the same unit basis as the territorial men, though with smaller establishments.

Gradually the Little Russian Cossacks lost the identity and free-living character which had distinguished themselves from the rest of the people of the Ukraine. Their military qualities were rated poorly by Manstein and Rumyantsev, and in the middle of the eighteenth century they put forth just a spiritless mass of about 22,000 mounted men.

Much less biddable were the Cossacks of the lower Dnieper. They ranged with freedom across a wide tract of steppes, but they owed their name and allegiance to the *Sech*, or defensible settlement, of Zaporozhe (lit. 'beyond the cataracts'), which occupied an island set amid the rapids of the Dnieper. The Zaporozhians threw their support behind Mazeppa in 1708, and suffered terribly in consequence, but they survived as 'a very strong and indefatigable people' (Rondeau, 4 April 1736, *SIRIO*, 1891, LXXVI, 503) with their character and institutions essentially intact. Arable farming did not accord with the Zaporozhian character, but in compensation the Dnieper was teeming with sturgeon and other fish, and the plains formed 'one immense and fat pasture' (Masson, 1859, 301). Every man had his little stock of horses, which could be traded for corn or other necessities, or carry him on the plundering expeditions for which the Zaporozhians were chiefly famous.

The *Sech* was rebuilt after it had been destroyed by the Russians in 1709, and it formed the centre of the bizarre social life of the Zaporozhians. No woman was supposed to set foot in the settlement, and in ignorance of this custom a regular lieutenant-colonel brought his wife with him to the *Sech* in the 1730s.

He had no sooner arrived when all the Cossacks surrounded his house in a mob, demanding that he should produce all the women who were inside, so that everybody could have a share. The lieutenant-colonel was hard put to it to calm them down, and he succeeded only after he had given them several kegs of spirits. (Manstein, 1860, I, 29-30)

The able-bodied male population was nevertheless maintained at about 15,000, thanks to the constant influx of deserters and runaways from Russia, Poland, Turkey and their cousins of the Don, as well as through the offspring of the unions with the women who were allowed to live along the banks of the river.

The easternmost of the great Cossack peoples, the horsemen of the Don, supported the risings of Stenka Razin and Bulavin, and underwent the usual castigation from the Muscovites. The losses were more than made up through natural increase and the arrival of refugees, and by the end of the eighteenth century the stock of both sexes reached some 300,000, far outnumbering the eccentric bachelors of Zaporozhe. At the time of the Seven Years War the active Don forces amounted to about 15,700 men, who were divided into twenty-two regiments of five *sotnyas* apiece. Nine thousand were actually called up for the first campaign, and, under the authority of the Russian government, the administration and command were exercised by an *ataman* and elected *starshinas* and *sotniks*.

While the ways of the Zaporozhians attracted more attention from foreign travellers, these Cossacks of the Don were the people who accompanied the Russian armies when they campaigned in the West, and their attributes were inevitably attached to the Cossacks as a whole.

Lastly, almost unknown to the Westerners, small bodies of Cossacks and 'hussars' were created and re-created to see to the security of specific stretches of the Asian borders. They were known by the names of their principal settlements, or the rivers entrusted to their guard, and they rarely if ever appeared on a European theatre of war.

The decline of Cossackdom

In the eighteenth century the free and democratic traditions of the historic Cossack peoples became increasingly difficult to reconcile with the advance of Russian state power, and the strategic and economic needs of the time. The Zaporozhians and the Don Cossacks had settled where the mood had taken them and not where the government necessarily wanted them to be, and while the Tartars of the Nogai steppes and the Crimea presented a diminishing threat, new and exposed frontiers were opening to the south-east and east, towards the Caucasus and Siberia. It was all the more intolerable to find that the depredations of the Zaporozhians actually endangered the more settled peoples of the old frontiers, and that in 1769 twenty regiments of Don Cossacks adamantly refused to set off for the Turkish war. Destructive forces were also at work within the Cossack communities, with the spread of a conventional agricultural economy, and the emergence of a Russified and serf-owning class among the leaders.

Already in the 1730s, Münnich calculated that only 32,000 of the approximately 110,000 Cossacks turned out for service, leaving the rest to protect their homes against Tartar raids (see p. 49). He did what he could to make the Cossacks of some use. Three hundred Cossacks and two hundred baptised Kalmyks were brought together on the Donets to form the regiment of Chuguevskii Cossacks, which was given proper pay and a regular organisation. An observer wrote in the Seven Years War:

they are clothed in red, and the officers have commissions and rank like the other officers of the army. This pulk was not only very brave, but also particularly well disciplined. It would be doing them an unpardonable injustice to compare them in the least to the other Cossacks, who do not deserve to be honoured with the name of soldiers, being without either pay or discipline. (Tielke, 1788, II, 14)

However, regular Cossacks of this kind remained an exception in the hordes of Cossackdom, and even towards the end of Catherine's reign they still represented only about 1,245 men. The irregulars amounted to 73,651, of which the Don Cossacks (28,125) formed the largest single contingent.

Prince Potemkin did something to earn his title of 'the final protector of the Cossacks' (Masson, 1859, 304). In 1775 he gave Cossack officers equivalent status to their counterparts in the regular army, and amongst other indications of his benevolent concern he conceived the idea in 1787 of forming a regiment of Jewish Cossacks, the 'Israelovskii'. The Prince de Ligne remembers that: 'we already had a squadron with us, and it occasioned me endless amusement. They resembled nothing so much as monkeys, what with their beards descending to their knees, their short stirrups, and the terror they showed at being on horseback' (Ligne, 1890, 178). Otherwise the story is one of oppression. In a single year, 1775, the *Sech* was destroyed for a second and final time, and the Zaporozhians dispersed to the wind, while the Yaik Cossacks of the eastern frontier were savagely tamed on account of the support they had given to Pugachev. The very name of the Yaik River was changed to the 'Ural', and the town of Yaitsk became 'Uralsk'. Further drastic things were done after Potemkin's death. Russian 'governments' absorbed large tracts of traditional Cossack land, while the inhabitants were either enserfed, or resettled *en masse* in the newly annexed territories of the Crimea and the Kuban.

Cossack institutions and leaders

In the eighteenth century it is possible to discern three rather ill-defined periods in the relations between Cossackdom and the Russian state. In the first years the eastern Cossack leaders retained some vestiges of independent command. After Poltava the sovereign began to subject the Cossacks to centralised control, while allowing them considerable freedom in the running of their internal affairs. Finally, towards the end of the century, the Cossack ruling class became to some degree separated from the mass of its own people, while accepting honours and positions from the state.

At the beginning of the century the Cossacks lived by a code of rough democracy, electing regimental commanders (*starshinas*) and chiefs (*hetmans* or *atamans*) who combined civil and military authority. The *starshinas* were accustomed to working out whatever plans of campaign might prove necessary, though the local Russian commanders were likely to be brought into the deliberations as a matter of convenience and courtesy. Following the invasion of Charles XII, however, Peter began to assert Russian authority over all the Cossacks, regardless of whether or not they had supported the Swedes. The loyal Skoropadskii had contributed to the victory of Poltava, but he protested in vain when later in 1709 Peter placed the Little Russian *starshinas* under the command of Russian generals. By the end of the reign the Cossacks had to accept the fact that where the *hetmans* or *atamans* had not been abolished altogether, they were to be elected only with the consent of the Russian sovereign.

Having gained these essential points, the government was content to let the Cossacks run lesser matters themselves. The War College merely maintained registers of those Cossacks who were liable to serve, and when the time came to enter on campaign the bureaucrats dispatched a bare

43 Volga Cossack, described (1774) as wearing red hat and red caftan (Viskovatov, 1844-56)

minimum of instructions concerning the numbers to be raised (e.g., 'recruit as many Cossacks as possible from the up-river settlements', 1735), and indicated the assembly points of the regiments, and the route of the subsequent march. Once the Cossacks reached the field army, the body was placed at the entire disposal of the Russian commander, and the *ataman* was left with just the tactical command of one of the regiments. Finally, in the 1760s, precise orders began to go out, which defined the numbers of regiments to be raised, and the size of each.

Adrian Karpovich Denisov has left probably the

best account of the sort of thing which went on during these processes, and indeed of the life of the eighteenth-century Don Cossacks as a whole. He was born in 1763 to a famous military line. His uncle was the redoubtable Thedor Petrovich (see p. 152), while his father Karp Petrovich became a *starshina* and ended his career with the rank of major-general. While Westerners might imagine that family and race gave Adrian an instinctive knowledge of what a Cossack leader ought to do, he admits that he was totally nonplussed when in 1787 Colonel Platov sent him a quantity of clothing, cloth, leather and other equipment, and assigned him a village where he was to raise a regiment of 1,400 men.

Adrian Denisov's first measure was to seek out a number of reasonably intelligent and literate men who could draw up lists of such folk as were fit to serve, while making sure that every family was left with a breadwinner.

Having made out the effectives of the regiment, I divided them into *sotnyas*, and promoted two of the Cossacks from each *sotnya* to serve as commanders. I wrote out an instruction which detailed the duties of every individual, while at the same time I fitted out the regiment and distributed the saddles, and had the missing items manufactured. (Denisov, 1874, *RS*, X, 33)

It is surprising to hear that the new Cossacks were unable to manage their horses, which were wild, and that the veterans were unable to teach them what ought to be done.

In this as in all other matters I was in some perplexity, but I worked until I dropped. Our chief Platov had his regiment not far from me, and so I took steps to be informed of all the more important things his regiment was up to, and I made a point of being present, so that I could try the same exercises with my regiment. . . . Finally, at the beginning of 1788, in the spring, my regiment was fully equipped, and the number of horses brought up to strength.

The names cited by Adrian Denisov are frequently those of the emerging upper class of Cossackdom, which owed its status less to the consent of its fellow Cossacks than to the recognition conferred by the Russians. Denisov's father and uncle won high rank and honours, as we have seen, while the Platov so often mentioned in his memoirs became lieutenant-general and *ataman* of the Don Cossacks. The Cossack leaders were granted minor nobility in 1775, and hereditary nobility in 1796. In 1798 the junior officers were given the status of gentry as well, and the peasants on the *starshinas'* estates were legally enserfed. Philip Longworth calculates that by 1802 these developments had formed a Don Cossack upper class amounting to more than one thousand generals and officers.

Denisov gives us some indication of the outlook on life of a young Cossack leader at this interesting period. He was still illiterate at the age of twelve, but over the next few years he picked up the rudiments of an education from a regimental officer in St Petersburg and at two *pansions* in the same place. He returned to his home on the Don still largely ignorant of the manners of polite society. His father suggested that it was time to find a wife, and agreed that Adrian should travel to Moscow to learn something of the way of the world. Adrian attended the theatre two or three times, and made the acquaintance of several great men, but he sadly misread the welcome he received from a wealthy hostess and the three daughters of the house. He was amused to hear the girls chatting about him in French, which (unknown to them) he could understand:

Encouraged by this circumstance, and by the fact that the second daughter had taken a great fancy to me, I made bold to propose to her in a letter. The refusal was not slow in coming. . . . Taking stock of my condition and the place of my abode, I thereupon concluded that it was not a wise thing to go wooing in Moscow. (*RS*, 1874, X, 24)

After his excursion into a Westernised Russia, Denisov discovered unsuspected virtues in the girls of his homeland, with their natural good manners and their skill at dancing. He eventually married a young lady from the Volga, and with his usual honesty he tells us that the match turned out to be a complete disaster. The girl was a neurotic slut, and Denisov became so bored with her that he was glad when the summons came to go to the wars.

Equipment and tactics

It seemed impossible to imagine the trained Cossacks as entities separate from their mounts: 'Their horses are small and thin, incapable of great effort, but utterly tireless. Having being raised in the steppes, they are indifferent to the rigour of the climate, and used to putting up with thirst and hunger — pretty much like their masters' (Masson, 1859, 308). Every Cossack had two of these animals — one for riding, and the other for carrying the supplies which gave the Cossacks such a useful degree of self-sufficiency. The saddles were light, and in place of spurs the rider urged his horse forward with a large whip which hung from his left wrist.

The Cossack usually provided his own weapons and equipment, which consequently gave some clue as to his status. The wealthy officers could be identified by signs like a fine sabre of Persian or Turkish manufacture, an armoured coat of mail or plate, a mace, a small ornamental axe (*chekan*), or perhaps a superior musket or brace of pistols. However, the majority of the Cossacks went to war clad in long woollen coats, and carrying the traditional weapon of the lance. This was a pine shaft, about one-and-a-half inches thick, and between twelve and eighteen feet long. The butt was furnished with a loop, to facilitate carrying, and the upper end terminated in a three-sided iron head. A plume of horsehair or black silk waved from the point where the shaft entered the tip. Cossacks employed the lance with great dexterity when they vaulted into the saddle, when they caught a hat in the air in play, and when they levelled the weapon at an enemy, in which eventuality 'many a cavalryman or hussar was liable to find himself skewered and hoisted into the air' (Wonzel, 1783, 180-1). Adrian Denisov conceived a very un-Cossack-like distaste for the lance after an incident in Bessarabia in 1789, when his weapon caught in the clothing of a Turk and he was unable to tug it free.

The standard of equipment actually declined in the course of the century, with the expansion of the eastern Cossacks. Some folk had to make do with lance points of sharpened wood, and in many localities the Cossacks still put their trust in the bow as their main missile weapon. The shafts of the arrows were made of reed or birch, and were fitted with four flights and a warhead of iron or bronze with four edges. Bows were obtained variously from the Mongols, Kalmyks, Bashkirs or Chinese, but the compound Turkish bows were regarded as the best of all.

In open battle against regular forces the Cossacks proved more useful than might have been supposed. They hung annoyingly around the enemy cavalry, fleeing whenever they came under threat of charge, but using their individual prowess to lethal effect if the troopers got out of formation. We have seen how at Gross-Jägersdorf the Don Cossacks on the far left under Serebryakov were able to draw the Prince of Holstein's cavalry on to the fire of fifteen battalions and forty-four guns. Again at Novi in 1799, Denisov made devastating use of the retreat and the counter-attack against the French. These were the tactics of the 'fish trap' which the Cossacks had learnt from the Tartars. Once an enemy formation was broken, the long lances of the Cossacks came into their own: 'In an instant the Cossacks litter the field with dead, and they would be capable of wreaking greater execution still if they did not give themselves over to searching the men they have killed or wounded' (Langeron, *RS*, 1895, LXXXIII, 192).

Experts harboured the most various opinions concerning the value of Cossacks on campaign. The Cossacks ought to have been able to form impenetrable screens around the army, throwing out swarms of patrols, and reporting the movements of the enemy. In the Seven Years War, however, the Cossacks worked as effective light cavalry only in the final campaigns, and in Potemkin's Turkish expeditions the Prince de Ligne noticed that the Cossacks were surprisingly bad at relaying any kind of information. In part, at least, the failings of the Cossacks proceeded from the way the regular commanders split up the regiments in order to use the manpower for

44 Charge of the Don Cossacks at the battle of Trebbia, 1799

convoy escorts, fatigues and other menial duties.

The most serious reservations of all concerned the Cossacks' penchant for despoiling innocent civilians. Indeed, the presence of Cossacks on a theatre of war often did more harm than good, for they wasted the resources of the countryside, and their reputation for infamy was liable to cling to the army as a whole. Here again, the Cossacks were not entirely at fault, since the men received no pay at all, and less than the barest minimum of subsistence. Langeron points out that whereas a Cossack regiment could be a model of discipline, under a good colonel or *starshina*, a number of regular commanders actually encouraged the Cossacks in their frightfulness, like Suvorov in Moldavia and Poland.

The Cossack character

If the savagery of the Cossacks burst forth in the heat of sack or battle, the Russian soldiers distinguished themselves by the merciless way they could go to work in cold blood. On occasion there seemed little in common between the two peoples except the Orthodox religion and the Russian language.

Taken as a whole the Cossacks are more handsome, tall, active and agile than the Russians, and individually more brave. Being unaccustomed to servitude, they are more open, proud and outspoken. Their cast of features is less uniform than the Russians, and does not yet show the deformities . . . that are imprinted by slavery. (Masson, 1859, 300)

The Cossack at his best was mild, impulsively generous and capable of extraordinary devotion. Langeron remembered how at the battle of Machin (1791) he had a Cossack attendant who remained constantly at his side:

However there was a time when I launched a charge with the hussars and we were surrounded by Turks. The Cossack was unsaddled, wounded and thrown to the ground, losing in the process one of the pistols I had entrusted to his keeping. When he found me again he cast himself at my feet, and begged me to forgive him for having lost the pistol, uttering not a word about his wounds or the perils he had undergone. I raised him up and gave him a ducat. He was amazed. He crossed himself ten or a dozen times and rushed off to retail the story to his comrades — he was unable to recover from his astonishment that I had not ordered him to be soundly thrashed for losing the weapon. (*RS*, 1895, LXXXIII, 193)

The Asiatics

Occasionally a Western theatre caught a glimpse of some of the most authentic remnants of the Golden Horde, summoned up from the wilds of Asia by their Russian masters. Ethnically quite distinct from the Russians and Cossacks, the principal groupings of the 'various nations' comprised the Kazan Tartars, the Bashkirs of the Urals and the Irtysh, and above all the Kalmyks of the Astrakhan steppes:

As to their persons, they [the Kalmyks] are of low stature, and generally bow-legged, occasioned by their being so continually on horseback, or sitting with their legs below them. Their faces are broad and flat, with a flat nose and little black eyes, distant from each other like the Chinese. They are of an olive colour, and their faces full of wrinkles, with very little or no beard. They shave their heads, leaving only a tuft of hair on the crown. (Bruce, 1782, 24)

The Kalmyks were at perpetual war with their tribal neighbours, the Kirgiz, and although firearms were known to them, they put their trust in bow and arrow, with which they could achieve considerable accuracy and range in calm and dry weather.

Heavily escorted by regular Russian cavalry, parties of these tribesmen made their way towards the theatre of operations early in the Seven Years War. Perhaps as many as 2,000 Kalmyks were ultimately dispatched to the army, together with 2,000 more of the other Asiatics. Apraksin desired their presence with the army less for their value in combat than 'because their very name instils terror among the enemy' (Maslovskii, 1888093, I, 35).

Eight   Catherine II, 'the Great' 1762-96

The new empress

Historians and students of human affairs have been fascinated by the work and character of Empress Catherine II. They accord her the title of 'the Great', but otherwise they find in her reign a multitude of paradoxes — how the perfect pupil of the Enlightenment became the enslaver of the eastern Poles, or how, without fighting an aggressive war in the West, she became the doyenne of the crowned heads of Europe after the death of Frederick the Great. Her army, never committed in action against the Prussians or French, grew by up to 200,000 men, and evolved a philosophy of warfare which commands respect two centuries later.

Sympathetic observers noted that Catherine lacked something of the magic of a Maria Theresa, but they felt that they had ample compensation in a generous and commanding personality. Already by the 1770s she was something of a tourist attraction in her own right:

Though she is now become rather corpulent, there is a dignity tempered with graciousness in her deportment and manner, which strikingly impresses. . . . She does not exceed, if she reaches, the middle size. Her features are small, and her eyes blue, but her neck is exquisitely white. (Wraxall, 1776, 201, 205-6)

Her capital began to assume the neo-classical air which accorded strangely well with the cold light

45 Catherine the Great

of the North, and her court became a model of agreeable luxury and public decorum.

The Prince de Ligne, who was no respecter of reputations, expressed genuine admiration for her intelligence, grasp of reality and sense of duty. With undue modesty she dismissed his praise of her sense of judgment in public affairs, but she did admit to a certain skill in choosing men for high military command.

It is all the more surprising to find that these finely attuned instincts were so often swayed by private passion. Amid an atmosphere of gossip and speculation she liked to select personable young men from the Guards and train of adjutants, and reward them with a generosity that was totally incommensurate with their modest talents and services. Physical allure certainly helped to account for the honours paid to Grigorii Grigorevich Orlov, the second of a set of brothers who had startled St Petersburg by their extravagance and splendid looks in the 1750s, and who helped to engineer the palace revolution of 1762.

Grigorii Orlov had 'every advantage of figure, countenance and manner' (Lord Cathcart, 29 December 1769, PRO, SPF 91/82), and his influence knew scarcely any bounds. His knowledge was of the most superficial kind, yet in 1765 he became Master General of the Ordnance. He failed to pay so much as a nominal attention to his duties, and during his seventeen-year tenure as director of the technical arms the artillery stood in danger of losing the impetus which had been given to it by Petr Shuvalov, while the engineers and fortresses suffered from a total neglect. Orlov ultimately lost his power to Grigorii Aleksandrovich Potemkin, who was a much more considerable character, and he died in a state of dementia in 1783.

The army in the early years of the reign

We are acquainted with the term 'Potemkin villages', which signifies the construction of a deceptively impressive facade, with little of substance behind it. The term originated from the show villages which, according to legend, Prince Potemkin was supposed to have built for Catherine on her journey to the Crimea in 1787, but it applies with particular relevance to the work of the Military Commission which first met under the presidency of Field-Marshal Petr Saltykov in 1763.

Saltykov and his colleagues reorganised the peacetime administration of the army into an initial eight divisions. They began to break up the useless Land Militia, they set up novel units of jaegers and the unarmoured heavy cavalry called 'carabiniers', and they issued new tactical codes for the foot and horse (1763). Also, they undertook to remedy something which had been sadly lacking in the Seven Years War, when in 1763 they re-made the old department of the quartermaster-general into a permanent general staff. Six years later the German staff officer Major-General Friedrich Wilhelm Bauer came to Russia at the invitation of Zakhar Chernyshev to review the progress which had been made. Bauer had considerable experience of this sort of thing from his service with Prince Ferdinand of Brunswick in the Seven Years War, and on 30 January 1770 he constructed a new staff establishment which provided for a corps of thirty-seven senior officers, and increased the number of the vital column guides to sixty. Bauer's main objective was to augment the number of officers who could be attached to the field armies.

46 Grigorii Grigorevich Orlov

47 Zakhar Grigorevich Chernyshev

48 Field-marshal, period of Catherine the Great (Viskovatov, 1844-56)

Within a few months Bauer was called on to apply his talents to actual warfare, as chief of staff to Rumyantsev. He not only became Rumyantsev's 'sole adviser, and the moving spirit behind all his actions' (Sabatier, 14 September 1770, *SIRIO*, 1913, CXLIII, 188), but proved himself to be an aggressive divisional commander at Ryabaya Mogila and other actions. 'General Bauer ... has an extreme solicitude for the honour and glory of our arms. In his activity, skill is invariably combined with daring' (Semen Vorontsov, 18 June 1770, *AKV*, 1870-95, XVI, 118).

Meanwhile the War College grew in independence and power under the presidency (1763-74) of Zakhar Chernyshev, who was 'active, artful, designing', and 'suspected of deep foreign connections' (Cathcart, 31 December 1770, 29 December 1769, PRO, SP 91/86 and 91/82). However, Chernyshev 'had an innate and unfailing gift of being able to reduce everything to order, and you could say that under his leadership military affairs proceeded as harmoniously as a musical composition' (Dolgorukov, *RS*, 1889, LXIII, 509). He gained the right of weekly access to the sovereign, and he set up a college printing press to facilitate communications with the army.

These achievements were undermined by the state's withdrawal from the management of the forces, a process of contracting out which went far beyond anything that might have been expected even under a woman sovereign. The effect of the regulations of the middle 1760s was to dismantle the rigorous economic controls which had been set up by Peter the Great, and over the following years the colonels found all kinds of means to exploit their new freedom to their own advantage, to the damage of the state and their soldiers. From 1767 promotion in the whole state service proceeded by the automatic working of seniority, or rather seniority modified by corruption, and Catherine left her servants to enrich themselves as they saw fit from the resources at their command.

Rumyantsev's War, 1768-74

Count Petr Aleksandrovich Rumyantsev (1725-96) has a key place in our story, as a channel by which some of the most advanced military thinking of the West reached Russia, and the founder of a new military tradition which was to be developed in full by Potemkin and Suvorov.

Peter was the legal son of Aleksandr Ivanovich Rumyantsev, who sprang from an obscure Little Russian family to become *generalanshef*, lieutenant-colonel of the Preobrazhenskii Regiment, and one of Peter the Great's closest advisers. He is described as 'a man of cheerful disposition', who 'owed rather more to luck than was consistent with somebody having the management of such high affairs' (Nashchokin, 1842, 91; see also p. 153). The mother was an intelligent and lively lady, who in the middle 1780s could still entrance people with tales of Louis XIV, Mme de Maintenon, Marlborough and the day that Peter the Great laid the foundation stone of St Petersburg. She liked to hint that this energetic monarch had enjoyed her favours, which raises intriguing possibilities concerning the true paternity of her son.

The young Rumyantsev soon proved that he had a will of his own, and he contrived to sign himself up with the Prussian army before he was brought back home under a cloud (see p. 140). After a period of mostly unsung service, Petr Aleksandrovich went on to play an active part in the Seven Years War, commanding a brigade at Gross-Jägersdorf, and the central division at Kunersdorf. Finally, in 1761, he had complete charge of the well-managed campaign which reduced the fortress-port of Colberg. Between times, Rumyantsev was chiefly occupied with organising and training bodies of cavalry, and leading them to the theatre of war.

For a young general, Rumyantsev made a considerable impression on the Westerners who saw him during this period. The Prussian spy Lambert characterised him as being hot-headed, ambitious and well-read, while Messelière witnessed a revealing incident in the spring of 1758, when the Prussians were on the move, and Rumyantsev came across a body of Russian troops who were resting along the banks of a frozen river, waiting for the ice to break so that they could cross on rafts:

He said in his own language to the soldiers: 'My children, I hardly think you are going to let an icy little river hold you up for three days from getting at the Prussians!' At these words the twelve hundred men got to their feet, crying *pobeda*!, which means victory, and *pruki*!, signifying that the Prussians were scum. On the instant, they broke the ice with their axes and sticks. . . . Rumyantsev made a lavish distribution of money, and announced 'I will tell our army that some good comrades are coming to join them!' (Messelière, 1803, 251)

For one who is upheld by Soviet historians as an exemplar of a purely Russian art of war, Rumyantsev was to a remarkable degree fascinated by the ways of the Prussian army. Wiegel points out that Rumyantsev was educated in the Cadet Corps in the Germanising period of Anna:

He then fought under the command of Count Fermor against Frederick the Great, but even during our victories over this royal commander he admired his skill and genius. Later Rumyantsev had the opportunity to become personally acquainted with Frederick, and he could not speak of him without enthusiasm. He had no great opinion of his fellow countrymen, and he invariably lived surrounded by Germans. (Wiegel, 1864-6, I, pt 1, 80)

Following the dethronement of Peter III, Rumyantsev actually debated for a while whether to return to the Prussian service of his youth (see p. 140). Frederick certainly considered it worth his while to cultivate Rumyantsev's good opinion, and he sent him a message of congratulation after the victory of Kagul. Langeron thought it significant that Rumyantsev retained the Prussian-style locks and pigtail for his Little Russia Grenadier Regiment, when the rest of the army had gone over to the unpowdered basin cut.

Elsewhere Langeron describes Rumyantsev as, beyond doubt:

the most brilliant of all the Russian generals, a man endowed with outstanding gifts. He possesses a most serious and broad education, high intelligence, astonishing powers of memory, sound judgment, considerable resolution and the art of inspiring respect. He owes this latter advantage as much to his open and attractive exterior and refined manners, as to a well-considered and civil firmness. I cannot think of any other man with whom it is so interesting and entertaining to converse. (Langeron, *RS*, 1895, LXXXIII, 153)

While it sometimes amused Rumyantsev to play the Little Russian peasant, he accumulated a great fortune, and renovated or built nine or more residences. He always kept 'from eight to ten musicians, with a set of Russian comedians, and a number of domestics, and from his mode of living, gives one a very adequate idea of the ancient feudal magnificence' (Anon., c.1787, 37).

In fact Rumyantsev's rare qualities were accompanied by a dry, detached and selfish temperament, which held him aloof from human commitments. His wife corresponded with him assiduously, but Langeron claims that at bottom he 'loved and respected nobody in the world' (Langeron, *RS*, 1895, LXXXIII, 155). Rumyantsev was certainly a stranger to his offspring:

One of his sons, upon completing his studies, sought him out to find employment. 'Who are you?', asked Rumyantsev. 'Your son!' 'Yes, how pleasant. You have grown'. Rumyantsev went on to pose a number of questions in a passably paternal fashion, after which the young man asked where he could put up, and what he was to do. 'Certainly', said his father, 'you must surely know some officer or other in the camp who can help you out.' (Masson, 1859, 146)

Rumyantsev read and reflected deeply upon his chosen profession. He maintained that a high commander must be fully informed of all relevant developments in the external relations of his country, and he once gave vent to the almost Clausewitzian statement:

A man who simply looks at what lies immediately before his eyes will be unable to see what advantages may derive from the perception of the less obvious attendant circumstances. I could easily go astray if I left myself in ignorance of the political side of affairs, for this lays down the guidelines for the military aspect. (To N. I. Panin, 2 February 1771, Rumyantsev, 1953-9, II, 226)

Though he kept himself abreast of modern military thinking, Rumyantsev rejected the tendency towards geometric and 'scientific' formalism which was beginning to grip some lesser minds in the West:

Our trade has its rules, but they are in many cases indeterminate, and devoid of concrete substance and precision, for they proceed essentially from the judgment of the commander. What the whole art of war comes down to is this . . . to hold the main objective of the war constantly in view, to be aware of what proved useful or damaging in similar cases in past times (giving due weight to the lie of the ground and the associated advantages and difficulties), and to evaluate the intentions of the enemy by working out what we might do if we were in his place. (To N. I. Panin, 27 January 1769, Rumyantsev, 1953-9, II, 64)

Rumyantsev was also an enemy to what became known as the 'cordon system' — the Austrian strategy of stringing out troops in defensive positions over wide stretches of ground. He maintained as a matter of principle that attacking forces held a constant moral ascendancy over those that were defending (Rumyantsev, 1953-9, I, xviii).

However, Rumyantsev remained a man of his time to the extent that he was willing to assert

CENTRAL DIVISIONAL SQUARES AT KAGUL

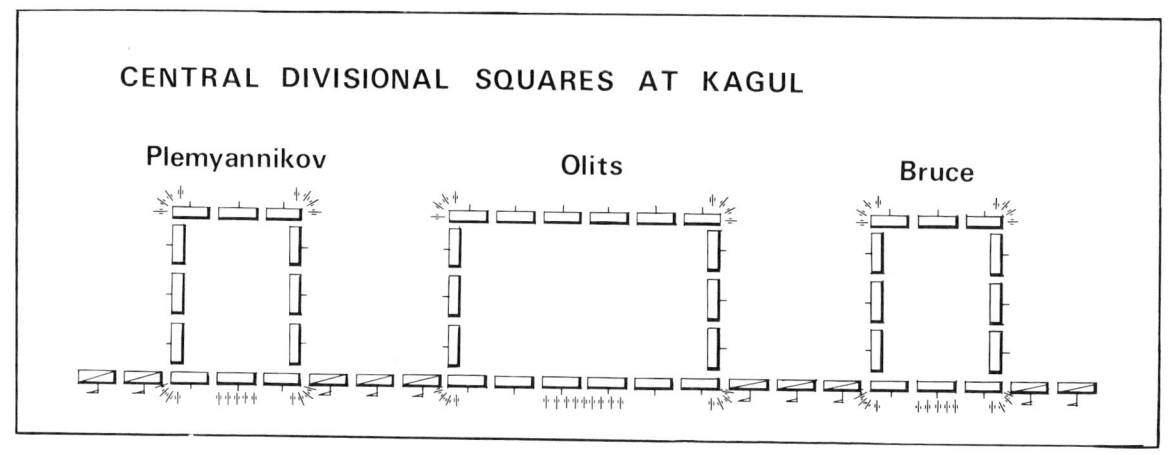

Plemyannikov   Olits   Bruce

49 Central divisional squares at Kagul

that 'nothing is more imprudent than to despise an enemy, or by any means to excite his indignation, revenge, or any other passions of a violent nature, which may make up for any deficiency in skill or courage' (Anon., c.1787, 36). While some hideous scenes of carnage were staged after the Russian victories, Rumyantsev set his face against unnecessary bloodshed, even if the blood happened to be Turkish.

In two respects Rumyantsev's conduct of his Turkish campaigns represents an important advance on the doings of Münnich a generation before. Already in the approaching winter of 1761 he contrived to keep his troops in temporary quarters close to the Prussian positions around Colberg, and in Catherine's Turkish wars he developed the technique still further when it was a question of holding the army throughout the winter months on the approaches to the Balkans. As well as keeping the troops adequately fed so far from home, he had to dispose them in compact groups so as to be ready to assemble in case of a Turkish attack. Many of the soldiers suffered severely in these advanced winter quarters, at least during the first years. However, the losses were probably a small price to pay for the facility of maintaining the army within such close reach of the theatre of war. Münnich sacrificed far more men during the inordinately long marches he had to prosecute every year in order to reach the scene of operations, and then return again to the point of departure.

Second, Rumyantsev evolved a flexible and responsive alternative to the massive army block of Münnich's time, bristling with *chevaux de frise* and encumbered with hundreds of waggons as it made its stately way across the steppes. At the battle of Ryabaya Mogila (1770) Rumyantsev carried the Turkish camp by an assault delivered in a dispersed formation of four squares, which were able to 'attack the enemy from different directions, while being close enough to lend mutual support' (Klokman, 1951, 96). The tactic was employed with no less success at Larga, and again at Kagul, where he formed five squares of divisions. These advances were summed up in Rumyantsev's *General Rules* of 1773, where he explained that 'every corps must be arranged in oblong square, in such a way that the lateral sides must correspond to half the face'. The sides in question were usually composed of infantry regiments with cannon in the centre, and howitzers on the flanks. Between the squares the jaegers were disposed in battalion squares, and the cavalry in lines two ranks deep. Rumyantsev taught the infantry to maintain the impetus of their advance unchecked, relying on the cavalry to counter the Turkish horse, and on the fast-moving artillery to subject the entrenchments to enfilade fire. The baggage train came up in the rear, where it could not encumber the army. One of Rumyantsev's generals, Aleksei Khpuschov, testifies that: 'in place of a beautifully-formed line he substituted an habituation to battle, and by his constant run of successes he engendered that courage which nothing has so far extirpated from the hearts of our troops' (Klokman, 1951, 173).

In the field of minor tactics Rumyantsev had above all to make provision to stave off the mass assaults of the Turkish hordes, 'for if the Turks once break in, there is no resisting their impetuosity' (Anon., c.1787, 37). From the beginning Rumyantsev doubted whether *chevaux de frise* were the most effective counter to the threat. In November 1768 he asked the War College to send him a quantity of these devices, but at the same time wrote to N. I. Panin:

I must confess that some able generals hold that they seem to be an unnecessary burden for the soldiers, and cause more trouble than they are worth. However I have never campaigned against the Turks, and all those who have so served are ready to affirm that *chevaux de frise* form the best and most reliable kind of obstacle. (Rumyantsev, 1953-9, II, 54)

In the event Rumyantsev decided to put his trust in firepower instead, though not with total conviction. He wondered whether Plemyannikov's square at Kagul had suffered unduly through the neglect of the *chevaux de frise*, and many years later he asked for Potemkin's opinion. Potemkin answered that he would always defer to Rumyantsev's authoritative decision on this point, and that the

50 Rumyantsev in battle against the Turks

battle of Kagul would always redound to his glory. Once Rumyantsev had made the break, the *chevaux de frise* disappeared not only from the Turkish theatre but also from the repertoire of tactics to be employed against Western enemies.

Rumyantsev simplified still further the methods ordained in the *Infantry Code* of 1763, and fined down the number of ranks in a line from three to two. While his line infantry was trained to deliver formal volleys by rank, battalion or platoon, Rumyantsev employed his jaegers with increasing freedom, in association with parties of grenadiers, dragoons and batteries of guns. These mobile formations scouted ahead of the army on the march, securing river crossings and other passages, and in time of battle they helped to guard the flanks of the squares, and the communications between them.

While Rumyantsev was 'a great admirer of the Prussian army ... this admiration was always free of the prejudices which weigh down lesser spirits' (S. Vorontsov, 'Zapiski', 1802, *AKV*, 1870-95, X, 482-3). In particular, Rumyantsev was an implacable opponent of the Prussian-style heavy cavalry which had been such a notable feature of the period immediately after the Seven Years War. Towards the end of the campaign of 1770 he wrote to Catherine:

The cuirassier and carabinier regiments are mounted on breeds of horses which are at once expensive, delicate and heavy, and which are better for parades than operations. During the whole campaign we had to feed them on dry fodder, since they wasted away when they grazed on pasture. The very equipment of the heavy cavalry is burdensome, weighing down both rider and horse. (Rumyantsev, 1953-9, II, 382)

Potemkin shared these views, and as President of the War College he effected a lightening of the cavalry, reorganising the cuirassiers as carabiniers, and restoring the historic primacy of the dragoon in the Russian army.

When Rumyantsev took over the First Army from Prince Golitsyn at the end of 1769, he found a wide diversity of practice obtaining among the regiments, in spite of all the regulations and instructions of recent years. To put things right he issued a supplementary *Order of Service* (*Obryad Sluzhby*) in March the next year. The *Order* was composed of seventeen passages for the infantry and four for the cavalry, and laid down clear rules for the management of marches, baggage trains, camps, pickets, sentries, hospitals and foraging, as well as simplified tactical formations. This excellent document received the approval of the War College in 1776, and was adopted by Potemkin for the field army in 1788.

Rumyantsev was much concerned with the physical conservation of his troops, and it was his misfortune that he commanded Russian armies at a time when it was beyond the power of an individual to stay the appalling mortality. Doctors were so scarce that whole corps of several regiments were left without any medical assistance whatsoever, and between 1769 and 1773 a devastating plague overtook the Russian and Turkish armies and spread to much of Russia. Rumyantsev devoted sums of money to setting up improvised hospitals, but otherwise he had to be content with ordering the officers to pay close attention to the cleanliness of their men.

In the exercise of man-management, Rumyantsev resorted variously to corporal punishment, telling rebukes, and surprises and compliments of the most agreeable kind. 'Promotions and decorations were certainly difficult to come by, when he was in command, but in compensation he awarded them justly, and to such men as deserved them for real service' (Engelhardt, 1868, 93). An Englishman once heard Rumyantsev say:

'A general must be easy and affable to his troops, without descending to meanness, or being too often seen by them, which must render him less respected.' He himself had learned so much affability by practice, and so rigidly observed his own rules, that he constantly took off his hat to the very children of his own peasants when they bowed to him. (Anon., c.1787, 36)

Rumyantsev's successes in this respect became legendary, and a generation later Aleksandr Mikhailovich Turgenev remarked that his style of command was 'not what you find nowadays. He knew every single one of his clerks, and every captain of the army which was entrusted to him' (Turgenev, *RS*, 1886, LII, 49). On the march, Rumyantsev insisted that the officers must forsake their carriages and ride on horseback with their platoons.

The soldiers sang as the mood took them, and when the field-marshal rode by they usually struck up some martial song in his honour, like *Akh ty, nash batyushka, Graf Rumyantsev general!* Sometimes he gave the singers a couple of ten-rouble pieces, and he also deigned to chat with several officers of the staff and regiment. Indeed his friendliness drew the hearts and minds of all people towards him. (Engelhardt, 1868, 79)

This remarkable man represented probably the most important single formative influence on the Russian army in the second half of the eighteenth century. Many of the initiatives that were associated with Potemkin came in the first place from Rumyantsev. Greater still was the impression made on Suvorov, in whom he foresaw 'a worthy successor in glory and deed' (Saikin, 1818, 62-3). Suvorov commanded his officers to observe the *Order of Service*, and incorporated some of its thinking in his own *Art of Victory*, and in 1789, when his old chief had lost favour, he was sedulous in showing Rumyantsev every mark of attention and respect. Count Thedor Rostopchin once penned a gushing eulogy to the effect that 'where Rumyantsev was a hero for his own time, Suvorov is a hero for all times!' The statement was read to Suvorov. 'It's not true!' he exclaimed, 'tell them "Suvorov is the pupil of Rumyantsev!"' (Fuchs, 1827, 41).

Catherine's first military enterprise became known in popular parlance as 'Rumyantsev's War'. In fact, in the contest with the Turks between 1768 and 1774 Rumyantsev was just an executive instrument of Catherine, or rather of a Russian geo-political will which sought to exploit an almost uniquely favourable state of international affairs. In the one direction, Zakhar Chernyshev and the resurgent expansionist party sought some compensation for the sacrifices of the Seven Years

51 Musketeer, 1763-c.1786. Green coat with red collar, lapels (an innovation in Russia), cuffs and turn-backs; red waistcoat; red breeches; hat bordered with white, and white plume (Viskovatov, 1844-56)

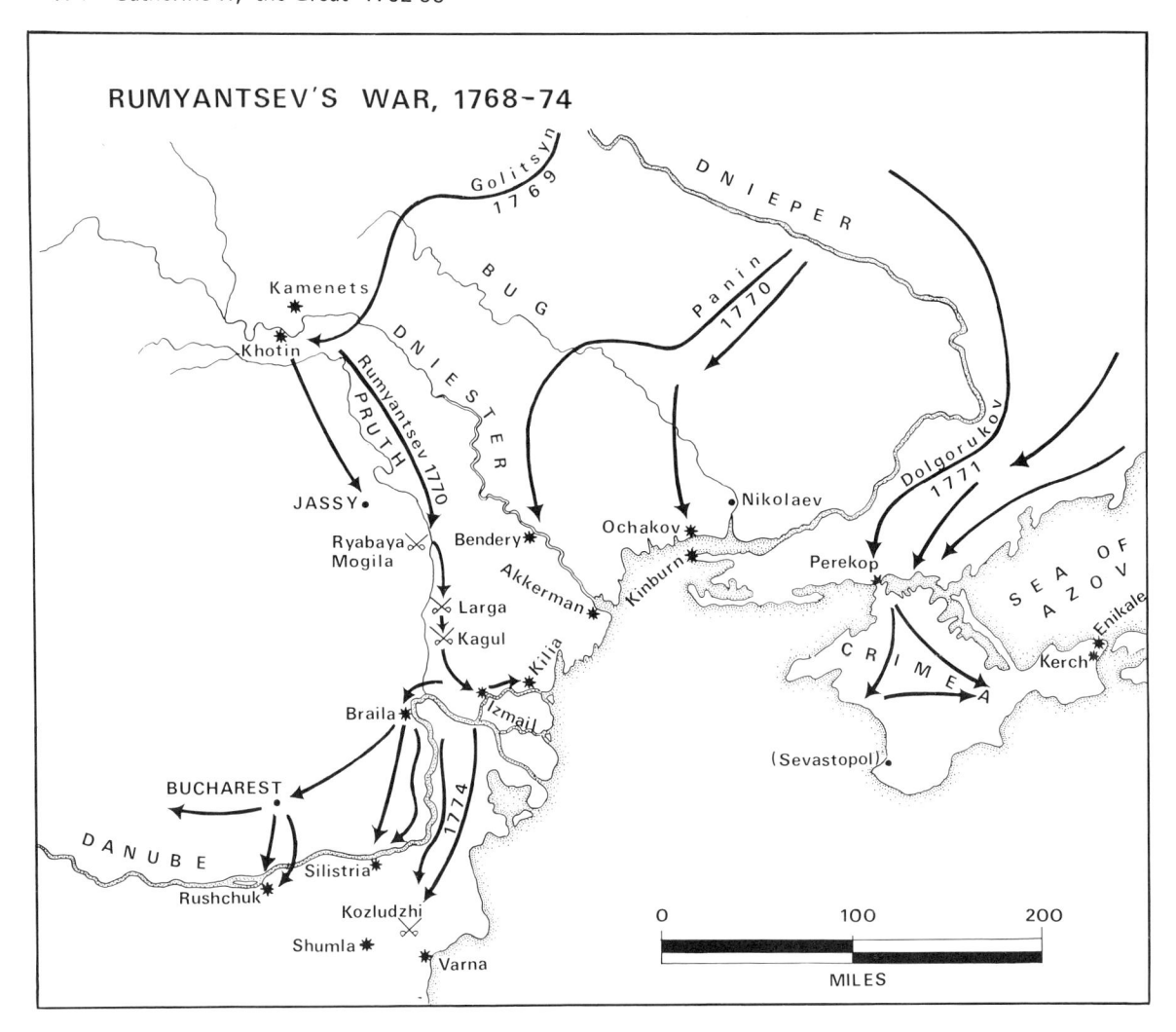

War, and spoke in favour of pushing Russian borders deep into anarchic Poland, so as to open water routes all the way from Riga to Kiev. To the south and east, commercial interests demanded an outlet to the Black Sea and the Mediterranean, to compare with the one which Peter had gained to the Baltic, as also the opening of trade with India, and the colonisation of the steppes, after the Tartars had been evicted from the northern Black Sea littoral. Little interference could be expected from the Swedes, or from the Prussians, Austrians or French, who had been enfeebled by the Seven Years War.

Catherine was satisfied for the moment to install a puppet king in Warsaw, and leave Polish sovereignty nominally intact, but a party of Polish irreconcilables looked to Turkey for support, and by the end of 1768 a major border incident helped to draw Russia and Turkey into direct confrontation. Now that she was committed to war, Catherine could no longer deny her lust for aggrandisement.

The Russian schemes certainly developed on a spectacular scale in 1769, what with the main armies campaigning on the river lines at the northwest corner of the Black Sea, a corps operating in the northern Caucasus, and squadrons being got ready for the Mediterranean.

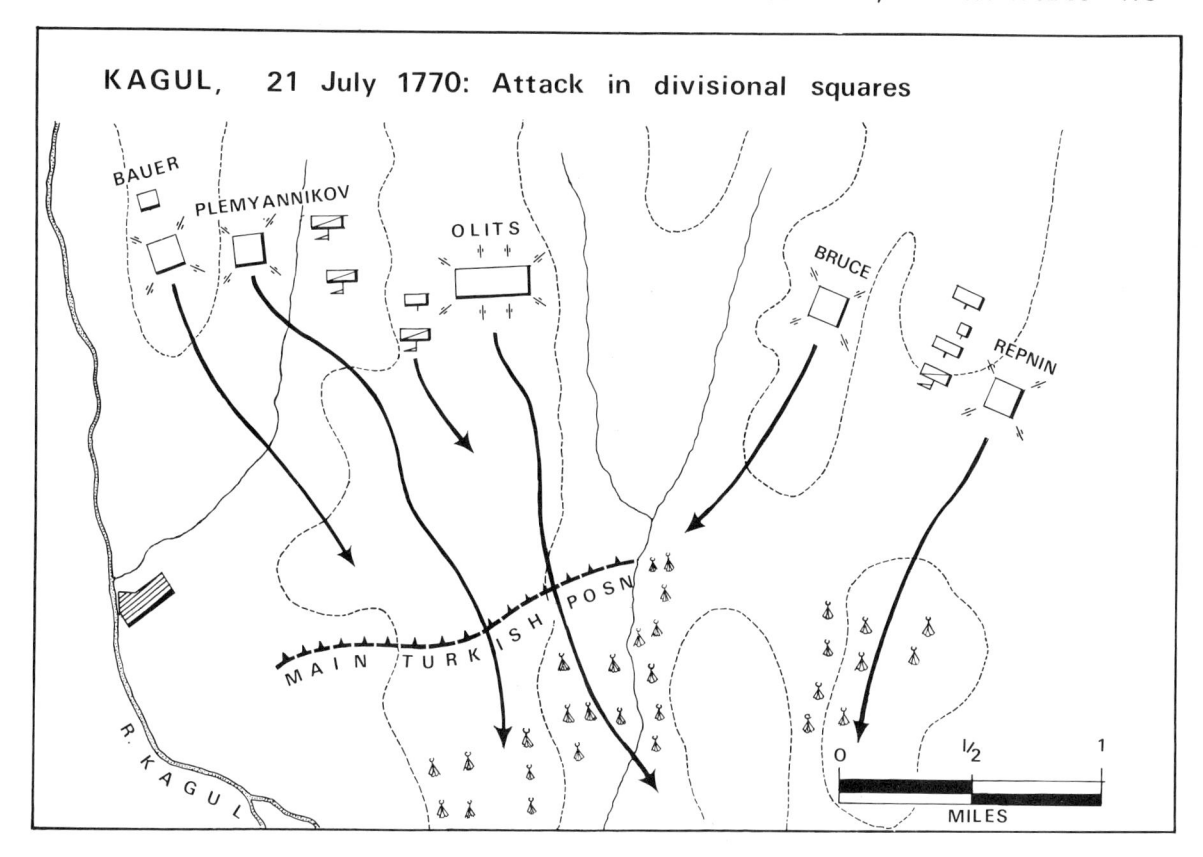

KAGUL, 21 July 1770: Attack in divisional squares

On the principal theatre of war, the Dniester, Prince Aleksandr Golitsyn and his First Army of 80,000 men finally entered into possession of Khotin after a laughably muddled campaign. Rumyantsev assumed control after Golitsyn was recalled to St Petersburg, and in the autumn he sent detached corps ranging over Moldavia and into Wallachia, awakening hopes of the overthrow of Turkish domination in the Balkans.

The successes of 1770 turned out to be some of the most brilliant which the Russians ever attained in the century. The main operation of that year was supposed to be the siege of the fortress of Bendery, which was sited on the lower Dniester, and the capture of which would complete the work of 1769, and give the Russians the command of the whole river. Prince Petr Panin moved slowly against it with a powerful and well-found army, and he finally reduced it by storm on 16 September.

Rumyantsev had meanwhile been given a free hand with his First Army, which amounted to between 35,000 and 40,000 men. Taking a route well to the rear of the garrison of Bendery, he advanced with extraordinary confidence towards the Danube. Again and again he overcame the forces in his path by dint of fixing them frontally by one of his divisional or corps squares, while turning their flanks and rear with the rest of the army. Seventy-two thousand Turks and Tartars were evicted from their camp at Ryabaya Mogila on 17 June, and the process was repeated at a position beside the river Larga on 7 July. Finally the main Turkish army of 150,000 warriors met Rumyantsev in a murderous battle near the Kagul on 21 July. The day ended with the surviving Turks in flight, and 138 guns, 2,000 prisoners and perhaps as many as 20,000 of their dead and wounded left on the field. This victory earned Rumyantsev the rank of field-marshal, and the felicitations of Frederick of Prussia. Rumyantsev was now free to move to the lower Danube, and in the course of three weeks he prised Izmail, Kilia and Braila from the nerveless grip of the Turks.

Catherine's joy was crowned by news from the Mediterranean, where by May 1770 the Russians had assembled four squadrons, which had sailed all the way from the Baltic. On 26 June Admiral Greig assailed the Turkish fleet in its refuge in the Bay of Chesmé in Asia Minor with a force of four of the line, two frigates, one bomb vessel and four fireships. One of the Turkish vessels caught alight during the exchange of gunfire, which disordered the Turkish array, and the sparks and the advent of the fireships completed the work of destruction. The Turks lost fifteen of the line, and nearly forty smaller craft, and before long they found themselves blockaded in the Dardanelles and cut off from Greece, which was in full revolt.

In 1771 the main offensive role on land was assumed by *Generalanshef* Prince Dolgorukov, whose Second Army stormed into the Crimea in the middle of June, and proceeded to overrun the peninsula. The plan of operations and the system of supply had been carefully worked out by Chernyshev at the War College, so as to avoid the collapse of administrative arrangements which had been seen in the 1730s. The resistance was minimal, because the main Tartar hosts were away on the Danube theatre, getting themselves killed by Rumyantsev.

Faced with military collapse, the Turks entered into peace negotiations. These dragged on from the spring of 1772, and finally broke down on the Turks' refusal to cede their rights over the Crimea. When fighting resumed in 1773, Rumyantsev had at his disposal scarcely 35,000 combatants, and with these he made a short-lived excursion beyond the Danube.

At last in 1774 Rumyantsev was given not just a respectable army, but a high degree of military and political freedom. He used the opportunities to the full. While a separate force operated against distant Ochakov and Kinburn, Rumyantsev fed the main army of 55,000 men across the Danube by carefully calculated detachments — first Kamenskii's division in April, and then commands under Suvorov, Saltykov and others. On 10 June Suvorov's division of 8,000 men defeated the 40,000-strong army of Abder-Rezah at Kozludzhi, which placed Shumla in peril, while Rumyantsev moved against Silistria, and Saltykov blockaded the upstream fortress of Rushchuk.

The Grand Vizier feared that nothing short of major concessions would stop the Russian army from advancing on Constantinople. Using his plenipotentiary diplomatic powers, Rumyantsev was therefore able to bring the Turks to immediate terms of peace at Kutchuk-Kainardji and win two major advantages on behalf of Russia. He eroded the Turkish strategic bridgehead on the northern shores of the Black Sea by having the Tartars of the Crimea and the Nogai steppes declared independent of Turkey, and gaining the outright cession to Russia of Azov, Kerch, and Kinburn with a stretch of land between the Bug and Dnieper. Second, he advanced Russian influence into the Balkans when he won favoured treatment for Russian subjects in Turkey, as well as the right to speak on behalf of the Christian peoples of Moldavia and Wallachia.

The long-term economic benefits were still more significant. Not only were the southern steppes opened to settlement, and the raising of cattle, sheep and grain, but the extinction of the age-old Tartar threat opened to a full interior colonisation the historic Russian lands south of the Muscovite forests. 'The soil of this region is probably the most fertile in all Russia, and as black as coal. Except for occasional hills, the terrain is virtually one continuous plain, so level and huge that it extends beyond the limit of your sight' (Strandmann, *RS*, 1882, XXXV, 291). Thus Russia began to exercise the mastery of the whole belt of lowlands from the Baltic to the Black Sea.

For all the waste and blunders, 'Rumyantsev's War' had given ample proof of a new style and confidence in Russian campaigning. The staff work reached a high standard (indeed, it declined afterwards), and the orders were issued as coherent 'dispositions', systematically outlining the tasks of each element of the army. The field guns were employed not just in large batteries, as in the

Seven Years War, but they moved with freedom on the battlefield, achieving impressive concentrations of fire. A French officer considered the Russian emphasis on artillery important, 'particularly in a century when this element in warfare has the principal influence on all operations' (Anon., 1788, 327). For the acknowledged expert, the Marquis da Silva, the performance of the troops of the line yielded further proof that the Russian infantry had become 'one of the finest in Europe. It has a consistency and endurance of its own. It is a veritable wall' (Silva, 1778, 53).

However, the light forces were the ones which had shown to the best advantage. In 1774 the scattered companies of jaegers were accordingly brought together into six battalions, and later in the reign the number of such battalions was increased to the extremely large total of forty.

52 Jaegers, 1765-c.1786. Drab green jacket, greatcoat and trousers; black felt cap with green edges (Viskovatov, 1844-56)

New regiments of hussars, lancers and other light horse were raised during the war, which effectively reversed the policies of the 1760s, and after the peace the number of dragoon regiments was augmented to ten, and those of hussars to sixteen.

'Rumyantsev's War' was staged at a time of peace elsewhere in Europe, and the Westerners had every opportunity to evaluate the significance of what was going on. A large number of foreign volunteers had accompanied the Russian armies and fleets, and the record of their experiences helped to swell the growing military literature of the period. Furthermore, Western commentators and statesmen were somewhat exercised by the threat to European interests and security implicit in what later became known as 'The Eastern Question'. Some of the French, Swedes, Prussians and Austrians began to look with a little trepidation on the changes in the balance of power on Europe's Asian borders, and on the further proofs of the endurance of Russian armies: 'A nation of men of such powerful physical constitution is very suited to conquering whole empires' (Wonzel, 1783, 22-3).

Other observers maintained that there was as yet no real cause for alarm. An anonymous English author certainly wrote:

> It is not without reason that many politicians dread the further aggrandizement of the Russian Empire. No power, within the century past, has made such important acquisitions. It has also adopted those very principles which rendered Rome the mistress of the world: the first of which was, to borrow from its neighbours every useful institution; and the second, to embrace every opportunity, whether fair or otherwise, of adding to its territory and its power. (Anon., c.1787, 15)

He added, however, that Russian ambitions were directed towards the east, and that if the Russian armies turned against Europe a million troops would stand in their way in Germany alone. The British ambassador, Lord Cathcart, likewise maintained that Russia's eastward enterprises were harmless to British interests, and that the same held true of the worm-eaten Russian fleet, which must always be dependent on British expertise (PRO, SPF 91/80-7).

Most detailed of all was the special report which Sabatier de Cabres, the French envoy in St Petersburg, drew up for Louis XV in 1772. As a hostile witness, he maintained that Russia could never become a great power, since all classes were ignorant and vicious, trade and the useful arts were sunk in irredeemable backwardness, and the population of eighteen million could never fill the vast geographic extent of the empire. On the military side, Sabatier had always entertained a low opinion of the Russian performance, and by dint of a series of careful calculations he put the strength of the Russian army in regular troops at no more than 210,000, which was probably not far off the mark. If the Russians ever sought to intervene again in Europe, they would present merely:

an auxiliary force of 50 or 60,000 men, badly organised, incomplete, demanding, expensive and extravagant. They will be a burden for the country which feeds them, and their intervention will be clumsy and short-lived. With commanders of suspect loyalty and boundless greed, they will let a whole campaign pass before delivering a few tardy blows, and then they will go home again. In other words, they will act just as they did when they were allies of the Austrians. (*SIRIO*, 1913, CXLIII, 613)

The first partition of Poland, 1772

During the Turkish war Russia had made a significant though bloodless westwards advance of her boundaries at the expense of Poland, which was now entering on the last anarchical years of its independent life. For several years now the anti-Russian party among the Poles had been disputing the virtual Muscovite protectorship over their land, but the impetus for a partition came not from Major-General Suvorov's storm of the castle of Cracow in February 1772, which put an end to the rebellion, but from the desire of Frederick the Great to establish a land corridor between the main body of his states and East Prussia.

The notion of a theft of Polish territory fitted in well with the desires of Chernyshev and the military party, and in August 1772 Russia, Prussia and Austria signed an unholy agreement by which they helped themselves to large slices of the outer Polish territories. Catherine's share amounted to 40,000 square miles, and the new frontier along the Dvina and the Dniester usefully eliminated the wriggling salients of Polish land which intervened between Livonia and the Ukraine. For the first time for half a century Russia's 'way to the West' was therefore expressed in territorial terms.

Young Russian officers like Pishchevich were astonished by the flirtatiousness of the Polish girls, 'but I must do them justice by saying that in addition to their agreeable manners and careful education, which are obvious to all, they draw one still more through their great sweetness of character' (Pishchevich, 1885, 31).

The Russians repaid the Poles most brutally. In the little towns and villages the Russian soldiery used to tyrannise the people on whom they were billeted, smashing up their houses, and making free with their property and womenfolk. Wiegel noted how in the cities the commanders of German blood behaved with the cruel oafishness of their ancestors in the Thirty Years War, while in Warsaw, still nominally independent, even the gracious Prince Repnin, the Russian ambassador, subjected Polish society to the most pointed snubs. 'A proud people may resign itself to being beaten,' commented de Ségur, 'but never to seeing itself humiliated' (Ségur, 1824-6, III, 17).

Pugachev's rebellion, 1773-4

The St Petersburg government was soon given further occupation by the last, and one of the most dangerous of the great peasant revolts of Russian history. The impetus was given by a man of charismatic gifts, the Don Cossack deserter Emilian Pugachev, who appeared among the Yaik Cossacks in the guise of the dead Peter III. His initial band of three hundred supporters grew rapidly to a force of 30,000, drawing in elements of nearly all those who had been alienated over the years by the enforced modernisation of Russian society — Old Believers, Cossacks, serfs, workers from the Ural mines and factories, and dispossessed Bashkirs and Kalmyks. The choice of the persona of Peter III was significant, for that monarch had freed the nobles from their obligations, and so (reasoned the downtrodden) he would surely do the same for the masses.

Some time before the outbreak, a council of war had dismissed the first reports of unrest, declaring 'the feeling of malcontency will have no consequences apart from occasioning some disorder in the levy of recruits, and increasing the number of dissidents and outlaws' (Andryshchenko, in Beskrovnyi, 1969, 341). The field army and the reserves were therefore committed without hesitation to the war against the Turks, delivering the initiative to the rebels from the autumn of 1773 to the high summer of 1774. The insurgents hounded the nobles and gentry, seized the towns of Kazan, Penza and Saratov, and blockaded the garrisons of Orenburg, Yaitsk and Ufa.

At last, however, Pugachev was defeated in the field outside Kazan, and the signing of peace with Turkey permitted the government to mass its forces to put down the revolt. The ferocious Colonel Ivan Ivanovich Michelson broke the power of the rebellion in an action at Tsaritsyn on the Volga, and Pugachev was delivered by his own companions to the vengeance of the government, which was carried out at Moscow in 1775.

Russia builds an army

We gain some inkling of the scale of the Russian military effort in the later part of the century from the huge demands made on industry.

In absolute terms, the production of domestic concerns was impressive, that of pig and cast iron rising from an annual 15,000 tons during Peter's reign to nearly 160,000 at the end of the century. By that time between fifteen and seventeen factories were casting artillery, four were producing small arms, and seventy more were supplying other military needs. The most important of these concerns were established in the Urals, and the majority were managed through private contractors. Russian artillery was capable of meeting the need for ordnance and most of the ammunition, though three million roubles-worth of foreign gunpowder had to be purchased in the 1780s and 1790s.

By the nature of things the manufacture of small arms had more the character of a craft industry, and even after it underwent reconstruction in 1767 and 1776 the famous and ancient factory at Tula could not satisfy the demand for smooth-bore weapons, let alone the requirement of rifles for the jaeger NCOs. Rumyantsev testified 'from actual experience, that the muskets in every infantry regiment are completely unfit for use', and that the soldiers spent a great deal of time and a lot of their own money in vain attempts to effect repairs (17 October 1768, *P. A. Rumyantsev. Dokumenty*, 1953-9, II, 15). In the 1780s an Englishman reported 'their firearms are very bad, and one thousand men are never exercised without two or three muskets bursting, and killing or wounding some of their men' (Anon., c.1787, 9).

During the same period, however, native cloth manufactures developed on a significant scale, more especially through the establishment of twenty contract factories which were permitted to employ peasant labour, thus avoiding some of the feudal restrictions which tended to hold back heavy industry. As regards both quantity and quality, the Russian soldiers could now be properly fitted out with uniforms of domestic manufacture.

In the domain of finance, the expanding resources of the nation were finally outpaced by increasingly urgent military demands, and the result was the abandonment of the glorious self-sufficiency of cash and kind which had seen the state through the wars of the earlier part of the century. The taxable male population rose from less than 8,000,000 in 1762, to 12,500,000 in the early 1780s, and to the 17,800,000 of the census of 1794-6. The costs of active military operations varied greatly from year to year, but they were much easier to bear than the price of the annual maintenance of the army, which after having been held at or under 10,000,000, climbed rapidly in the 1780s and reached a new plateau of 28,100,000 in 1792. The government had recourse to large foreign loans and the issue of paper money or 'assignations'; 210,000,000 roubles of paper money were in circulation in 1799, and they exchanged hands at just 65½ kopeks each.

It is sad to reflect that so much of the produce of the taxation of peasant 'souls', earned in circumstances of dreadful hardship, was allowed to run to waste in a supply system of notorious corruption and inefficiency. (Paul I has the credit of bringing the reign of misrule to at least a temporary end, when in 1797 he installed the offices of Food Supply (*Proviant*) and the Commissariat in St Petersburg, and reduced them to the rank of 'expeditions' of the War College.)

Catherine's Russia was rich most of all in gifted commanding personalities, who make a much greater impact on the imagination than the leading men of the Seven Years War. If Rumyantsev has a claim to be considered the founder of a new way in warfare, then Field-Marshal Prince Potemkin was the individual whose name was most often on the lips of contemporaries. He has a place in our story as coming closest to a purely Russian ideal of what many officers would have liked to have been.

After toying with the idea of entering the church, Grigorii Aleksandrovich Potemkin (1739-91) enlisted as a trooper in the Regiment of Horse Guards, and it was as a young officer in this splendid unit that a chance encounter brought him into conversation with the empress. She was much taken by his passion, boldness and colossal height. As Masson remarked, these two larger-than-life characters seemed to be made for one another. 'He is the only man that the empress stands in awe of, and she both likes and fears him' (Anon., c.1787, 29).

Potemkin reached field rank in 'Rumyantsev's War', and in the early 1770s it became evident that his radiant presence had eclipsed the Orlovs in the imperial favour. The year 1774 brought the rank of *generalanshef* and the Vice-Presidency of the War College, and ten years later he became full President and field-marshal.

Far less of the European than Rumyantsev,

53 Grigorii Aleksandrovich Potemkin

Chernyshev or even Suvorov, Potemkin seemed to luxuriate in all the trappings of Asiatic despotism. In his garb he variously affected a favourite bearskin wrap, a luxurious version of a Cossack hetman's clothes, or the plain uniform of an ordinary soldier, such as the one he had made up in 1787, so as not to shame the poorer officers. His suite of adjutants, lackeys, spongers and confidants amounted to two or three hundred.

With all of this:

No great man up to that time had put his power to less evil ends. He was devoid of vengeful or rancorous feelings. . . . He was daring and lustful for power. On some occasions he was insouciant to the point of immobility, and on others capable of putting forth incredible exertions. . . . Altogether he summed up everything which redounds to the glory of the Russian nation, and everything for which it has justly been reproached. (Wiegel, 1864-6, I, pt 1, 291)

He could not hear a cannon shot without fearing that it might have cost the lives of some of his soldiers, and his dislike of corporal punishment went so far as to endanger discipline. He dispensed his wealth with the same unconcern as he received it, and while affecting the greatest delicacy, he ignored the extremes of heat and cold and every personal danger whenever he felt his presence was needed.

Potemkin's headquarters were notable for their dirt and disorder, and he showed little aptitude for the detail of military operations. However, the prince had the undeniable gift of creating excitement and activity in those about him: 'When he was absent, he was the sole topic of conversation. When he was present, he was the cynosure of all eyes' (Masson, 1859, 103). Pishchevich began to perceive a pattern:

I saw him in the Crimea, lying on a sofa, surrounded by fruits and apparently oblivious of all care — yet amid all the unconcern Russia conquered the peninsula. I saw him again in idle mood at Elizavetgrad, looking on while the thirty-four generals, who were residing at headquarters without any command, took it in turns to play at billiards — and shortly afterwards the bitterly-contested storm of Ochakov signalled his spirit of enterprise to the world. (Pishchevich, 1885, 128)

Indeed, it was easy for a less astute observer to overlook the vast range of Potemkin's activities, which embraced diplomatic and administrative affairs, as well as the command of the army.

Towards the end of his life, Potemkin remarked at table to a circle of friends:

Is there a man who has been more fortunate than me? Everything I have ever wanted, all my whims, have been fulfilled as if by magic. I desired high ranks — I have them. Orders of chivalry — I have them also. I loved to gamble — I won incalculable sums. I loved to stage festivities — and they turned out to be magnificent ones. I liked to buy up estates — I have them. I was fond of building houses — and I have built veritable palaces. I craved precious things — and no other private person has had so many of them or such rare ones.

(Zatvornitskii, in Skalon, 1902-c.1911, III, pt 6, 94)

At this he hit the plate in front of him with his fist, breaking it in pieces. He left the table and went to his bedchamber.

From 1774 until he died in 1791 Potemkin was effective head of the War College, a position which, as somebody put it, 'gave him to some degree the power to bind the whole body of generals to him, and offered him the opportunity to assist and oblige the junior officers and even the private soldiers' (Anon., 1792, 35). In 1781 he re-created the College's accounting department (*Schetnaya Ekspeditsiya*), which had been formed by Münnich but abolished in the reign of Elizabeth, and in 1785 he appointed an inspector-general and four ordinary inspectors who were to enforce standards in the army, aided by an *Inspektorskaya Ekspeditsiya* of the War College. Unfortunately Potemkin's talents were not of a nature to shine in routine administration. His dislike of paperwork, his favouritism and his lack of system combined to reduce the running of the army to 'hopeless confusion' (Langeron, *RS*, 1895, LXXXIII, 150). The War College lost track of appointments, and the processes of promotion were upset by the intervention of Potemkin, Suvorov, Zubov and others on behalf of their protégés.

Operational management likewise fell into some disorder. Friedrich Wilhelm Bauer, as virtual chief of staff, had alienated Potemkin and other native Russians by his pushy and independent ways, and in 1774 he found it expedient to leave the country. Catherine retrieved him in the following year, but for the rest of his career (he died in 1783) he was employed merely on works of civil engineering and public building. The staff corps was virtually moribund by the end of the reign, and Langeron ruminated:

The French and Austrian general staffs are brilliant organisations, but in our own corps I have never encountered the kind of officers who were capable of putting together far-reaching dispositions or plans of campaign, of or leading the columns with any degree of skill. This corps was in an excellent state when it was set up by General

Bauer in 1769 [sic, actually 1770], but now in Russia it scarcely exists, even though it ought to be the nursery of future generals. (Langeron, *RS*, 1895, LXXXIII, 165)

In fact the staff always had the nature of an alien graft, and it was ultimately rejected by the Russians. The Duc de Richelieu went so far as to declare: 'Prince Potemkin is a declared enemy of tactics and science in military affairs. He has succeeded in inculcating this opinion throughout almost the whole army, which could occasion considerable inconveniences' (*SIRIO*, 1886, LIV, 149).

Potemkin's instincts were much more sure when he turned to more comprehensible matters like arming, equipping and training troops, and imbuing them with a warlike spirit. In 1778 he began to create new regiments of grenadiers, by dint of selecting peasants from the former monastic estates of Little Russia. Extraordinary transformations were wrought in this unpromising material, as was the Russian way, and the new grenadier regiments took a leading place in the assaults that were delivered on Ochakov and Izmail. Otherwise, Potemkin's inclination was to form bodies of troops that were capable of acting with facility in difficult terrain, and sustaining the long marches which the army had to prosecute on the Turkish theatre. These considerations led to a vast increase in the number of jaegers, and a lightening of the cavalry (see p. 172) which caused a revival of the cross-bred dragoons, for 'being trained to act both as infantry and cavalry, they may be used for both purposes as the situation demands, without having to borrow infantry or cavalry for assistance and support' (Mikhnevich, in Skalon, 1902-c.1911, IV, Introduction, 201).

In contrast to the developments among the other field arms, Catherine's artillery held largely to the organisation and regulations which had been worked out by Shuvalov and Fermor for the great war against Prussia. Only in June 1788 was the army issued with an official *Supplement concerning (Artillery) Fire*. This was the work of a deserving individual, *Generalanshef* Ivan Ivanovich Meller-Zakomelskii (1725-90). He was born of a middle class German Lutheran family, and rose from the ranks of the Russian artillery by long service. He commanded the guns at Rumyantsev's siege of Colberg, and afterwards he exercised a wide supervision over the ordnance as a whole, on account of the long absences of the nominal Master General, Grigorii Orlov.

The *Supplement* of 1788 was a practical document, devoted almost entirely to telling the gunners how to work the greatest execution among the Turks, and perhaps it also helped the Russians to derive some benefit from the first significant improvements which had been effected in the artillery for thirty years. The secret canister howitzer was taken out of use, which cut the size of the field (medium) artillery to 244 pieces, and an extensive programme of recasting reduced the weight of the 12-pounder cannon barrel from eighty *puds* to sixty, and that of the 6-pounder from fifty to thirty-one. The intermediate 8-pounder cannon was abolished altogether, as was the cumbersome 9-*pud* mortar.

Potemkin reminded his officers that 'the name of "soldier" is an honourable one'. He was as severe in punishing officers who maltreated their men, as he was attentive in distributing medals among the rank and file after victories. By 1788 'none of the officers or staff dared to punish the soldiers, for these folk had the right of carrying their complaints direct to His Highness' (Tsebrikov, *RS*, 1895, LXXXIV, 172).

The most characteristic product of the age of Potemkin was in fact the radical transformation which he undertook in the uniforms of all the troops save the Guards and the Cossacks, beginning in 1786 with the forces he had under his immediate command in the southern provinces. The changes concerned not just cut and style, but a rejection of Western values and a fundamental reorientation of the purpose for which military clothing was worn at all. Potemkin explained that when

the concept of regularity was first introduced to Russia, there came also some foreign officers who were imbued with all the pedantry of their time. Our own officers were ready to honour all of this as something holy and secret, for they did not know what military order was really about. It seemed to them that it had to do with pigtails, hats, facings, the manual drill of arms, and things like that . . . altogether the clothing and equipment of our army were ideally suited to torment the soldiers.

The outfit looked well on parade, but Potemkin maintained that 'the true beauty of military dress consists in its uniformity, and the extent to which the component items correspond to their use. Clothes are for dressing a soldier, and not for loading him with a burden' (Mikhnevich, in Skalon, 1902-c.1911, IV, Introduction, 198-9).

54 Musketeers in the 'Potemkin' uniform, c.1786. Green *kurtka* coat with yellow shoulder strap and red collar, lapels, cuffs and turn-back stripes; red trousers with yellow braid; white belts (Viskovatov, 1844-56)

The standard coat of the new uniform was a short drab green tunic, or *kurtka*, which could be closed across the chest with buttons in winter. The eminently practical trousers were edged with leather at the bottoms, and the shoes or light boots were of soft but durable leather. The hair was done in a rather ugly, unpowdered basin cut, and the ensemble was crowned by a round felt helmet with a peak. The commodity of the uniform was admired by foreign observers, and looking back on the former fashions, Langeron wrote that, 'it now seems quite incomprehensible to me how we could for such a long time have subjected ourselves to such a torment, forcing ourselves to curl, pomade and powder our locks, and lose two hours of every day in this ludicrous occupation' (Langeron, *RS*, 1895, LXXXIII, 146).

The summer exercise camps were another expression of the spirit of the times. These useful institutions had fallen out of use under Peter's successors, but they entered a new lease of life in the new reign. The biggest affairs of the kind were held in the 1760s, at Tsarskoe Selo, Smolensk, Kazan, Orenburg, Moscow and other places, and they involved infantry and cavalry to the number of as many as 30,000 at a time. When they were not engaged in the larger assemblies, the individual regiments called in their component companies to camp sites designated by the War College, and they exercised from about the middle of May to the middle of August.

On such occasions the senior officers enjoyed a considerable freedom of interpretation:

Every regimental commander uses his own discretion to make up whatever rules he desires for his unit . . . one might wish to introduce his regiment to the principles of the French codes of 1773 or 1788, while others would try to imitate Prussian tactics, and so on. (Langeron, *RS*, 1895, LXXXIII, 196)

This creative ferment engendered some initiatives which became famous in their own generation, or which reveal the thinking of men who later rose to high rank. Semen Vorontsov's *Instruction for Company Commanders* of 1774 was originally composed for the First Grenadier Regiment (see

55 The 'Potemkin' cap, showing the brass band and the yellow transverse crest of wool. The long black cloth flaps at the back could be tied under the chin to protect the ears against the cold (Viskovatov, 1844-56)

p. 129), but the approval of Rumyantsev commended it to a wider audience. Rumyantsev's own *Order of Service* achieved semi-official status, and his memoranda on artillery, as also K. B. Borozdin's *Precept* (*Nastavlenie*) of 1769, helped to make up for the long silence of the War College on this important branch of the service.

Considerable biographical interest attached to the instructions and tactical drills of Aleksandr Suvorov (see p. 191), and to the teachings of Mikhail Ilarionovich Kutuzov, who was already known by the 1770s for the breadth of his military knowledge. As commander of the Bugskii Jaeger Corps, Kutuzov composed a set of *Notes on Infantry Service in General, and that of Jaegers in Particular* (dated 1782 or 1785). Kutuzov regarded accurate fire as the essence of jaeger tactics, and he maintained that the purpose of the jaegers' life was to second the work of the troops of the line by operating in woods, villages, defiles and other kinds of difficult terrain that were inaccessible to their heavier-footed brethren.

Knowledge of a wider military world was diffused through translations of the classics of foreign lands and Antiquity. The middle decades of the century saw the appearance in Russian of editions of Vauban (by Vasilii Suvorov, 1744), de Saxe (1751), Montecuccoli (1760), Vegetius (1764) and Folard (1781). Frederick's instructions to his generals were published four times between 1761 and 1791. Journals of every description flourished in later years.

The New Byzantium, the Turkish war of 1787-92

In 1775 Potemkin was made governor-general and viceroy of the southern provinces of New Russia, Azov and Astrakhan. Two years later he toured these extensive territories, and revolved schemes for the implementation of a grandiose 'Greek Project', which might expel the Turks from Europe, and re-establish the Byzantine empire under a sovereign of Russian blood. Romantic and chimerical in appearance, Potemkin's design embodied something of the irresistible southward drive of Catherine's Russia, as expressed in the colonisation of the steppes, and the striving to rid Russia once and for all of the surviving Moslem bridgeheads on the northern shores of the Black Sea.

On two occasions after the peace of 1774 Catherine's armies invaded the Crimea on behalf of the Russian party among the Tartars, and finally in 1783 the Russians dared to annex the Crimea and the Kuban outright, and extend their protectorship into Georgia. A further reaching-out of Russian ambitions was implicit in the creation of the Black Sea Fleet, which owned bases at Nikolaev, Kherson and Taganrog on the mainland, and the newly founded port of Sevastopol in the Crimea.

Catherine travelled south in 1787, and by her imperial presence she drew international attention to the importance of the annexations. At the rebuilt town of Kherson she met Emperor Joseph II of Austria, no less, and she continued her famous progress into the Crimea. The journey was attended with all the tasteful details that Potemkin could provide — new flotillas swimming on the southern waters, gardens that sprang up overnight, and Balkan and Caucasian princes who prostrated themselves at her feet. The Prince de Ligne was glad to see that Catherine did not permit her judgment to be swayed.

All of this was achieved without battles or sieges, and during the whole period Western Europe showed an astonishing complaisance towards the extension of Russian power. Maria Theresa and Joseph II were glad to have the good offices of Catherine to bring to an end the costly little War of the Bavarian Succession with Prussia. Russia promised to act as a guarantor of the accord, and on 13 May 1779 the Russian delegate Prince Nikolai Repnin could report that an agreement had been reached at Teschen:

The peace has been signed. . . . I make bold to congratulate Your Imperial Highness for this achievement — indeed the credit belongs to no one more properly than to Yourself. It was the exertion of Your power, directed by Your genius, which gave peace to that part of the world, and now Germany will unite with Russia to bless Your reign. Your glory is already immortal, and now it has acquired a new brilliance. Admiration, respect and love are the sentiments which will draw towards You not just the hearts of Your own subjects, but of Europe in its entirety. (*SIRIO*, 1888, LXV, 487)

The episode lent further encouragement to the Russian perception of herself as a lofty arbiter in the quarrels of Western Europe.

The grateful Austrians went on to conclude a defensive alliance with Russia in 1781, and six years later they became a partner in the new war against the Turks. Britain and France were meanwhile engaged in a struggle of their own. The British looked to Russia for help in concluding the Peace of Versailles in 1783, and the impoverished French went on to sign a treaty of trade with the mighty eastern empire in 1786.

After so many years of provocations on their part, it is odd to find the Russians taken by surprise when the Turks finally opened hostilities in 1787. The new annexations stood in some danger, and

186   Catherine II, 'the Great' 1762-96

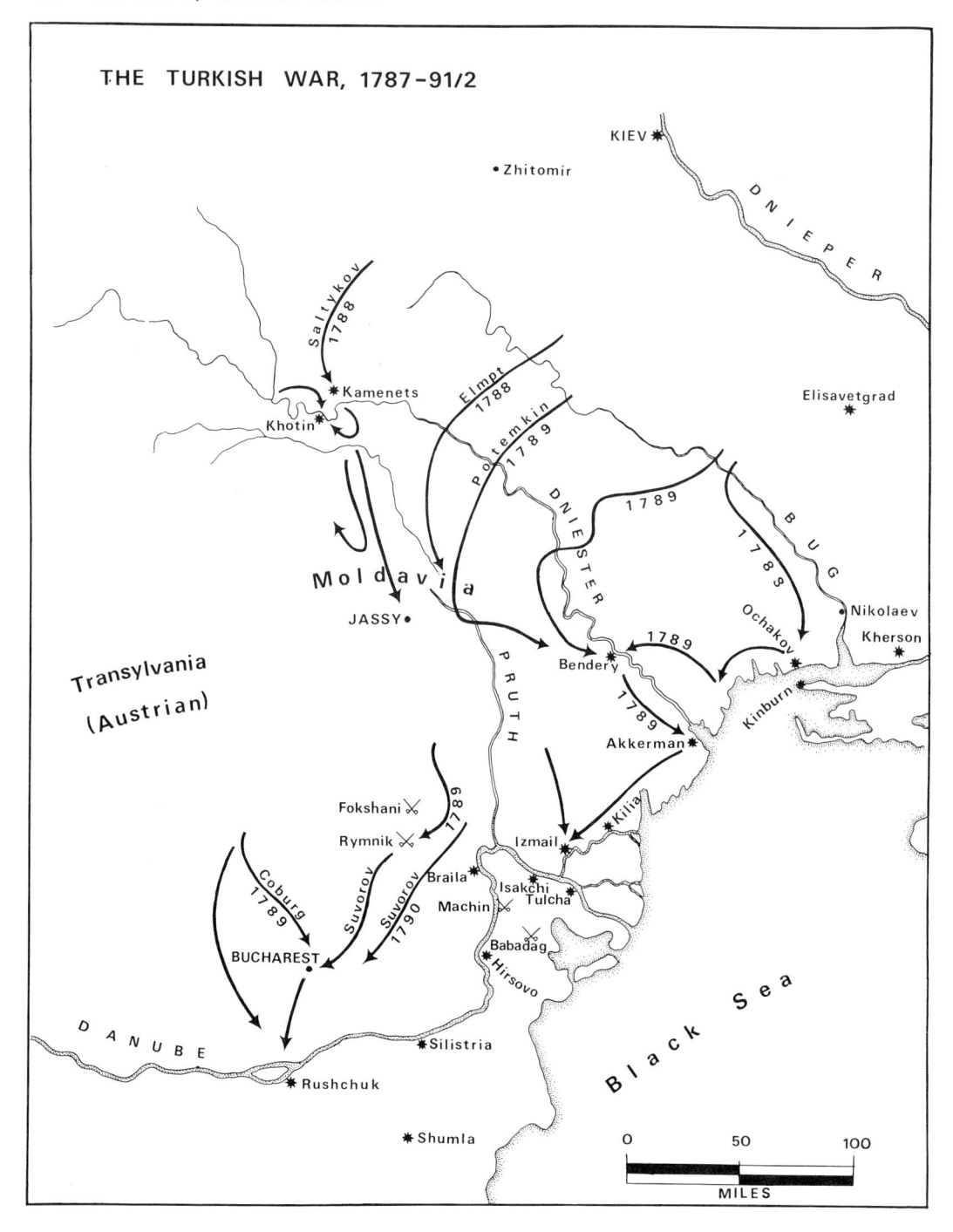

notably the Crimea and its hinterland, which formed a vulnerable appendage within easy reach of the Turkish fortress-port of Ochakov. Aleksandr Suvorov had the command in the Crimea, and he performed a valuable service when in the late autumn he beat off and ultimately destroyed a Turkish amphibious force at Kinburn.

The Russians therefore won the time to build up two forces to act against the Turkish holdings on the north-west corner of the Black Sea in 1788. The veteran Rumyantsev led 37,000 men across the Dniester, while Potemkin in person assumed command of a host of 93,000 troops, or two-thirds of the available force. His objective was to reduce Ochakov, and so eliminate the possibility of the powerful new Turkish fleet throwing forces on to the northern shore of the Black Sea.

Potemkin arrived before Ochakov in June, but he was so unwilling to compromise his reputation by any risky venture that he established the army into an entrenched camp for what turned out to be a long stay. On a bitterly cold 6 December, after he had exhausted every other expedient, Potemkin was reduced to throwing six columns at the fortress. The Russians stormed over the Turkish entrenchment, the fortress ramparts proper, and finally the Hassan Pasha Castle at the tip of the peninsula behind. They lost 956 dead and a nominal 1,829 wounded, though many more men probably died over the following days from wounds and cold. The Turks had more than 4,000 of their men captured, and over 9,500 killed. When the carnage was over,

piles of naked corpses were heaped on the frozen Liman. They remained there until the thaw, and the Russian ladies made circuits of the human pyramids in their sleighs, so as to admire the fine bodies of the Moslems, all rigid with cold.
(Masson, 1859, 199)

Potemkin returned to St Petersburg in triumph, and ribbons, gold crosses and silver medals rained down on the army. Ochakov was an undeniable gain, but the inordinate delays and the final bloody storm revealed a total lack of Russian competence in formal siegework, and consequently an important gap in the repertoire of Catherine's armies.

In 1789 Rumyantsev was eased out of the command against the Turks, and Potemkin was invested with the direction of all the forces on the southern theatre. The Turks were in an aggressive mood, being determined to strike at the junction between the Russian and Austrian forces, and in the event the hottest combats and the most strenuous marches were endured by the division of Suvorov, which was assigned to co-operate with the Austrian corps of Saxe-Coburg. This Third Division, or the 'Suvorov division', became something of an elite force, and it twice executed forced marches to come to the help of the Austrians, and twice joined with them to defeat the Turks in the open field — at Fokshani on 20 July, and again at Rymnik on 11 September, when the allies killed 5,000 of the enemy. These victories helped to secure Moldavia for the Russians, and Suvorov was rewarded with the St George first class, and the title of count with the suffix of 'Rymnikskii'.

In 1790 Catherine stood in need of spectacular and clear-cut victories. She aimed no longer to implement the 'Greek Project', but to enable her diplomats to free Russia from its military entanglements on honourable terms. France was in a state of revolution, which was fraught with incalculable consequences, and elsewhere in Europe the mood of acquiescence had passed. Prussia was building up concentrations of force in Silesia and in the Baltic provinces, while the British Prime Minister Pitt was wondering whether to resort to some military action on behalf of the Turks (even if he was unable to find Ochakov on his map). Sweden made peace with Russia on 14 August, which put an end to an irritating diversion in the Baltic (see p. 189), but in the next month Russia's Austrian allies dropped out of the war with Turkey.

The Russian army of 31,000 men was set the task of reducing the newly strengthened fortress of Izmail, which offered the Turks a bridgehead on the north bank of one of the main arms of the Danube delta. The Russians arrived before Izmail very late in the season, and the lack of shelter and the mounting sickness so depressed the generals that they decided to call off the operation. On 2 December, however, Suvorov arrived to take over the local command. He rejected all the defeatist counsels, and his presence made an immediate impact on the spirit of the troops. To the Duc de Richelieu it seemed that his style was that of a Cossack or Tartar chieftain, rather than the commander of a European army.

Suvorov did not hesitate to pronounce that the place must be taken by assault. Within ten days the troops had put together 27,000 fascines for filling the ditches, and forty ladders for scaling the walls, and they were made to carry out mock attacks on a facsimile of a fortress rampart which was built nearby. 'In these rehearsals Suvorov carried realism so far that he trained the recruits to thrust their bayonets into fascines which had been set up specifically for the purpose' (Richelieu, *SIRIO*, 1886, LIV, 174).

The assault on Izmail was delivered under cover of a dense mist at half past five on the morning of 11 December 1790. The nine columns came in from all sides at once. By the late morning the Russians had mastered three of the gates, but the fight was prolonged inside the town for several hours more, and the Russians frequently had to bring up artillery to overcome the resistance of the Turks in the narrow streets and the stone-built houses. One of the bloodiest days of the century ended with an estimated 26,000 Turkish soldiers and civilians dead, and 9,000 more prisoners in the hands of the Russians. The assailants themselves lost 1,815 dead and 2,445 wounded, 'but it is impossible to deny, from the political and military point of view, that they were more than compensated by the total destruction of an army of nearly 40,000 men, and the conquest of one of the keys of the Ottoman empire' (Richelieu, *SIRIO*, 1886, LIV, 192).

In 1791 the last campaign of the Turkish war was prosecuted in an atmosphere of international tension, for it seemed quite possible that Prussia was about to open hostilities on the northern theatre. The Russians, therefore, had to do something energetic to break up the concentration of 80,000 men that the Turks were building up in the neighbourhood of Izmail. First of all Kutuzov sallied out of Izmail with 12,000 men, and on 3 June he turned 10,000 Turks out of their camp at Babadag. Then Prince Repnin assembled the entire army, and advancing in the customary Russian formation of squares he broke the main Turkish force at Machin on 28 June.

After long negotiations, Turkey and Russia signed a treaty of peace at Jassy on 29 December 1791/9 January 1792. The new and advantageous Russian borders ran along the Dniester to the west, and the further edge of the Kuban plain to the east, and in between Russia gained undisputed possession of the Crimea, Ochakov and all the northern coast of the Black Sea.

Concerning the Russian military performance, we have detailed evaluations from the Frenchmen Richelieu and Langeron, and the Austrian de Ligne. They expressed their admiration for Potemkin's new uniforms, for the spirit and cheerfulness of the troops, and the excellent quality of the infantry, and especially the grenadiers. They deplored the feebleness of the cavalry, the excessive quantities of baggage and hangers-on, the lack of care for the welfare of the men, and a disregard for professionalism and military science which seemed to bode ill for the Russians in any confrontation with a Western army. As a student of military history, the adopted Russian Pishchevich concluded that the Turks had been a considerable offensive force in the early eighteenth century, and that they were still capable of putting up a good fight in Rumyantsev's War. During the last war, however, they had shown themselves to be timorous in combat, and thus 'the fates decreed that Russia should complete the process of destruction which had been begun by Prince Eugene of Savoy' (Pishchevich, 1885, 143).

Catherine was aware of the kind of thing that people were saying about her armies, and she put the more unfavourable comments down to the West's hatred and ignorance of Russia. She pointed out how after recent wars the Russians had restored vast conquests which it had been in their power to retain — namely East Prussia and part of Pomerania to Frederick, and the Greek archipelago to the Turks. As for the capacity of her military leaders, our generals have some claim to the esteem of the critics, taking into account the manifold wars in which they have served, all the battles they have won, all the towns they have taken, the variety of European and Asiatic troops they have beaten, and the multitude of provinces they have conquered. Altogether it has been possible for a single individual in our own time to have done more and seen more than entire generations in times past. (To J. Zimmermann, 26 Jan. 1791, *SIRIO*, 1888, LV, 274)

Westward diversion — the Swedish War 1788-90

At a time when Russia's main forces were engaged on the southern theatre, Catherine was presented with an annoying and potentially dangerous threat from Sweden in the Baltic. In 1788 King Gustavus III of Sweden made some patently impossible demands for the restitution of all Finland to Sweden, and of the Crimea to the Turks. When Russia refused, he opened hostilities on land and sea.

The embarrassment to the Russians came not from any major resurgence of Swedish military power, but from the fact that Catherine's best forces and best generals were committed against the Turks, and because the theatre of war so directly concerned Russia's outlets to the West. Semen Vorontsov wrote that for this reason the smallest reverse in the Swedish war would prove more serious than a full battle lost against the Turks: 'I would be prepared to yield up thirty Crimeas for the gain of Helsingfors and Sveaborg, without which St Petersburg will never live in security against a coup de main' (to A. Vorontsov, 31 May 1790, *AKV*, 1870-95, IX, 173-4).

As things turned out, the fighting on land was confined to feeble demonstrations on either side of the border. In the perilous first year of the war the Russians held their part of Finland with less than 20,000 men, standing under the command of *Generalanshef* Musin-Pushkin, who was 'certainly no sage, but at least an honourable and brave man' (Petr Zavadovskii, 1 June 1789, *AKV*, 1870-95, XII, 62). Gustavus III crossed the border of Russian Finland in the midsummer of 1788, but he essayed nothing more than a feeble bombardment of Fredrikshamn and a vain siege of Nyslot before the sickly and demoralised forces had to retrace their steps.

More interesting were the events at sea, where the Swedes made their main effort with their well-found fleet and galley flotilla. However, the Swedes lost most of the encounters in the more open waters, and their galley flotilla, after a spirited performance, was finally shut up in the Bay of Rochensalm. Gustavus had to contend with a vociferous political opposition at home, and on 3 (14) August 1790 the Swedes came to terms at Verela, and recognised the line of the border as it had run before the war.

The Western world was changing fast. Two years after the peace, Gustavus III was killed by an assassin. Catherine was horrified by the deed, which she attributed to Jacobins, and she began to cast about for allies as a security against the bellicose Revolution which had overtaken France.

The emergence of Suvorov

In the last decade of the century the Russian army lost two of its heroes of olden times. In the autumn of 1791, after a final glorious reception in St Petersburg, Potemkin travelled south to the territories which he had helped to make secure for Russia. On 5 October he was taken ill on the way to Nikolaev. He was helped from his carriage, and died on a cloak that was spread out for him on the road.

For years now the crusty old Field-Marshal Rumyantsev, as governor of Little Russia, had seen his officers starved of promotion, and his ragged troops suffer from material want. The preference was given in every way to the armies and provinces lying at the disposal of Potemkin. The final disappointment came in 1789, when Rumyantsev was removed from active field command in the war against the Turks. He retired to his estates, where he was sought out only by friends like Suvorov, or curious foreign tourists. An Englishman succeeded in tracking him down in one of his castles in Little Russia, and found that the field-marshal's conversation was easy and undogmatic, and enlivened with a caustic humour.

Even the dishabille of such a man is worth remembering. It consisted of a white cotton night cap, a brown old greatcoat, a grey silk quilted waistcoat, dark casimir breeches and boots. In his stature he is tall and lusty, though his tallness is concealed by his being so ill of foot. His face is large and protuberant so as to remind me, as his person likewise did, of old Mr. Boucherett and Lord North. (Parkinson, 1971, 206)

Rumyantsev was recalled to the service in 1794, but he fell into disfavour with the new Emperor Paul, after some remarks he made on the subject of the novel infantry code, and he died on 8 December 1796.

Long afterwards veteran commanders used to assert that 'Potemkin's soldiers were quite different from those of Rumyantsev' (Lubyanovskii, 1872, 92). Troops who knew them both used to recall Potemkin with affection,

but it cheered us up to go campaigning with our little father Count Petr Aleksandrovich, even though he filled us with terror. He was bursting with life, and when he looked in our direction he used to give us some roubles, and somehow he made us feel very brave. (Quoted in Engelhardt, 1868, 130)

A third leader, greater in his way than Rumyantsev or Potemkin, was shortly going to bring the Russian army to the attention of the West in a very dramatic manner. We have encountered Aleksandr Vasilevich Suvorov as the victor of Fokshani and Rymnik. He was born in 1725 to a noble family settled in reasonably comfortable circumstances in the province of Orel. His father, Vasilii Ivanovich, was a well-read soldier, who was the author of the first Russian translation of the works of Vauban. Young Aleksandr devoured the tales of military heroes in his father's library, and after studies in the Cadet Corps and a long spell as a supernumerary NCO in the Semenovskii Regiment, he was commissioned into the army proper in 1754. He saw his first real soldiers in the Astrakhanskii and Ingermanlandskii regiments, which were old and famous units, yielding in prestige only to the Guards.

Suvorov was given his practical schooling in the Seven Years War. He received his baptism of blood in 1759, in the campaign of Kunersdorf, and two years later he experienced independent command as leader of bodies of Cossacks and hussars against Platen and other elusive enemies. In August 1762, immediately after the war, Suvorov was appointed colonel of the Astrakhanskii:

He was most desirous to show the regiment how a storm ought to be carried out. On the march they came across a monastery, and from his ardent imagination Suvorov immediately conjured up a plan of assault. At his signal the regiment threw itself at the walls, according to the accepted rules for storming a fortress, and the victory was crowned by the capture of the monastery. Catherine expressed a desire to see the madman who was responsible for this deed, and their first meeting, as Suvorov says, opened for him the road to glory. (Fuchs, 1827, 115. This was a good exercise, since monasteries constituted some of the very rare stone-walled buildings in Russia.)

A few months later Suvorov assumed command of the Suzdalskii Regiment, and put it through a rigorous programme of training according to his '*Suzdal Regulations*' of 1763-4. At the beginning of the troubles in Poland, in the early winter of 1768, Suvorov executed a celebrated one-month forced march from Lake Ladoga to join a corps at Smolensk. He went on to become one of the few leaders to emerge with an enhanced reputation from these peculiarly frustrating campaigns, first as brigade commander, then, from January 1770, as major-general.

After the Polish and Turkish wars, Suvorov held manoeuvres in the conquered southern provinces, and for the sake of the participating regiments he issued his new instructions 'for the Kuban and Crimean corps' on 16 May 1778. Suvorov here allowed himself considerable freedom, because the official codes had little to say on the subject of warfare against the Turks.

The early 1790s brought Suvorov the St George,

and fame and a certain amount of notoriety for the bloody storms of Izmail and Praga. Suvorov used the subsequent lull very much as he had done in similar circumstances twenty years before, training his command of troops in southern Russia, and putting together his notions on warfare. The product in this case was the celebrated *Art of Victory* (*Nauka Pobezhda*), which was first circulated in 1795. The document comprised two sections – a *Vakht-Parad*, instructing the officers on tactical formations, and then an exposition of the underlying principles of combat. No less revealing were the many instructions which Suvorov penned for the benefit of the astonished Austrians who found themselves under his command in north Italy in 1799. In all of this Suvorov wrote and spoke in his characteristically lapidary style, which comes across well in Russian, with its lack of articles, but is reduced to clumsy circumlocutions when rendered into English.

For Suvorov, training was the foundation of the military art: 'Train hard, fight easy. Train easy, and you will have hard fighting' (Mikhnevich, in Skalon, 1902-c.1911, IV, Introduction, 208). The process of military education embraced everyone, from recruit to army commander, and it was to be systematic and realistic throughout. Progress was to be achieved through patience, repetition and practical demonstration. During the season of summer manoeuvres, Suvorov assembled the regiments under his command in three or four camps, and put the troops through the complete repertoire of military operations – forced marches, mock battles, and storms on fortresses and camps. Lives were always lost in the process. No other army of the age subjected itself to such an ordeal in peacetime, and Langeron admits that he had been horrified by some of Suvorov's practices, like sending cavalry to charge flat out against infantry. He afterwards recognised that there could have been no better training for real combat.

From Suvorov's teachings and campaigns we can arrive at some comprehension of the great man's way of warfare. Speedy movement was fundamental to Suvorov's strategy, and many were the famous marches to his credit. Like Marlborough, Stonewall Jackson and other commanders of the kind, Suvorov attained his results not by driving his men into the ground, but through regular, easy progress, and good administration.

Suvorov gave much thought to the choice of tactical formations. In his Crimean and Kuban instructions of 1778 he was willing to uphold an essential distinction between the methods to be employed on Western and Eastern theatres.

Against regular armies we use lines – as in the late war with Prussia. Against irregular forces we employ the formations in use in the last Turkish war. Deep squares are clumsy. Regimental squares are the most flexible of all, but battalion squares are best for laying down a cross-fire. . . . Such formations worked to terrible effect against whole hosts of Stamboulers in the recent war. Woods, water, mountains, ravines – nothing was capable of stopping them (Gippius, in Skalon, 1902-c.1911, IV, pt 1, bk 2, sect. 3, 118).

The advent of the Revolutionary Wars induced Suvorov to consider applying something of the same principles on the Western theatre as well. In The *Art of Victory* he wrote that the lunatic French were in the habit of using columns in regular warfare, which might compel the Russians to do the same, and on arriving in Italy in 1799 he advised the Austrians to attack the enemy in multiple columns or ranks. In his more detailed prescriptions, however, he recommended that the army should deploy at one thousand paces from the enemy, and continue the advance in a formation of two lines, with the cavalry drawn up on the flanks, or placed in the rear as a third line. Perhaps he believed that the Austrians were not sufficiently schooled in his methods to be able to abandon the conventional linear tactics.

Suvorov had no such hesitations about recommending the use of the bayonet in Western warfare, maintaining that this weapon had decisive moral and physical advantages over the musket ball, that 'crazy bitch'.

We must attack!!! [he urged the Austrians in 1799] Cold steel – bayonets and sabres! Push the enemy over, hammer them down, don't lose a moment! Overcome everything that stands in your way, however insurmountable it might appear! Follow on their heels, destroy them to the last man! The Cossacks will catch the fugitives and all their baggage. Forward without rest, exploit the victory! ... As for drawing up the order of battle, that's Chasteler's affair [Chasteler was Suvorov's Austrian chief of staff]. (Suvorov, 1949-53, IV, 13)

It is by no means certain that Suvorov really expected that his men would be engaged at bayonet point. In the wars of the period the number of verifiable instances of such encounters is extraordinarily rare, for it is not in human nature to withstand the ordeal. The one exception is offered by the fighting for fortifications or entrenchments, since the defenders were often inclined or forced to stand their ground. When Suvorov advocated his 'through attack' with cold steel, he probably intended to overcome the natural instinct of the infantry, which was to come to a wavering halt at about three hundred paces from the enemy, and open a ragged and ineffective exchange of fire. It seems likely that Suvorov's bloodthirsty exhortations were designed to carry his troops through this zone with momentum undiminished, which would indeed have caused the enemy to collapse in the way he so often described.

In fact all of Suvorov's operations were 'so disposed as to work on the morale of men — whether his own troops or the enemy's' (Engelhardt, 1868, 183). He had at his command a range of artful effects, calculated to strike the imagination of the soldiers. Deliberately rejecting pomp and state, he stumped around the army in a ragged soldier's coat, and when he had to go somewhere on horseback he borrowed the first nag to come to hand. He shared likewise the soldiers' belief in the 'Russian God', and was ready to take issue with anybody who maintained the superiority of the French language and manners. 'Speak and read French, by all means, but do so in such a way that everybody knows that you are a Russian' (Fuchs, 1827, 145). He rejected a suggestion that the Russians should rid themselves of their customary hosts of musicians: 'No! Music is both necessary and useful, providing it is very loud. Music doubles, trebles the force of the army. When I took Izmail, it was with the cross in the hands of the priest, with flying colours, and with loud music' (Fuchs, 1827, 45).

In the tradition of Rumyantsev, Suvorov got his officers and doctors to keep the welfare of the men in the forefront of their attentions. Officers who failed in this respect were placed under arrest, and NCOs were flogged. Suvorov prided himself, with no very good reason, on the extent of his herbal and medicinal knowledge. Some of his peasant remedies probably did more harm than good, and on occasion Suvorov chased the patients from the hospitals, declaring that his soldiers were not allowed to be sick. However, the troops only accepted these attentions as further evidence of their commander's concern. 'Suvorov was a barbarian and a clown, but at the same time possibly the general best suited to the genius of the Russians. The soldiers loved him. The officers thought he was odd, but they fought with confidence under his command' (Masson, 1859, 331).

It was characteristic that Suvorov reserved his sharpest asperities for his officers rather than his men. Nothing was better calculated to arouse his ire than vagueness or irresolution — 'God save us from the "don't knows"!' (Engelhardt, 1868, 183). He liked to test people by putting to them the most arcane questions, and he was delighted when he received an answer which betrayed expert knowledge, or at least confidence and a ready wit:
'How many fish are there in the Danube?'
'Forty-two-and-a-half million!'
'How far is it to the sky?'
'For Suvorov, two campaigns!'
'How many stars are there in the heavens?'
'I'll begin counting — one, two, three, four ...'
'What do they eat in Revel on Thursdays?'
'Cabbage soup!' (This from an officer who knew that they consumed this substance on every day of the week.)

Suvorov wished operational orders to be clear and concise, and to allow plenty of freedom to the men on the spot. For general guidance, however, he stressed the importance of three fundamental principles of warfare, namely *coup d'oeil*, speed

56 Suvorov the man-manager

57 Suvorov in English caricature

and impact. By *coup d'oeil* Suvorov understood the ability to size up a military situation, and devise the appropriate response swiftly and accurately. As for the other two principles, 'speed and impact are the soul of present-day warfare. A fleeing enemy can be destroyed only through pursuit' (undated 1799, Suvorov, 1949-53, IV, 20).

Suvorov's behaviour and character were the subject of unfailing interest for his contemporaries. From his rough-sounding name ('Souworow') and his rougher reputation, English caricaturists used to represent him as a bullet-headed and bewhiskered thug, quite at variance with the thin, stooping figure which actually emerged from lodging or tent at about six every morning. The face had the wrinkled aspect of a Voltaire, and something of the taut intelligence of a von Moltke the Elder, but the gaunt cheeks and staring eyes imprinted the expression with the fanaticism of the Old Testament prophet. Oblivious of who might be present, Suvorov doused himself with cold water, and capered naked on the grass until he was dry and warm. He might then get his army under way by crowing three times like a cock.

Suvorov took his simple lunch on a wooden platter at any time between eight and eleven. He downed a large glass of vodka beforehand, and up to two glasses of wine during the actual meal, but his servant Timchenko was always at hand to prevent him from emptying a third. A less narrow-minded retainer, a Cossack, accompanied him into the field with a bottle of very strong punch.

58 Aleksandr Vasilevich Suvorov. The decoration on the far right is the Austrian Military Order of Maria Theresa

'Suvorov called it his "lemonade", and drank it unceasingly, as a result of which he rapidly attained what you might term an excitable condition' (Langeron, *RS*, 1895, LXXXIII, 159).

In the late afternoon Suvorov selected his next resting place, in which matter he had certain preferences. The first man on the scene was an officer, who was careful to remove the windows and any other objects of glass, whereupon an orderly brought in a mobile thunderbox, and a bale of straw which he dumped on the floor to serve as Suvorov's bed.

When Suvorov wished to put on a special performance, some of the details almost surpass belief:

All sorts of oddities might be seen. At the head of his army or on parade Suvorov could stand for half an hour at a time on one leg, shouting or singing. In a salon, in the midst of a most numerous company, he was liable to jump onto a table or chair, or throw himself flat on the floor. On one occasion he gave vent to lamentations on the death of a turkey, which had been decapitated by a soldier. He kissed the defunct fowl, and tried to set the head back on the neck. (Langeron, *RS*, 1895, LXXXIII, 156)

Those who knew Suvorov were aware that he was not the lunatic that he pretended to be. Fuchs was at a loss to account for the eccentricities, but Engelhardt and Ségur believed that they were a device to disarm potential enemies in the army and at court. Langeron noticed how Suvorov exploited these occasions to convey some sharp comments or telling lessons, and he suspected that the inspiration went back to a comment of Catherine, who once said in Suvorov's hearing that all great men were slightly odd.

Behaviour of this kind encouraged a belief that Suvorov's knowledge of the art of war was purely instinctive. In fact, Suvorov was one of the best-read commanders of the time, being acquainted with the doings and writings of the military heroes of classical antiquity, as well as more recent authorities like Vauban, Coehoorn, Montecuccoli, Turenne, Eugene and Frederick the Great. He had a fluent command of French, German, Greek and Turkish, in addition to the Latin of his Roman authors, and his knowledge of current military events enabled him to pass some extremely acute judgments. Count Rostopchin once asked him to select the greatest commanders of history, and himself made a few suggestions to that end. At each contribution Suvorov crossed himself, and then he whispered a few words in Rostopchin's ear — to wit, Hannibal, Julius Caesar — and Napoleon Bonaparte.

As a man of wide culture, Suvorov was able to converse with the Austrian general Zach on Cervantes' *Don Quixote*, and talk sensibly about the canvases he saw in the Italian galleries on his campaign of 1799. Like Bonaparte and other men of action at the time, he was also given to occasional 'Ossianising' — best described as moods of faintly melancholy reflection on the mutability of human affairs.

It was therefore with the authority of a true intellectual that Suvorov could maintain that brainpower alone had a very limited capacity to influence events in the real world. He was scornful of the proliferation of French literature on the art of war:

> It is amazing ... how more was written about tactics in the reign of Louis XV than at any other time, and yet how appalling was the role of the French army in military events. Who were its leaders? My God, Soubise and Clermont! What were it's examples of the military spirit? Why, Rossbach and Minden! (Fuchs, 1827, 101).

The extinction of Poland, 1792-5

Having annihilated the Turkish army at Izmail, Suvorov and his Russians before long wrought the same carnage among the Poles. Now that she was free of the war in the south, Catherine made ready to send her armies into Poland, where a party of Patriots was taking active steps to reverse the process of decline and partition which threatened to destroy their country. Russian columns marched briskly into Poland in the high summer of 1792, defeating the Patriot commander Thaddeus Kósciuszko with his inferior forces at Dubienka on 18 July. On 23 January the next year Russia and Prussia concluded the second of the series of infamous treaties of Polish partition. The 1793 version enabled the Prussians to occupy the salient of Polish territory between West Prussia and Silesia, while Russia's new border was carried westward by an average of two hundred miles, taking in the extensions of White Russia and the Ukraine, and giving the Russians a direct and secure avenue to the Balkans. The rump of Poland came under Russian and Prussian 'protectorship'.

Polish defiance burst forth in an insurrection in the spring of 1794. General Tormasov with about 3,500 Russians were defeated at Racławice on 4 April, which gave the signal for a general uprising, and on 17 and 18 April the Russian and Prussian garrisons were evicted from Warsaw. The Patriots did remarkably well, considering that their leaders were given to seeking ill-judged actions in the open field, and that their small forces of regular troops and Polish ex-Russian deserters had to be filled out with masses of scythe-wielding peasants. Kósciuszko was defeated at Rawka on 6 June, which led to the loss of Cracow, but the spread of the insurrection to western Poland caused the Prussians to steal away from the scene of operations at the beginning of September.

While the Poles fortified Warsaw as a central point d'appui, the Russians were active on two theatres — in the east, where Suvorov was coming up with an army from the Ukraine, and in the south, where the Russian forces lay under the command of the German general Johann Fersen, a quiet man with a tremendous presence, who was 'genuinely attached to our great fatherland, and served it not as a mercenary but as a devoted son' (Wiegel, 1864-6, I, pt 1, 96).

Seeking to prevent a junction of the Russian forces, Kósciuszko and his 7,000 men were caught at Maciejowice on the Dniester by Fersen, who enjoyed a two-fold superiority. The Poles were attacked and annihilated on 10 October. Kósciuszko himself was gravely wounded, and shortly afterwards he fell into the hands of a party of marauding Cossacks. Colonel Adrian Denisov was the first Russian officer to arrive on the scene,

59 Catherine tempted by the Devil

and found that Kósciuszko was alive but so pale that he looked like a corpse. His head was covered with blood, and his feet were without boots. He was dressed in a kaftan, done up with a great number of buttons, and in satin waistcoat and pantaloons. I remembered that I had with me an engraving of his portrait for just such an eventuality. I took it out, and found a very strong likeness. (Denisov, *RS*, 1874, XI, 407)

The disaster of Maciejowice left Warsaw as the only major seat of the insurrection. Here about 30,000 Poles were ensconced on the east bank of the Vistula in the bridgehead fortifications at Praga, determined to resist to the last. Suvorov came up with an army reduced by its exertions to perhaps as little as 16,000 men, but in compensation these troops were infuriated by the Polish resistance, and by the tales of the atrocities inflicted on the Russian garrison in Warsaw in the spring.

Without going through so much as a pretence at formal siege, Suvorov committed his army to an outright assault on 24 October (4 November) 1794. In three hours of fighting, and in the subsequent butchery, an estimated 13,000 rebels and unarmed civilians were killed, about 14,500 were captured, about 2,000 more perished in the Vistula in the attempt to reach the Warsaw bank.

You would have had to have been an eyewitness, to form a picture of the frightfulness of the storm towards the end. Every conceivable form of violent death had been perpetrated on every yard of ground as far as the Vistula, while the bank of the river was piled with heaps of the bodies of the dead or dying – warriors, townspeople, Jews, monks, women and lads. (Engelhardt, 1868, 177)

Warsaw surrendered without resistance, and the remnants of the Polish army were overhauled and forced to lay down their arms. For this achievement Suvorov received the rank of field-marshal, and a vast estate at Kobrin with 6,922 male serfs. A superb new uniform arrived as a personal present from Catherine, and as was his wont, Suvorov greeted the object with hugs, kisses and signs of the cross.

A third, complete and final partition was accomplished by Russian treaties with Austria on 3 January 1795, and with Prussia on 24 October. In the process Poland disappeared from the map altogether. Russia's new borders now marched for about 360 miles each with those of Prussia and Austria, taking in 45,000 square miles of Kurland, Samogitia, Lithuania, Podlesia and Volhynia. Between 1772 and 1795 the process of partition had advanced Catherine's frontiers three hundred miles to the west on a frontage of no less than six hundred miles, and acquired six million new subjects for the delights of Russian rule. Poles made up more than half of the 800,000 serfs who were granted to the nobles in Catherine's reign.

The last years of Catherine

The Russians were scarcely likely to be downcast by the work of killing Poles and Turks, or by the disapprobation of men of sensibility. The empress herself is supposed to have criticised Prince Nikolai Vasilevich Repnin for the *sainte humanité* he displayed in Lithuania. The undeniable malaise of the final years of Catherine's army proceeded not from any events in the field, but from an all-pervading atmosphere of corruption. The scandals could be attributed in general terms to the weakening of Catherine's physical and moral forces, as the future Emperor Alexander believed, but more specifically to the failings in the commissariat.

The frightful abuses and waste which crept into this branch of the state first took root and developed from 1775. They proceeded by no means from the institutions as such, but from the influence of powerful favourites, and so they became general, extending beyond the military machine to all departments of government. (S. R. Vorontsov, *AKV*, 1870-95, XXIX, 465)

In the matter of the commissariat proper, the frauds endemic in the equipment department were far exceeded by those perpetrated in that of food supply (*Proviant*), where the fraudulent dealings alienated 'all those honest contractors

60 Catherine the Great with her family and leading courtiers, 1782. Left to right: Potemkin, Bezborodko, the juvenile grand princes, Alexander and Constantine, Grand Princess Maria Theodorovna, Catherine the Great, Betzkoi, Grand Prince Pavel Petrovich (the future Paul I), Repnin, Panin, Lanskoi, Naryshkin, Ostermann. In the background is the 'bronze horseman', Catherine's monument to Peter the Great

who were willing to provide the sustenance of the army at an infinitely cheaper rate' (Rzhevskii, *RA*, 1879, XVII, pt 1, 358). Altogether, wrote Langeron, 'there never existed, and never will exist, more barefaced swindlers than the personnel of these departments' (Langeron, *RS*, 1895, LXXXIII, 150). The glorious example of the chiefs was sedulously imitated by the petty functionaries at the regimental level.

As for the favourites, we have seen how the reign of the Orlov dynasty was succeeded in the 1770s by that of Potemkin, which lasted until 1791. The existence of these virtual *aimants en titre* by no means deterred Catherine from seeking a little variety in her menfolk. Nobody could say much to the discredit of Aleksandr Dmitrevich Lanskoi or Semen Gavriilovich Zorich, who were reasonably honest as well as handsome. However, a great deal of harm was done by the last of the lesser favourites, Platon Aleksandrovich Zubov. This fortunate young gentleman was said to have been introduced to the empress by Nikolai Saltykov in 1789, at a time when he was the only presentable junior officer in sight, and Catherine accordingly made him an aide-de-camp and installed him in the customary apartment of her favourites at Tsarskoe Selo. Zubov became lieutenant-general in 1792, and in the following year he was appointed Master General of the Ordnance instead of the far better-qualified Melissino.

In such an atmosphere, well-placed generals attracted trains of toadies of the sort described in unbridled terms by one of Potemkin's secretaries in the Ochakov campaign of 1788:

My God! What outbursts of temper, what defamations and slanders gush forth at headquarters and in the staff when the officers consider the new promotions. If one of them has received a rapid advancement, the others in their rage will invent and attribute to him every possible shortcoming. (Tsebrikov, *RS*, 1895, LXXXIV, 201-2)

There existed no individuals or organisations

strong enough to withstand the tide of corruption. At the War College, the upright but ineffective Nikolai Ivanovich Saltykov (not the same as the celebrated Peter Semenovich) took over as acting president after the death of Potemkin in 1791, and he left affairs in the same state of disorder as before. At a lower level of military administration, the inspectors neglected their fundamentally important duty of enforcing standards throughout the army. Typical of the level of interest of these people was the case of Prince Vasilii Vasilevich Dolgorukov, who had the inspectorate of Little Russia. Engelhardt remembered how pleasant it was for young officers to come under his authority,

since instead of carrying out strict inspections, he was interested only in holding festivities in the camp, so as to entertain his wife, whom he had just married. He always announced beforehand which regiment was to undergo inspection, and for this event the colonels prepared feasts, illuminations and fireworks. (Engelhardt, 1868, 60)

If an inspector went so far as to insist on viewing the regiments, the respective colonels conspired to cover their deficiencies. 'In 1796,' says Langeron, I saw with my own eyes how a very strict inspector ended up by rejecting one and the same horse in four different regiments, without ever noticing the animal's identity' (Langeron, RS, 1895, LXXXIII, 199).

In these circumstances, all effective authority was invested in the colonels of the individual regiments, which resulted in atrocious abuses that were explained in detail by Langeron and Lieutenant-General Stepan Matveeich Rzhevskii. Even where outright corruption was held within bounds, standards of professionalism were eroded by officers who took themselves off on long leaves, or to early retirement, or who simply left the performance of their duties to others.

There was seldom any doubt as to the battle-worthiness of Suvorov's lean and ferocious infantry. Elsewhere, however, outward appearances were all that mattered.

It is impossible for the soldier to stand, sit or walk comfortably. His sword seems to shine like fire, but the blade is rusted into the scabbard. His musket is as bright as a mirror, but it cannot be fired with accuracy, on account of the deformation of the stock, which is purposely designed to make the weapon impossible to aim, but merely to seat it directly on the shoulder. (Rzhevskii, RA, 1879, XVII, pt 1, 359-60)

By the nature of things, the mounted arm suffered the most from the indifference and criminality of the colonels. The horses were under-fed and under-exercised, which made for feeble mounts and inexperienced riders. Most cavalrymen rode just five or six times a year, and Langeron could name only four regimental commanders who were actually capable of staying in the saddle.

Among the gunners, Semen Vorontsov observed that the standard of expertise of the officers was pitiable:

I have known some of those people who were ignorant of what elevation to give to their cannon for ricochet fire. As for the science of higher mathematics — so indispensable for mortar fire, where you have to calculate the trajectory of the bombs — it is something totally unknown to us. (Vorontsov, 'Zapiski', 1802, AKV, 1870-95, X, 483-4)

If the artillery was spared the full degradation of the cavalry, it was because the ordinary gunners were chosen from the strongest and most lively of the recruits, and because at different periods the arm had enlightened leadership from men like Meller-Zakomelskii or the exotic Petr Ivanovich Melissino.

Born to a Greek family of Cephalonia, Melissino was educated in Russia in the Cadet Corps, where he excelled in the celebrated amateur theatricals of that institution. He picked up his practical knowledge of gunnery in the later campaigns of the Seven Years War, and in 1770 as a major-general he commanded the artillery of Rumyantsev's army, and contributed greatly to the victories of Larga and Kagul. 1783 brought the rank of lieutenant-general and the post of Director of the

Artillery and Engineering Cadet Corps, though he never attained the final prize of the Master Generalship of the Ordnance.

This vain, showy and extravagant individual commanded genuine respect on account of his military record, his fluency in eight languages, and his knowledge of gunfounding, mechanics and chemistry, as well as the mumbo-jumbo of fashionable Freemasonry. Melissino improved the method of boring out the artillery in the St Petersburg works, and, braving the contempt of Zubov, he went on to establish six large companies of horse artillery in the last three years of the reign.

Empress Catherine died on 6 November 1796. Looking back on her life, people were willing to set aside the weaknesses of the final period, and wonder at the great cumulative achievement of her reign — the westward and southward expansion of lands and population, the foundation of 250 towns, the build-up of the army (from a nominal 303,529 in 1765 to 413,473 in 1795), the advance in society and national self-esteem, and the place secured for Russia in the regard of Europe. Even the stern critic Masson had to admit:

Taken together, the generosity of Catherine, the brilliance of her reign, her magnificent court, her institutions, monuments and wars constituted for Russia what the century of Louis XIV was for Europe. But Catherine was personally greater than that monarch. The French were the glory of Louis XIV, whereas Catherine was the glory of the Russians. (Masson, 1859, 83)

Nine Paul I 1796-1801

The new Potsdam

The career of the 'great and most wise mother' was followed to the end by the unblinkingly hostile gaze of the heir apparent, Grand Prince Pavel Petrovich. Paul had always considered himself far less the son of Catherine than the successor of his putative father, Emperor Peter III. His bent towards things military had been cultivated by some devoted tutors – men like Semen Andreevich Poroshin, and Nikolai Ivanovich Saltykov. Models of all the types of Russian ordnance had been prepared for the edification of the tsarevich, and likewise a number of simplified editions of the standard books on fortification. However, the most formative experience of Paul's life was undoubtedly a visit to Prussia in 1776. On this occasion Old Fritz explained that he and Paul's father had been the best of friends, and he put his perfectly drilled troops through their paces for the benefit of his young visitor. Paul returned home more dissatisfied than ever with what he saw of the Russian army. 'Everything proceeds according to individual whim,' he complained to General Petr Panin, 'and this fancy consists of doing nothing except gratifying one's unbridled passions. This is the deplorable condition to which our armed forces have sunk' (P. S. Lebedev, *RS*, 1877, XVIII, 577).

It is interesting to observe how Paul, apparently so Prussian in all his instincts, reverted to the practice of the young Peter the Great a century

61 Grenadier and musketeer of the Gatchina Corps, 1793. Sober, neo-Prussian uniforms of green, with red facings and white breeches. The 'Union Jack' on the grenadier's mitre cap is the St Andrew's cross of blue on a red field (Viskovatov, 1844-56)

62 Inspection of the guard indoors at Gatchina

before, and set up a private army to give concrete form to his fantasies. He assembled his first recruits at the palace of Petrovsk in 1782, and then in the next year he purchased from the Orlov family the dank estate of Gatchina, lying about forty miles from St Petersburg. Here Paul established the base of the 'Gatchina Corps', a complete miniature army which reached the strength of 1,601 infantry, 590 cavalry and 214 gunners.

Catherine permitted the existence of the Gatchina Corps, to provide the tsarevich with a measure of occupation and diversion, but this force, organised and trained on the Prussian model, represented a kind of silent protest against Catherine's military system. (Kvardi, in Skalon, 1902-c.1911, II, bk 1, 261)

Among the curious beings who flourished amid the drill squares, lakes and soggy woods of Gatchina the most prominent was the gargoyle-like Aleksei Arakcheev, who arrived in 1792 with a good character from Melissino as an expert in artillery. Arakcheev threw himself into the work with brutal zeal, and in 1795 he was rewarded with the title of 'Governor of Gatchina'. Scarcely less influential were ex-Prussian dugouts like Steinwehr, Diebitsch and Lindener, who lent a certain authenticity of antique detail, and fascinated Paul by telling him how Frederick used to spend his day. Paul learnt his role to seeming perfection, and he liked to station himself on a terrace near Pavlovsk, from where he could examine the palace guards with his telescope. When he noticed that something was wrong, he would dispatch a lackey with an appropriate message, or arrive on the scene in person to do or undo a button, or correct the carriage of a musket. Altogether, nothing could have been calculated to afford Paul greater pleasure than the comment of the Prussian veteran Baron Driesen, who, at the sight of the emperor riding past, once cried out *Ganz wie der Alte Fritz!*

In Catherine's last hours Paul and a party of the Gatchina inmates hastened to St Petersburg to secure the imperial palace. The whole Gatchina circus then undertook a forced march on St Petersburg, and on 9 November Paul brought about its mass incorporation into the Guard, which signified to the capital that he was at last firmly in command. At court

the former atmosphere of freedom, ease and gallantry gave way to an intolerable repression. Almost at once the yelling of orders, the noise of iron and soldiers, and the clatter of great boots and spurs rang through the apartments where Catherine had just entered on her eternal sleep. (Masson, 1859, 77)

Paul and his officials got down to work early each day,

and opposite the Winter Palace, in the building of the Vice-Chancellery, you could see all the chandeliers and fireplaces glowing brightly. The Senators were in session at their fine mahogany table from eight in the morning. The renaissance in military affairs was even more striking — and it began at the top. Silver-headed commanders, wearing the star of the Order of St. George, had to learn how to march, deploy, and salute with the spontoon. (Lubyanovskii, 1872, 94)

The new administrative structures were less complicated than they appeared, for they were all designed to enable Paul to reassemble the military machine in a manageable form. In January 1797 the Chancellery of Artillery and Fortification, and the notoriously maladministered offices of the Commissariat and the *Proviant*, were reduced to 'expeditions' of the War College. Paul retained his old tutor Saltykov as President of the College, but he kept him under close supervision, and made the College give up much of its authority to a new and more responsive body, the Mobile Military Chancellery of His Imperial Highness. The competence of the Chancellery was much wider than its title might suggest. It exercised the higher management of military affairs, as well as a degree of civil administration when Paul took it with him on his travels, and it represented an important stage of the transformation of the old collegiate form of administration into the modern ministerial one, which was accomplished early in the next reign.

On 13 November 1796 the General Staff was abolished and its personnel dispersed, and the maps, plans and registers were delivered up to General-Adjutant Kushelev as head of a novel organisation, the Suite of His Imperial Highness Concerning the Affairs of the Quartermaster. Lying at the direct disposal of the sovereign, the members of the Suite were liable to find themselves on distant military or diplomatic missions, as well as being appointed inspectors, or assigned the job of arranging the imperial journeys. The break from the old system was no great crime, for

63 Paul I

the General Staff was almost defunct (see p. 181), but Paul was much at fault in failing to make sure that the Suite fulfilled its essential task of planning and directing military movements. Thus, when his armies went to war in 1799, they were to be fatally dependent on such guidance as might be provided by the Austrians.

Under Paul the daily watch parade at St Petersburg assumed extraordinary significance, being at once an endurance test for the officers, the chief ceremony of state, and a means by which Paul could exercise direct personal control of the

The *Flügel-Adjutant du Jour* or another aide did his best to keep up with the flow of instructions, scribbling heavily abbreviated words in a notebook, ultimately to be written up by the Chancellery into proper decrees.

Where Paul could not be present in person, he sought to inculcate habits of obedience and uniformity through the inspectors — one for each of the three arms of the service — who were established in the twelve former administrative 'divisions' of Catherine's reign. A number of junior officers from Gatchina were among those appointed to carry out this work, which exacerbated the resentment of Suvorov and other veteran generals.

As regards the outward appearance of the troops, 'the form of a hat, the colour of a plume, the height of a grenadier cap, and boots, gaiters, cockades, pigtails, belts and things like that became great matters of state' (Masson, 1859, 124). A series of *Règlements* imposed on the army the Gatchina uniforms, which were themselves modelled on the Prussian dress of the period of the Seven Years War. Captain Gryazev conveys a good impression of the garb when he described the

64 Paul I in front of the Winter Palace. Behind him are (left to right): Count C.A. Leiven (head of the Mobile Military Chancellery), T. P. Uvarov (the general-adjutant *du jour*), and the *Flügel-Adjutant*, A. I. Gorchakov

empire. The issue of the *parole*, or password, had always been an essential feature of Frederick's watch parades, but when Paul transferred it to Russia he used the opportunity to dictate instructions of the widest possible import, ranging from grand state affairs, to kindly messages like:

Lieutenant Shepelev, of the Preobrazhenskii Regiment, is transferred to the Eletskii Musketeer Regiment on account of his ignorance of his duties, his sloth and his negligence — habits picked up in the company of the princes Potemkin and Zubov. (Kvardi, in Skalon, 1902-c.1911, II, bk 1, 281)

65 Paul I

uniform in which his regiment marched to Italy late in 1798:

a heavy dark green coat with lapels, turned-down collar and cuffs of brick red with white buttons. Also a long waistcoat and short breeches of a uniform yellow colour. Our hair was cut close in front and covered with stinking grease ... a pigtail twenty-eight inches long was tied down as far as the nape of the neck and powdered with flour. We had a hat with wide bands of silver braid, a large buttonhole of the same material and a black bow — this headgear was of an amazing form and gave our heads little cover. A flannel stock was pulled as tight as possible around the neck. Our feet were pushed into snub-nosed black shoes, and the leg as far as the knee was encased in black cloth gaiters which were done up along the whole length with red buttons. (Orlov, 1898, 27)

Traditions were dealt a further blow by a decree of 20 August 1798, which did away with the old denomination of regiments according to place of origin, and imposed instead the name and person of a new dignitary, the Prussian-style *chef*, or colonel in chief. The *chef* was invariably a general, and so was usually absent on business elsewhere, but his very existence curbed the authority of the acting colonel — which was probably no bad thing. Less happy was the effect on the soldiers. Semen Vorontsov recalled:

When I had the misfortune to take over the command of the corps which returned from the North Holland Expedition [1799], I went to see the soldiers in the hospital at Portsmouth, and asked them what regiment they belonged to. A typical reply would run as follows: 'I used to belong to such and such a regiment (supplying the name). But now, little father, I don't know where I am. The emperor has given it to some German or other.' ('Zapiski', 1802, *AKV*, 1870-95, X, 470)

Paul's new infantry code was issued on 29 November 1796, or in other words just twenty-three days after his accession. This apparently remarkable promptitude is explained by the fact that the document had already been printed for the use of the Gatchina Corps. It was a compila-

66 Musketeer, period of Paul I (Viskovatov, 1844-56)

tion of Grigorii Kushelev and the restless and fussy Thedor Vasilevich Rostopchin, and derived mostly from a poor French translation of the Prussian infantry code, which had appeared in 1760. Another text of the Gatchina days, *Tactical Rules* (1794), was published as a supplement.

The Pauline tactics came straight from the era of the Seven Years War, what with the platoon column for approach marches, the simple two-line order of battle, and the companies drawn up three ranks deep, with the component platoons firing in the order 1 – 2 – 3 – 4. By 1799 the innovations of Catherine's era had disappeared as if they had never been, at least where Suvorov was not present with the armies in person. Sir Henry Bunbury wrote of the greencoats in North Holland as:

exactly the stiff, hard, wooden machines which we have reason to figure to ourselves as the Russians of the Seven Years War. Their dress and equipments seemed to have remained unaltered. They waddled slowly forward to the tap-tap of their monotonous drums; and if they were beaten they waddled slowly back again, without appearing in either case to feel a sense of danger, or of the need of taking ultra tap-taps to better their condition. (Bunbury, 1927, 145)

The codes held sway until 1808, or in other words well into the Napoleonic era. Thus in 1805 the Russian army advanced over the fields of Austerlitz in Frederician arrangement of open platoon column, and was caught in this formation when the French irrupted out of the mist.

As regards organisation, Paul abolished the grenadier regiments outright, and reduced the battalions of jaegers to so many companies. Altogether the general down-grading of the infantry reduced the establishment in 1800 to 203,228 men, as opposed to 218,386 in 1786.

A matching series of reductions in the lighter elements of the cavalry brought the establishment down to 32,968 mounted regulars, and thirty-nine regiments instead of the original fifty-four, which probably corresponded to the number of horses actually available. Paul's genuine interest in the cavalry arm is shown by the relevant regulations – the principal *Military Code of Field Cavalry Service* of 1796, and the supplementary *Rules* and *Precepts*. The tactical line was reduced to two ranks, as opposed to the three of 1755 and 1763, and the *Code* rightly scorned foot drill, 'since experience shows that the employment of dragoons as infantry is virtually impossible'.

The essential principles of the new dispensations were inculcated at special classes for senior officers which were staged by Arakcheev in St Petersburg from 1796. The incongruity of the scenes was still capable of raising a laugh fifty years later. Suvorov declared that the classes were a case of the blind leading the crippled, but Kutuzov, assiduous courtier that he was, could not say enough in their praise, and was assiduous in his attendance.

In the field the ordeal of the watch parades was writ large at the major manoeuvres that were staged by several regiments at a time. The units were disposed as they actually tried to fight in 1799 on the Adda, Tidone and Trebbia, and at Zürich and Bergen, namely in an advance guard pushing ahead, and a main force marching in two parallel columns as a prelude to the 'processional' deployment into line.

The management of the artillery at first promised well. On 6 December Paul ousted the hateful Zubov from his post as head of the artillery, and replaced him by Melissino, who enjoyed the power, if not the title, of Master General. Having waited so long for a position that was rightfully his, the Greek was forced by ill health to give up office on 24 September 1797, and died on 26 December of the same year.

The care of the artillery now passed to the veteran gunner major-general Aleksandr Ivanovich Chelishev, who wrought changes in a routine of business which had remained unaltered since the time of Petr Shuvalov. He was probably also responsible, with Melissino, for a number of useful technical improvements – the gun carriages were given longer trails, for the sake of stability, the capacity of the ammunition chests was increased to thirty rounds, and the ammunition itself was rendered more effective through more powerful gunpowder, and the substitution of canister shot of iron instead of lead.

The reign of Chelishev came to an end on 4 January 1799, when he was ousted by Arakcheev. This grotesque being too was dethroned on 1 October, after he was detected in an attempt to cover up for the negligence of one of his brothers. Thus the artillery was left without effective direction at the time of the War of the Second Coalition. The gunners lent inadequate support to the other arms at Zürich and elsewhere, and the neglect of the horse artillery is notable, in view of the fine state to which Paul had brought the Gatchina detachments as tsarevich.

At times Paul almost seemed to be at war with elements in his own army. The Guard, as the home of the 'parasite nobility', was subjected to immediate and far-reaching transformations.

Gentlemen [Paul once said], word reaches me that the Guards officers grumble and complain that I am freezing them to death on the watch parade. But you can see for yourselves just how badly the Guard does its service. Nobody knows anything. To make you do your duty, it is not enough to explain and demonstrate things to you — you have to be led by the hand. (Volkonskii, *RS*, 1876, XVI, 183)

The first mass transfer of Gatchina officers to the Guard was effected in November 1796, and Paul went on to reshape the household troops into a coherent fighting force, compelling the golden lads to think for the first time about serious military service. De Sanglein exclaimed indignantly that:

to convert Guards officers from imperial to army soldiers, to introduce strict discipline, and in short to turn everything upside down, signified a contempt for public opinion, and the destruction of a whole prevailing order that had been sanctified by time. . . . The consequence was that the greater part of the Guards officers entered into retirement. Who was to replace them? (De Sanglein, *RS*, 1882, XXXVI, 475)

The answer was readily supplied by a fresh influx of the Gatchina product, which gave rise to all sorts of bizarre juxtapositions of young resentful nobility, and the inarticulate and awkward men from Gatchina, who hung about the palaces like lumpish ghosts.

The army as a whole was purged of no less than seven field-marshals, 330 generals and 2,261 junior officers, many of whom were reinstated after Paul felt the lesson had sunk home. Suvorov's order of dismissal came on 6 February 1797. His offence was to have spoken so loudly about the new order of things. He described the *Infantry Code* of 1796 as a rat-chewed parchment, found in a castle, and at the sight of the new uniforms he declared: 'You can't explode hair powder! You can't shoot buckles! You can't bayonet somebody with a pigtail!' (Masson, 1859, 130).

In some circles a notice of dismissal was considered a sign of honour, and there were officers who deliberately appeared at court in irregular and untidy dress, or talked and argued on the watch parade. Löwenstern writes proudly of a deceit he practised when his squadron of cuirassiers joined the rest of the regiment on a march through Riga in parade order. The cobblers had been unable to make enough of the new, Prussian-style boots, but:

then I was seized with the inspiration of dressing each cuirassier in just one of the high boots, since

67 Paul I and Suvorov

they rode in the usual order by ranks of two at a time. I had them wear the high boots on the outside leg, while retaining the half-boots on the inside leg. Nobody detected this ruse, which was taken up by the whole regiment. The emperor received from the military governor a report on the exemplary martial bearing of our regiment, and he showered us with eulogies. (Löwenstern, *RS*, 1900, CIII, 283)

Bearing in mind the theme of our book, the Pauline episode is of crucial importance in evaluating the impact of the outside world on Russian military affairs. Soviet historians regard it as a totally foreign intrusion, misconceived at the outset, and completely harmful in all its workings. Certainly there was a good deal that was odd in its outward manifestations, which made it appear a reproduction of Peter III's counterfeit, an imitation at two removes of an alien Frederician original, valid only in its own time and place. Semen Vorontsov makes the telling point that Paul missed the true significance of Frederick's achievement, which lay in the field of grand tactics, while copying externals which Old Fritz had inherited from his father and never bothered to change.

In justice, however, it is worth making some effort to discover what exactly Paul set out to do. His *oeuvre* makes sense only in the context of the run-down, mismanaged army which he had inherited from the last reign, 'when, thanks to the lack of vigilance, the fitful gleams of glory were everywhere interspersed with dark shadows ... you must agree that it was a good idea to stir things up and give them a new impetus, especially in the red glow of the French Revolution' (Lubyanovskii, 1872, 92-3). Wiegel disliked the new uniforms, but he too conceded that 'along with such measures there were introduced a number of reforms which were most useful for the service' (Wiegel, 1864-6, I, pt 1, 82). If the experience of the older generation was set at naught by the novel codes, younger officers found that 'the new evolutions were simple, demanding only a certain accuracy and attention to detail in the execution' (Engelhardt, 1868, 208).

In this context, there was a lot to be said for the objectives which Paul put before himself. These may be summed up as follows:

(a) to subject the army to the control of the sovereign;
(b) to eradicate the corruption and tyrannical power of the colonels and senior officers;
(c) to recall the officers as a whole to their professional obligations, and curb their notorious drinking and gambling (here Langeron was in no doubt as to the necessity and effectiveness of the Pauline visitation);
(d) to improve the lot of the private soldier, who had been so cruelly abused in the reign of Catherine.

Striving towards the last aim, Paul augmented the musketeer's pay to 9 roubles 40½ kopeks a year. He increased the number of pupils in the garrison schools to 16,500, and on 23 December 1798 he founded a Military Orphanage, accommodating 200 sons of officers and 800 of private soldiers. His *Code* of 1796 spoke of the importance of spurring on the troops by encouraging words, instead of belabouring them with the stick, and the *Tactical Rules* of the following year, so often cited as evidence of blind reaction, told the officers, 'The soldier must always be regarded as a human being, for almost anything can be attained through friendly dealings. Soldiers will do more for an officer who treats them well, and receives their trust, than for one whom they merely fear.'

What of the person of Paul, outwardly ridiculous with his pug nose and bald box-like cranium, his stick and his hat à la Old Fritz? Much has been made of the personal savagery of Paul in his dealings with the army, and of his readiness to assail his officers with the stick. There were actually just three cases of the kind, and on each occasion the emperor later relented and expressed his apologies. Indeed, there is much evidence to show that Paul was a man of idealism, honesty and (we have to say) sweetness and courtesy. Some of the worst asperities of the time are associated not with Paul or the Prussian freaks from Gatchina, but with men of old-fashioned Muscovite cast like the simian Arakcheev, or Paul's son, Grand Prince

Constantine, the leader of the xenophobic party. In all seriousness, Constantine once propounded two basic *Maxims on Military Discipline*:

First Maxim. The officer is purely and simply a machine

Second Maxim. Everything which a superior commands of his subordinate must be carried out, even if it is an atrocity

Constantine drew a number of monstrous consequences, and rounded off by declaring that 'education, reasoning, and feelings of honour and justice are prejudicial to good discipline.... An officer must never make use of his good sense or intelligence. The less he has of honour the better he is. (*SIRIO*, 1870, V, 58-9)

War against the Revolution

It took some years for the monarchies of old Europe to appreciate that in Revolutionary France a power of quite extraordinary malevolence had emerged — an armed people interested no longer in readjusting borders and maintaining the balance of power, but in overthrowing states and the social and religious order upon which they had been founded. The early and middle 1790s found Russia preoccupied with affairs in Poland, and the anti-French First Coalition came and went before Catherine or Paul could take a direct hand in affairs. Prussia dropped out of the league in 1795, and the alliance collapsed altogether after Bonaparte beat the Austrians in north Italy in 1796 and 1797.

As Suvorov already sensed, the advent of Bonaparte signified a marriage between supreme military genius and the crusading enthusiasms of the Republic. In 1798 this bold Corsican embarked on the expedition which took a French army to the shores of Egypt. Paul was now at last awakened from his torpor by the news that on their way to the Orient the French had captured the island of Malta, and expelled the Knights of St John from their seat. The thing appealed to the emperor's love of lost causes, and he not only accepted the Grand Mastership Extraordinary from a party of refugee knights, but approached Britain with a view to joint action against the French.

The British Cabinet was willing to accommodate this 'natural ally', and in the middle of 1799 it undertook to make over £181,000 per month for 90,000 Russian and 20,000 Swiss troops to act against the French in central Europe, and an additional £44,000 for an army of 17,500 Russians for service in Holland. Other agreements linked Russia with the kingdom of Naples and with Turkey, the ancient enemy, and the battered Austrians joined the league as well.

The War of the Second Coalition was to be fought on a truly continental scale, with the peripheral forces of Russia, Austria and Britain seeking to concert operations against 240,000 French troops who were arrayed across a wide tract of Europe — of whom 27,000 stood under Brune in Holland, 45,000 under Jourdan and Bernadotte on the Rhine, 48,000 under Masséna in Switzerland, 58,000 under Schérer in north Italy, as well as 25,000 in garrison in the north Italian fortresses, and 34,000 under Macdonald in southern Italy (all figures approximate).

It was some comfort that at least the French army in Egypt was incapable of returning to add to these considerable masses. The sealing-off process was accomplished by Admiral Nelson, who closed with Brueys in the Battle of the Nile on 1 August 1798. As the Soviet historians would have it, 'at Aboukir, using the methods of Ushakov, Nelson defeated the French fleet as it lay at anchor' (Beskrovnyi, 1958, 600). Suvorov liked the style of the thing, and was much taken with Nelson's exclamation before the battle: 'Tomorrow I shall be a lord or an angel!' This, at least, was how it was transmitted to him. The original (less telling) ran: 'Before this time tomorrow, I shall have gained a peerage or Westminster Abbey.'

This victory isolated the French garrisons in the Mediterranean, and spared the Russian Black Sea Fleet, when it arrived on the scene, the ordeal of having to face the French in the open sea. The fleet in question was that of Admiral Ushakov, consisting of six of the line and seven frigates. At Constantinople it picked up a number of Turkish vessels, and in the autumn the united armada proceeded to the Ionian Islands, which guarded the access to the Adriatic and thus to the eastern flank of Italy. Cerigo, Zante and Marva were secured with no great difficulty, but the blockade and siege of Corfu dragged on until the capitulation of 3 March 1799. The Russians then sailed without hindrance to the Italian coast, where they seized Brindisi and laid Ancona under blockade. Ushakov had a landing force of Russian troops on board his vessels, but the prowess of Paul's army was not to be tested until it came to grips with the French on three theatres of mainland Europe.

Some dismal sentiments were being expressed concerning the outcome of such a confrontation. Rzhevskii had little hope of finding courage in such a debauched army. Masson doubted the Cossacks' ability to cope with the conditions of war in western Europe, and Langeron argued that the Russians were too accustomed to easy victories over backward opponents like the Turks and Poles.

Where are our officers and generals? [asked Count Rostopchin] The last Turkish war spoilt even those commanders who showed some glimmerings of talent. The leaders displayed no other merit than that required to sustain the cold and hardships of those long campaigns, which ended with assaults in which the meanest soldier counted for as much as his general. (O. V. Rostopchin, 5 November 1796, *AKV*, 1870-95, VII, 148-9)

North Holland, 1799

Paul did not share the fainthearts' reservations.

The crazy tsar was at this time at the highest pitch of his ardour for crushing French democracy. He was eager to send his Muscovites everywhere and anywhere, provided that other governments (and the English in particular) would bear a large share of the expenses. Paul seems never to have doubted of the superiority of his rude soldiers over those of Western Europe. He expected his Russians to conquer, if they found the opportunity to fight, as a matter of course. (Bunbury, 1927, 26)

Unfortunately for Paul's stability of mind, a contingent of his troops was engaged in a disastrous enterprise against the northern flank of French-dominated Europe. This took the form of an amphibious descent on Holland, and more specifically North Holland — the tongue of land which enclosed the western side of the Zuider Zee. The initiative throughout rested with the British, who effected the first landing at The Helder on 27 August 1799. They soon found that they had underestimated the defensive strength of this terrain of ditches and dykes, and that they had overestimated in equal proportion the willingness of the Dutch to rise in their favour.

Meanwhile, the Russian transports had been making their way from the Baltic, attended by some of the oafish pupils of Gatchina, one of whom demanded to see the King of Hamburg in passing. The Russian force was commanded by Lieutenant-General Johann Hermann, a Saxon who had entered the Russian service in 1769, and was described as being 'a brave, zealous and straightforward fellow' (Bunbury, 1927, 15), though bad at maintaining discipline and ignorant of the higher reaches of the military art. The last of the 11,000 or so Russians came ashore on 26 September, by when the British had had the opportunity to form some opinions of these apparitions from the East.

Edward Walsh wrote that the Russians were 'robust and muscular ... to those who were unaccustomed to view them, they seemed even repulsive and ferocious'. However,

the general appearance of the Russian army, when drawn up under arms, announced at the first glance that it was composed of troops formed altogether for service, and not for show. There appeared to have been established throughout all ranks the most absolute subordination. (Nostitz, 1976, 239)

Those with an eye for detail noted that these sallow, smelly people ate a bread that looked like an oily cattle cake, and that they were delighted to be able to smear this substance with axle grease. William Surtees, as a light infantryman, took a professional interest in a party of their jaegers:

if we appeared irregular and grotesque, I know not well how to describe *them*. Their riflemen were

NORTH HOLLAND, 1799

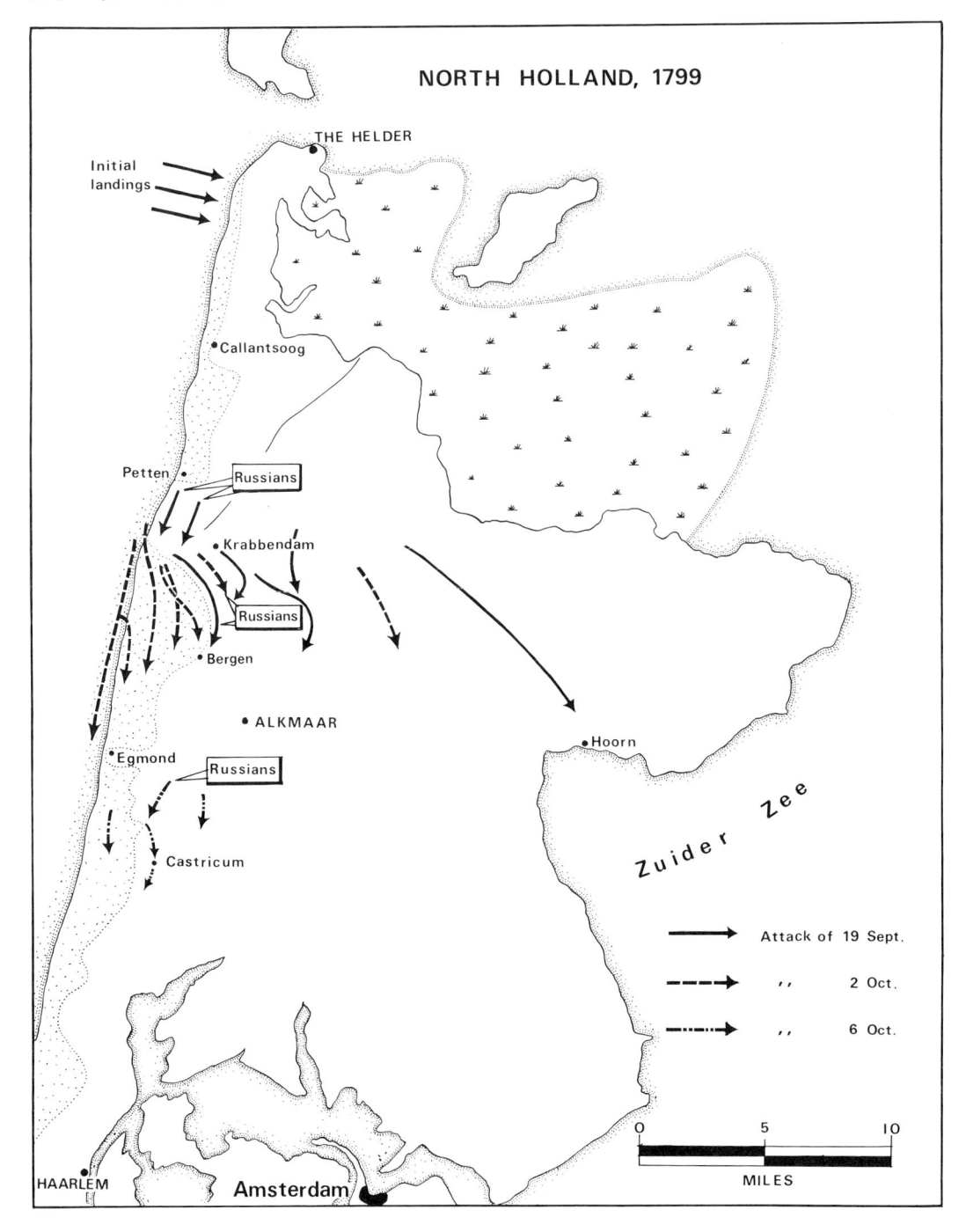

- THE HELDER
- Initial landings
- Callantsoog
- Petten — Russians
- Krabbendam
- Russians — Bergen
- ALKMAAR
- Egmond — Russians
- Castricum
- Hoorn
- Zuider Zee
- HAARLEM
- Amsterdam

→ Attack of 19 Sept.
⇢ ,, 2 Oct.
⇢ ,, 6 Oct.

0   5   10
MILES

shod with boots very much resembling those of our fishermen, coming up considerably higher than the knee, thus rendering them, I should say, incapable of celerity of movement, one of the chief requisites in a rifle corps. They also wore large cocked hats and long green coats. Their grenadiers were dressed [no] more apropos, having high sugar-loaf caps, mounted with a great deal of brass, and projecting forward at the top, with long coats, and gaiters reaching above the knee. Their regular infantry were nearly similar to the grenadiers, only they wore cocked hats instead of caps. The regiment we saw on this occasion had with it, I should think, full half as many followers as soldiers, some of whom carried immensely large copper kettles.... The officers, I remember, carried what was formerly used in our service, a long sort of pole, with a head like a halberd, and called, I believe, a 'spontoon'. This, on passing a general at a review, the officer twists and twirls around his head, precisely as a drum-major in our service does his cane. (Surtees, 1973, 8-9)

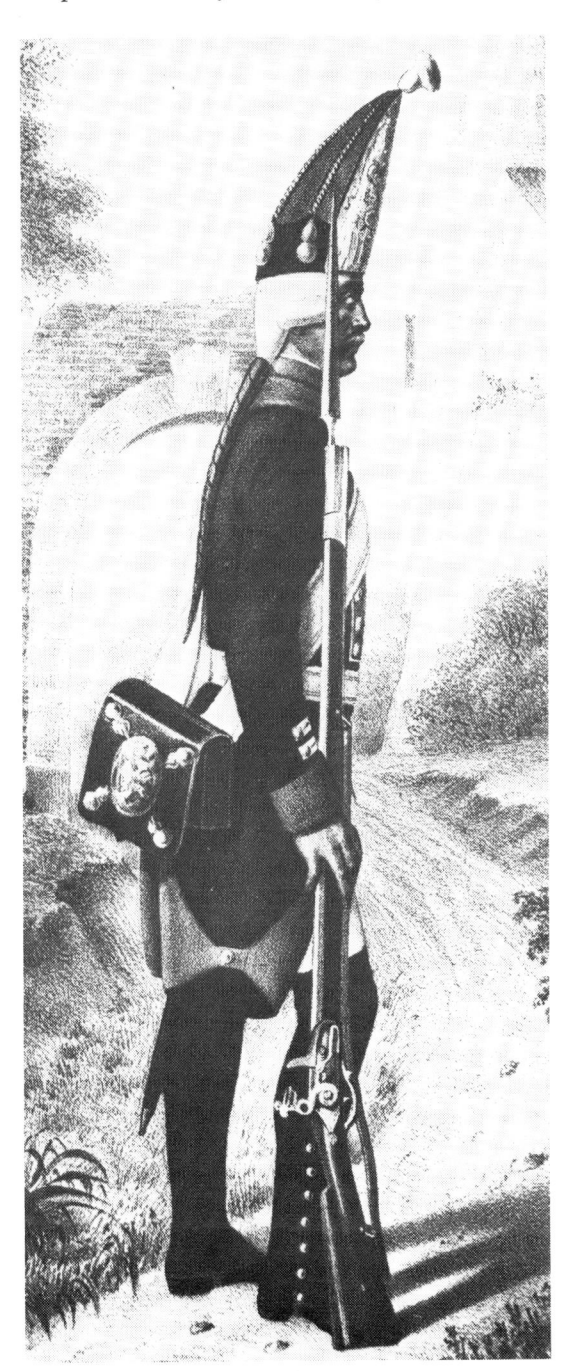

The first offensive action was launched on 19 September, and its outcome was to be fatal to the working together of the allies. The scheme for this Battle of Bergen was a fairly complicated one, involving a frontal attack by three main columns, and a sweeping movement by a fourth column by way of Alkmaar so as to exploit any opportunities on the eastern flank. Hermann's Russians were massed on the corresponding western flank, in the coastal sand dunes, and they constituted the first of the columns of the principal force.

On the appointed day of the attack the Russians got under way two hours before sunrise, stampeded by one of Hermann's subordinates. The agile French delivered a deadly cross fire from the sand dunes, and the Russians, unable to deploy into line, pushed forward in a single confused mass as far as the village of Bergen. Russian corpses were everywhere, and Captain Herbert Taylor 'observed

68 Grenadier of the Shlyushelburgskii Musketeer Regiment, period of Paul I. Dark green coat with light green collar, lapels and cuffs and red turn-backs; red stock; mitre cap with light green and dark green back, white metal frontal plate and white pompom; the devices on the cartridge pouch are of brass (Viskovatov, 1844-56)

to General Hermann that the troops in the rear must have fired upon those in front, which he admitted was more than probable' (20 September, 'Dropmore Papers', V, 1906, 418). Under pressure from the enemy the Russians then executed a fighting retreat, leaving behind about 1,700 dead and wounded and their chief, Hermann, a prisoner of the French. Elsewhere along the front the British columns failed to reach their objectives.

General Essen, who took the place of Hermann, was said to be 'false, intriguing, and ill-disposed towards the British' (Bunbury, 1927, 15). His conduct, wrote Semen Vorontsov, was 'a mixture of ignorance, base conduct and pride ... what hurts me the most is to know that our contingent has been totally disgraced by the incapacity of the commander and those dreadful officers who make up nine-tenths of all the commissioned ranks' (30 October 1799, *AKV*, 1870-95, X, 64-5).

A little ground was gained in a further assault on 2 October, in which the Russians were committed well inland, but the territory was lost again towards the close of a confused and unplanned fight which broke out on 6 October. Twelve days later an agreement was reached with the French, in virtue of which the demoralised allies were evacuated from The Helder.

The British had little idea what to do with the contingent of Russians, which was now left on their hands. The Cabinet actually contemplated sending 5,000 of the troops to help to hold down Ireland, but the scheme was rejected by the Chief Secretary for Ireland, and by Lord Cornwallis, who wrote that it would give rise to scenes of 'indescribable plunder and murder' (Nostitz, 1976, 82). The Russians were finally decanted in the isle of Jersey, which at least served to forward the education of one of the Gatchina officers, who had always assumed that the place was part of the mainland.

Disaster at Zürich, 1799

The main Russian striking force was destined to act in association with the Austrians in Switzerland in the heart of Western Europe. The theatre had a triple appeal for the British paymasters. First of all, the St Gotthard Pass offered a much more direct line of communication between Italy and Germany than the Brenner. Second, the allies, once masters of Switzerland, could open up a weakly fortified sector of the French frontier. Finally the Swiss, 'the gallant poor little fellows in the little cantons' (Lord Mulgrave, 15 September 1799, 'Dropmore Papers', V, 1906, 406) were already invested with a certain aura of cleanliness and the love of liberty, and it was hoped that up to 20,000 of these virtuous people would join with the Austrians and Russians to evict the French under Masséna, who were holding on to a corner of Switzerland along the River Limmat, in the neighbourhood of Zürich.

The main army of 45,000 Russians was admitted to be composed of 'the best and finest Russian troops' (Sir Charles Whitworth, 30 April 1799, PRO FO 65/42), and 'the march of the force was held up, so as to bring the drill to a final peak of perfection' (Masson, 1859, 357). The command was invested in *Generalanshef* Rimskii-Korsakov, who had commended himself by his enthusiasm for Paul's methods, and his confidence that the Russian troops, with their high morale and superior discipline, would surely acquit themselves better than the Austrians, whom he had seen in the Netherlands in 1794. As if these recommendations were not enough, Paul was entranced by a slow march which Korsakov (a member of a musical family) had composed for the Semenovskii Guards, and he had it played over on many occasions.

Lieutenant-General John Ramsay came out to see that the British got good value for their subsidies, and in the third week of July he watched the Russian columns as they wound through Prague in Bohemia. The weather was hot, and the march was hurried, but Ramsay was impressed by the generally sound state of the army, and he assured his masters that 'good justice has been done, both with respect to the selection of the troops, as also in respect to the essential part of their equipments'. He liked what he saw of the artillery, and noted that the regular cavalry was fitted out in the Prussian style (20 July 1799, PRO, FO 74/28).

ITALY AND SWITZERLAND, 1799

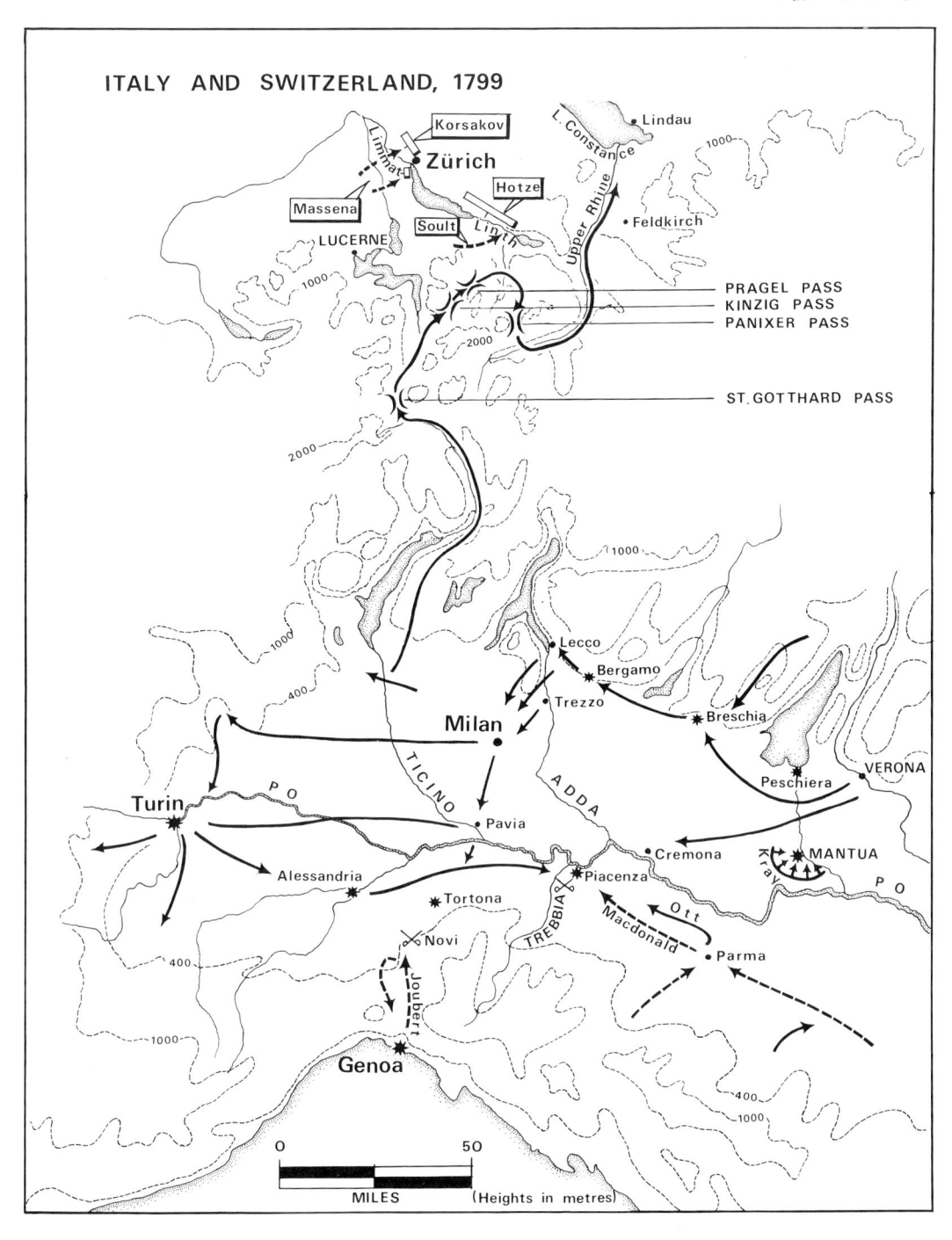

One of the cuirassiers, the young officer Waldemar Löwenstern, found time to make the rounds of polite society in Prague, where he caused a sensation in the circle of French émigrés.

It is difficult to imagine the absurdity of the kind of question that was put to me. One of the ladies asked me in all seriousness 'Is it true that your soldiers eat young children?' 'Not only small ones', I replied, 'but big ones as well, if they are as pretty as you, *mesdames*!'

At their request he produced his batman for inspection, so that they could see what an ordinary Russian looked like. The company stood in appalled fascination, and Löwenstern had to admit that with his slit Kalmyk eyes 'he really did look rather like a cannibal' (Löwenstern, *RS*, 1900, CIII, 288).

It was no fault of the Russians that the coalition strategy now fell apart. The Austrian chancellor, Thugut, conceived of the war in purely dynastic terms, and he was displeased to hear of the impetuous progress of Suvorov in Italy (see p. 217), and the field-marshal's eagerness to restore the House of Savoy as ruler of Piedmont. As the best means of removing the Russians from Italy, and simultaneously forwarding the Habsburg designs on Alsace and Lorraine, Thugut decided to transfer Archduke Charles with the main body of the Austrians from Switzerland to the middle Rhine, and bring up Suvorov from Italy to replace him at Zürich, in the meantime leaving only a number of Austrian staff officers and a corps of 23,000 troops under Hotze in support of Korsakov.

This complicated reshuffle of the allied armies gave Masséna the time to build up his own strength to 70,000 men, and exploit the advantages of his central position to the full. As a first move, he sent General Lecourbe and 12,000 troops marching south in late August to seize the St Gotthard. Meanwhile, the main force continued to hold its positions near Zürich in the close proximity of the Cossack outposts. 'Sometimes the French musicians came to play martial airs on the banks of the beautiful Limmat. Then the Cossacks would spring to their feet of their own accord, and dance and jump in circles' (Masson, 1859, 437-8).

Meanwhile some disturbing evidence was coming to light concerning the leadership of the Russians. Ramsay was pained to see that Korsakov was not particularly

aware of the necessity of those precautions which other armies adopt in particular circumstances, and which he will in all probability feel inclined to attend to, when more acquainted with the stratagems and proceedings of an active and clever enemy who acts scientifically and with system. The same deficiency appears evidently to be general among the officers, from the manner in which the service is carried on, and particularly that of the advanced posts, where we have seen the troops with their baggage and baggage waggons as if in perfect security. The pickets of Cossacks, notwithstanding the reputation they have for this species of service, having their horses unsaddled and at grass, within pistol-shot of the enemy's vedettes. (5 September 1799, PRO, FO 74/28)

During the peaceful weeks of late summer, Löwenstern's regiment of cuirassiers progressed slowly towards the theatre of operations in Switzerland. He spent two agreeable weeks in Lindau, 'the Venice of Lake Constance', and halted again at Schaffhausen, beside the famous Rhine Falls. 'Sitting on a fragment of rock, I was struck by the melancholy character of the noise produced by the falling water. People explain it by reference to a hidden affinity with the onward rush of our life' (Löwenstern, *RS*, 1900, CIII, 291).

Löwenstern soon heard a noise of a more melancholy nature still carrying from the direction of Zürich, where early on 25 September Masséna launched about 39,000 troops against the Russian positions. From 7.30 a.m. Korsakov's left, or southern flank, was heavily engaged with the division of Mortier, which made a heavy demonstration attack against the Russians at Wollishofen, between Mont Albis and the Lake of Zürich. The Russians responded to the invitation, and counter-attacked in force in the direction of the mountain. They ran up the heights like madmen, and, says Wickham,

the hedges and vineyards all about the village

were full of wounded and dead Russians, though I do not recollect having seen five dead Frenchmen on the whole ground. This is easily accounted for from the nature of the country, which is particularly well calculated for the French manner of fighting, and from the mode of attack of the Russians who appear to trust wholly to the bayonet, which the French never attempt to stand. (30 September 1799, 'Dropmore Papers', V, 1906, 441)

Meanwhile, on the Russian right, the French division of Lorge effected a crossing of the weakly held Limmat at Dietikon, and by two in the afternoon, when Korsakov finally became aware of the threat, the French had already pushed dangerously far in the direction of Zürich. Instead of making a stand on the commanding Zürichberg, Korsakov elected to fight in the confined space close under the town walls, feeding his troops to their destruction by dribs and drabs. The British and Austrian observers watched with admiration and horror while the French tirailleurs and batteries of horse artillery ravaged the dense Russian formations. 'Whole files collapsed forwards, and entire ranks were struck down in enfilade. The Russians trampled their dying comrades underfoot so as to close up in good order and reload by platoons and divisions' (Masson, 1859, 364). By nine in the evening the Russians were shut up in Zürich, and before midnight the able-bodied survivors forced their way out of the trap and retreated on Eglisau.

At the same time as these combats were raging on the north-west side of Lake Zürich, a French detachment under Soult meted out much the same treatment to the troops of Hotze, holding the line of the Linth as it ran into the opposite corner of the lake. Over the following days Korsakov and the Austrians were bundled back towards Schaffhausen and the upper Rhine, leaving the French in firm command of central Switzerland, and Suvorov in deadly peril.

With Suvorov through Italy and Switzerland

The third element of the Russian forces, amounting to about 25,000 men, had meanwhile made its way to Italy. At the request of the Austrians the command was given to the sixty-nine-year-old Suvorov, who was thereby rescued from his disgrace. In other circumstances Suvorov would have been content to remain in his opulent retirement, but in taking up the charge he said that he was

influenced alone by an anxious wish for the emancipation of Europe, and the deliverance of an extensive empire from a savage and ambitious government, pretending to the name of a republic, but being in fact the tyranny of usurpation of the meanest birth and basest minds. (Mulgrave, 12 September 1799, PRO, FO 74/27)

The old field-marshal received at Mitau the blessing of the exiled Louis XVIII on his enterprise, which probably encouraged Masson to make the ignorant charge that when Suvorov confronted the Revolution, he thought that he was dealing with a band of mutinous slaves. On the contrary, Suvorov was a man of cosmopolitan culture, very well acquainted with the historical and philosophical origins of the beast in question. He also grasped some important truths about the nature of ideological totalitarianism. Earlier generations had encountered Moslem religious fanaticism, but 'it has been left to us to witness another phenomenon, just as frightful, namely political fanaticism' (Fuchs, 1827, 36). He deplored the vandalisms perpetrated by Berthier in Rome, and drew attention to the way the French concealed their crimes through the distortion of language, using paranyms like *gagner* or *républicaniser* where 'outright thievery' would have been more in order. 'Can you show me,' he asked, 'a single Frenchman who has been made a whit happier by the Revolution?' (Fuchs, 1827, 160).

Suvorov maintained that any war against enemies like these must be prosecuted with the utmost seriousness, and he scarcely dared mention what he knew of the military genius of Bonaparte (see p. 194). As for the manner of operations, he made some notes for the eyes of Paul:

1   act only on the offensive
2   be speedy on the march, and attack furiously with cold steel
3   abhor methodicism — see and decide on the instant
4   give full authority to the commander-in-chief
5   attack and beat the enemy in the open field
6   don't waste time in sieges . . . . (Meerovich and Budanov, 1978, 253)

Suvorov followed in the track of his troops through Vienna and so over the Alps. The Austrian capital found him laconic in conversation, 'but this singularity was disregarded, thanks to the confidence which everyone reposed in his military talents and personal bravery' (Runich, *RS*, 1901, CV, 329). On reaching the Italian plain in April, Suvorov was enraptured by the sights and sounds of a land which he had come to know so well from his books. Every landscape spoke to him of the glorious campaigns of the past, and he loved to hear the peasant songs as they carried across the fields, for they reminded him of the melodies of home. Chasteler, his borrowed Austrian chief of staff, travelled with him in his coach and tried to draw his attention to matters in hand, but Suvorov just muttered 'Bayonets! Bayonets!'

In an access of enthusiasm the Austrians had made Suvorov a field-marshal in the Austrian service, and commander-in-chief of all the forces in north Italy. The Austrian staff officers Chasteler, Zach and Weyrother learnt to value some of Suvorov's unusual qualities, and some at least of the Austrian rank-and-file responded to Suvorov's attempts to enkindle their enthusiasm. In private he told William Wickham of his admiration for the professionalism of the Austrian officers, and the efficiency of their administration.

Many sources of friction remained. On arriving at the army Suvorov issued the first of the series of tactical instructions to which he expected the Austrians as well as the Russians to conform. Wenzel Anton Radetzky, who was then a young officer, explained that

the order of the day was dictated to a victorious and confident army, and it worked disadvantageously on the morale of the troops. The army felt itself humiliated, offended. Trust in the leadership disappeared. The consequence was an extraordinary division between the allied forces — a division which extended all the way up to headquarters. (Regele, 1957, 58)

The general Austrian opinion was that the Russian troops were savage marauders, and that their leaders were blockheads. Even Chasteler attracted the hatred of his former comrades by taking the part of Suvorov.

On the Russian side, Captain Gryazev harboured what was probably the common opinion of the middle ranks of Suvorov's officers. He was ready to praise the good condition of the Austrian muskets, the practicability of their greatcoats, and the imposing appearance of their grenadier bearskins, but he maintained that the Austrians had forgotten that 'what is needed in action against the enemy is not hair powder, polished belts, or glittering metal accoutrements, but courage, daring and composure'. If the Hungarian troops made a good impression, the native Austrians struck him as being spiritless and sheep-like, and their officers self-indulgent — 'everything reeks of phlegmaticism and pedantry' (Orlov, 1898, 162, 163). It was all the more galling for the Russians, who lacked trained staff officers, to be so dependent on the Austrians for everything that had to do with supply, movement and the mechanics of military operations.

Tensions were also inherent in the conduct and objectives of the campaign. Suvorov's strategy was conceived as a 'right-flanking' movement, designed to carry the allies around the Alpine flank of the Lombard plain, beating the French field forces, and leaving their isolated garrisons to wither away. It appeared quite incomprehensible to the Russians how their allies were determined to fritter away their field forces for the sake of conducting 'irrelevant' sieges in accordance with the dictates of the *Hofkriegsrath*, sitting in far-off Vienna.

More was at stake than a divergence of military technique. The Austrians, as we have seen, were interested above all in consolidating once more their mastery of Lombardy, and delaying or frustrating the return of the King of Sardinia as ruler of Piedmont. Suvorov, on the contrary, wished to restore the old order of things in its entirety, after which he would be free to launch the allied army in an outright invasion of France by way of Dauphiné.

By now we have stolen somewhat ahead of our story, having left Suvorov in mid-April when he assumed command of the Austro-Russian army in north-east Italy. He had at his disposal a combined force of 48,500 troops, of which the active Russian element comprised about 24,500 men and forty-four pieces of field artillery. The French commander was the rigid and unimaginative Schérer, who had 28,000 troops dispersed along the length of the Adda, a north-bank tributary of the Po. In front of this main defensive position there was a scattering of garrisons — Brescia and Bergamo towards the Alpine foothills, Peschiera on the southern shore of Lake Garda, and the powerful fortress of Mantua.

In the whole of the French army there was probably 'not a single officer who knew the different branches of the Russian army, who possessed the slightest notion of their language, or of their ways of marching, camping or fighting' (Masson, 1859, 431). The ignorance was sustained by the work of the Cossacks, who, far more successfully than their comrades in Switzerland, prevented the French from taking prisoners and conducting reconnaissances. Suvorov had instructed Adrian Denisov to manage the business in close concert with Chasteler, and Denisov now had to tell the Austrian that the Cossack officers could not read maps, and that most of them were too poor to own watches. In place of these conventional means of orientation, Denisov therefore divided the Cossacks into four or five handy commands, with instructions to explore passages across rivers and canals, to bring back prisoners, and to make detailed descriptions of the places they had seen, even if they were unable to ascertain the names. From these clues the Italians on Chasteler's staff were able to identify the localities in question, and build up an accurate picture of the land and the enemy.

While Kray was detached with 20,000 Austrians to garrison the base at Verona, and mask Peschiera and Mantua, the main force concentrated against the northern flank of the French positions. Brescia was seized on 20 April, and a little later Denisov took Bergamo by a *coup de main*. By late April, therefore, Suvorov was ready for his intended blow against a thirty-five-mile stretch of the upper Adda. Here the river formed a kind of sump of Lake Como, where the long south-eastern arm narrowed into sheets of water and reedy bogs. Inside the chosen sector, Suvorov built up heavy local concentrations of troops. The operation was inaugurated on 25 April, when Suvorov sent Prince Bagration with 3,000 men to attack the powerful French forces on both banks of the Adda upstream at Lecco. On the 26th, aided by this auxiliary attack, the allies effected crossings downstream at Trezzo and Cassano. The French were unable to redispose their forces in time, and the day ended with their beaten army in retreat, prodded on its way by the Cossacks. French losses were estimated at 2,000 dead, 5,000 captured and twenty-seven guns. 'Those famous *demi-brigades* the terror and admiration of Europe ... now presented to the Russian army no more than scattered bands' (Masson, 1859, 334-5).

Suvorov exclaimed, 'the Adda is our Rubicon!', meaning that the passage of the river had opened the plain of Lombardy. General Moreau, Schérer's successor, withdrew the chastened French army to the approaches to Genoa, leaving garrisons in the citadels of Milan, Turin, Alessandria and Tortona, but abandoning everything outside their confines to the enemy. The allied army entered Milan, the capital of Austrian Lombardy, on 29 April.

Suvorov found in the Austrians 'an army bigotted to a defensive system, afraid even to pursue their successes, when that system permitted them to obtain any' (Mulgrave, 12 September 1799, PRO, FO 74/27). Seeking to consolidate the ground which had been won already, Thugut insisted that the allies must provide for the sieges of Mantua and the citadels — a strategy which reduced Suvorov's concentration around Alessandria to less than 40,000 troops. This state of affairs encouraged the French to regain the initiative by taking him between the two jaws of a strategic pincers. While Moreau with a 'western' force of 25,000 men threatened Suvorov from the direction of Genoa, General Macdonald was to strike across the Apennines with the French troops from central and southern Italy and come at the allies from the east. In early June 1799 Macdonald irrupted into the plain, and gathering troops to the number of about 35,000, he chased the small Austrian detachments from Modena and Parma. The main Austrian force in that part of the world stood under the command of Kray, and it was inextricably committed by the *Hofkriegsrath* to the siege of Mantua, leaving the defence of the middle Po entirely to Ott's command of an initial 6,000 Austrians.

The sun of mid-June beat down with relentless heat as the armies disputed the outcome of the campaign on the levels south of the Po — an expanse of poplar-lined fields, interspersed by drainage channels, and the broad white gashes where shallow rivers made their way northwards through beds of white pebbles. For Suvorov the first priority was to get help to Ott, as he recoiled in the face of Macdonald. Suvorov could spare only 17,000 men to leave under Bellegarde to mask Genoa, and with the remaining 22,000 he hastened east, covering thirty miles a day.

The first clash was staged on the afternoon of 17 June, and took the form of an encounter battle, in which the Russian advance guard and Cossacks came to the help of the hard-pressed Ott, and persuaded the French to withdraw across the Tidone.

On 18 June the allies undertook a full offensive against the French, as they stood beside the Trebbia. Suvorov disposed the main body in three columns, or divisions, along a frontage of five or six miles, and stipulated that 'if, contrary to expectations, the enemy encounters us, we are to form line immediately in an orderly fashion, though without pedantry or an excessive appearance of exactitude' (Suvorov, 1953, IV, 154). The approach march was hot and exhausting, and the armies came into contact only at three or four in the afternoon. For two hours almost the whole weight of the battle was borne by the allied right wing, where Prince Bagration with the Cossacks and other elements of the right-wing advance guard launched an attack against the hated émigré Poles of Dombrowski. Macdonald brought his forces in this sector up to a strength of 15,000, and in their turn the allies advanced Schweikowsky's Austrians and Rosenberg's Russians from the main body of the right wing. Altogether the French counter-attack burst twice across the Trebbia, but it was unable to overcome the 'Russian impassivity, that herd-like stubbornness against which the discipline of the Prussians and the tactics of Frederick the Great had so often failed' (Masson, 1859, 344). Fröhlich and Ott, standing respectively to the centre and left, were engaged too late to affect the outcome, and the combat ended with the armies facing each other across the Trebbia.

The contestants had all their forces at hand for the final combat of 19 June. Macdonald now had 33,000 troops to match Suvorov's 28,000, and he built up a crushing concentration of 12,000 men on the southern flank of the field with the intention of turning Suvorov's right. Once more Dombrowski's division was the first major formation to make contact, and once more it was defeated by Bagration. The very impetus of the Russian counter-attack opened a gap in the allied line, and Schweikowsky was for a time surrounded by the divisions of Victor and Rusca. Suvorov hastened up in person and helped to push the French back towards the Trebbia, but 'Papa' Melas, the overall commander of the Austrian contingent, was very slow about feeding the central division of Fröhlich into the action, and the French were able to consolidate along their start line. Much the same thing had happened the day before.

Although Suvorov resigned himself to a further battle on the next day, Macdonald made off eastwards during the night, having lost 6,000 dead and wounded and 5,000 men prisoner over the three days of combat, as compared with the allied butcher's bill of 5,000 casualties. Before Macdonald could escape across the Apennines, a further 7,500 French were overtaken and captured at Piacenza.

The events on the Tidone and Trebbia represented a fair trial of strength between Suvorov and the Revolutionary French, and the happy outcome enabled him to return west and settle accounts with the French lurking in the Ligurian Alps. The Austrians now began to reap the reward of their persistence in the matter of the sieges, and news began to arrive on the surrender of the isolated French garrisons — at the citadels of Turin and Alessandria, and most welcome of all at the fortress of Mantua, which set free General Kray to join Suvorov with his 20,000 Austrians. The reinforcements brought the allied army to about 50,000 combatants, a respectable total with which to face General Joubert, the third and least lucky of the French commanders.

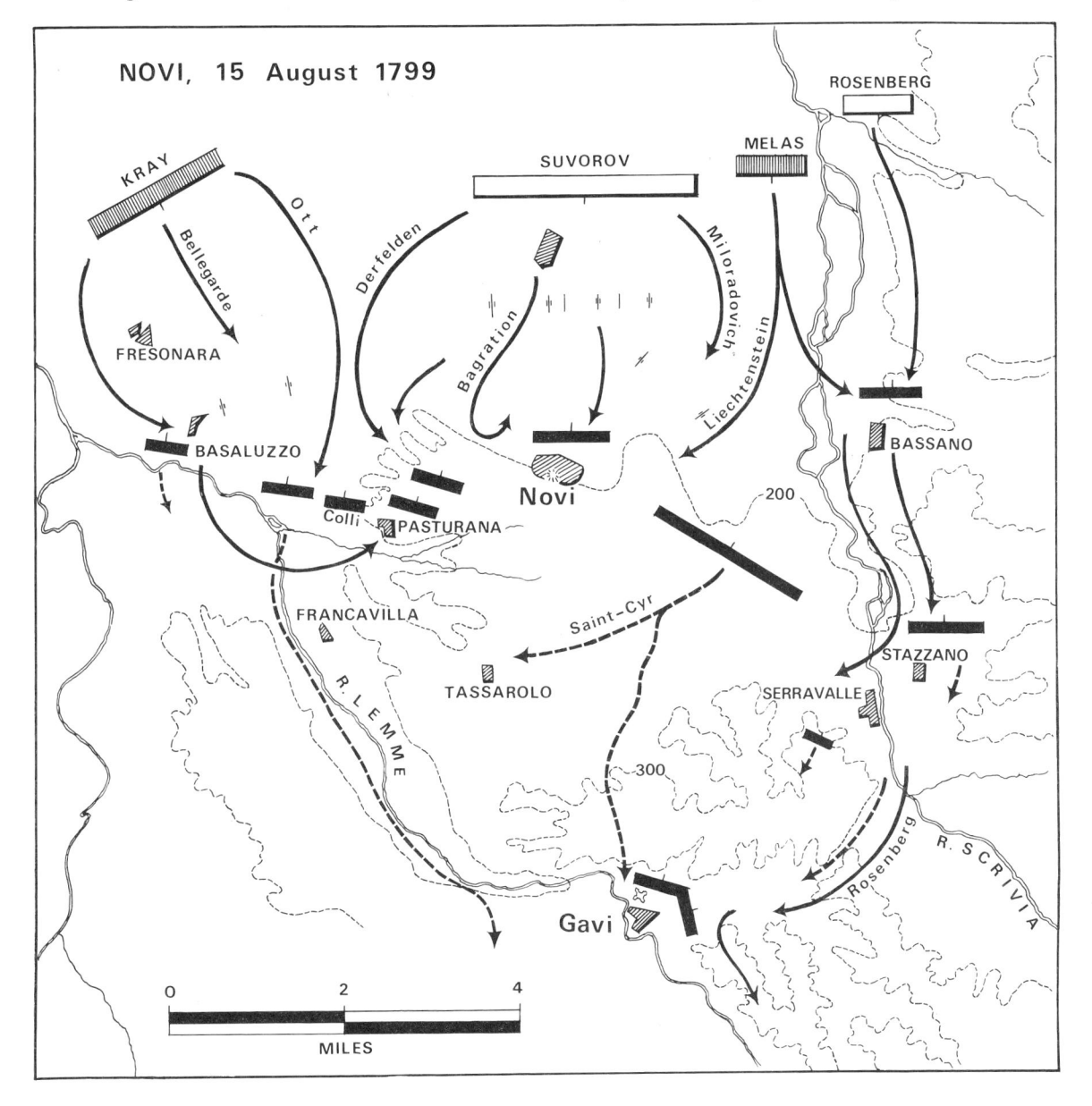

As Suvorov looked south in the direction of Genoa, the verdant plain of Marengo was rimmed along the horizon by the bluish hump-backs of the peaks of the Ligurian Alps, where Joubert could have offered a strong resistance with his 40,000 or so French. Instead, the doomed young man advanced to the edge of the plain, and ensconced himself along a frontage of a dozen miles in a region of low, grassy foothills. The one post of any great strength was on the French right centre at Novi, where a little town crowded into a perimeter of medieval walls of brown brick. Inside the town, a steep little hill was crowned by the remains of a castle, partially adapted into a renaissance fort.

Suvorov's army converged on the Novi position on 14 August. Kray's Austrians were in possession of a little verse from Suvorov, in praise of their leader, and indeed the combat turned out to be a latter-day Kunersdorf, with Russians and Austrians working together in harmony to produce a resounding victory. The thing could be done, if only once in every generation.

On the next day Suvorov impatiently fed his forces into the attack as soon as they arrived, and the battle gradually unfolded from west to east until almost the whole of the Novi position was taken in the allied embrace. Kray begged, and received, the permission to open the action with his Austrians against the French left. He began the first of ten attacks at five in the morning, and ultimately forced his way to the valley between Pasturana and the River Lemme. At the outset of the combat General Joubert had rushed up to encourage his tirailleurs, only to be shot dead for his pains, and his successor, Moreau, became so alarmed by developments on this flank that he sent thither the brigade of Colli from his right, thereby massing no less than 20,000 men in the west.

From eight in the morning the centre of the French position at Novi came under attack by Bagration and Miloradovich. This sector was held by the division of Gardane, which could dart out from the perimeter of the town walls at will, and which enjoyed the support of three batteries on the castle hill, 'erupting in flames and incessant thunder like some fire-spitting Etna' (Gryazev, in Orlov, 1898, 66). Much against his will, Adrian Denisov obeyed orders to position his regiment of Don Cossacks within lethally close range of 1,600 French infantry. Sixty of his men were hit, and his horse, 'terrified by the shot striking in the earth nearby, made three or four involuntary bounds, and on one occasion reared up so high that it was

69 Novi Castle

70 Base of the interior tower at Novi Castle, looking at the western side. The surface is pitted with hundreds of holes from the action of cannon shot, canister and musket balls, with particularly heavy concentrations at waist height, indicating a heavy, accurate and short-range fire coming from the west and north (the regularly spaced oblong holes are for scaffolding)

with difficulty that I could keep in the saddle'. Denisov ordered his men to pull back some way, which had the effect of luring a swarm of French tirailleurs from the security of their position. Seizing his opportunity, he launched his Cossacks in a charge, and the enemy were 'so astonished that they made no attempt to stand their ground, but took to their heels. Nearly all the Cossacks managed to kill two or three Frenchmen apiece' (Denisov, RS, 1874, XII, 33, 34).

This was poor consolation for the allies, who saw Bagration's command shot up and beaten back when it tried to approach the walls. Even the advent of the rest of the Russian infantry, from about eleven in the morning onwards, failed to dislodge the French from their defences. The last remaining resource was the Austrian division of Melas, which worked its way around to the east of Novi, and delivered a deadly attack against the weakened French right at three in the afternoon.

The enemy line was now so depleted that the Russians were finally able to break through the town and assault the castle hill. They overcame the French resistance in the castle compound in a firefight of the utmost ferocity, and a party of Austrian hussars was able to get across the path of the enemy retreat to Gavi, which contributed to swell the French losses to 6,600 dead and wounded and 3,000 prisoners. The allied casualties amounted to 8,750, most of whom were Austrians.

The bloody but little-known battle of Novi brought Suvorov the title of Prince, with the suffix of 'Italiiski', and it secured the Papacy and the royal thrones of Naples and Sardinia. It might also have led Suvorov and the Austrians on to an outright invasion of France, if the machinations of Count Thugut (see p. 214) had not forced them to part – the Austrians remaining in Italy, there to be beaten by Bonaparte in 1800, and Suvorov taking off with his Russian regiments to Switzerland, where the winter was already closing in.

Affairs in Switzerland were beginning to assume a still worse aspect than Suvorov had anticipated. He had put the enemy forces in that part of the world at a mere 60,000, whereas Masséna had 70,000 in his main concentration on Lake Zürich, and he had another 12,000 under Lecourbe disposed behind the St Gotthard Pass, by which Suvorov proposed to enter Switzerland. On the allied side, the doomed Korsakov and Hotze had 43,000 troops on either side of Lake Zürich, and a scattering of smaller Austrian detachments extended some way in the direction of Suvorov — namely those of Jellačić (5,000), Linken (3,500), Strauch (4,500), Auffenberg (3,000) and Haddik (4,500). Of these forces, Suvorov hoped to join Strauch and Auffenberg soon after his entry into Switzerland (as actually happened), and to meet Linken at Schwyz before proceeding to unite with Korsakov.

Travelling north, Suvorov bade an ironic farewell to Italy, the land of hospitality, pasta and 'sublime natural beauty' (Fuchs, 1827, 183-4). On 15 September, having marched 116 English miles in five days, Suvorov's command reached the little Swiss town of Taverne, set amid round tree-covered hills on the road to the St Gotthard. After this considerable effort, he was chagrined to have to lose five precious days in the place, sorting out transport arrangements. The Austrians had failed to furnish him with the promised supplies and train of 1,429 mules he needed for the push on Schwyz. On the suggestion of Grand Prince Constantine, the Russians therefore helped themselves out with 1,500 horses from the Cossacks, leaving their masters to fight on foot as infantry. The Russian artillery was sent on a circuitous route in the direction of the Upper Rhine, and for the fighting ahead Suvorov relied on twenty-five mountain pieces, which he had borrowed from the Piedmontese.

The Austrian commissaries seem to have been at fault in the affair, but in any case the break with the system of Austrian support would have occurred very soon. The Russians had marched to Italy

to act merely as auxiliaries, and unprovided with staff, commissariat, pontoniers, pioneers and in short with almost everything requisite for an army to enter into campaign, consequently from the moment of their quitting the Austrian army in Italy, the regularity of which prevented the marshal [Suvorov] from perceiving these deficiencies, everything has been one scene of confusion. The want of arrangement in procuring provisions . . . has authorised and even encouraged pillaging in a ferocious soldiery . . . the Russian soldier is brave and hardy in a great degree, but the officer is [just] as ignorant [as he is], and without any of those qualities which might occasionally supply the want of knowledge in the field.
(Clinton, 10 October 1799, PRO, FO 74/27)

The one advantage of the delay at Taverne was that it enabled Suvorov to compile a long instruction for his army, detailing the orders of march and tactics to be adopted in mountain warfare. In contrast to movement in the plains, where the Cossacks could go scouting ahead, the Russians now had to move in a tight, well-regulated march formation of three divisional columns, each consisting of an advance guard (twenty-five Cossacks, twenty pioneers, a battalion of jaegers or grenadiers, and one gun) and a main body (in order of march — three battalions, one gun, two battalions, one gun, two battalions, one gun, and two spare guns). In most eventualities the columns were to proceed along the same route, one after another, separated by an interval of only sixty paces. When the allies had to attack a mountain, the breadth of their deployment was to be in proportion to that of the French. The troops were to assault uphill with the bayonet, if the sharpshooters failed to dislodge the enemy by fire, though 'it will be evident to all that it is not necessary to ascend a mountain frontally, when it is possible to turn it from the sides' (20 September, Suvorov, 1949-53, IV, 333). The document shows a remarkable degree of perception, considering that it originated from an army of plain-dwellers. At the same time

the Russians, as foreign to the Alps as the Austrians would have been to the Caucasus,

71 At the gates of Switzerland. Dismounted Cossacks burning their useless lances

inevitably had to allow themselves to be directed in this respect by their allies, who had been campaigning for a considerable time in the very mountains that would have to be crossed. And so the enterprise was directed by a numerous and well-qualified Austrian staff. (Anon., 'Rélation Raisonnée de la Marche de l'Armée de Suwarow', in Jomini, 1840, IV, 142)

The little army set out from Taverne on 21 and 22 September. The mountains began to rear impressively on either side of the road, and with the knowledge of the fearsome barrier of the St Gotthard lying ahead, Suvorov decided to take the position by a pincer movement. The Russian general Rosenberg with a detachment of 6,000 men struck out on an easterly circuit by way of Disentis and the Oberalp Pass, with the commission to come at the St Gotthard from the rear.

The main body of 15,000 (including the Austrian brigade of Strauch), held on its path, and made ready for the frontal assault.

At Airolo the road deserted the Ticino valley, and climbed the wall-like massif to the right, zigzagging through a landscape of bare rocks, thin grass, and dark upland ponds. Lecourbe was taken completely by surprise by the advent of the allies, but when they set themselves at the slopes on 24 September he was able to build up the equivalent of a brigade in their path. Bagration with the advance guard was supposed to turn the positions of the French from their left, or eastern flank, and according to some authorities he actually did so. However, the heaviest fighting was occasioned by the direct assault on the 2,108-metre-high pass, which cost the allies some twelve hundred men.

We flew up like eagles, and pressed them back ever

SUVOROV IN SWITZERLAND, 1799

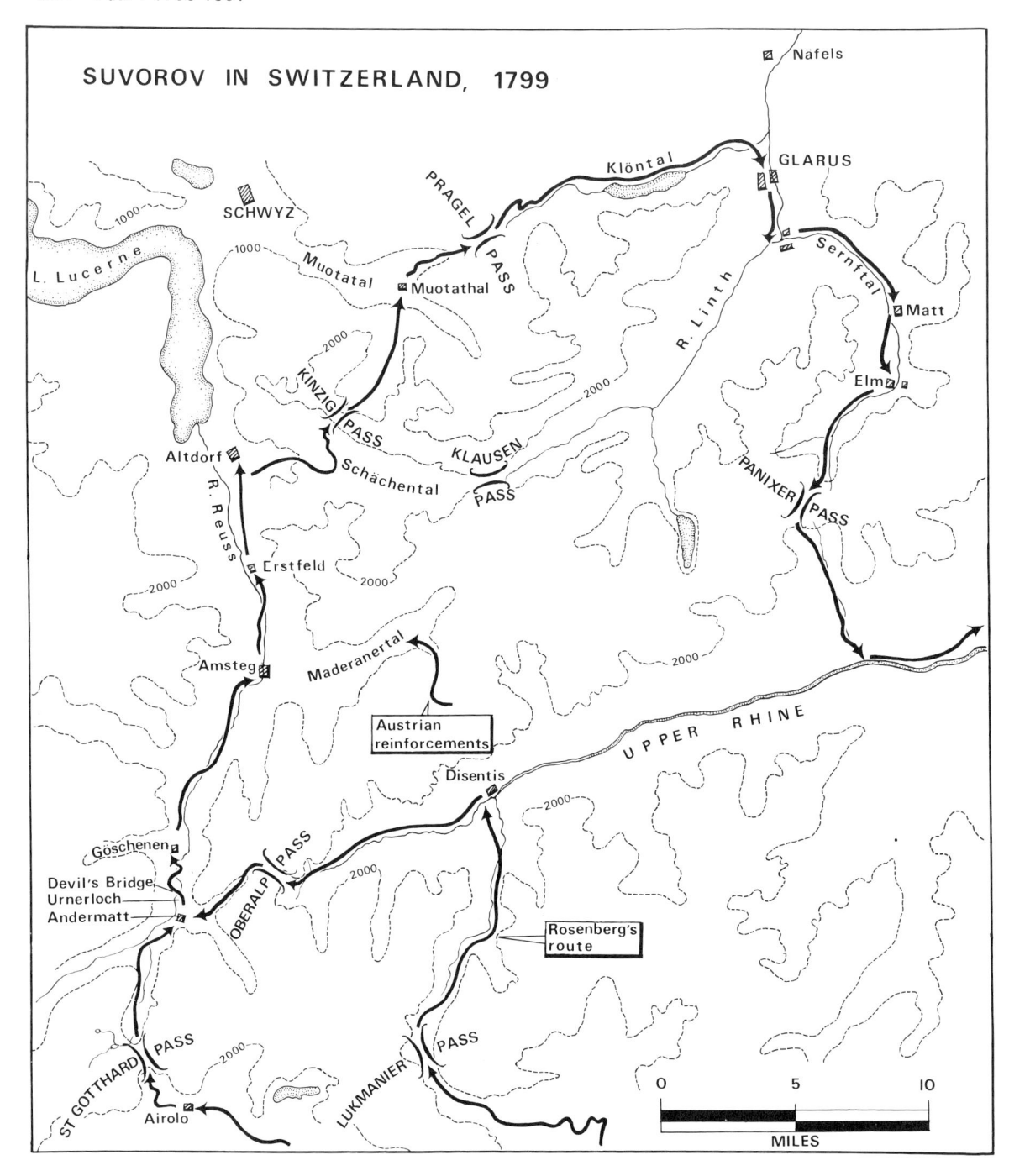

further and higher towards the heavens. Indeed, every now and then the operations were interrupted by wandering clouds, which enveloped us or glided over our heads.... Climbing steadily in this way we reached a summit, which to all appearance was the last one, but there succeeded another that was steeper still, and so on, until we finally came to the loftiest of them all, where the enemy held the steep and rocky eminence, and put up a long and bitter resistance. Our brave and tireless warriors, helping each other up the stony crags and bare rocks, beat them and forced them back. (Gryazev, in Orlov, 1898, 86-7)

The Russians pushed on for five exhausting miles downhill as far as Hospenthal, where the leading troops spent the night. On the same day Rosenberg had accomplished his passage of the Oberalp, and so the two wings of the force were reunited.

The northern exit from the mountain-rimmed amphitheatre of Hospenthal and Andermatt lay by a V-shaped cleft, beset by a remarkable series of natural and artificial phenomena. Converging sheets of grey-green rock closed in on the little River Reuss so narrowly that the industrious Swiss had been forced to drive a 190-yard-long tunnel, the Urnerloch, to enable the road to pass to the right. Considering the natural strength of the position, the number of defenders (two battalions), and the steep slopes on either side, an expert Swiss authority has reckoned that the French must have been ultimately forced back by two wide outflanking movements, over the Bäzberg from the west and from the Oberalp valley from the east (Reding-Biberegg, 1895, 45, 172). However, this circumstance does not detract from the drama of 25 September, when a force of Russians came at the Urnerloch from the front.

The French were ready with a gun at the far end of the rocky tube, and greeted the Mansurov Regiment with a blast of canister. About 260 yards short of the reeking entrance, Colonel Trubnikov is said to have led three hundred men up the cliffs to the right, and picked his way to the 'French' end of the tunnel. Miloradovich seconded the attempt by rushing a fresh wave of troops through the tunnel, whereupon the enemy threw their gun into the Reuss and retired.

Emerging into the open air, the Russians came under fire that crackled from cliffs to their left front, dominating a gulf where the stream plunged half right into a narrow gorge. The road clung to the walls of the torrent on its dizzy descent, and on the way down it passed to the left side over the hump-backed Devil's Bridge, and thence over two arches which had been built on to the far

72 Forcing the Devil's Bridge, Andermatt. The picture correctly shows the bridge itself as intact

side of the gorge. One of these arches had been considerately broken by the French. Below it, the Reuss surged 'with great impetuosity and noise down to the stony bottom of the gorge, where, meeting the rocks that rose out of the water, it rebounded in spray, and coursed around them in foaming waves' (Gryazev, in Orlov, 1898, 92).

Major Trevogin took charge of two hundred men, and splashed across the Reuss to the left bank, just before the waters gathered themselves for the plunge into the void. This move gave the French sharpshooters some occupation while a number of gallant souls addressed themselves to the task of binding together some planks of a dismantled shed with officers' sashes, so as to serve as a crossing for the gap in the arch. Major Meshcherskii was the first to attempt the passage, and he paid for it with his life, as did the Cossack behind him. The third man survived, and the rest of the Russians followed in the path of the heroes, regardless of casualties. The action ended with the Russians chasing the French down the rocky descent to the floor of the wide but gloomy valley that led to Lake Lucerne.

Colonel Strauch had been left behind to secure the St Gotthard, but in compensation Suvorov was met at Amsteg by General Auffenberg with 2,000 Austrians who had come to join him from the Upper Rhine valley by way of the Maderanertal. Suvorov now had a combined force of about 22,500 troops.

On the afternoon of 26 September Suvorov reached Altdorf, less than two miles short of Lake Lucerne, and he made ready to intervene in the quarrels of Korsakov and Masséna.

He wore a shirt, with an open black waistcoat, and hose which were open at the sides. As he rode past he held a whip in one hand, and with the other he dispensed blessings like a bishop. . . . He then delivered himself of a speech in broken German, announcing himself as the saviour and liberator of the world, which he had come to free from the tyranny of the infidels. (Dr Lusser, in Reding-Biberegg, 1895, 49)

The standard accounts claim that through some oversight of the Austrian staff, Suvorov only now discovered that it was impossible to strike directly for Schwyz and Zürich, because the expected road along the east side of Lake Zürich simply did not exist. Since the waters of Lake Lucerne were commanded by the French, Suvorov and the generals met in council of war on the evening of the 26th, and decided to make for Schwyz by an anti-clockwise circuit inland over mountains and valleys. The matter was something more than an inconvenience, for the troops had eaten all the food they had carried with them, and the supply train of pack animals stretched all the way back to Airolo.

The supposed oversight of the staff has always been difficult to explain, if only because the rest of the march argues a very considerable local knowledge on the part of the Austrians. The French certainly had the advantage of being able to consult the Pfyffer relief model of Switzerland, and the corresponding Johann Meyer map (the best of the land until 1864), but:

did Suvorov really end up in a cul de sac as a result of ignorance of the terrain and inadequate maps? We should not assume that the Austrian liaison officers, who knew the region in detail from their earlier operations, had not acquainted him with the fact that Schwyz could be reached from Altdorf only by mountain paths. In that period it was a matter of routine for whole armies to traverse passes which to-day are frequented only by occasional hikers. (Schweizerische Verkehrszentrale, 1974, 3)

On 27 September Suvorov's leading troops addressed themselves to the first stage of the march, making the steady climb eastwards up the grassy Schächental, then striking left in disorderly columns along drovers' tracks which took them through a landscape of rocky fangs, grey scree and sheets of snow to the Kinzig Pass (2,073 m.; 6,800 feet). On the downward path beside the Hüribach a cleft in the rocks gave access to a final zig-zag which led to the pretty, flat-bottomed valley of Muotatal. It is easy to imagine the astonishment of the population when, towards the middle of the afternoon of the 27th, a black mass flooded through the gap, with Prince Bagration and the

73 Descent to the Muotatal from the Kinzig Pass. The course of the Hüribach is indicated by the diagonal line of trees on the right

advance guard leading the way for a host of 'hard, tough, warlike folk . . . dark brown in complexion', and all decked up in antique garb (Fassbind, in Reding-Biberegg, 1895, 355). The chaplain of the Franciscan convent of St Joseph told a little gathering that the day of deliverance from the French was at hand. He was still speaking when a party of Cossacks appeared, stretched him out on the ground, and relieved him of his shoes with their silver buckles. A party of forty or fifty French were unaccountably slow in getting away. They were wiped out in the night by a patrol of Cossacks, who afterwards laughed wildly as they washed their sabres in the waters of the Muota.

Lecourbe still had about 7,500 troops hovering dangerously about the lower Reuss. Luckily, the Swiss people refused to enlighten him as to the allies' movements, and the mist and the heavy, continuous rain concealed from him the march up the Schächental. To keep the Frenchman in perplexity was the task of Infantry General Rosenberg, who guarded the rear of the army with his own corps and the rearguard proper under Förster.

Of all the Russian commanders, Andreas Rosenberg was apparently the one least likely to be able to live up to this important responsibility. He was an old German, who had visited St Petersburg only in his younger days, and who for more than twenty years now had held insignificant and quiet commands in the Caucasus and the Crimea. People were unsettled by his dry humour. He was thrifty, not to say mean, and although he never married he liked to summon pretty girls to serve him tea and other commodities.

Now, in Switzerland in 1799, Rosenberg's 'calm and courageous management of military affairs caused Suvorov to bemoan that he had not made use of him earlier' (Wiegel, 1864-6, I, pt 1, 101). On 27 September Rosenberg imposed monstrously on Lecourbe by a show of aggressive activity. He made soundings along the Reuss, he put in a feint attack against the hamlet of Erstfeld, and when the French responded by seizing Altdorf, he promptly pushed them out again. On the next day he made good his escape over the Kinzig Pass, leaving Förster to follow up with three regiments of infantry and a body of Cossacks. Lecourbe remained passive on the lower Reuss, allowing the Russians to get clean away.

74 Convent of St Joseph, Muotathal village, seen from the west

On 28 September Suvorov crossed the pass on a litter borne by peasants, and he and his staff made their headquarters just outside the village of Muotathal in the convent of St Joseph, with its neat and fragrant rooms of wood panelling. The troops were fit and lively, but the march over the Kinzig had taken a heavy toll of the footwear, and the only food readily available was the white and green cheese of the locality, which was not to the Russian taste. The memories of those days are still strong in the Muotatal, and the taciturn peasants occasionally relate how the Russian soldiers stripped the unripe fruits from the trees, and founded the stock which, so they say, is perpetuated in the high cheekbones and slant eyes of certain families. However, the Russians were:

most restrained and pious, and did not the slightest violence to clergy, sacred property or women ... they were willing to pay amply for everything, but since the Muotatalers asked exorbitant prices, and the Russians were driven by hunger, they changed their tune, and took by force what the people were unwilling to offer at a reasonable rate. (Fassbind, in Reding-Biberegg, 1895, 353)

Early on the 29th, Suvorov and his generals met in an anxious council of war in the meadows outside the convent. On the day before they had suffered a double disappointment. Not only was there no sign of Linken's command of Austrians (they had fallen back to the Upper Rhine), but a series of reports left no doubt that Korsakov and Hotze had been broken by the French. Thus the whole scheme of campaign had collapsed, and the French were now free to locate and destroy Suvorov's little army. From being a participant in a grandiose scheme for a general offensive, Suvorov was in danger of becoming the quarry in a hunt in which his own survival was at stake. The council therefore decided to strike eastwards to the valley of the Linth, there to orient themselves afresh.

By itself the initial stage was one of the most difficult operations that could be imagined, for the long drawn-out columns had to traverse the Muotatal from south to north-east, exposing their flank to the French who were advancing up the valley from the open western end.

75 Eastern end of the Klöntalersee, viewed from near the French blocking position of 30 September - 1 October

As commander of the advance guard, Prince Bagration had the task of ensuring that the allies were able to make their escape at all. On the 29th General Auffenberg's brigade led the way over the Pragel Pass, which formed the north-eastern exit from the valley, and initiated two days of heavy fighting in the Klöntal against General Molitor, who ultimately brought up eight or more battalions (5,500 men) to dispute the passage. On the evening of the 29th, Molitor was able to make a stand at the near end of the fiord-like waters of the Klöntalersee, and when Bagration arrived on the 30th the French merely fell back to a new position at the eastern end of the lake. The allies renewed the frontal assault on 1 October, this time in conjunction with a turning movement by way of the steep slopes to the north, all covered with larches, and ancient mossy beeches. Bagration now carried the position, and in a day of bloody fighting he pushed on to the relative civilisation of the Linth valley and Glarus.

On the night of the 29th Förster's Cossacks were still leading their ponies by hand over the Kinzig. A scattering of what appeared to be stars could be seen in the gloom below. These were the fires of Rosenberg's command in the Muotatal, resting before it faced the enemy. The French first tested the resistance of the rearguard on the following day, when the division of Mortier advanced up the Muotatal from the west. Rosenberg hung back for some time before supporting his outposts, but once he got on the move he threw the French back smartly by the way they had come.

The arrival of Förster's division brought Rosenberg's force in the Muotatal to 8 or 9,000 effectives (sixteen depleted battalions, three regiments of Cossacks, and a nominal fifteen guns). Every last man was needed, for Masséna in person concentrated 9-10,000 troops (Mortier's division and a brigade of Molitor's) for a new sweep up the valley on 1 October. The French were checked for a time by the Russian outpost regiment, which occupied a feature which barred the narrow valley of the lower Muota. However, Rosenberg deliberately made his stand well up the valley, knowing that if he fought too far forward he would be exposed to any outflanking move on the part of the French, who were probably the superior of the Russians in grand tactical move-

ROSENBERG IN THE MUOTATAL, 1 October 1799

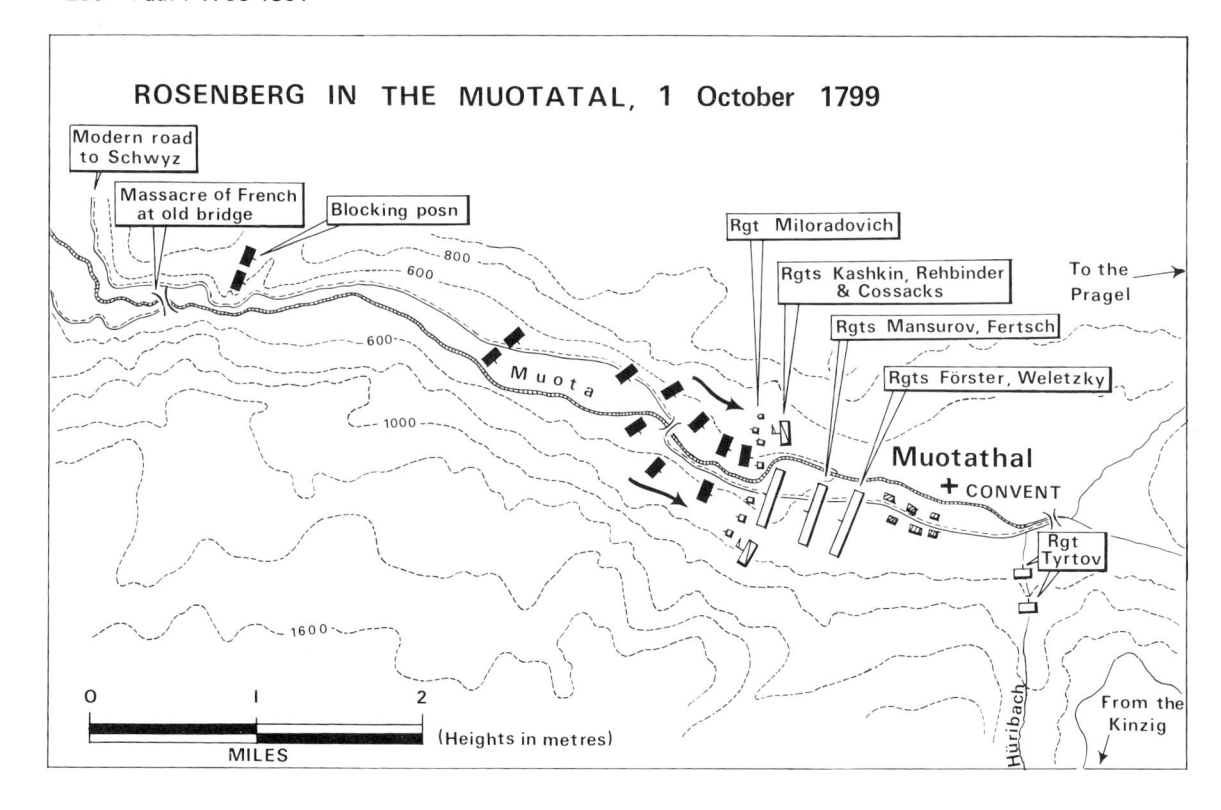

ment. Conversely, the Russian infantry, and even the Cossacks, were proving surprisingly adept in making use of the ground, and launching short-ranged hooks through steep and woody terrain. Rosenberg accordingly ranged his forces just in front of Muotathal in two lines, filling the 1,000-yard-wide valley from one side to the other. The valley floor was more heavily wooded then than now, and the villagers noted that the Russians were well concealed.

The French advanced in three dense columns, preceded by a thick cloud of skirmishers. They were checked and surprised in the first exchanges of fire, but they renewed the attack with the help of reinforcements, and began to make a perceptible impression on the Russians. The Russian second line was now brought up three hundred paces to be incorporated in the first, and after an interlude of musketry the whole rushed forward with loud cries. The Swiss looked on with admiration as the Russians scoured the valley floor like a wave, and the Cossacks darted ahead, executing mighty bounds over hedges and ditches. The French made off down the narrowing valley, and jammed together on a stone bridge which carried the track high above the waters of the Muota. Whole clumps of panic-stricken soldiery plunged into the gorge, and many of the men who reached the far side were shot down by the laughing Russians. Altogether the little battle of 1 October cost the French five guns, one thousand dead and wounded and at least as many taken prisoner. The Russians also had about one thousand casualties in this, their last indisputably victorious passage of arms in the eighteenth century.

Having won precious time for the escape of the main army, Rosenberg followed in Suvorov's muddy tracks over the Pragel, leaving the floor of the Muotatal littered with the bodies of men, horses and mules. Finally on 4 October the entire Russo-Austrian forces assembled at Glarus, where the leading troops had already spent two days' rest.

On the same 4 October Suvorov assembled a

76 The entry to the Panixer Pass (left centre), seen from the Sernftal

council of war. He and his Austrian staff officers wished to rescue something from the campaign by barging northwards down the Linth valley and joining up with Jellačić's isolated command of Austrian troops. However, the Grand Prince Constantine and the rest of the Russian generals could think of nothing but putting the greatest possible distance between themselves and the French, in other words, taking a route south to the Upper Rhine. Indeed, Auffenberg and his Austrians had already taken off in that direction. Suvorov could only give way.

This time Bagration was assigned with his 2,000 or so jaegers and grenadiers to constitute the rearguard, enabling the main force of 15,000 to scuttle southwards up the narrow Sernftal by way of Matt and Elm. On 6 October the army turned up a gorge-like valley, skirted the eerie little Häxenseeli water, and made the strenuous crossing of the Panixer Pass (2,407 m.; 7,900 feet), lying under two feet of fresh snow. The artillery, the pack animals and more than two hundred men were lost on the passage, many of them very probably on the steep descending zig-zag which lay beyond the pass. A final push through a forest of conifers brought the Russians on 7 October to the valley of the Upper Rhine at Ilanz, where not even the French would venture to follow them.

Suvorov and his survivors trailed down the valley by way of Chur, and on 18 October he was joined by the sorry remnants of Korsakov's army near Lindau. From here the view across Lake Constance to the snowy peaks reminded every man of the ordeal he had endured in Switzerland. For the winter the army was withdrawn to quarters in southern Bavaria, while Suvorov in person was summoned back to Russia. He stopped for some time in Prague, feasting and conversing with the many foreigners who had collected there. 'But this was a swan song on the waters of the Meander. In Cracow there awaited him both physical and mental collapse, which hastened the end of his notable life' (Fuchs, 1827, 46).

The ailing soldier travelled on to his estate at

Kobrin, and so to his final place of rest at St Petersburg. Paul had created him generalissimo for his last achievements, but he did not feel bound to wait on Suvorov in his final hours. Suvorov died at two in the afternoon on 6 May 1800, 'the greatest commander which Russia had ever produced' (Langeron, *RS*, 1895, LXXXIII, 160).

There was no prospect of the orphaned army being employed once more against the French. Paul's unstable temperament had been a prime moving force in the creation of the Second Coalition, and it was now the cause of its disintegration. The Austrians had angered him by their blatant pursuit of short-term ends in the late campaign, while the British infuriated him still more when they refused to deliver Malta to his keeping as Grand Master of the Order of St John. He laid an embargo on British shipping, and sent an armed expedition some way on the path to India, and only the lack of time and resources prevented an all-out shooting war between the former allies.

Russia was returned to normality in the most drastic way, when a group of palace conspirators assassinated Paul on 11 March 1801. One of his general-adjutants, Count Christoph Lieven, was summoned to the Winter Palace to see Paul's son Alexander, who had been deposited on the throne in the place of his murdered father. Lieven knew nothing of the change in affairs, and:

he found Grand Prince Constantine and a number of generals in the waiting room. The grand prince was bathed in tears, but the generals were in a state of almost drunken exaltation at their deliverance. It took half a minute to inform Lieven that Emperor Paul was dead, and that he must pay his respects to his successor. The door of the office opened, and Emperor Alexander emerged, asking 'Where is Lieven?' The emperor fell on his shoulder and sobbed 'My father, my poor father!' (Kvardi, in Skalon, 1902-c.1911, II, bk 1, 310)

Captain Gryazev, a survivor of Suvorov's campaign, tried to sum up the prospects for his nation in the new century. He conceded that the French were very formidable enemies, and he was:

unaware of any other nation, save the Russian, which is capable of withstanding them. With the passage of time we may well see my prophecy come to pass. We shudder at the extraordinary chains of events, the revolutions which may lie ahead of Europe in all its turmoil. We draw comfort from the many things that elevate us above the other civilised nations of that continent — the good state of our monarchy in every respect, our inexhaustible riches, power and constancy, the inviolability of property which is enjoyed by all classes of society, and the nobles in particular, and our condition of unshakeable repose.... God grant that we may continue to live as we do now — enjoying the protection of a wise government. Then the coming century will proceed in the same way as the last one, and we may always take pride in the name of *Russian*! (Gryazev, in Orlov, 1898, 166-7)

Ten Conclusions

Russia's military way to the West

Now that we have spent some time in the company of eighteenth-century Russian armies, it is probably evident how very little outright combat with the Western powers had to do with Russia's territorial gains in Europe, at least after Peter the Great's push to the Baltic. When Lacy and Münnich besieged Danzig in 1734, it was in the interest of puppets and allies, and if Elizabeth's Russia began to harbour designs on East Prussia, this very considerable prize was cast away with unconcern by Peter III, and not retrieved by Catherine the Great. However, by participating so mightily in the Seven Years War Russia had secured an entrée into the ranks of the greatest European monarchies, and in the later part of the century she joined Prussia and Austria as a more than equal partner in the dismemberment of Poland. The only enemy blood that was shed in the process was Polish, and then by way of suppression rather than conquest. Hence the unresisted westwards encroachments of Catherine's realm. We may apply to Russia as a whole the comment which Wiegel made about Potemkin: 'He was feared not so much for what he really did, as for what he might have done' (Wiegel, 1864-6, I, pt 1, 291).

Less obvious to the West was the generation in Russia of a concept of herself as a kind of pantomime fairy queen, alighting on the European stage to sort out the tangled affairs of other nations. The expeditions of 1735 and 1748 helped to bring satisfactory ends to the wars of the Polish and Austrian Successions, while Catherine's good offices in the Teschen peace conference of 1779 drew the most flattering expressions from diplomats and sovereigns. In the new age of ideological and national war, the same interventionalist urge was transmuted into the messianic crusades of Paul I, Alexander I and Nicholas I, which carried Russian armies into so many parts of Europe.

When we attempt to evaluate the degree to which Russia acquired European military modes, it is perhaps better to employ the term 'modernisation' than 'Westernisation'. This is because Peter the Great made the fundamentally important decision, which shapes Russia still, to adopt what was useful from European practice, while rejecting many of the values and the kind of society which had accounted for the technical advance of the West in the first place. The contradictions were overcome by the autocratic power that lay at the disposal of the Mongol-Muscovite monarchy, enabling it to concentrate national effort on the armed forces. An Englishman travelled through Russia in the 1770s and noted that:

in point of education, the military science is the most cultivated. In absolute governments the army takes the lead in everything; by the prevailing argument of a musket, submission is obtained; the regulation and discipline of that army, will ever be a primary interest in those governments.
(Richard, 1780, 30)

Society was militarised to a degree unknown in the West outside Prussia, and even in the nineteenth century a military career offered many gentlemen the only alternative to the tedium of work in the civil service or life on a provincial estate. Thus the military episodes in the lives of writers like Tolstoy, Lermontov and Dostoevsky.

In Russia peculiar circumstances forced into the regular army men who, in other countries, would scarcely have dreamed of it. Amongst such men there were inevitably those who would, in due course, emerge as writers. In consequence we have an imaginative and interpretative literature about the occasions and emotions of regular soldiering such as is to be found in no other country.
(Luckett, in Best and Wheatcroft, 1976, 30)

How complete was the modernisation of the Russian army? With the impetus given to it by Peter, the process extended to the acquisition of Western-style ranks, tactics, weapons, and (with some modifications) regimental organisation and uniforms. Self-sufficiency in war production was already well advanced in Peter's time, and by the end of the century the independence was nearly complete. However, certain areas remained largely untouched. It would be difficult to maintain, for example, that the Russian officers took as readily to the Western aristocratic military ethos, or a Prussian sense of responsibility, as they did to European languages and manners. More happily, the private soldier retained his primitive virtues in full measure, deriving not just from physical constitution, but a sense of community which he carried from his village life.

Two things above all distinguished the Russian army from its Western counterparts. The first was the fact that it was constituted as a national army, which further promoted the extraordinary toughness and consistency of the Russian infantry. Peter the Great recognised the priceless value of this asset when he preserved local loyalties in the nomenclature and recruiting of his regiments.

Second, whole generations of commanders were shaped by campaigning against the Tartars and Turks. On the positive side, the steppe experience habituated the Russian armies to wide-ranging operations, and encouraged generals like Fermor, Münnich, Rumyantsev and Suvorov to develop an offensive philosophy of warfare, which stood in interesting contrast to the outlook of some of the Austrians, who had been campaigning against the Turks on the Danube. Unfortunately, the otherwise praiseworthy self-sufficiency of Russian logistics became a liability in the Seven Years War, when the huge trains of waggons obstructed the operations, and restrained the commanders for far too long from looking for means of subsistence better suited to a Western theatre. It also appears likely that the comparative ease of victories over people like the Turks and Poles left the Russians unprepared for combat against disciplined enemies like the French. Here the very needful tightening of standards by Paul I probably stood the Russians in better stead than most commentators have been prepared to admit.

We shall touch later on the sterile controversies about the alleged conflict between Western and national Russian influences on the army of the eighteenth century. In his own age, Peter the Great was seen as neither a Muscovite nor a Western European, but a frightful phenomenon *sui generis*. It is just as difficult to detect the supposed polarisation in later generations. If the arch-Teuton Münnich worked for the Russification of the officer corps, then the native Russians Rumyantsev and Suvorov were neither totally self-sufficient pioneers (as the Soviets claim), nor passive recipients of a superior Western knowledge, but active and creative members of the cosmopolitan European military community. Only in the person of the semi-Oriental Potemkin do we encounter somebody who deliberately set himself against some Western ways of doing things.

As for the impact of the Russian army on the West, we have noticed again and again how men who saw the Russians with their own eyes commented on the urbanity of the officers, and (with the occasional failing) the fine discipline of the men. Western public opinion in general was, however, persuaded otherwise, thanks to the effective propaganda of Frederick the Great, and the misdeeds of the Cossacks, which were wrongly laid to the account of the entire army. Some genuine alarm was occasioned in the West by the Russian destruction of Swedish power in the Great Northern War, and (in certain circles) by the revelations of Russian potential in the Seven Years War, but in general the *frissons* were calmed by the risible incompetence of the Russians in matters of military detail, and the fact that Russian ambitions were so strongly diverted towards the East.

Without detracting from the achievements of Russian armies in the Seven Years War, or the heroism so often displayed in 1799, it is worth asking why Russia, with her immense geographical extent, failed to make a greater impact on campaigns in Europe than she did. In the first place, the available resources of manpower were modest, and badly conserved, permitting the Russians to emerge on Western theatres in adequate but by no means overwhelming force. More surprising still, the stock of native horses was not only small in numbers, but poor in quality, which had far-reaching consequences for the tactical efficiency, security and logistic support of the army. Much effort must have been required to build up the cavalry that launched the devastating charge at Kunersdorf, and to provide the motive power which enabled the excellent artillery of Shuvalov to engage the Prussians to such good effect.

Good staff work would have enabled the commanders to make the best use of what troops and horses lay at their disposal. However, this kind of mental activity remained totally alien to the Russian temperament, as witness the failure of Shuvalov to interest the government in his projects for a staff college in the 1750s, or the persecutions undergone by Bauer in the 1770s. It was a pity that the Russian officers were frequently on bad personal terms with their most steadfast allies, the Austrians, who were qualified and willing to help them out in this respect.

No firm operational guidance came from above, after the end of the Great Northern War. Peter the Great was the only true soldier-king that Russia knew in the eighteenth century, and even he was very slow to intervene directly in the business of command. Under his successors, the element of political stability itself could no longer be guaranteed, a failure evident in the dramatic withdrawals from the Seven Years War and the War of the Second Coalition.

While the sheer size of the Romanov empire lent Russia, if not St Petersburg, a high degree of invulnerability, the distance which separated the Russian heartland from the Western theatres of war told heavily on every operation of an offensive kind. The face of military and political affairs was liable to change considerably by the time Russian armies approached their objectives. Active operations ceased while the expeditions of 1735 and 1748 were still on the march, which occasioned a measure of frustration. However, outright disaster stared Suvorov and Kutuzov in the face, when they finally arrived in the depths of Europe in 1799 and 1805, only to find the allied plans in disarray, and themselves the object of the enemy's undivided attention.

The Russians could have done a lot to assist themselves through suitable structures and strategies. Instead of the small, Western-type regiment, a super-large unit establishment would have made allowance for the inevitable wastage of manpower, as Semen Vorontsov suggested. Third battalions, of the kind evolved in the Seven Years War, could have been retained permanently to serve as reception and training centres for the recruits marching to the theatres of war. Lastly, no Russian commander, save Rumyantsev, seems to have grasped the importance of establishing forward bases, where the army could have restored its strength during the winter months, instead of losing time and men by prosecuting a lengthy retreat at the end of each campaign.

Movements within Russia themselves called for prodigious efforts. When Paul ordered 100,000 troops to assemble for a review outside Moscow in May 1799 most of the regiments which were summoned to the event had to traverse seven or eight hundred versts to the place of assembly, and there was not a single one which had to march less than five hundred. This diversion cost millions of roubles, and we commented at the time that the burden was borne not by the treasury, but by the people of the areas through which the forces marched. The regiments had to set out from their garrisons in March, according to the movement orders . . . and anybody who has the slightest acquaintance with Holy Russia knows that in this season it is almost impossible to progress by road, a state of affairs summed up in the ancient proverb: 'In Russia, March is a month without water, and April is a month without grass'. By this we mean that in March the rivers are still frozen, and cannot be navigated by rafts, and yet the ice is too thin to bear your weight in safety. As for the absence of grass in April, this comes from the continuous thawing of the snow, which transforms the soil into a liquid dough . . . there were instances when the barrels, wheels and appurtenances had to be removed from the gun carriages, and the whole lot carried by hand — and in this case the hands were those of peasants. Nobody can estimate how many of these folk were killed or crippled by the labour. Peasants are not soldiers, and so in Russia they are not accounted human beings. (Turgenev, *RS*, 1885, XLVIII, 74-5)

The historians' verdict

To a greater or lesser extent, every historian of the old Russian army has lived parasitically off the mighty product of the Russian scholars of the second half of the nineteenth century. In those years a series of voluminous record publications brought to light a great quantity of memoirs and other documents, and helped to furnish ammunition for two contending schools of military history. One band of scholars became known as the 'academics', and maintained that they could trace a 'single highway' through Russian military affairs, by identifying successive periods of foreign influence — Scandinavian, Byzantine, Mongol, Swedish and so on. For them, the eighteenth century was clearly an epoch when Prussian fashions were in the ascendancy (G. A. Leer, P. A. Geisman, P. O. Bobrovskii, M. Bogdanovich, N. P. Mikhnevich, A. Baiov, etc.).

The 'Russian' school, on the other hand, was stridently nationalistic, drawing attention to a Russian way of war that was original, and generally superior to that of the West. Probably the most productive of such 'Russians' was Dmitri Fedorovich Maslovskii, who edited several collections of material from the archives, and wrote a heavily documented history of the Seven Years War.

In the early twentieth century, by when passions had abated somewhat, the formidable capacities of Russian military scholarship and, indeed, of Russian printers found their final expression in two multi-volumed works. The centenary of the War Ministry in 1902 prompted the moderate 'academic' D. A. Skalon to supervise the publication of a detailed and wide-ranging collective study of Russia's military past, the *Stoletie Voennago Ministerstva*. A more straightforwardly narrative approach was adopted for the *Istoriya Russkoi Armii i Flota* (A. S. Grishinskii, V. Nikolskii, N. L. Klado), which began publication in 1911.

The Great War, the Bolshevik Revolution and the Civil War between them accomplished an apparently complete physical eradication of the sturdy growth of Russian military history. From 1934, however, the first new shoots struggled into the light, encouraged by some resolutions of the Central Committee of the Communist Party of the USSR, which spoke of the usefulness of the study of military history in the schools and in the services. The *Voenno – Istoricheskii Zhurnal* was founded in 1939, and the next year saw the publication of N. M. Korobkov's useful new study of the Seven Years War.

Military history became a prime governmental concern when Stalin sought to marshal older national enthusiasms behind the Party in the ordeal of the Great Patriotic War of 1941-5. The shade of Suvorov was conjured up to give his name to a new order for military bravery, which was instituted in 1942, and again to a system of junior military academies which came into being in 1943. The tsarist military uniforms were re-introduced, and Stalin himself assumed the Suvorovian title of generalissimo, and gave out that the retreat of 1941 was a carefully considered move, inspired by

Kutozov's fabian strategy of 1812.

The historians responded with an enthusiasm that was to embarrass some of their successors. A title like *The Destruction of the Prussian Forces by the Russians 1756-1762* (Korobkov) is sufficient explanation by itself, while E. V. Tarle and his associates completed *Napoleon's Invasion 1812* with the declared aim of 'popularising one of the most brilliant pages of Russian military history in terms that would broaden the struggle of the Russian people against the German fascists'. In the 1960s and 1970s scholars found it necessary to point out that the old Russian army was, after all, an upholder of the 'feudal' absolutism.

The era of patriotic enthusiasm was succeeded by that of the peacetime Stalinist personality cult, which engendered some undeniably useful editions of printed documents relating to famous leaders like Rumyantsev and Suvorov. The year 1955, however, produced a revolution that was as far-reaching in historical studies as it was in politics. 'The overcoming of the error of subjectivism began after the Twentieth Session of the Communist Party of the USSR, which signified a new stage in the development of the historical art' (Klokman, in Beskrovnyi, 1969, 42). Researches now became more wide-ranging in character, as a matter of policy, and they resulted in the publication of works like the collective commemorative volume *Poltava* (1959). Most active and influential of the newer generation was Lev Beskrovnyi, a slightly-built and intense man who was the teacher of Lieutenant-General Pavel Zhilin and other prominent historians, and who was himself the author of important bibliographical studies (1957 and 1962), and the sizeable *Russian Army and Fleet in the Eighteenth Century* (1958).

The value of the post-Stalin military-historical oeuvre is by no means easy to assess. The school is remarkably good (thanks to Beskrovnyi) on the bibliographical side, and has much of worth to say on war production, recruiting, and military training and education. Regarded as a whole, however, it is nationalistic, uneven and unconvincing, and given to attaching undue importance to certain developments, while ignoring such episodes as do not serve its purpose, like the hammering of the Poles in 1794.

It is perhaps of interest to see what judgments the Soviet historians have passed on the Russian army of the eighteenth century. With some reservations, the work of Peter the Great has always been held up for admiration. The Soviets write that this energetic gentleman appreciated that Russia's general backwardness was derived from an economic backwardness, and that this in turn proceeded from the denial of access to the seas. Hence he opened the Baltic as a national task. Furthermore, Peter founded heavy industries, and, while making a modicum of borrowings from the West, he determined the application in the light of his own experience and the particular needs of Russia. Peter saw the Great Northern War as a school for the nation, not just the army, and in his supreme effort against the Swedes in 1708-9 he was in turn powerfully aided by the people at large. Indeed, 'Soviet historiography is favourably distinguished from the pre-Revolutionary and bourgeois historiography, which grossly underestimated the significance of the struggle of the popular mass against the Swedish aggressors in the course of the Great Northern War' (Klokman, in Beskrovnyi, 1969, 33).

Most far-reaching of all, Peter is supposed to have founded a specifically Russian school of war, characterised by a search for a 'general battle', and an emphasis on offensive action and moral qualities. The torch is alleged to have been taken up in later generations by Rumyantsev, Potemkin, Suvorov, Kutozov and the admirals Spiridov and Ushakov. The contrary school is represented by foreign, and more particularly Prussian leaders, and those who fell under their influence. Harsh, cold and alien, the foreigners are described as defensively-minded, blind to the virtues of the native Russian, and obsessed with routine, linear tactics, and a discipline which held the soldier in robot-like subjection. (The Soviets' attempt to fit Münnich into the latter category undoubtedly renders a severe disservice to the man who alleviated the lot of the recruits, and who, by founding the Cadet Corps and raising the pay of the native officers, sought to break the domination of the foreigners in military affairs.)

Moving to the middle of the century, we find that, with the exception of Saltykov, the commanders of the Seven Years War have aroused little enthusiasm among the Soviets, which possibly helps to account for the comparative neglect of this important episode in Russian military history. Hence the best of the modern insights come from Western historians like Mediger, Bangert, Kaplan, Oliva and Kunisch.

However, there is a good deal of solid worth in Soviet evaluations of the leaders of the reign of Catherine the Great, and indeed some of the more extravagant claims of the 1940s have since been repudiated. No longer do historians seek to establish a direct correspondence between Suvorov's enlightened military practice, on the one hand, and his social and political aims, which are now admitted to have been devoted to the interests of his class and the monarchy.

As might have been expected, the wretched Emperor Paul is comprehensively damned as one who set himself against common humanity and the principles of the 'Russian school of war'. Little account is taken of Paul's idealism, or his ambitions to destroy all that was cruel and rotten in the army that was left by Catherine. Interestingly enough, the Soviets here range themselves alongside the true reactionaries of the 1790s — the xenophobes and the corrupt nobility — and they reject the opportunity to construct what could have been a passably convincing 'proletarian' interpretation of the eighteenth-century army, based on the worth of the private soldier and his enlightened champions.

Anomalies of this kind give some clue as to the inspiration behind the work of Soviet historians. Marxism-Leninism defines the eighteenth century as a period of equilibrium, when neither the decaying feudalism nor the rising bourgeoisie had the upper hand, and when both had an interest in strengthening the new bureaucratic state. The Russian monarchy is said by the Soviets to have played a progressive role at that time, for its desire to develop the economy demanded a forward foreign policy, a centralised governmental apparatus, and a regular army. The detailed application of the analysis, however, carries little conviction. Thus the dismal phenomenon of desertion is glorified as a proletarian instrument in the 'class war'. Thus, in accordance with Lenin's views on the direct relationship of tactics and technology, Beskrovnyi and his school enter into considerable detail on the production of pig-iron and the like, but fail to establish any credible connection between the alleged superiority of Russian weaponry and the Suvorovian art of war.

There is reason to suspect that in Russia the ramshackle apparatus of Marxism-Leninism is driven not by its own feeble motive power, but by some much more powerful forces. Chief among these is the outright nationalism which sustains the Soviet historians as strongly as it did the 'Russian' school of the 1880s and 1890s. 'These historians,' writes Beskrovnyi, 'were correct to emphasise that military affairs in Russia bore a national character, that their development reflected internal needs and not foreign influences, and that the Russian school of war was in no way inferior to that of Western Europe' (Beskrovnyi, 1957, 154).

Altogether Marxism-Leninism has served merely to complicate the task of the Soviet military historians. It compels them to search for formulae that will reconcile the paradox of the imposition of Germanic materialism on Holy Russia, forcing them to establish connections between Russian nationalism and a whole variety of disparate technical, economic, social and military processes. The many consequent absurdities throw the credibility of the whole into doubt, and do the greatest possible disservice to the memory of some of the truly remarkable phenomena of eighteenth-century Russia — the national army, the victories of the Seven Years War, the inspirations of Shuvalov and Potemkin, the timeless genius of Suvorov, and the endurance of the ordinary soldier, a man who never knew when he was beaten, and who by his fortitude so often made good the blunders and negligence of his chiefs.

Continuities and discontinuities

The Russian army survived until 1917 as recognisably the same animal which had gone to war in the eighteenth century. Did the October Revolution and the consolidation of the new regime then mark a complete break with the old continuities? In many fields of national activity this was apparently the case, not least concerning the ease with which the bulk of the population seemed to transfer its loyalty from tsar and church to the new gods of Soviet atheism. However, some enduring constants have become more evident with every decade which separates us from the Revolution.

The old tyrannies of distance, terrain and climate have been eroded, but not destroyed, by modern technology, leaving Russia still (by Western standards) a vast, underpopulated, underdeveloped and ill-articulated mass, where space acts at least as much to the disadvantage of the regime as in its favour. Tyranny of a governmental kind was taken over almost without a break from the old order. 'Dissidents' and the like remain a tiny, unrepresentative minority, and the people have proved perfectly ready to accept the apparatus of controls, passports and directions with which they have lived for centuries. The rulers — Peter, Catherine or Stalin — have not shrunk from removing whole populations from the map, changing or annihilating in the process the very names of their old habitations.

The ancient hatreds and suspicions of the outside world endure unabated, and in the twentieth century have been extended to such Soviet soldiers who have ever fallen into the hands of the enemy, or who have come into contact with alien civilian populations. Writing of the dangers of such contamination, a Russian explained that 'it could happen all too easily that our troops could absorb dangerous principles in foreign countries, where the form of government differs from ours, and bring these ideas back to our own land' (Mediger, 1952, 273). The words might have come from Stalin, but they were penned by Vice-Chancellor Vorontsov in 1745.

As regards warlike affairs in particular, the sentiment of J. Richard concerning Russian military priorities (see p. 233) applies with equal force to a government which devotes many of its best brains and a substantial proportion of public expenditure and resources to its armed forces. On its side, the army still helps to repay the attention by lending itself to be used as an instrument of civilian control and support. The result is an overdirected nation which excels at one thing only — acquiring the capacity to wage war.

A continuity of practice between the old and new regimes was reinforced by the influence of ex-tsarist officers like Brusilov and Tukhachevsky, and it is evident in the primacy given to mobility and mass, as well as the principle of the rolling deployment, and significant details like the symbols used to denote military units on maps. We have noticed how patriotic Russians were also unable to ignore the achievement of their remoter military past. Indeed, military history in the Soviet Union has assumed dimensions that are now unknown in the West, being considered at once a source of patriotic inspiration, and a fund of experience from which military doctrine may be extracted or supported. Suvorovian formations are still upheld as praiseworthy examples of the vital principle of depth, and with extraordinary consistency the peculiarly Russian concept of the *corps volant* has reappeared in almost every generation since Peter first wrote about it in the 1700s. This type of fast-moving, semi-independent formation took Berlin from the Prussians in 1760. It is seen again in Rumyantsev's Turkish campaigns. It was employed in various guises in the two World Wars, and it has assumed its most modern guise in the shape of the units of *reidoviki*, designed to roam around in the rear of NATO forces. If the *corps volant* was one expression of the impact of distance and space on the Russian art of war, we may also trace in the eighteenth century the forces which made for the emergence of the later concepts of 'theatre' (see p. 126) and 'front', and the force of meaning behind the word 'operation' (subtly different from the Western understanding of 'campaign'), which conveys the idea of a sequence of military activity pursued through to the accomplishment of a set objective — a term probably fixed by the exhaustion of supplies. The designation of 'operation', therefore, applies as usefully to Fermor's seizure of East Prussia in 1758 as to the Russian push from the Oder in 1945.

In the eighteenth century the artillery offered the one occasional exception to the almost uniformly depressing story of Russian technical backwardness, and with their stress on the weight of artillery and missile fire the present generation of Soviet gunners has placed itself in the direct line of descent from Shuvalov, Martinov, Glebov, Melissino and the other gifted artillerymen of two centuries ago. As for the infantry, the tales of tenacity from Brest and Stalingrad do not differ in kind from those that were current at the time of Zorndorf or Borodino. The present intakes of Soviet recruits have nine or more generations of conscription behind them, enough to invest the young mens' entry into military life with something of the aura of the sacrament of confirmation, even if the soldiers of peasant stock are now outnumbered by the townsmen.

The Soviet concern for traditions is both fascinating and amusing. Sergei Bondarchuk and other directors have created films of the tsarist past with an almost unfailing sense of period, and with rather less discrimination.

the new regime appropriates whatever was good and universally recognised as such ... the old onion-domed churches, Pushkin and Tolstoy, ballet and caviare are wrenched from their historical contexts and become creations of the Russian people in so far as it is now represented by the Soviet regime ... if an *izba* is gracefully proportioned, it is the creation of the Russian people; if it is full of vermin, it is the creation of capitalism (Besançon, 1978, 82).

Alain Besançon regards such manifestations as sterile and artificial, a mere dressing-up of the crudities of the Soviet present with artefacts from a museum. Solzhenitsyn would probably agree. However, it is possible to argue at least as convincingly that over the decades the Soviet regime has chosen to respond to a quiet, spontaneous but ultimately irresistible popular demand for the symbolic and immaterial. The nationalistic revival of 1942 was just one manifestation of a phenomenon which has surrounded every major stage in the course of military and civilian life with a sense of ritual, and causes people to invoke the sacrifice of the Great Patriotic War with a reverence that was once reserved for the Divinity.

One of the most remarkable continuities of all resides in the very potent attractions and repulsions which have coloured relations between Russia and Germany over the ages. We have often noticed the emotions generated by this connection in the eighteenth century. In the succeeding Napoleonic period, in an episode much celebrated in propaganda today, parties of liberty-loving Prussian officers sought refuge in Russia, and before long the Prussians as a whole welcomed the Russians as comrades in arms in the crusade which freed Europe from The Ogre in 1813 and 1814. In the second quarter of the century the German way in public affairs was upheld as a model by Nicholas I, and in the 1880s the Germans and Balts, having braved the onset of Pan-Slavism, occupied the majority of posts in the Foreign Office and the systems of transport and communication, and held about one-third of the senior commands in the army (the same proportion as a century before). General Rennenkampf led the Russian First Army to its doom at Tannenberg in 1914. The corresponding Second Army, on the left flank, was originally entrusted (according to Solzhenitsyn) to a General Rausch von Traubenberg, who did not bear the most Muscovite of names.

After the Great War the German army and the new Soviet Red Army embarked on eleven years of very profitable association, the Soviets deriving as much benefit from the German military instruction as the Germans did from their secret testing grounds and industrial plants in Russia. As Tukhachevsky remarked: 'The Reichswehr has been the teacher of the Red Army, and that will never be forgotten' (Laqueur, 1965, 131). There existed no inherent ideological antagonisms between the early Nazis and the Soviets, whom Josef Goebbels was prepared to see as companions on the road to socialism, and when the breach came in September 1933 it was largely at the instigation of Alfred Rosenberg, who was himself a German Balt, and not untypical of that brand of Russian.

Employing the term 'military culture' in its widest sense, we discover all sorts of details which confirm the impression that the Russian and the Prusso-German armies partake of a common north-east European tradition. Families like the Mansteins and Manteuffels contributed with distinction to both armed forces. The typically 'German' goose-step and spiked helmet were in fact joint productions, and the Germans turned again to certain Russian motifs for inspiration for the uniforms of the Nazi regime. An historian of costume believes that 'it is not surprising that both the German National Socialists, and the Italian Fascists, should have modelled their uniforms on those of Russia, when they had already imposed on their respective countries a totalitarian system of a kind that had flourished in Russia for centuries' (J. Mollo, 1972, 232). The parallel is enlightening, even if some might prefer to describe the Russian regime as 'authoritarian', rather than 'totalitarian'.

In Russian military history, Germany has been at once the arch-enemy and guide and helpmate, a necessary check on the extravagances of what the poets called 'vagabond Russia', and the ultimate standard by which Russia's military efforts must be measured. It is almost as if the Russians have had to render constant account to this foremost representative of the hated West.

Appendix

Measurements

Time

The Russian calendar ran eleven days behind that of western Europe. In the present work the Russian old style dates have been retained for events in Russia and the East, and the Western new style adopted for campaigns and actions in western Europe.

Weight

The Russian pound approximated to the pound as known in other European countries (itself subject to national deviations). It comprised ninety-six *solotnik*. Forty Russian pounds made one *pud* (not to be confused with 'pound'), which was a unit much in use in the artillery.

Length

Of the measurements in most common use, the *sazhen* was the equivalent of seven feet, and the *verst* (of 500 *sazhens*) corresponded to two-thirds of a mile.

Money

One hundred kopeks made one rouble, and two roubles made one ducat. The subsidy agreement with the Maritime Powers in 1747 put the value of the British pound sterling at 4½ roubles, though it is very difficult to establish the equivalents in purchasing power.

Select Bibliography

Abbreviations

AKV   *Arkhiv Knyazya Vorontsova* (1870-95), 40 vols, Moscow. An important collection of documents from the archives of the Vorontsov family.
PRO   Public Record Office, Kew.

(Periodicals)
RA   *Russkii Arkhiv*, Moscow.
RS   *Russkaya Starina*, St Petersburg.
SIRIO   *Sbornik Imperatorskago Russkago Istoricheskago Obshchestva*, St Petersburg.
VS   *Voennyi Sbornik*, St Petersburg.

Adamczyk, T. (1936), *Fürst G. A. Potemkin*, Emsdetten.
Altshuller, R.E. 'Kutuzov kak Voennyi Pedagog-Direktor Kadetskogo Korpusa', in Beskrovnyi (1969).
Amburger, E. (1961), *Beiträge zur Geschichte der deutsch-russischen kulturellen Beziehungen*, Giessen.
Amburger, E. (1966), *Russische Regierung und Entwicklung von Anfang des 17ten Jahrhunderts bis 1917*, Leiden. Especially for national origins of Russian nobility.
Anderson, M. S. (1958), *Britain's Discovery of Russia 1553-1815*, London.
Anderson, M. S. (1978), *Peter the Great*, London. The most reliable and accessible guide.
Anderson, R. C. (1910), *Naval Wars in the Baltic during the Sailing Ship Epoch, 1552-1850*, London.
Anderson, R. C. (1952), *Naval Wars in the Levant*, Princeton.
Andolenko, C. R. (1967), *Histoire de l'Armée Russe*, Paris.
Andryshchenko, A. I., 'Pugachevskoe Vosstanie i Kyuchuk-Kainardzhiiskii Mir', in Beskrovnyi (1969).
Anon. ('By an officer on board the Russian fleet') (1772), *An Authentic Narrative of the Russian Expedition against the Turks by Sea and Land*, London.
Anon. (c.1787), *General Observations Regarding the Present State of the Russian Empire*, London.
Anon. (from a French ms.) (1788), *Historisches Tagebuch des Krieges zwischen Russland und der Pforte von 1768 bis 1774*, Vienna.
Anon. (1792), *Anecdoten zur Lebensgeschichte des Ritters und Reichs-Fürsten Potemkin*, Freistadt.
Anon. (wrongly attributed to the 'Sieur de Villebois') (1853), *Mémoires Secrets pour Servir à l'Histoire de la Cour de Russie*, Paris.
Anon. (1872), 'Petr Velikii i ego Armiya', *VS*, LXXV, pt 1, St Petersburg.
Anon. (1883), 'Petrovskaya Brigada: Polki Leib-Gvardii Preobrazhenskii i Semenovskii, 1683-1883', *RS*, XXXVIII, St Petersburg.
Archenholtz, J. W. (1840), *Geschichte des Siebenjährigen Krieges in Deutschland*, 2 vols, Berlin.
Auty, R., and Obolensky, D. (eds) (1976), *An Introduction to Russian History* (*Companion to Russian Studies*, vol. 1), Cambridge. A useful guide to the present state of scholarship.

Avtorkratov, V. N., 'Voennyi Prikaz', in Beskrovnyi (1969).

Baiov, A. (1906), *Russkaya Armiya v Tsarstvovanie Imperatritsy Anny Ioannovnyi*, 2 vols, St Petersburg. A detailed and important study by a pro-Münnich member of the 'academic' school of historians.

Bangert, D. E. (1971), *Die Russisch-Österreichische Militärische Zusammenarbeit im Siebenjährigen Kriege in den Jahren 1758-1759*, Boppard. An excellent work. Contains many illuminating details.

Basov, P. (1874), 'Suvorov i ego Obraz Deistvii', *VS*, XCVIII, St Petersburg.

Beauclair, P. (1774), *Histoire de Pierre III*, London.

Bellamy, C. (1979), 'Seventy Years on: Similarities between the Modern Soviet Army and its Tsarist Predecessor', *RUSI Journal of the Royal United Services Institute*, London, September.

Bescançon, A. (March 1978), 'Soviet Present and Russian Past', *Encounter*, London.

Beskrovnyi, L. G. (1957), *Ocherki po Istochnikovedeniyu Voennoi Istorii Rossii*, Moscow. A good survey of sources.

Beskrovnyi, L. G. (1958), *Russkaya Armiya i Flot v XVIII Veke*, Moscow. A massive and indispensable work, though marred by the selective coverage and the heavy Marxist-Leninist bias. To be used with caution.

Beskrovnyi, L. G. (as ed.) (1959a), *Poltava. K 250-Letiyu Poltavskogo Srazheniya*, Moscow. A useful collection of commemorative essays.

Beskrovnyi, L. G. (1959b), 'Strategiya i Taktika Russkoi Armii v Poltavskii Period Severnoi Voiny', in Beskrovnyi (1959a).

Beskrovnyi, L. G. (1962), *Ocherki Voennoi Istoriografii Rossii*, Moscow. A most valuable bibliographical summary.

Beskrovnyi, L. G. (essays presented to) (1969), *Voprosy Voennoi Istorii Rossii. XVIII i Pervaya Polovina XIX Vekov*, Moscow.

Bestuzhev, N. I. (1961), *Opyt Istorii Rossiiskogo Flota*, (new edn), Leningrad.

Billington, J. H. (1966), *The Icon and the Axe. An Interpretive History of Russian Culture*, London.

Bobrovskii, P. O. (1900), *Suvorov na Kubanu v 1778 godu i za Kubanyu v 1783 godu*, St Petersburg.

Bogdanovich, M. (1873), *Russkaya Armiya v Veke Imperatritsy Ekateriny II*, St Petersburg. Very elementary.

Bolotov, A. T. (1870-3), *Zhizn*, 4 vols, St Petersburg. One of the most vivid of all eighteenth-century military memoirs.

Bruce, P. H. (1782), *Memoirs of Peter Henry Bruce, Esq.*, London.

Buerja, A. (1785), *Observations d'un Voyageur sur la Russie*, Berlin.

Buganov, V. I., 'Streletskoe Vosstanie 1698 g. i Nachalo Likvidatsii Streletskogo Voiska', in Beskrovnyi (1969).

Bunbury, H. (1927), *Narratives of Some Passages in the Great War with France*, London.

Buturlin, G. (1819-23), *Voennaya Istoriya Pokhodov Rossiyan v XVIII Stoletii*, 4 vols, St Petersburg.

Cook, J. (1770), *Voyages and Travels through the Russian Empire*, 2 vols, Edinburgh.

Curtiss, J. C. (1965), *The Russian Army under Nicholas I, 1825-1855*, Durham, N. Carolina. Highly recommended.

Danilov, M. V. (1842, written in 1771), *Zapiski Artillerii Maiora Mikhaila Vasilevicha Danilova*, Moscow. Especially on the conditions of technical education, and the development of Shuvalov's new ordnance.

Danilov, N. A., 'Istoricheskii Ocherk Razvitiya Voennago Upravlenie v Rossii', in Skalon (1902-c.1911), I.

Denisov, A. K. (1874), 'Zapiski Donskago Atamana Denisova', *RS*, X-XII, St Petersburg. An impressive evocation of an upper-class Cossack's life.

D'Eon (1837), *Mémoires du Chevalier D'Eon*, 3 vols, Brussels.

Dirrheimer, G., and Fritz, F. (1967), 'Einhörner und Schuwalowsche Haubitzen', in *Maria Theresia. Beiträge zur Geschichte des Heerwesens ihrer Zeit*, Graz. On the Austrian evaluation of Shuvalov's artillery.

Dolgorukov, Yu. V. (1889), 'Zapiski Knyazya Yuriya Vladimirovicha Dolgorukova, 1740-1830', *RS*, LXIII, St Petersburg.

Donnelly, A. S. (1968), *The Russian Conquest of Bashkiria, 1552-1740: A Case Study in Imperialism*, New Haven.

'Dropmore Papers' (1906), Historical Manuscripts Commission, *Report on the Manuscripts of J. B. Fortescue, Esq., Preserved at Dropmore*, V, London.

Dyadichenko, V. A., 'Ukrainskoe Kazatskoe Voisko v Kontse XVII – Nachale XVIII v.', in Beskrovnyi (1959a).

Eelking, M. (ed.) (1854), *Correspondenz des Kurfürstlich Sächsischen Premier-Ministers Grafen von Brühl mit dem Sächsischen General-Lieutenant Freiherrn von Riedesel*, Leipzig.

Engelhardt, L. N. (1868), *Zapiski Lva Nikolaevicha Engelgardta 1766-1836*, Moscow. One of the best of the many good memoirs of the period.

Fabritsius, I. G., 'Glavnoe Inzhenernoe Upravlenie. Istoricheskii Ocherk', in Skalon (1902-c.1911), VII, pt 1.

Fisher, A. W. (1970), *The Russian Annexation of the Crimea 1772-1783*, Cambridge.

Frisch, E. (1919), *Zur Geschichte des russischen Feldzüge im Siebenjährigen Kriege nach den Aufzeichnungen und Beobachtungen der dem russischen Hauptquartier zugeteilten österreichischen Offiziere*, Heidelberg. Disappointingly impersonal.

Fuchs (Fuks), E. (1827), *Anekdoty Knyazya Italiiskago Grafa Rymnikskago*, St Petersburg. Affectionate and informative.

Funcken, L. and T. (1977), *Arms and Uniforms. The Lace Wars*, pt II, London.

Gippius, A. I., 'Ustavy i Nastavleniya', in Skalon (1902-c.1911), IV, pt 1, bk 2, sect. 3. Helpfully reprints long extracts from rules and regulations.

Glinoetskii, N. (1871), 'Nekotorya Svedeniya ob Obuchenii Russkikh Voisk vo Vtoroi Polovine Proshlago Veka', *VS*, LXXXII, pt 1, St Petersburg.

Golikova, N. B., 'Iz Istorii Klassovykh Protivorechii v Russkoi Armii (1700-1709 gg.)', in Beskrovnyi (1959a). Good on the conditions of private soldiers.

Golitsyn, N. S. (1890), 'Russkie Soldaty v Prusskoi Sluzhbe', *RS*, LXVI, St Petersburg.

Gordeev, N. V., and Portinov, M. E., 'Pamyatniki Poltavskogo Srazheniya', in Beskrovnyi (1959a).

Gotzkowsky, J. C. (1768-9), *Geschichte eines Patriotischen Kaufmanns*, 2 vols, Augsburg. For the allied occupation of Berlin in 1760.

Grosser Generalstab (1890-1914), *Die Kriege Friedrichs des Grossen*, 20 vols, Berlin.

La Harpe, F. C. (1978), *Correspondance de Frédéric-César de la Harpe et Alexandre 1er*, Neuchâtel.

Hasenkamp, X. (1886), *Ostpreussen unter dem Doppelaar*, Königsberg.

Hatton, R. M. (1953), 'Captain James Jefferye's Letters to the Secretary of State, Whitehall, from the Swedish Army, 1707-1709', *Historiska Handlingar*, pt 31, i, Stockholm.

Hatton, R. M. (1968), *Charles XII of Sweden*, London.

'H. D.' (1877), 'Voina Rossii s Turtsieyu ... Vtoraya Voina v Tsarstvovanie Imperatritsy Ekateriny II 1787-1791 gg.', *VS*, CXII, CXIV, St Petersburg.

Helbig, G.A. (1917), *Russische Günstlinge*, Berlin. Unreliable but entertaining.

Hellie, R. (1971), *Enserfment and Military Change in Muscovy*, Chicago.

Hingley, R. (1978), *The Russian Mind*, London.

Hordt, Comte de (1805), *Mémoires Historiques, Politiques et Militaires de M. le Comte de Hordt*, 2 vols, Paris.

Horward, D.D. (ed.) (1980), *Proceedings of the Consortium on Revolutionary Europe*, Tallahassee.

Jenkins, M. (1969), *Arakcheev. Grand Vizier of the Russian Empire*, London.

Jomini, Lt.-Gen. (1840), *Histoire Critique et Militaire des Guerres de la Révolution*, 4 vols, Brussels. Especially for 'Rélation Raisonnée de la Marche de l'Armée de Suwarow, d'Italie en Suisse', by an eyewitness, in vol. IV.

Jones, D.R. (ed.) (forthcoming), *The Military-Naval Encyclopedia of Russia and the Soviet Union*, Gulf Breeze, Florida.

Josselson, M., and Josselson, D. (1980), *The Commander. A Life of Barclay de Tolly*, Oxford. Michael Josselson's untimely death deprives us of something almost unique in military history – an independent writer who has pursued researches into the Russian army and its campaigns from original sources. Although primarily concerned with the Napoleonic period, Josselson has much of value to say about the viewpoint of the Baltic Lutherans in general.

Kaplan, H. H. (1968), *Russia and the Outbreak of the Seven Years War*, Berkeley.

Kapustina, G. D., 'Guzhevoi Transport v Severnoi Voine', in Beskrovnyi (1969).

Keep, J.L. 'Response of the Russian Army to the French Revolution', in Horward (1980).

Keralio, L. (1773), *Histoire de la Guerre entre la Russie et la Turquie*, St Petersburg.

Khevenhüller-Metsch, J. J. (1907-72), *Aus der Zeit Maria Theresias. Tagebuch des Fürsten Johann Josef Khevenhüller-Metsch, Kaiserlichen Obersthofmeisters 1742-1776*, 8 vols, Vienna.
Klokman, Yu. R. (1951), *Feldmarshal Rumyantsev v Period Russkogo-Turetskoi Voiny*, Moscow.
Klokman, Yu. R., 'Voprosy Voennoi Istorii Rossii XVIII-Nachala XIX v. V. sovetskoi Istoriografii', in Beskrovnyi (1969).
Klugin, L. (1861), 'Russkaya Soldatskaya Artel', *VS*, XX, no. 7, July, St Petersburg.
Korb, J.-G. (1863), *Diary of an Austrian Secretary of Legation at the Court of Czar Peter the Great*, 2 vols, London. For the defects of the old military organisation.
Korobkov, N. (1940), *Semiletnyaya Voina (1756-1762 gg.)*, Moscow. Detailed and very useful.
Koslov, E. E. (1959), 'Artilleriya v Poltavskom Srazhenii', in Beskrovnyi (1959a).
Kunisch, J. (1978), *Das Mirakel des Hauses Brandenburg*, Munich. Balanced and well-informed.
Kvardi, V. V., 'Imperatorskaya Glavnaya Kvartira. Istoriya Gosudarevoi Svity', in Skalon (1902-c.1911).
Langeron, A. (1895), 'Russkaya Armiya v God Smerti Ekateriny II', *RS*, LXXXIII, St Petersburg. Possibly the most detailed and judicious contemporary account of the Russian army in the eighteenth century.
Lantzeff, G. V., and Pierce, R. A. (1973), *Eastwards to Empire*, London.
Laqueur, W. (1965), *Russia and Germany. A Century of Conflict*, London.
Lebedev, A. (1898), *Russkaya Armiya v Nachale Tsarstvovaniya Imperatritsy Ekateriny II*, Moscow. Has useful lists of senior and middle-ranking officers.
Lebedev, P. S. (1877), 'Preobrazovateli Russkoi Armii v Tsarstvovanie Imperatora Pavla Petrovicha, 1796-1801', *RS*, St Petersburg. Very good.
Lehndorff, A. H. (1910-13), *Dreissig Jahre am Hofe Friedrichs des Grossen ... Nachträge*, 2 vols, Gotha.
Lemcke, J. F. (1909), 'Kriegs und Friedenbilder', *Preussische Jahrbücher*, CXXXVIII, Berlin.
Ligne, C. J. (1795-1811), *Mélanges Militaires, Littéraires et Sentimentaires*, 34 vols, Dresden.
Ligne, C. J. (1890), *Oeuvres Choisies*, Paris.
Lloyd, H. (1781), *History of the Late War in Germany*, 2 vols, London.
Longworth, P. (1965), *The Art of Victory. The Life and Achievements of Generalissimo Suvorov 1729-1800*, London.
Longworth, P. (1969), *The Cossacks*, London. Another valuable work from an outstanding authority.
Longworth, P. (1980), 'War and Cossack Society in the Eighteenth Century', *Brooklyn College Studies on Society in Change*, Brooklyn.
Löwenstern, V. I. (1900), 'Zapiski V. I. Levenshterna', *RS*, CIII, no. 3, St Petersburg.
Lubyanovskii, Th. P. (1872), *Vospominaniya Th. P. Lubyanovskago*, Moscow.
Luckett, R. (1976), 'Pre-Revolutionary Army Life in Russian Literature', in *War, Economy and the Military Mind*, Best, G., and Wheatcroft, A., eds, London.
Lukyanov, P. M., 'Proizvodstvo Porokha v Rossii v Pervoi Chetverti XVIII v.', in Beskrovnyi (1959a).
Lyons, M. (1968), *The Russian Imperial Army. A Bibliography of Regimental Histories and Related Works*, Stanford.
Mackesy, P. (1974), *Statesmen at War. The Strategy of Overthrow, 1798-1799*, London.
McNeill, W. H. (1964), *Europe's Steppe Frontier, 1500-1800*, Chicago.
Madariaga, I. de (1981), *Russia in the Age of Catherine the Great*, London.
Manstein, C. H. (1860), *Mémoires Historiques, Politiques et Militaires sur la Russie*, 3 vols, Paris. One of the classics of military literature.
Maslovskii, D. F. (1888-93) (trans. and ed. Drygalski, A.), *Der Siebenjährige Krieg nach Russischer Darstellung*, 3 vols, Berlin.
Maslovskii, D. F., *Sbornik Voenno-Istoricheskikh Materialov*, especially vols II (1892), III and IV (1893), St Petersburg. Helpful collections of military documents.
Masson, C. F. (1859), *Mémoires Secrets sur la Russie pendant les Règnes de Catherine II et de Paul Ier*, Paris. Good for details of military life, but heavily prejudiced against Catherine.
Mediger, W. (1952), *Moskaus Weg nach Europa*, Brunswick. A first-class study.
Meerovich, G. I., and Budanov, F. V. (1978), *Suvorov v Peterburge*, Moscow. Good on the contemporary background.
Menning, B. W., 'G. A. Potemkin and A. I. Chernyshev: Two Dimensions of Reform and

the Military Frontier in Imperial Russia', in Horward (1980).

Messelière, M. (1803), *Voyage à Petersbourg*, Paris. Experiences of a French diplomat in the interesting years of 1757-8.

Meshcheryakov, G. P., 'Iz Istorii Voenno-Teoreticheskoi Mysli v Rossii v Pervoi Chetverti XVIII V.', in Beskrovnyi (1969).

Mikhnevich, N. P., 'Vooruzhenyya Sily Rossii do Tsarstvovaniya Imperatora Aleksandra I', in Skalon (1902-c.1911), IV, Introduction.

Mikhnevich, N. P., 'Komplektovanie Vooruzhennykh Sil v Rossii do 1802 g.', in Skalon (1902-c.1911), IV, pt 1, bk 1, sect. 1.

Minzloff, R. (1872), *Pierre le Grand dans la Littérature Etrangère*, St Petersburg.

Mollo, B. (1979) (illus. Mollo, J.), *Uniforms of the Imperial Russian Army*, Poole.

Mollo, J. (1972), *Military Fashion*, London.

Mollo, J. (1977) (illus. McGregor, M.), *Uniforms of the Seven Years War*, Poole.

Montalembert, M. R. (1777), *Correspondance de Monsieur le Marquis de Montalembert*, London.

Myshlaevskii, A. Z. (1896), *Petr Velikii. Voina v Finlandii v 1712-1714 gg.*, St Petersburg.

Nashchokin, V. A. (1842), *Zapiski Vasiliya Aleksandrovicha Nashchokina*, St Petersburg.

Neplyuev, I. I. (1893), *Zapiski Ivana Ivanovicha Neplyueva (1693-1773)*, St Petersburg.

Nolde, B. (1952-3), *La Formation de l'Empire Russe*, 2 vols, Paris.

Nostitz, F. A. (1976), *Der Westfeldzug Suvorovs in der Öffentlichen Meinung Englands*, Wiesbaden. Contains many interesting insights and details.

Obolenski, M. A., and Posselt, M. C. (eds) (1849-51), *Tagebuch des Generals Patrick Gordon*, 2 vols, Moscow and Leipzig.

Oliva, L. J. (1964), *Misalliance. A Study of French Policy in Russia during the Seven Years War*, New York.

Oreus, I. I. (1876), 'Ivan Ivanovich Mikhelson. Pobeditel Pugacheva', *RS*, XV, St Petersburg. Uncritical.

Orlov, N. (1898), *Italyanskii Pokhod Suvorova v 1799 g.*, St Petersburg. Prints extensive quotations from Captain Gryazev's high-flown account, which cannot always be taken literally.

Pallas, P. S., et al. (1774), *Histoire des Découvertes Faites par Divers Savans Voyageurs*, 2 vols, Berne.

Parker, W. H. (1968), *An Historical Geography of Russia*, London.

Parkinson, J. (1971), *A Tour of Russia, Siberia and the Crimea 1792-1794*, London.

Pavlenko, N. I., 'Produktsiya Uralskoi Metallurgii v Nachale XVIII v.', in Beskrovnyi (1959a).

Peter the Great (1887-1975), *Pisma i Bumagi Imperatora Petra Velikogo*, 12 vols, Moscow.

Petrov, P. V., 'Glavnoe Upravlenie Voenno-Uchebnykh Zavedenii', in Skalon (1902-c.1911). Important.

Pinter, W. M. and Rowney, D. K. (eds) (1980), *Russian Officialdom: The Bureaucratisation of Russian Society from the Seventeenth to the Twentieth Century*, Chapel Hill.

Pipes, R. (1974), *Russian under the Old Regime*, London. Lively and controversial.

Pishchevich, A. S. (1885), *Zhizn A. S. Pishchevicha 1764-1805*, Moscow.

Podyapolskaya, E. P. (1959), 'Voennye Sovety 1708-1709 gg.', in Beskrovnyi (1959a). Shows councils of war as part of the educational process of Peter and his army.

Porfirev, E. I. (1959), *Poltavskoe Srazhenie 27 Iyunya 1709 g.*, Moscow.

Poroshin, S. (1844), *Semena Poroshina Zapiski*, St Petersburg.

Pososhkov, I. T. (new edn 1951, written 1701), 'O Ratnom Povedenii', in *Kniga o Skudosti i Bogatstvie i Drugie Sochineniya*, Moscow.

Preobrazhenskii, A. A., 'Voennye Postavki Nevyanskogo Zavoda Nakanune Poltavskogo Srazheniya', in Beskrovnyi (1969).

Prittwitz, C. W. (1935), *Unter der Fahne des Herzogs von Bevern*, Berlin.

Prokofev, A. S., 'O Deistviyakh Povstantsev Pravoberezhya k Krestyanskoi Voine pod Predvoditelstvom E. I. Pugacheva', in Beskrovnyi (1969).

Rabinovich, M. D., 'Formirovanie Regulyarnoi Russkoi Armii Nakanune Severnoi Voiny', in Beskrovnyi (1969).

Raeff, M. (1966), *Origins of the Russian Intelligentsia. The 18th Century Nobility*, New York. Especially valuable on the relaxation of service obligations.

Rambaud, A. (1895), *Russes et Prussiens. Guerre de Sept Ans*, Paris. Still worth reading. Catches the flavour of the time and place.

Reding-Biberegg, R. (1895), 'Der Zug Suworoffs durch die Schweiz', in *Der Geschichtsfreund*,

L, Stans. The most detailed and reliable account of the famous campaign.
Regele, O. (1957), *Feldmarschall Radetzky*, Vienna. For Austrian opinions on the Russians in Italy, 1799.
Reimers, H. (1883), 'Peterburg pri Imperatore Pavle Petrovich 1796-1801 gg.', *RS*, XXXIX, St Petersburg.
Repninskii, G. K. (1885-9), 'Gr. Gotlob-Kurt-Genrikh Totleben v 1715-1763', *RS*, XLVII, XLVIII, XLIX, LII, LIII, LX, LXI, LXII, LXIV, St Petersburg.
Retzow, J. A. (1802), *Charakteristik der Wichtigsten Ereignisse des Siebenjährigen Krieges*, 2 vols, Berlin.
Richard, J. (1780), *A Tour from London to Petersburgh*, London.
Richelieu, A. E. (1886), 'Dokumenty i Bumagi', *SIRIO*, LIV, St Petersburg.
Rozhdestvenskii, S. V. (1912), *Ocherki po Istorii Sistem Narodnago Prosveshcheniya v Rossii v XVIII-XIX Vekakh*, vol. 1, St Petersburg.
Rumyantsev, E. M., (1888), *Pisma Grafina E. M. Rumyantsovoi k eye Muzhu, Feldmarshalu Grafu P. A. Rumyantsov-Zadunaiskomu 1762-1779 g.*, St Petersburg.
Rumyantsev, P. A. (1872), 'Perepiska Grafa Petra Aleksandrovicha Rumyantseva s Grafom Nikitoyu Ivanovichem Paninym v 1765 i 1771 godakh', *SIRIO*, IX, St Petersburg.
Rumyantsev, P. A. (1953-9), *P. A. Rumyantsev. Dokumenty*, ed. Fortunatov, P. K., 3 vols, Moscow. A rich source.
Runich, D. P. (1901), 'Iz Zapisok D. P. Runicha', *RS*, CV, vol. 1, St Petersburg.
Rzhevskii, S. M. (1879), 'O Russkaya Armiya vo Vtoroi Polovine Ekaterinskago Tsarstvovaniya', *RA*, XVII, pt 1, Moscow. A scathing indictment of the state of the army, by a Russian general.
Sabatier de Cabres (1913), 'Catherine II. Sa Cour et la Russie en 1772', *SIRIO*, CXLIII, St Petersburg. Also printed Berlin 1869. All Sabatier's reports must be treated with some caution.
Saikin, I. (1818), *Anekdoten und Charakterzüge des Feldmarschalls Grafen Peter Alexandrowitsch Rumänzow-Sadunaiskoi*, Dorpat.
Sanglein, J. J. de (1882), 'Zapiski', *RS*, XXXVI, St Petersburg.
Saul, N. E. (1970), *Russia and the Mediterranean, 1797-1807*, Chicago. One of the few works to do justice to Paul I.
Scheffner, J. G. (1823), *Mein Leben*, Leipzig.
Schmidt, C. (1770), *Briefe über Russland*, Brunswick.
Schweizerische Verkehrszentrale (1974, September), 'Auf Suworows Spuren', in *Schweiz*, Zürich. A fascinating study of topography and Suvorovian relics. Typical of the lively interest which the campaign of 1799 still commands in Switzerland.
Ségur, Comte de (1824-6), *Mémoires, ou Souvenirs et Anecdotes*, 3 vols, Paris.
Semenyik, G. I., 'Oruzhie, Voennaya Organizatsiya i Voennoe Iskusstvo Kazakhov v XVIII-XIX vv.', in Beskrovnyi (1969). Good.
Semevskii, M. (1862), 'Protivniki Fridrikh Velikago. Apraksin i Bestuzhev-Ryumin', *VS*, XXV, XXVIII, St Petersburg.
Sheremetev, B. P. (1808), *Zhizn, Anekdoty, Voennya Politicheskiya Deyaniya Rossiiskago General-Feldmarshala Grafa Borisa Petrovicha Sheremeteva*, St Petersburg.
Shmidt, S. O., 'Proekt P. I. Shuvalova o Sozdanii v Rossii Vysshei Voennoi Shkoly (1755 g.)', in Beskrovnyi (1969).
Shuvalov, I. I. (1872), 'Iz Bumag Ivana Ivanovicha Shuvalova', *SIRIO*, IX, St Petersburg.
Silva, Marquis da (1778), *Pensées sur la Tactique, et la Stratégique*, Turin.
Skalon, D. A. (ed.) (1902-c.1911), *Stoletie Voennago Ministerstva 1802-1902*, St Petersburg. This vast compilation covers almost every aspect of the organisation, regulation and training of the army from the time of Peter the Great, and may be seen as the crowning achievement of the pre-Revolutionary military historiography. The total number of volumes and the final publication date are difficult to ascertain.
Solovev, N. (1893), 'Kratkii Istoricheskii Ocherk Organizatsii Russkikh Regulyarnykh Voisk v Pervoi Polovine XVIII Stol. (1700-1761 gg.)', *VS*, CCIX, St Petersburg.
Stein, F. (1885), *Geschichte des Russischen Heeres*, Hanover. Especially good for lists of regiments and changes in organisation.
Stiessius, C. (1706), *Relation vom dem Gegenwärtigen Zustande des Moscowitischen Reichs*, Frankfurt.
Strandmann, G. (1882-4), 'Zapiski Gustava fon-Shtrandmana 1742-1803', *RS*, XXXV, XLIII, St Petersburg. The publication of this interest-

ing account appears to have been discontinued prematurely.

Strukov, S. P., 'Glavnoi Artilleriiskoe Upravlenie. Istoricheskii Ocherk', in Skalon (1902-c.1911), VI, bk 1, pt 1.

Strumilin, S. G., 'K Voprosu ob Ekonomike Petrovskoi Epokhi', in Beskrovnyi (1959).

Surtees, W. (1973), *Twenty-Five Years in the Rifle Brigade*, London. For descriptions of the Russians in North Holland 1799.

A. V. Suvorov. Dokumenty (ed. Meshcheryakov, G. P.) (1949-53), 4 vols, Moscow. One of the useful Stalin-period documentary collections. No authoritative text of the *Art of Victory* yet exists. Versions were published in 1806 and 1809, and in 1940 the Soviets first brought out a new but unreliable edition, allegedly based on authentic material from the late eighteenth century.

Täge, Pastor (1864), 'K Istorii Semiletnei Voiny. Zapiski Pastora Tege', *RA*, II, Moscow.

Tarle, E. V. (1958), *Severnaya Voina*, Moscow.

Thilo von Trotha (1888), *Zur Geschichte der Russisch-Österreichischen Kooperation im Feldzuge von 1759*, Hanover.

Tielke, J. G. (1788), *An Account of some of the most Remarkable Transactions of the War between the Prussians, Austrians, and Russians from 1756 to 1763*, vol. II, London. The vivid testimony of a Saxon officer who was on attachment with the Russians.

Tomasic, D. (1953), *The Impact of Russian Culture on Soviet Communism*, Glencoe.

Totleben, G. K. (1762), *Mémoires de la Vie du Comte de Totleben*, 2 pts, Zalt Bommel. Entertaining.

Tschitschagoff (Chichagov, P.V.) (1862), *Mémoires de l'Amiral Tschitschagoff (1767-1849)*, Leipzig. Of doubtful authenticity.

Tsebrikov, R. M. (1895, July), 'Vokrug Ochakova 1788 god', *RS*, LXXXIV, St Petersburg. A critical and deeply-felt account by one of Potemkin's secretaries.

Turgenev, A. M., 'Zapiski Aleksandra Mikhailovicha Turgeneva' (1885-9), *RS*, XLVII, XLVIII, XLIX, LII, LIII, St Petersburg.

Venturi, F. (1979), *Settecento Riformatore III. La prima Crisi dell'Antico Regime 1768-1776*, Turin. For the effect on Italy of the arrival of the Russian fleet in the Mediterranean in 1770.

Vischer, M. (1938), *Münnich. Ingenieur, Feldherr, Hochverräter*, Frankfurt. Good.

Viskovatov, A. V. (1844-56), *Peremeny v Obmundirovanii i Vooruzhenii Voisk Rossiskoi Imperatorskoi Armii*, 30 vols, St Petersburg. Compiled at imperial command, this is the most detailed review of Russian military costume. Well, if stiffly, illustrated.

Vodarskii, Ya. E., 'Sluzhiloe Dvoryanstvo v Rossii v Kontse XVII-Nachale XVIII v.', in Beskrovnyi (1969).

Volkonskii, P. M. (1876), 'Razskazy Knyazya P. M. Volkonskago', *RS*, XVI, St Petersburg.

Volz, G. B., and Küntzel, G. (1899), *Preussische und Österreichische Acten zur Vorgeschichte des Siebenjährigen Krieges*, Leipzig.

Vorontsov, S. R. (1871, November), 'Instruktsiya Rotnym Komandiram' (of 1774), *VS*, LXXII, St Petersburg.

Vorontsov, S. R. (1870-95), 'Zapiski S. R. Vorontsov o Russkom Voiske, Predstavlennaya Imperatoru Aleksandru Pavlovichu v 1802 godu', *AKV*, X, Moscow. Heavily patriotic in tone. Foreshadows the interpretations of the 'national' school of military historians.

Warnery, C. E. (1770), *Rémarques sur le Militaire des Turcs*, Leipzig and Dresden.

Warnery, C. E. (1788), *Campagnes de Frédéric II Roi de Prusse*, Amsterdam.

Weber, F. C. (1744), *Das Veränderte Russland*, 3 pts, Frankfurt and Leipzig.

Weymarn, H. H. (1794), 'Ueber den ersten Feldzug des Russischen Kriegsheeres gegen die Preussen im Jahr 1757', in *Neue Nordische Miscellaneen*, Riga. An honest and descriptive relation by Apraksin's chief of staff.

Wiegel, F. F. (1864-6), *Vospominaniya F. F. Vigela*, 3 vols, Moscow. Excellent.

Wonzel, P. (1783), *Der Gegenwärtige Staat von Russland*, St Petersburg and Leipzig.

Wraxall, N. (1776), *A Tour through some of the Northern Parts of Europe*, London.

Young, P. (1970), *History of the British Army*, London.

Yukht, A. I., 'Russkaya Promyshlennost i Snabzhenie Armii Obmundirovaniem i Amunitsei', in Beskrovnyi (1959a).

Zatvornitskii, N. M., 'Voennye Ministry i Glavnoupravlyayushchie Voennoyu Chastyu v Rossii s 1701 po 1910 god', in Skalon (1902-c.1911), III, pt 6.

Zhuravskii, D. P. (1858-9), 'Statisticheskoe

Obozrenie Raskhodov na Voennyya Potrebnosti (s 1711 po 1825 god)', *VS*, St Petersburg, II, pt 2, X, pt 2. On military budgeting.

Zweguintzow, W. (1967), *L'Armée Russe*, vol. I, Paris. A useful compilation, too little known outside France.

NB. This bibliography does not attempt to reproduce the full range of articles and conference papers recently published in the West. Details are available in the excellent *Newsletter: Military and Society, Russia and East Europe*, ed. Prof. B. W. Menning, Dept. of History, Miami University, Oxford, Ohio, OH 45056, USA.

Index

Åbo, 36; peace of (1743), 57
Adda River, action (1799), 205, 217
Åland Islands, 28, 36
Alessandria, siege (1799), 217, 219
Aleksei Mikhailovich, Tsar, 4, 6-8, 9, 11, 158
Alexander (Aleksandr Pavlovich), Grand Prince (later emperor), 196, 232
Allenburg, 78, 95
Altdorf, 226, 227
Altranstadt (Peace of, 1706), 20
Ancona blockade (1799), 209
Andermatt, 225
Anhalt-Bernburg, Count F., 144, 146
Anna, Empress: accession, 42-3; character, 43; War of Polish Succession, 48; death, 48, 53
Apraksin, family, 2
Apraksin, Stepan Fedorovich, 54, 59, 67, 73-4, 75, 78, 81, 93, 95, 98, 126, 131, 164
Archenholtz, J.W., 103
Arakcheev, Aleksei Andreevich, 103, 201, 205, 207
army, Russian, and related topics
    administration, 32-4, 35, 45, 56, 60, 62, 73, 93, 94, 126, 128, 148, 166, 167, 180, 181, 196-7, 202-4; Conference, 92-3, 119; War College, 13, 32-4, 35, 56, 128, 147, 148, 160, 167, 180, 181, 198, 202
    artillery, 17-18, 23, 47, 66-72, 79, 81, 89, 90-1, 102, 121-2, 166-70, 172, 177, 182, 198, 205, 212, 235
    cavalry (regular), 17, 22, 23, 35, 46-7, 63-7, 100, 121, 128, 166, 170, 172, 177, 182, 198, 205, 212, 235; hussars, 47, 64, 101, 128, 177
    codes and regulations, 6-7, 18, 20-2, 62-3, 100, 118, 129, 133, 137, 166, 170, 172, 183-4, 190, 191-2, 204-5, 206, 207
    Cossacks: character, 163-4; Chuguevskii Cossack Regiment, 47, 81, 106, 111, 159; Dnieper, or Zaporozhian, Cossacks, 22, 24, 49, 102, 158, 159; Don Cossacks, 48, 53, 81, 102, 106, 119, 158-9, 161, 162; indiscipline, 75, 82, 85, 87, 95, 98, 101-2, 104, 227, 234-5; Israelovskii, or Jewish, Cossacks, 159; organisation, 157-8; origins, 158, 159-61; tactics and proficiency, 78, 79, 80-1, 85, 101-2, 119-20, 162-3, 192, 214, 217, 221, 222, 230; Ukranian Cossacks, 102, 151, 157, 158; Yaik Cossacks, 178; mentioned, 64, 81, 82, 157-64
    disease and medical services, 46, 53, 74-5, 96-8, 129, 132, 172
    evolution and experiences: medieval and early modern origins, 1, 6-8; modernisation by Peter the Great, 10-14, 17-18, 22-3, 29-41; Great Northern War (1700-21), 19-28; Pruth campaign (1711), 27; under Münnich, 45-7, 54; Polish Succession 1733-5, 48; Swedish War (1741-43), 48-9, 56-7; Turkish War (1735-9), 48-53; march to Germany (1748), 57-9; preparation for Seven Years War, 56, 62-74; Seven Years War (1756-63), 74-124; in reign of Catherine the Great (1762-96), 166-78, 179-85, 196-9; Turkish War (1768-74), 168-74; against Pugachev (1773-4), 178-9; Turkish War (1787-92), 185-8; Swedish War (1788-90), 188-9; against the Poles (1792-4), 195-6; in reign of Paul I (1796-1801), 200-8; War of Second Coalition (1798-1800), 208-31; Turkish theatre, conditions and influence of, 6, 27, 49-52, 73, 95, 119, 126, 153, 162, 170-2, 176, 188, 189, 191, 209, 234; Western impressions of, 7, 14, 17, 23, 26, 48, 58, 63, 72, 73, 74, 80-1, 82-3, 86, 90, 103-4, 115, 125, 134-5, 152-6, 177, 188-9, 193, 205, 209-15, 216, 227, 228, 234-5
    finances, taxes and subsidies, 36-7, 38, 45, 56, 57, 58, 60, 61, 95, 126, 179-80, 208, 235-6
    flying corps, 30, 172, 239
    Garrison Army, 35, 73, 96
    Guard, 32, 34, 42, 43, 54, 123-4, 137, 138, 140-2, 144, 201, 206; Chevalier Garde, 141; Ismailovskii Regiment, 43, 124, 140; Preobrazhenskii Regiment, 10, 12, 13, 42, 43, 54, 140, 141, 203; Semenovskii Regiment, 10, 12, 13, 42, 124, 212
    industry, war, 37-8, 179, 238
    infantry, 23, 34-5. 62-3. 120-1, 128-9, 170-2, 177, 204-5; grenadiers, 44, 46, 63, 172, 182, 205, 211; jaeger, or light infantry, 117, 120-1, 170,

251

172, 177, 182, 184, 205-6, 209-11, 222
Land Militia, 35, 43, 47, 73, 125, 166
logistics (supply and transport), 6, 31, 50, 51, 52, 58, 64, 68, 73, 74, 80, 81, 85, 86, 94-5, 98, 116, 117, 119, 120, 131, 176, 188, 196-7, 198, 226, 228, 234, 235-6
maps and topography, 49, 52, 57, 61, 94, 96, 98, 202, 217, 226
men: conditions of life, morale, 90, 91, 129-30, 131-5, 190, 192, 234, 238; desertion, 38, 46, 133; discipline and punishments, 32, 115, 117, 132, 182, 207, 228, 234; education, 130; pay, 46, 130; recruitment, 6, 7, 12-13, 38, 46, 96, 118, 125-39, 235-40
military literature, 30, 120, 140, 142, 185, 190, 194
navy, 26-8, 35-6, 57, 177-8, 185, 189, 208-9
Observation Corps, 73, 86, 87, 89, 90, 91, 96, 104, 109, 118, 121
officers: corruption of, 126, 132, 147, 148-51, 154, 167-8, 196-8; decorations and rewards, 10, 42, 81, 151-2, 187, 196; education, 45, 60, 138-45; foreign officers and Balts, 27, 38-9, 43, 45, 54, 56, 58, 81, 132, 145-7, 178, 182, 227, 237; origins and service obligations, xii, 6, 7, 13, 14, 39, 40, 45-6, 81, 130-43, 147, 152; proficiency, 38, 95, 96, 119, 135, 141-2, 155-6, 182, 188, 198, 214; promotion and ranks, 14, 30-1, 51, 64, 119, 145-51, 179, 197; social life, 58, 82-3, 103-4, 136-42, 148, 151, 152-5, 234
regimental organisation, 13, 34-5, 46, 58, 65-6, 97, 99, 100-1, 102, 123, 127, 134, 141, 143, 148, 149, 152, 153, 157, 160, 161, 162, 169, 173, 177, 180, 182-3, 184, 188, 200, 203-4, 206-7, 209-11, 227, 241
regiments (mentioned in text): Akhtyrka Hussars, 128; Apsheronskii Infantry, 97; Astrakhanskii Infantry, 134, 190; Astrakhanskii Cuirassiers, 128; Bugskii Jaeger Corps, 184; Butyrskii Infantry; Grenadier Regiment, First, 79, 89, 126, 134, 183; Grenadier Regiment, Second, 80, 89; Grusinskii (Georgian) Hussars, 101; Hungarian Hussars, 101; Ingermanlandskii (Ingrian) Infantry, 134, 190; Kazan Grenadiers, 64; Kharkov Hussars, 128; Kuban Jaeger Corps, 134; Ladozhskii Dragoons, 147; Lefort Infantry, 17; Little Russian Grenadiers, 169; Moldavian Hussars, 101; Narvskii Carabiniers, 147; Narvskii Infantry, 80; Nevskii Infantry, 79; Novgorod Cuirassiers, 64; Olonetskii Dragoons, 147; St. Petersburg Infantry, 62; Saratov Fusiliers, First, 133; Serbian Hussars, 101; Shlyushelburgskii Dragoons, 147; Shlyushelburgskii Infantry, 211; Sibirskii Grenadiers, 142; Sibirskii Infantry; Suzdalskii Infantry, 190; Tverskii Carabiniers, 147; Vyborgskii Dragoons, 147
staff work, 96, 166, 176, 181-2, 202, 216, 235
strategic and political geography, 2, 4-6, 11, 14-15, 20, 23-4, 26, 27, 28, 29, 36, 37, 49, 53, 57, 61, 74, 83-4, 94, 117-18, 173, 176, 185, 188, 189, 196, 235-6
strategy, 19, 30-1, 93-6, 105, 112, 116, 172, 176, 202, 239
tactics, 22-3, 31-2, 46, 50-2, 62-4, 79-81, 90, 98, 100, 106-7, 108, 112, 120-2, 170-2, 204-5, 211-12, 214-15, 222-3, 230
uniforms, 6, 13, 34-5, 39, 46, 58, 65-6, 97, 99, 100-1, 102, 122, 123, 127, 134, 141, 143, 148, 149, 152, 153, 157, 160, 161, 162, 167, 169, 173, 177, 180, 182-3, 184, 188, 200, 203-4, 206-7, 209-11, 227, 241
westward advance of Russian power, 14, 20, 26, 28, 40-1, 47, 48, 55, 58-9, 61-2, 83, 112, 124, 177-8, 185, 187, 196, 233, 235, 237, 239
Astrakhan, 4, 164, 185
Auffenberg, General, 222, 226, 229, 231
Augustus II, King of Poland, 15, 20, 44
Augustus III, King of Poland, 48
Austria, 11, 13, 47, 59, 93-4, 105, 178, 185, 187, 196, 233
Avramov, M.P., 30
Azov, Sea of, 4, 11, 49, 53

Azov, 27, 35, 37, 176, 185; sieges (1695 and 1696), 11; (1736 and 1737), 51-2

Babadag, battle (1791), 188
Bagration, P.I., 217, 218, 220, 221, 223, 226-7, 229, 231
Baiov, A., 236
Baku, 29
Baltic Sea, 4, 14, 35-6, 126
Bangert, D.E., 238
Bashkir tribesmen, 164, 179
Bauer, F.W., 146, 166-7, 181, 235
Bavarian Succession, War of (1778-9), 185
Behring, I.I., 29
Belgorod, 67, 158
Belgrade, Peace of (1739), 53
Bendery, siege (1770), 175
Berezina, River, 22
Bergamo (seized, 1799), 217
Bergen, action at (1759), 118
Bergen, action at (1799), 205, 211-12
Berlin, 85; raided (1760), 114-16
Beskrovnyi, L.G., 237
Bestuzhev, Aleksei Petrovich, 56, 57, 58, 59, 60-1, 73, 81, 93, 95, 126
Bestuzhev, M., 93
Betzkoi, I.I., 144
Bibikov, A.I., 129
Biron, E.J., 43, 49, 54, 147
Black Sea, 4, 27, 49, 50, 173, 176, 186, 188
Bobrovskii, P.O., 236
Bolotov, A.T., 78-80, 82-3, 138, 155
Bondarchuk, S., 240
Borozdin, K.B., 67, 184
Braila, siege of (1770), 176
Brescia (seized, 1799), 217
Brindisi (seized, 1799), 209
Browne, G. (Yurii Yurevich), 78, 81, 87, 94, 95
Bruce, James, 18, 34, 39
Brusilov, General, 239
Bryansk, 24
Bug, River, 26, 50, 52, 53, 176
Bukhvostov, S.L., 9
Bulavin, K., 35, 158
Bunzelwitz, camp (1761), 117
Burkersdorf, action at (1762), 118
Buturlin, Aleksandr Borisovich, 32, 54, 55, 83, 95, 100, 116, 117, 119, 120
Byzantium, 1, 2, 4, 236

Caspian Sea, 4, 29, 35, 49
Cathcart, Lord, 177
Catherine I, Empress, 20, 42, 151
Catherine II, 'the Great', Empress, 41, 137, 138, 139, 152; accession, 74, 92, 123-4; achievement, 165,

Index   253

199; character, 165-6, 180; Crimean journey (1787), 166, 185; favourites, 166, 180-1, 197; military reform, 142; and Swedish War (1788-90), 189; and Turkish War (1768-74), 173-4; and Turkish War (1787-91/2), 187-9
Charles, Archduke of Austria, 214
Charles, Prince of Saxony, 86, 89, 91, 98, 101-2
Charles XII, King of Sweden, 15-16, 19, 22-6, 27, 28, 139
Chasteler, staff officer, 216
Chernyshev, Zakhar Grigorevich, 59, 62, 73, 82, 89, 94, 95, 114, 115, 117, 120, 123, 124, 140, 166, 167, 173, 176, 178
Chesmé, naval battle of (1770), 176
Chichagov, P.V., 139
Choiseul, Duc de, 83
Coehoorn, M., 30, 194
Colberg (Kolberg), 95, 113; siege of (1758), 91, 102, 145; (1759), 105; (1761), 116-18, 119, 120, 168, 170, 182
Constantine (Konstantin Pavlovich), Grand Prince, 49, 50, 145, 207-8, 222
Corfu, siege of (1799), 209
Cracow, 23; siege of (1772), 178; siege of (1794), 195
Crimea, 4, 6, 24, 49-52, 160, 176, 188, 189, 190; annexed (1783), 131, 185
Crimean Tartars, 4, 29, 49, 53, 159, 173, 185
Croy, Duc de, 16
Cüstrin (Küstrin), 83, 85, 98; siege of (1758), 86, 91, 102

Danilov, M.V., 67, 69, 71, 142
Danube, River, 175-6
Danzig, 83, 91; siege of (1734), 48, 233
Dardanelles, 176
Dashkova, Princess E.R., 122, 124
Daun, L., 72, 108, 112
Defoe, D., 26
Démicoud (Demiku), T., 85, 96
Denisov, Adrian Karpovich, 140, 160-2, 195-6, 217, 220
Denisov, Karp Petrovich, 161
Denisov, Thedor Petrovich, 152, 161
Denmark, 15, 123
Deptford, 11
Derbent, 29
Dnieper, River, 26, 47, 50, 51, 124, 176
Dniester, River, 53, 175, 178, 187, 188
Dobroe, action at (1708), 23
Dohna, C., 86, 89

Dolgorukov, family, 1, 42, 136
Dolgorukov, Vasilii Mikhailovich, 176
Dolgorukov, Vasilii Vasilevich, 198
Dolgorukov, Ya.F., 32, 33
Don, River, 4, 11, 27, 37, 47, 51
Dorpat, siege of (1704), 20
Dresden, siege of (1759), 112
Dubienka, battle of (1792), 195
Durakov, F., 127
Dvina, River, 74, 124, 178

East Prussia, 68, 75, 81-3, 90, 94, 103, 116, 119, 123, 124, 233
Egypt, 208
Elbing, 104
Elizabeth Petrovna, Empress: accession, 54; character, 41, 54, 55-6, 59, 63; death, 122; and military reform, 56, 64, 119; and Seven Years War, 59, 92-3, 95, 112, 118; and Swedish War (1741-3), 57
Engelhardt, L.N., 138, 140, 145, 146, 147, 151, 198
Eniseisk, River, 29
Eristfer, action at (1701), 19
Erstfeld, 227
Essen, I.I., 212
Esterhazy, Count, Austrian ambassador, 61, 92-3, 95
Estonia, 4, 15, 27
Eugene, Prince of Savoy, 13, 32, 44, 49, 139, 140, 188, 194

Fedor Alekseevich, Tsar, 7, 9
Fénelon, Archbishop, 44
Fermor, Villim Villimovich, 50, 71, 72, 75, 78, 81-2, 85, 86, 87, 89, 91, 93, 95, 96, 98, 103, 104, 114, 115-16, 119, 121, 239
Fersen, J., 195
Finck, F., 108-9, 110
Finland, 4, 15, 20, 26, 28, 36, 48
Finland, Gulf of, 4, 15, 20, 26, 28, 36, 48
Fokshani, battle of (1789), 187
Folard, J.C., 63, 185
France, 48, 61, 105, 112
Frankfurt-an-der-Oder, 85, 108
Fraustadt, action at (1707), 134
Frederick II 'the Great', King of Prussia, 14, 41, 59, 74, 78, 83, 85, 86, 91, 92, 93, 103, 105, 108, 109, 111-12, 114, 115-16, 118, 119, 123, 124, 151, 168-9, 176, 178, 185, 194, 200, 207, 218, 234
Fredrikshamn: captured (1742), 57; bombarded (1788), 189

Gatchina Corps, 201, 203, 204, 206, 207, 212
Geisman, P.A., 236
Genghis Khan, 1, 2
Genoa, 217, 218, 219
Georgia, 49
Glebov, A., 121, 240
Glogau, 83, 112, 113, 114
Golitsyn, Aleksandr Mikhailovich, 95, 96, 172, 175
Golitsyn, Boris Alekseevich, 17
Golitsyn, family, 42, 136
Golitsyn, Mikhail Mikhailovich, 23
Golitsyn, Vasilii Vasilevich, 7
Golovin, Avtomon Mikhailovich, 12, 14, 39
Golovin, family, 136
Gordon, P., 10, 11, 13
Gotzkowsky, J., 115-16
Graudenz, 104
Great Britain, 28, 185, 187
Greece, 176, 188
Greenwich Observatory, 11
Greig, S.K., 176
Grishinskii, A.S., 236
Grodno, 22, 31
Gross-Jägersdorf, battle of (1757), 67, 71, 76-81, 92, 96, 98, 100, 102, 121, 134, 162, 168
Gryazev, Captain, 132, 216, 232
Günter, J., 45
Günter, Captain, 142
Gustavus III, King of Sweden, 189
Hallart, General, 16
Hangö, Cape, action at (1714), 28
Hannibal, A.P., 33, 67
Helsingfors, 36, 189; captured (1713), 28; captured (1742), 57
Hennin, W., 47
Hermann, J., 209, 211-12
Hessen-Homburg, Prince L. of, 94, 118
Holland, North, expedition (1799), 205, 209-12
Holovzin, action at (1708), 22, 23
Holstein, Duke G.L. of, 79
Holy League, 7
Hotze, General, 215, 228
Hummelshof, action at (1702), 19

Ingria (Ingermanland), 15, 34
Ionian Islands, 209
Ireland, 212
Irtysh, River, 29
Ivan III, Grand Prince, 2
Ivan IV, 'The Terrible', 4, 6
Izmail, siege of (1770), 176; siege of (1790), 41, 133-4, 187-8, 195

Jassy, Peace of (1791-2), 188
Joseph II, Emperor of Austria, 185
Joubert, B.C., 220

Kagul, battle of (1770), 41, 169, 170, 171, 175-6, 198
Kalicz, action at (1706), 21, 31
Kalmyks, tribesmen and auxiliaries, 49, 58, 81, 82, 162, 164, 179
Kamchatka peninsula, 29
Kamenskii, M., 153, 156, 176
Kanitz, H.W., 89
Kant, I., 82
Kaplan, H.H., 238
Karelia, 15, 37, 48, 57
Kaunitz, W.A., 61
Kay, *see* Paltzig
Keith, James, 43, 48, 56, 57
Kexholm, siege of (1710), 26
Kerch, Straits of, 4, 176
Kharkov, 24, 139, 158
Kherson, 185
Khotin (Choczim), 50; siege of (1769), 175
Khpuschov, A., 171
Kiev, 1, 2, 4, 37, 53, 67, 173
Kilia, siege of (1770), 176
Kinburn: siege of (1774), 176; action at (1787), 187
Kinzig Pass, 226, 227, 229
Kirgiz tribesmen, 164
Klado, N.L., 236
Kleist, E.C., 104
Klöntal, 229
Kochmin, V., 11
Kolin, (battle 1757), 89, 140
Königsberg, 78, 81, 82, 83, 102, 104, 124
Korb, J.G., 17
Korff, N.A., 83, 119
Korobkov, N.M., 236, 237
Korsakov, *see* Rimskii-Korsakov
Kósciuszko, T., 195-6
Kostyurin, General, 91, 98, 104, 119
Kovno, 74, 75
Kozludzhi, action at (1774), 176
Krasnoshchekov, I.M., 48
Kray, P., 218, 219, 220
Kronstadt, 28, 36
Kuban, River, 160, 188, 190
Kunersdorf, battle of (1759), 41, 67, 96, 97, 104, 108-12, 118, 119, 120, 121, 134, 168
Kunisch, J., 238
Kurland, 59, 196
Kursk, 24
Kushelev, G., 202, 204
Kutchuk-Kainardji, Peace of (1774), 176
Kutuzov, Mikhail Ilarionovich, 144, 184, 188, 235, 236-7
Kyumen, River, 57

Lacy, Boris Petrovich, 146
Lacy, Francis Maurice, 44, 114
Lacy, Peter (Petr Petrovich), 43-4, 48, 49, 51-2, 56, 57, 104, 233
Ladoga Canal, 29, 45
Ladoga, Lake, 37, 190
Lambert, Captain, 63, 64, 100, 102, 103, 120, 154, 168
Langeron, Alexandre, 125, 129, 132, 133, 142, 148, 153, 154, 156, 163, 169, 188, 191, 194
Lanskoi, A.D., 197
Larga, (battle 1770), 170, 198
Lecourbe, C.J., 214, 222, 227
Leer, G.A., 236
Lefort, F., 10, 13, 146
Lehwaldt, H., 75, 78, 81-2
Leibniz, G.W., 15, 33
Lemcke, J., 103
Leontev, family, 2
Leopold, Prince of Anhalt-Dessau ('Old Dessauer'), 32
Lesnaya, action at (1708), 24, 30, 31
Lewenhaupt, A., 22, 23, 24, 26, 30
Libau, 68
Liegnitz, battle of (1760), 114
Lieven, Matvei, 79
Lieven, Christoph (Khristofer Andreevich), 232
Lieven, Yurii, 62, 78, 80
Ligne, C.J. de, 145, 162, 165-6, 185, 188
Limmat, River, 212, 215
Lindau, 214
Linth, River, 215, 229, 231
Lithuania, 74, 196
Livonia, 4, 19-20, 26-7, 28, 43, 59, 73, 178
Lloyd, H., 95
Lopukhin, V.A., 78
Loudon, G.E., 108, 111, 113, 117
Louis XVIII, 215
Löwenstern, W., 139, 140, 148, 206-7, 214, 226

Macdonald, E.J., 226
Machin, (battle 1791), 163, 188
Maciejowice, battle of (1794), 195
Malet, A. Manesson, 30
Malta, 208, 232
Manstein, C.H., 44, 145, 146, 158
Manteuffel, family, 241
Manteuffel, J., 79
Mantua, siege of (1799), 217, 219
Maria Theresa, Empress of Austria, 58, 61, 62,
Marienwerder, 72, 104
Martinov, technician, 67, 71, 240
Maslovskii, D.F., 236
Masséna, A., 212, 214, 222, 229
Masson, C.F., 154, 199, 209
Masurian Lakes, 78
Maxen, capitulation of (1759), 94
Mazeppa, hetman, 22, 24, 158
Mecklenburg, 28

Mediger, xi, 238
Mediterranean, 173, 208-9
Melas, General, 218, 221
Melissino, Petr Ivanovich, 142, 197, 198-9, 201, 205, 240
Meller-Zakomelskii, I.I., 120-1, 146, 182, 198
Memel, 81; siege (1757), 75, 95
Menshikov, Aleksandr Danilovich, 20, 22, 25, 26, 31, 32-3, 34, 42, 151
Meshcherskii, Major, 226
Michelson, I.I., 179
Mikhailov, O., 6
Mikhnevich, N.P., 236
Milan, 217
Modena, 218
Mogilev (Mohilev), 23
Moldavia, 49, 53, 176, 179, 187
Molitor, G.J., 229
Mongols, *see* Tartars
Montalembert, M.R., 114
Montecuccoli, R., 185, 194
Mordaunt, General, 58
Moreau, J.V., 217, 218, 220
Mortier, A.E., 214, 229
Moscow, 2, 4, 10, 20, 22, 24, 37, 40, 43, 183
Münnich, Burchard Christoph, 29, 56, 153, 159; achievement, 54, 237; character and rise, 44-5, 54; and military reforms, 45 7, 124, 126, 135, 158, 159; and Turkish War (1735-9), 48-53; preparations for Swedish War (1741), 48; fall, 54, 123
Muotatal valley, 226-30
Muotathal village, 228, 230
Muscovy, 1-8, 15
Musin-Pushkin, V.P., 189

Napoleon Bonaparte, 194, 208, 221
Narva, battle of (1700), 15-17, 19, 22, 140
Neva, River, 20
New Russia, province, 185
Niemen, River, 22, 74, 94
Nikolaev, 185, 189
Nikolskii, V., 236
Nile (Aboukir), battle of (1798), 208
Nolcken, Swedish ambassador, 48
Nöteborg (Schlüsselburg), siege of (1702), 20
Novgorod, 1, 2, 15
Novi, battle of (1799), 162, 219-21
Numsen, Th. M., 146
Nyslot, siege of (1788), 189
Nystadt, Peace of (1721), 28

Ob, River, 29
Oberalp Pass, 223, 225
Ochakov, 50, 176, 188; siege of

(1737), 52, 53; siege of (1788), 133-4, 187
Oder, River, 83-94, 86, 91, 108, 111-12, 113, 117, 119
Ogilvy, G.B., 18, 31
Oliva, L.J., 238
Onega, Lake, 37
Orenburg, 151, 179, 183
Orlov, Grigorii Grigorevich, 166
Ostermann, H.J., 43, 49, 53, 54, 146
Ott, General, 218

Pacific Ocean, 4
Palmenbach, General, 91, 145
Paltzig (Kay): action at (1759), 67, 103, 105-8, 112, 120, 121
Panin, Nikita Ivanovich, 103, 171
Panin, Petr Ivanovich, 103, 175
Panixer Pass, 231
Parma, 218
Patkul, J., 15, 20
Paul I, Emperor, 7, 8, 126, 133, 152; accession, 201; character, 200, 207; and Gatchina Corps, 201, 206; and military reforms, 141, 144-5, 200-7, 234, 238; and War of Second Coalition (1798-1800), 208, 209, 232; murder of (1801), 232
Penza, 138-9, 179
Perekop Lines, 6, 51
Perevolochna, capitulation of (1709), 26
Pernau, 16; siege of (1710), 27
Persia, 4, 29, 46
Peschiera, blockade of (1799), 217
Peter I, 'the Great', Emperor, 7, 8, 126, 133, 152; achievement, 28-9, 40-1, 42, 44, 124, 234, 237; character and early years, 9-12; and Cossacks, 158, 160; and military administration, 32-4, 126; and military education, 139, 142; and military reform in general, 10, 12-14, 17-18, 22-3, 29-39; navy, 35-6; regulations, 22-3, 29-32; St Petersburg, 20, 36; social organisation, 137, 139, 151; strategy and tactics, 22, 23, 25, 30-2; war industry, 36-8; Azov campaigns (1695-96), 11; Narva campaign (1700), 14-17; Poltava campaign (1708-9), 22-6; Pruth campaign (1711), 27; victory over Sweden in Great Northern War, 28-9
Peter II, Emperor, 42
Peter III, Emperor, 41, 42, 73-4, 92, 122-4, 137, 200, 233
Petrovsk, 201
Pfister, J., 146
Piacenza, 218

Piedmont-Sardinia, 214, 217
Pishchevich, A.S., 131, 138, 140, 147, 154, 178, 181, 188
Platen, D.F., 111, 116-17
Platov, M.I., 161
Plemyannikov, P.G., 174
Pochep, 24
Podlesia, 196
Poland, 4, 48, 94, 119, 124, 173, 174, 190, 195-6; First Partition (1772), 178; Second Partition (1793), 195; Third Partition (1795), 196
Poltava, campaign, siege and battle of (1708-9), 19, 23-6, 28, 31, 32, 41, 160
Polyanskii, A.I., 117
Pomerania, 83, 91, 94, 113, 117, 188
Poroshin, S.A., 200
Portsmouth, 204
Posen, 85, 120
Pososhkov, I.T., 7, 14
Potemkin, Grigorii Aleksandrovich, 138, 139, 140, 145, 147, 172; achievement, 237; character and early years, 180-1, 233; leadership, 133, 134, 182, 190; and military reforms, 126, 144, 172, 181-3; and origins of Turkish War (1787), 185; and Ochakov (1788), 187; death (1791), 189
Pozharskoi, family, 138
Praga, storm at (1794), 125, 142, 191, 196
Pragel Pass, 229
Prague, 214, 231; battle of (1757), 74
Pregel, River, 78, 80
Preobrazhenskoe, 9, 12
Prussia, 178, 195, 196, 208, 233
Pruth, campaign and Peace of (1711), 27
Pskov, 15, 17
Pugachev, E.I., 133, 178-9
Pushkin, A.S., 33

Racławice, action at (1794), 195
Radetzky, W.A., 216
Ramsay, J., 212
Rawka, battle of (1794), 195
Razin, Stenka, 158
Razumovskii, K.G., 124, 150, 151
Repnin, Anikita Ivanovich, 13, 139
Repnin, Nikolai Vasilevich, 136, 154-5, 178, 185, 196
Repnin, Vasilii Anikitich, 57, 140
Repnin, Yurii Anikitich, 140
Reshut, 29
Reuss, River, 225-6
Revel, 36, 61; siege of (1710), 27; action off (1790), 139
Rhine, River, 48, 226, 231

Richelieu, A. du P., Duc de, 188
Riga, 11, 20, 44, 61, 98, 173, 206; siege of (1700), 15; siege of (1710), 26
Rimskii-Korsakov (Korsakov), A.M., 212, 214-15, 222, 228
Rosen, C., 146
Rosenberg, Alfred, 240
Rosenberg, Andreas, G., 218, 225, 227, 229-30
Rostopchin, family, 2
Rostopchin, O. 209
Rostopchin, Thedor Vasilevich, 204
Rumyantsev, Aleksandr Ivanovich, 32, 153, 168
Rumyantsev, Petr Aleksandrovich, 63, 65, 74, 79, 86, 91, 95, 96, 100-1, 116-18, 119, 120, 128, 148, 156, 158; achievement, 173, 237; character and early years, 140, 168-9, 182; leadership, 133, 168, 172-4, 190; military thought and practice, 126, 129, 169-72, 176-7, 184; Turkish War (1768-74), 167, 173-6; retirement and death, 187, 189-90
Rushchuk, 176
Ryabaya Mogila, battle of (1770), 167, 170, 175
Rymnik, battle of (1789), 187
Rzhevskii, S.M., 145, 148, 198

Sabatier de Cabres, 155-6, 178
Sabatky, I., 116
St André, General, 89
St Gotthard Pass, 214, 222, 233-5
St Petersburg, 20, 22, 26, 29, 36, 37, 40, 43, 55, 67-8, 123, 139, 168, 189, 199, 201, 232, 235
Saint-Rémy, S., 49, 69
Saltykov, Ivan Ivanovich, 136, 154
Saltykov, Nikolai Ivanovich, 197, 198
Saltykov, Petr Semenovich, 95, 104-5, 106, 107, 108, 109-10, 112, 113, 114, 116, 119, 120, 133, 166, 238
Samogitia, 196
Saratov, 147, 179
Saxe, Marshal M. de, 185
Schächental, 226, 227
Scharf, Colonel, 10
Schérer, B.L., 217
Schlüsselburg (Nöteborg), 20
Schwedt, 86
Schweidnitz, storm of (1761), 117-18
Schwyz, 222, 226
Serebryakov, hetman, 79, 162
Sernftal, 231
Sevastopol, 185
Seydlitz, F.W., 89, 90, 104
Shapirov, P., 30

Sheremetev, family, 136, 138
Sheremetev, Boris Petrovich, 17, 19, 24, 26, 27, 39
Shklov, 145
Shumla, 176
Shuvalov, Aleksandr Ivanovich, 59-60, 91, 93
Shuvalov, Ivan Ivanovich, 59
Shuvalov, Petr Ivanovich, 54, 55, 90, 93, 95, 96, 121, 122; career and character, 60; artillery reform, 67-72; officer education, 60, 142; Infantry Code (1755), 62-3
Siberia, 4, 29, 151, 159
Sibilsky, cavalry commander, 74, 78, 79, 96
Silistria, 176
Skalon, D.A., 236
Smolensk, 139, 183, 190
Solzhenitsyn, Aleksandr, xiii, 75, 240
Sophia, regent, 9, 10, 12
Sozh, River, 24
Spiridov, G.A., 237
Stalin, 236-7
Starodub, 24
Stavitzkii, Colonel, 147
Stavuchanakh, storm of (1739), 53
Stettin, 83, 105; siege of (1713), 27, 33
Stoffeln, General, 52, 96
Stralsund, siege of (1715), 28
Streltsy, 6, 12, 15, 134
Strauch, Colonel, 222, 223, 226
Sumarokov, A.P., 144
Sumy, 158
Suvorov, Aleksandr Vasilevich, 147, 173, 176; achievement, 237; character and rise of, 139, 178, 184, 187, 188, 189, 190-1, 193-5, 226; field routine of, 193-4; leadership, 131, 133, 135, 192-3; principles of war, 192-3, 215-16; training and tactics, 188, 190, 191-2, 222-3; at Kinburn (1787), 187; at Moldavia (1789), 187; Izmail (1790), 188; Praga (1794), 125, 196; relations with Paul I, 203, 205, 206; against the Revolution, 208, 215-16; Italy (1799), 216-21; Switzerland (1799), 222-31; death (1800), 231-2
Suvorov, Vasilii Ivanovich, 32, 33, 119, 185, 190
Sweaborg, 189

Sweden, 4, 14-15, 28, 48, 56-7, 189
Switzerland, 212, 214, 221-31

Taganrog, 11, 27, 53, 185
Täge, Pastor, 82, 87-8
Tannenberg, battle of (1914), 240
Tarle, E.V., 237
Tartars, 1-6, 53, 162; *see also* Crimean Tartars
Taverne, 222, 223
Teschen, Peace of (1779), 185, 223
Thugut, Chancellor, 214, 221
Tidone, battle of (1799), 205, 218
Tielke, J.G., 103
Timmermann, F., 10
Tolstoi, Matvei Andreevich, 54, 102
Tolstoy, L., novelist, 54, 102
Tormasov, A.P., 195
Totleben, G.K., 96, 111, 113, 114-15, 116, 145
Trebbia, battle of (1799), 163, 205, 218-19
Trevogin, Major, 226
Trezzo, 217
Trubnikov, Colonel, 225
Tsaritsyn, 179
Tsarskoe Selo, 197, 183
Tsebrikov, R.M., 51
Tukhachevsky, Marshal, 239, 240
Turenne, Marshal, 194
Turgenev, A.M., 172
Turgenev, family, 2
Turin, citadel besieged (1799), 217
Turkey, 4, 27, 29, 49
Tyutchev, Major (later Colonel), 78, 121

Ufa, 179
Ukraine, 4, 6, 74, 126, 137, 158, 178, 195
Ural, River, 159
Urals, 37, 164
Urnerloch, 225
Ushakov, F.F., 208-9, 237
Ustyak Tartars, 29

Vauban, S. le P., 185, 190, 194
Vegetius, 185
Velikolutsk, 37
Verona, 217
Versailles, First Treaty of (1756), 61
Versailles, Peace of (1783), 185
Vienna, 216
Vigel, *see* Wiegel
Vikings, 1, 236

Viliya, River, 74
Villebois (Vilbua), Aleksandr Nikitich, 146
Villebois, Nikita Petrovich, 80, 95
Vinius, A., 17
Vistula, River, 94, 116, 117, 119
Vladimir, Grand Prince, 1
Volga, River, 1, 4, 11, 29, 37, 49, 126, 147
Volhynia, 196
Volkonskii, family, 136
Volkonskii, General, 95
Voltaire, 40-1, 115
Vorontsov, Aleksandr Romanovich, 82
Vorontsov, Mikhail Ilarionovich, 61, 83, 95, 115, 122, 239
Vorontsov, Semen Romanovich, 41, 54, 126, 128, 129, 133, 134, 138, 148, 155, 183-4, 189, 198, 204, 207, 212
Vorskla, River, 24, 25
Vyborg, 36, 57; siege (1710), 26

Wallachia, 49, 176, 179
Warsaw, 195, 196
Warthe, River, 85, 94
Wedel (Wedell), J., 105, 106, 108
Weide, A.A., 13-14
Westminster, Convention of (1756), 61
West Prussia, 195
Weymarn, H.H., 74-5, 80, 96, 98
White Russia, 195
Wiegel (Vigel), F.F., 147, 154, 168, 178, 207
Willmanstrand, storm of (1741), 48
Woolwich Arsenal, 11, 18

Yaguzhinskii, P.I., 143
Yaik (Ural), River, 159
Yaitsk (Uralsk), 159, 179

Zante, 209
Zaporozhe, 158
Zhilin, P., 237
Zorich, S.G., 145, 197
Zorndorf, battle of (1758), 67, 70, 71, 86-91, 98, 100, 102, 104, 112, 118, 121, 124, 240
Zubov, P.A., 197, 199, 203, 205
Züllichau, 105
Zürich, battle of (1799), 135, 205, 214-15
Zürich, Lake, 226